FROMMER'S

COMPREHENSIVE TRAVEL GUIDE

MOROCCO '92-'93

by Darwin Porter
Assisted by Danforth Prince

PRENTICE HALL TRAVEL

NEW YORK • LONDON • TORONTO • SYDNEY • TOKYO • SINGAPORE

FROMMER BOOKS

Published by Prentice Hall General Reference
A division of Simon & Schuster Inc.
15 Columbus Circle
New York, NY 10023

PRENTICE HALL and colophon are registered trademarks of
Simon & Schuster Inc.

ISBN 0-13-334582-3
ISSN 1053-2447

Design by Robert Bull Design
Maps by Geografix Inc.

Manufactured in the United States of America

FROMMER'S MOROCCO '92–'93
Editor-in-Chief: Marilyn Wood
Senior Editors: Judith de Rubini, Pamela Marshall, Amit Shah
Editors: Alice Fellows, Paige Hughes, Theodore Stavrou
Assistant Editors: Suzanne Arkin, Peter Katucki, Ellen Zucker
Contributing Editors: Robert Daniels, Lisa Renaud
Managing Editor: Leanne Coupe

CONTENTS

LIST OF MAPS vii

1 GETTING TO KNOW MOROCCO 1

1. Geography, History & Politics 2
2. Art, Architecture, Literature & Language 17
3. Famous Moroccans 22
4. Religion, Myth & Folklore 23
5. Food & Drink 25
6. Recommended Books, Films & Recordings 28

SPECIAL FEATURES
- *Did You Know . . . ? 2*
- *Dateline 7*

2 PLANNING A TRIP TO MOROCCO 31

1. Information, Entry Requirements, Customs & Money 31
2. When to Go—Climate, Holidays & Events 36
3. Health, Insurance & Other Concerns 40
4. What to Pack 44
5. Tips for the Disabled, Seniors, Singles, Families & Students 45
6. Alternative/Adventure Travel 47
7. Getting There 48
8. Getting Around 52

SPECIAL FEATURES
- *What Things Cost in Marrakesh 35*
- *Morocco Calendar of Events 37*
- *Marrakesh Calendar of Events 39*
- *Frommer's Smart Traveler: Airfares 50*
- *Suggested Itineraries 57*
- *Fast Facts: Morocco 59*

3 TANGIER 64

1. A Brief History 65
2. Orientation & Getting Around 67
3. Accommodations 75
4. Dining 82
5. Attractions 90
6. Savvy Shopping 104
7. Evening Entertainment 106
8. Easy Excursions 109

SPECIAL FEATURES
- *What's Special About Tangier 65*
- *Fast Facts: Tangier 72*
- *Frommer's Smart Traveler: Hotels 81*
- *Frommer's Cool for Kids: Hotels 82*
- *Frommer's Smart Traveler: Restaurants 89*
- *Frommer's Cool for Kids: Restaurants 90*
- *Suggested Itineraries 91*
- *Did You Know . . . ? 94*
- *Frommer's Favorite Tangier Experiences 100*

4 THE NORTHERN COAST 111

1. Ceuta/Sebta (Spain) 112
2. Tetuán 117
3. Chaouen (Chefchaouen) 120
4. Asilah 122
5. Larache (El Araïch) 124

SPECIAL FEATURES
- *What's Special About the Northern Coast 112*
- *Suggested Itinerary 112*

5 RABAT, CASABLANCA & THE ATLANTIC COAST 127

1. Rabat 128
2. Casablanca 140
3. Essaouira 153

SPECIAL FEATURES
- *What's Special About Rabat, Casablanca & the Atlantic Coast 128*
- *Suggested Itinerary 128*

6 MEKNES, FEZ & THE MIDDLE ATLAS 155

1. Meknes 156
2. Fez 166
3. Taza 181

SPECIAL FEATURES
- *What's Special About Meknes, Fez & the Middle Atlas 156*
- *Suggested Itinerary 156*

7 AGADIR, THE SOUSS & THE ANTI-ATLAS 183

1. Agadir 184
2. Taroudannt 193
3. Tiznit 196
4. Tafraoute 197

SPECIAL FEATURES
- *Suggested Itinerary 183*
- *What's Special About Agadir, the Souss & the Anti-Atlas 184*

8 MARRAKESH 199

1. Orientation & Getting Around 200
2. Accommodations 207
3. Dining 214
4. Attractions 224
5. Savvy Shopping 236
6. Evening Entertainment 238
7. Easy Excursions 240

SPECIAL FEATURES
- *What's Special About Marrakesh 200*
- *Fast Facts: Marrakesh 205*
- *Frommer's Smart Traveler: Hotels 210*
- *Frommer's Cool for Kids: Hotels 213*
- *Frommer's Smart Traveler: Restaurants 219*
- *Frommer's Cool for Kids: Restaurants 222*
- *Did You Know . . . ? 224*
- *Suggested Itineraries 224*
- *Frommer's Favorite Marrakesh Experiences 225*

9 THE HIGH ATLAS & THE DEEP SOUTH 242

1. Vallée de l'Ourika 244
2. Asni 245
3. Ouarzazate 247
4. Zagora 249
5. El Kelâa des M'Gouna 250
6. Boumalne du Dadès 251
7. Tinerhir 252
8. Er Rachidia 253
9. Erfoud 254

SPECIAL FEATURES
● *What's Special About the High Atlas & the Deep South 243*
● *Suggested Itinerary 243*

10 THE WESTERN SAHARA 256

1. Goulimine 256
2. Laayoune 258

SPECIAL FEATURES
● *Suggested Itinerary 256*
● *What's Special About the Western Sahara 257*

APPENDIX 261

A. Glossary of Terms 261
B. The Metric System 263
C. Mileage Between Morocco's Major Cities 264

INDEX 265

General Information 265
Destinations 268

LIST OF MAPS

Morocco   4–5
Tangier
   Accommodations   76–77
Tangier Dining   84–85
Tangier Attractions   92–93
Walking Tour—
   Tangier   101
Rabat   129
Casablanca   141
Meknes   157

Fez   165
Walking Tour—New Fez (Fès El
   Jedid)   171
Marrakesh
   Accommodations   208–209
Marrakesh Dining   216–217
Marrakesh
   Attractions   226–227
Walking Tour—
   Marrakesh   233

INVITATION TO THE READERS

In researching this book, I have come across many wonderful establishments, the best of which I have included here. I am sure that many of you will also come across wonderful hotels, inns, restaurants, guesthouses, shops, and attractions. Please don't keep them to yourself. Share your experiences, especially if you want to comment on places that have been included in this edition that have changed for the worse. You can address your letters to:

Darwin Porter
Frommer's Morocco '92–'93
c/o Prentice Hall Travel
15 Columbus Circle
New York, NY 10023

A DISCLAIMER

Readers are advised that prices fluctuate in the course of time and travel information changes under the impact of the varied and volatile factors that affect the travel industry. Neither the author nor the publisher can be held responsible for the experiences of readers while traveling. Readers are invited to write to the publisher with ideas, comments, and suggestions for future editions.

SAFETY ADVISORY

Whenever you're traveling in an unfamiliar city or country, stay alert. Be aware of your immediate surroundings. Wear a moneybelt and keep a close eye on your possessions. Be particularly careful with cameras, purses, and wallets, all favorite targets of thieves and pickpockets.

CHAPTER 1

GETTING TO KNOW MOROCCO

- **DID YOU KNOW . . . ?**
1. **GEOGRAPHY, HISTORY & POLITICS**
- **DATELINE**
2. **ART, ARCHITECTURE, LITERATURE & LANGUAGE**
3. **FAMOUS MOROCCANS**
4. **RELIGION, MYTH & FOLKLORE**
5. **FOOD & DRINK**
6. **RECOMMENDED BOOKS, FILMS & RECORDINGS**

Although Humphrey Bogart and Ingrid Bergman have long ago departed from Casablanca, Morocco continues to entice travelers with its great beauty and a legendary sense of the exotic.

Strategically located at the northwestern tip of Africa, at the crossroads of many of history's most potent cultures, Morocco is simultaneously an Atlantic country, a Mediterranean country, and a North African country. Although it has a history thousands of years old, it is a young country, politically independent since 1956, with an overwhelmingly young population. Its last census (in 1987) counted 23,376,000 inhabitants, 60% of whom were under the age of 20. It is also a rural country, with 61% of its population living outside urban centers.

Its history of the past 3,000 years reads like an epic saga. At one time the Moroccan empire stretched from Tunisia to central Spain, and included some of the richest territories of the Sudan. Under its regime, mathematics, literature, architecture, and Islamic theology flowered in Spanish Andalusia, Marrakesh, Fez, and Tangier. Morocco's scholars, some of whom wrote noteworthy treatises on Aristotle's philosophy and on monotheism, became a deeply revered force throughout the Christian and Islamic worlds.

Known since medieval times for the ferocity of its warriors, Morocco developed dreaded cavalries and navies. It is the only country on the Mediterranean's southern shores never to have been dominated by the Turks. As late as the 18th century, the piratical corsairs of North Africa were the most feared vessels in the Mediterranean.

From a geographical point of view, Morocco is the closest Arab and African neighbor of the United States. It is the world's second country to have officially recognized the fledging U.S. republic. (The Caribbean's tiny island of St. Eustatius was the first.) Signed by both Jefferson and Madison in 1786, the U.S. "Treaty of Friendship" with Morocco is still in force. This treaty is one of the oldest such pacts the United States has signed.

America proved a friend indeed on November 8, 1942, when General Patton's armies landed on the Moroccan coastline to repel the Nazi offensive in North Africa. In 1943, Morocco was the site of the historic Casablanca Conference. The participants were the United States, the United Kingdom, and Free France. The commitments made at that conference altered the course of World War II and of world history. Adding to the drama were the secret meetings (which would

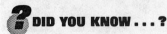

DID YOU KNOW . . . ?

- In 1661, King Charles II of Britain and Ireland was given Tangier as a wedding present, and called it "the richest jewel in my crown."
- The American novelist Edith Wharton wrote the first guidebook to Morocco.
- Ronald Reagan was originally slated to play the role of Rick in the film *Casablanca*, but lost the part to Humphrey Bogart.
- The English playwright Noël Coward, appearing in Tangier as an indiscreet society gossip, was actually spreading disinformation and spying for British and French intelligence during World War II.
- The most famous of movie Tarzans, Johnny Weissmuller, visited Morocco in 1958 for rest and relaxation but suffered a nervous breakdown instead.
- The old "law of the veil" for women in Morocco used to exempt only two groups: Jewish women and prostitutes.
- Moulay Ismail, whose brutal reign lasted for 55 years, had 500 women in his harem and fathered 700 sons. He didn't bother to count the daughters.

undoubtedly have horrified the French) between Franklin D. Roosevelt and the future King Mohammed V. At those meetings, the United States encouraged Morocco's future sovereign to reject the colonial yoke of France.

LAND OF THE EXOTIC

Longtime aficionados of Morocco consider it one of the world's most fascinating countries, rich in contrasts. Perfumed with Arabian Nights' legends and repository of some of the Muslim world's most interesting art and architecture, it is a culturally fascinating destination. Although in many ways a modern country well respected for the industry and ingenuity of its people, Morocco offers a riveting series of sometimes medieval images, much like an electrically charged kaleidoscope.

1. GEOGRAPHY, HISTORY & POLITICS

Although close to Europe, Morocco is set apart by its geography, history, politics, and religion. Sometimes the unspoken social and cultural rules in Morocco are different from what you are used to.

GEOGRAPHY

Situated between Algeria in the east, the Mediterranean's rugged coastline in the north, and the Sahara in the south, Morocco and its history have been shaped by the country's geography.

Morocco lies at the "bottom" of Europe, separated from Spain only by the strategically important Strait of Gibraltar. The Rif mountains are a continuation of the alpine system whose peaks are better known in Switzerland and Austria. In Morocco this system manifests itself as a crescent-shaped mountain range composed of several massifs whose highest altitude is 8,018 feet. At the other end of the country, overlooking Marrakesh, the Grand (or High) Atlas mountain range towers 13,619 feet at its highest point, Djebel Toubkal, with many individual peaks measuring more than 11,500 feet.

IMPRESSIONS

In Morocco, we find ourselves face to face with an independent and historic empire, jealous in the extreme of its independence and rebellious of all forms of servitude.
—MARECHAL HUBERT LYAUTEY, leader of French colonial forces in Morocco, writing to his superiors in Paris in 1916

The Middle Atlas range doesn't go this high. Locals call it the "water tower" of Morocco because, compared to the rest of the country, it receives heavy rainfall. The Anti-Atlas range reaches more than 8,541 feet at Djebel Aklin, and its southwestern location "shoulders" on the Grand Atlas.

Between these mountain ranges, the seemingly endless plains and flat plateaus of Morocco reach out in all directions. This is where much grain is raised, including the semolina products used in making couscous, the national dish. Vineyards, citrus trees, and vegetables are also grown here. In the Gharb plains there are rice fields.

In the south, Morocco is a dramatic land of oases and palm groves until it reaches the vast wastelands of the desert. That section of Morocco, bordering the Mediterranean stretches for 290 miles, facing Spain and Gibraltar on its northern coast. Atlantic Morocco encompasses a staggering 1,550 miles of coastline, where huge sand beaches are spread between the cliffs. Along this coast are found the heavily populated cities of Rabat and Casablanca, as well as one of the largest and wealthiest beach resorts in all of Africa, Agadir.

Moroccans speak of their country as the Maghreb, meaning "the West," a name that indicates Morocco's position as the most far-flung western region of the Arab world. Sometimes this name is used to describe the accumulated land mass of Morocco, Tunisia, and Algeria as well.

THE REGIONS IN BRIEF

The Northwest Most visitors enter Morocco through the Northwest, the closest point to Europe. Tangier is the leading gateway, and Tetuán is the region's second major city. The Rif mountain range, rising to the south, runs parallel to the Mediterranean coastline. For centuries, these mountains protected the folkloric heart of Morocco from the mainstream of Mediterranean civilization.

Ceuta (along with Melilla) is a Spanish enclave in Morocco. A victim of constant turmoil, Ceuta, it is said, has been under almost constant siege since 1580. Yet Spain tenaciously clings to these territories, even though its policy somewhat undermines its own claim to British-controlled Gibraltar.

The Atlantic Coast This is one of the most important regions of Morocco, stretching between Tangier and Agadir. The French called it Maroc Utile (Useful Morocco). The country's political and industrial belt, the Atlantic coast takes in both Morocco's capital of Rabat and its major city of Casablanca. Chaouia, Doukkala, and Gharb, all coastal provinces, are considered the bread basket of Morocco.

Meknes, Fez, and the Middle Atlas The imperial cities of Meknes and Fez, along with the Middle Atlas, form a rich tourist belt of the country, its heartland. Much of the culture of Morocco has centered around these two cities. The first Muslim kingdom of Morocco was founded here upon the ruins of Volubilis, an old capital of the Roman conquerors. The Middle Atlas lies north of the High Atlas mountains and is separated from the Rif by deep gorges that have been cut into the limestone by fast-flowing and very cold rivers. Dubbed "Little Switzerland" by homesick European visitors, much of this area has cool temperatures and alpine flora.

Marrakesh and the High Atlas The city and mountains form a barrier between the grassy lands and ports of the Atlantic coast and the Sahara. Home to a

IMPRESSIONS

Goldshot green of the Rif's slant fields here, vapor-blossom resinous and summery. . . . We've had a windfall of kif. Allah has smiled upon us.
—THOMAS PYNCHON, *Gravity's Rainbow*

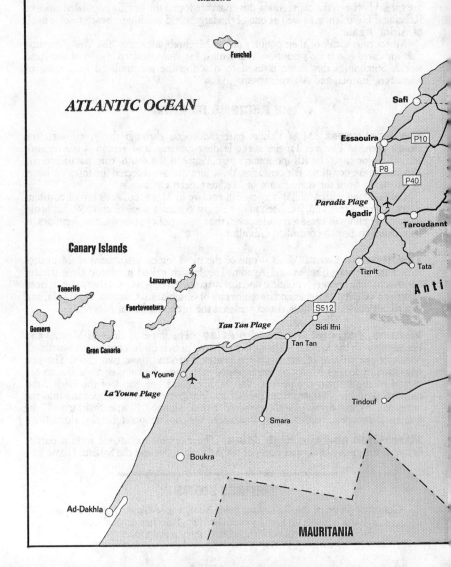

0 — 100 km
0 — 60 mi

MOROCCO

ALGERIA

MAURITANIA

Madeira

Funchal

ATLANTIC OCEAN

Safi

Essaouira   P10

P8

P40

Paradis Plage
Agadir

Taroudannt

Canary Islands

Tenerife

Lanzarote

Fuerteventura

Gomera

Gran Canaria

Tan Tan Plage

Sidi Ifni

Tan Tan

Tiznit   Tata

Anti

La 'Youne

La'Youne Plage

Tindouf

Smara

Boukra

Ad-Dakhla

MAURITANIA

S512

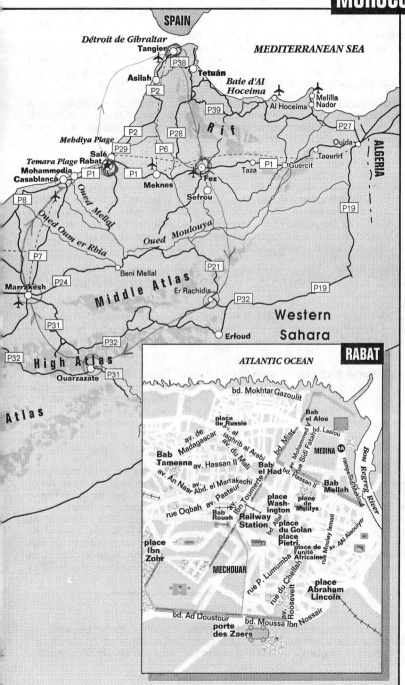

MOROCCO

SPAIN

Détroit de Gibraltar
Tangier
MEDITERRANEAN SEA
P38
Asilah Tetuán
P2
Baie d'Al
Hoceima
P39
Al Hoceima Melilla
Nador
Rif
P27
P2 P28
Mebdiya Plage Ouida
P29 P6 Taourirt
Temara Plage Rabat
Salé P1
Mohammedia P1 Taza P1 Guercit
Casablanca Meknes Fez
P8 Sefrou P19
Oued Mellal
Oued Oum er Rbia Oued Moulouya
P7
P24 Beni Mellal P21
Marrakesh Er Rachidia P19
Middle Atlas
P31 P32
Western
P32 Erfoud Sahara
P32 High Atlas
Atlas Ouarzazate P31

RABAT

ATLANTIC OCEAN

bd. Mokhtar Gazoulit
Bab
place el Alou
de Russie bd. Laalou
av. de av. al bd. Misr
Madagascar Taghrib al Arabi av. Mohammed V
av. du Mali rue Sidi Fatah MEDINA
Bab Bab bd. Hassan II rampe Sidi Makhlouf
Tamesna av. Hassan II el Had
av. An Nasr av. Abd. el Marrakechi Bab
av. av. Pasteur Mellah
rue Oqbah place place
Bab Ibn Toumerte Wash- de
Rouah ington Mellys
Railway bd. Alou
Station place
place du Golan
Ibn place
Zohr Pietri place de
l'unité
MECHOUAR Africaine
rue P. Lumumba place
Abraham
bd. Ad Doustour rue du Chellah Lincoln
porte av. Roosevelt av. Moulay Ismail
des Zaers bd. Moussa Ibn Nossair av. Al Alaouyin

Bou Regreg River

ALGERIA

large Berber population, the High Atlas is crossed at two major passes, both south of Marrakesh: the Tizi n'Tichka (7,390 feet) and the Tizi n'Test (6,841 feet). These crossings have been caravan routes since the 12th century.

"Marrakesh the Red," as it is called because of the color of its earth and its buildings, is the number-one tourist attraction in all of Morocco. The former capital and stronghold of several of Morocco's Berber dynasties, Marrakesh is one of the most interesting and legendary cities in Africa.

The Valleys of the Southern Oases North of the Sahara extends a region known for centuries to caravan drivers. Rainfall is almost nonexistent here. Almost all life is sustained by underground springs and underground streams that carry snowmelt away from the Anti-Atlas. Where the water bubbles to the muddy surface, an oasis—rich with date palms—is formed. Without these oases, most life would wither and die. The region incorporates the valleys of the Dadès, the Todra, the Rhéris, the Ziz, and the Drâa. Because of irrigation networks that required centuries of development, these valleys support agriculture and are even considered fertile.

The Souss Valley extends inland from Agadir, the celebrated west coast resort of Morocco. The valley survives because the High Atlas protects it in the north, as does the Anti-Atlas in the south. Fruits, vegetables, and olive trees are cultivated here. Three hundred years ago, the sugarcane produced in this region was considered the finest in the world, and eagerly sought out by the aristrocracy of Europe.

The Anti-Atlas The country's most self-contained region, it has been called a "platform" existing between the High Atlas and the desert wastelands that form the far northwestern extension of the Sahara.

Because of its relative geographical isolation, this area of Morocco has developed a strong regional personality. Its Chleuh tribe, inbred residents here for centuries, still retains highly characteristic physical features, the most noticeable of which is pronounced cheekbones. To some observers, the look suggests Central Asian or even Inca ancestry.

The Western Sahara Known as the Spanish Sahara until the time of Franco's death, this is the least populated part of Morocco. Relentlessly arid, and bordering the desperately poor African nation of Mauritania, it's considered a virtual wasteland except for the presence of almost unbelievably rich deposits of phosphates. Their presence within the borders of Morocco makes it the third-largest phosphate producer—after the United States and the Soviet Union—in the world. (Phosphates provide an essential ingredient in, among many other products, agricultural fertilizers.)

Goulimine, an old and rather dusty market town, is the gateway to the region, and the gathering place of many of its tribes. The waters of the nearby Atlantic are of virtually no help here. It never rains, and savage cliffs prevent the easy unloading of ships. Even worse, residual deposits of salt make the land unfit for cultivation.

During most of the 1980s, this land was made even more forbidding because of the savage guerrilla warfare between the region's Algerian-funded Polisario rebels and the newly empowered Moroccan army. Since then, the Moroccan military, at vast expense, has firmly dug in, and appears to have the district firmly under control. In fact, in a dramatic ideological display of his intent to retain permanent control of

---

IMPRESSIONS

It is spicy in the souks, and cool and colorful. The smell, always pleasant, changes gradually with the nature of the merchandise. There are no names or signs; there is no glass. . . . You find everything—but you always find it many times over.
—ELIAS CANETTI, *The Voices of Marrakesh*

the Western Sahara, the Moroccan king created a city of 100,000 residents at the far-flung town of Laayoune. Set several miles from the sea, surrounded by desert, it represents one of the most dramatic acts of urbanization in the 20th century. It's even touted as a resort. Sheer willpower and money keep such a city alive in this impossibly harsh environment.

HISTORY

The tides of change that have swept over North Africa could easily rival, in grandeur and complexity, the various eras of European history. Although the cradle of Islam lay much farther east, in what is now Saudi Arabia, it was in Morocco that the Arab and African worlds met and mingled with the European more freely and more profitably than anywhere else. See "Recommended Books," below.

THE PREHISTORIC ERA

Within excavations at Sidi Abd er Rahman, near Casablanca, and at the villages of Mougharet and Aliya, near Tangier, prehistoric graves indicate the presence, 300,000 years ago, of creatures possessing the same bone and cranial structure as their European contemporary, Neanderthal man. Other than the discovery of flint knives, spearheads, and some bone needles, however, very little is known about the Stone Age in Morocco.

Archeologists become more clear, however, about distinct cultural development in the region between 10,000 and 5000 B.C. One important tribe originated in the Nile Delta and gradually migrated westward.

ANCIENT MOROCCO

The era witnessed the construction of cromlechs in both western France and England and in Morocco. Mostly in ruins today, the remains of one of these can be found northeast of Larache, on the Atlantic coast. Whether the inspiration for these dolmen structures came from Druidic influences within Europe is one of the mysteries of modern archeology.

As early as 3000 B.C., North Africa was inhabited by groups of scattered and politically disorganized tribes to which anthropologists have given a catch-all name, the Berbers. The single element unifying these various tribes and social groups was a roughly approximate language— the basis for the Berber dialect, which is even today an oral, rather than a written, language.

From a series of cave drawings and graves found in such places as Figuig, Oukameden, and Foum el Hassan, it is known that the inhabitants of Morocco of 3,000 years ago probably sculpted their beards into points, shaved most of the hair off their heads (perhaps for religious rites), carried shields made from elephant hides, and—at least the wealthier ones—wore earrings, bracelets, necklaces, and (sometimes) ankle ornaments. The dead were buried in a fetal position, usually daubed with red-ocher paint before

DATELINE

• **Around 1200 B.C.** The Phoenicians establish their first colonies along the Moroccan coast. In Tunisia, they establish Carthage.

• **500 B.C.** Carthage emerges as one of the supreme military and economic powers of the Mediterranean world, and Morocco falls to an increasing degree within its orbit.

• **146 B.C.** Destruction of Carthage by the Romans.

• **33 B.C.** Beginnings of the Romanization of Morocco.

• **25 B.C.** The kingdom of Mauretania is established as a puppet government of Rome. Its long-lived Berber king, Juba II, marries the daughter of Cleopatra.

• **A.D. 40** The bloodiest of the many Berber revolts against the Romans. Incited by the murder of Juba's son and heir by Caligula.

• **250** In scattered pockets, Morocco begins a process of
(continues)

Christianization. Schismatic Christian sects begin to quarrel over theological doctrines.

- **300** Collapse of the western Roman Empire. Though Rome itself isn't sacked until a century later, the empire diminishes rapidly. Morocco's Romanized populace continues trade and cultural ties with the Christian rulers in Constantinople (Byzantium).
- **429–477** Vandal tribes originating in Europe conquer key cities on the Moroccan coastline.
- **533** Byzantium attacks the Vandals and reconquers Tangier and Ceuta.
- **622** The Prophet Muhammad flees from his enemies in Mecca. Debut of Islam.
- **683** First Arabic Islamic incursion into Morocco.
- **711** Enforced Islamization of the Berber tribes, first by the Omeyyhades, then by the Iraqi-based Abbasides.
- **788** Idriss I establishes the Idrissid dynasty and the first Moroccan empire.
- **1061** Establishment of the Almoravid dynasty. Morocco's influ-

(continues)

burial, perhaps to simulate the appearance of the blood covering a newborn infant; tombs were laid out along lines facing the rising sun.

The society was probably patriarchal and arranged into tribal units. There is a notable lack of evidence pointing to a single racial group, leading anthropologists to believe that the races and tribes mingled and merged, creating the genes for the modern social group known as the Berbers.

THE PHOENICIANS AND CARTHAGE

By 1200 B.C., the region of Morocco had cautiously and tentatively entered the Mediterranean world. This was partly due to Phoenician merchants who, sailing from a base in what is now Lebanon, spearheaded trading expeditions throughout the Mediterranean and as far as the central African coastline. The colony they established in Tunisia around 800 B.C. eventually evolved into the nerve and trading center of Carthage—after Egypt, the most potent military and cultural force of the North African coast. Direct influences of the Carthaginians upon the primitive Berber tribes inhabiting Morocco included the use of perfume, ceramics, and cloth. In fact, the ideas and values of the Carthaginians propelled Morocco from the Stone Age into the commerce and consciousness of the ancient world.

THE ROMANS

In 146 B.C., the Romans, under the leadership of Scipio Africanus Minor, demolished Carthage, leveling its buildings, enslaving its populace, and sowing its fields with salt to ensure their sterility for generations to come. The power struggles known today as the Punic Wars changed the power balance of the ancient world. Taking advantage of their newfound superiority in the Mediterranean, the Romans established colonies along the Moroccan coastline, most notably Tingis (Tangier), which received all the rights and prestige of an outpost of Rome. The puppet kingdom of Mauretania was headed by Juba II, an Algerian-born Romanized Berber who, as part of a political alliance engineered by the Romans, married Cleopatra Selene, the daughter of Marc Antony and Cleopatra VII, the last and most famous queen of Egypt.

Juba, like Cleopatra's son, Ptolemy, was later assassinated by the legendary Roman emperor Caligula. The assassination provoked a revolt against Rome by the inhabitants of Mauretania, which, after it was crushed, brought an increased Roman pressure and presence.

To better control their domain, Rome divided most of the western North African coastline into Caesarian Mauretania (modern Algeria) and Tingitian Mauretania (modern Morocco), a move that probably forever divided the two regions into culturally distinct entities. During the Roman regime, the administration of Morocco was conducted from Volubilis (whose ruins are fascinating for scholars of ancient history). Morocco was considered strategically important as a protection for the sea routes into Rome's rich colonies in southern Spain.

Morocco became famous as the source of many of the wild beasts that, while mangling early Christians and gladiators in the arenas of Rome, endlessly amused the Roman populace. It was also famous for its purple dye, animal hides, ivory, *garum* (a rancid fish sauce favored by the Romans), and a gastronomic delicacy eagerly acquired by wealthy Romans, the cartilage of the elephant's tusk. (Partly because of this, early in Morocco's recorded history, its few remaining elephants were hunted to extinction.)

These years led to an ever-increasing Romanization of ancient Morocco. Few written sources exist, but most historians believe that a Romanized Berber society probably became increasingly inbred within Morocco after the decline of Rome and before the conversion of Morocco to Islam. When Rome officially converted to Christianity in the 4th century, large colonies of Christians grew up within Morocco, especially in Tangier and Larache, justifying the establishment of four bishoprics. Today, the only recognizable remains of one of this era's early basilicas is in Lixus, near Larache, south of Tangier.

THE FALL OF ROME

After sacking Rome in the 5th century A.D., the Vandals tried briefly and without success to fill Rome's shoes as master of the Mediterranean world. Crossing the narrows of Gibraltar from Spain, they placed a dubious and transitory hold on territories formerly occupied by Rome, leaving almost no architectural traces.

The vestiges of the Roman Empire, from its new eastern base in Constantinople, schemed to regain control of the North African coastline, launching several military campaigns against the Visigoths. A general acceptance of some vague form of monotheism spread through the Berber populace, thanks to the constant presence of the frequently squabbling Catholic, Greek Orthodox, and Jewish traders. (The diaspora of Jerusalem had populated the North African coast with many of Israel's refugees.) Trade and cultural contacts continued between the Moroccan ports and Constantinople until around A.D. 600, when a decadent and weakened Christian regime could no longer withstand the tidal wave of emotion and passion that was Islam.

THE ISLAMIZATION OF MOROCCO

Morocco's schismatic and indecisive links to Byzantium did not give the country the leadership it needed to resist the Muslim armies coming from the east. From its origins in Saudi Arabia, Islam, under the banner of the Prophet Muhammad (who died around 630), conquered the Christianized/Hellenized territories of Egypt in 640. It is estimated that the regions comprising modern Iran, Egypt, and Syria fell to Islam after no more than a total of six battles occurring within two years.

DATELINE

ence stretches from central Spain to the borders of Tunisia.

- **1147** The Almohad dynasty. The Moroccan empire covers a larger land mass than ever before or since. The Andalusian-Muslim style in architecture, mathematics, and literature flourishes.
- **1248** The Merenid dynasty. The arts continue their ascent, but the Catholic forces of Europe begin to diminish the size of the Islamic empire.
- **1415** Conquest of Ceuta by the Portuguese.
- **1492** The Reconquest of Spain is completed with the conquest of Granada by a recently united Spain under Ferdinand and Isabella.
- **1548** Rise of power of the Saadian dynasty. Spain and Portugal invest fortunes to protect trading posts along the Moroccan coastline, many of which change hands several times.
- **1590** Destruction of the Sudanese kingdom of Timbuktu by the Saadian sultans. Morocco grows wealthy from increased trade with
(continues)

DATELINE

Europe and Central Africa.

• **1650** Growing strength of the North African corsairs, who operate from bases in Rabat and Tripoli in a quasi-legal gray zone tolerated by the sultans.

• **1667** Beginning of the Alaouite dynasty, ancestors of the present king.

• **1786** The sultan of Morocco's Alaouite dynasty represents one of the first foreign governments to officially recognize the new government of the United States. An American consulate opens in Tangier.

• **1830** The French occupy neighboring Algeria, eventually defining it as part of France.

• **1844** Defeat of Moroccan forces by the French at the battle of Isly.

• **1906** International agreement among the European powers at Algeciras regarding the establishment of foreign zones of influence within Morocco.

• **1907** The French occupy the Atlantic coast.

• **1911** The French invade Fez.

• **1912** Morocco's central region is completely occupied by France; its

(continues)

Reinforced by troops and provisions from the conquering territories, the Muslim armies moved westward. The stiffest resistance that Islam encountered was in Tunisia, Algeria, and Morocco. These regions, after 50 years of bloody battles, eventually accepted Islam.

Many of the soldiers of the opposing armies converted to Islam, and before the middle of the 700s, all but a few scattered pockets of Morocco had converted from either paganism, Judaism, or Christianity to Islam. Those scattered holdouts that did not convert were eventually slaughtered.

Reveling in their conquest of North Africa, the Arabs appointed an Islamized Berber named Tarik ibn Ziad to lead an army of 7,000 Muslim troops. In 711, they used Morocco as the departure point for the launching of a campaign against the vastly wealthy Catholic kingdoms of Iberia.

SCHISMS WITHIN ISLAM

The Arabic Empire now stretched across Africa and the Middle East, from Spain to the eastern edges of Persia, rivaling at its height the land mass controlled 800 years before by the Romans. Despite the unified religion and values that bound together this unwieldy empire, various cultural and racial differences began to show at the seams.

In Morocco, the Berber majority chafed under the political and cultural domination of the Arab minority, whose power was increasingly derived through reinforcements from Muslim strongholds to the east. Rebelling against taxation and the opulence of the caliphs ruling them from Damascus and Tangier, the Berbers were inspired by the teachings of a group of Islamic schismatics, the Khajarites, who preached egalitarianism and a severe austerity and piety.

Mingling political with religious passion, and always endorsing the unity of Allah, the Berbers of Morocco, and even more passionately, the Berbers of eastern Algeria and Tunisia, revolted against the Arabic newcomers. Though troops were sent in from as far away as Egypt and Iraq, the Berber revolt continued for more than 30 years, eventually ending in 772.

The political fragmentation of Morocco continued with the creation of several military strongholds controlled by highly competitive fiefdoms.

The communities that emerged in Morocco from these conflicts included three Berber kingdoms whose ruins can still be visited today: (1) Sijilmassa, in Morocco's southern sub-Sahara, which would grow rich on the caravan trades to Ghana and black Africa; (2) Berghouata, in the Rif mountains (today known as Chaouia), which survived virtually intact, unchanged, and unvisited by non-Muslims until the early 20th century; and (3) the Berber community that developed a stronghold at Oualila near the ruins of the former Roman capital of Volubilis. Although no one would ever have suspected it at the time, this last community would later rule Morocco under the name of the Idrissid dynasty.

THE IDRISSIDS

The Idrissid dynasty derived its moral imperative from its founding member, Idriss ibn Abdallah, a direct descendant of Ali (the Prophet Muhammad's favorite lieutenant) and Fatima (the Prophet's daughter). Narrowly escaping the dynastic bloodbaths near Mecca that continued for a century after the death of Muhammad around 630, Idriss ibn Abdallah escaped to what might have been the most distant corner of the Islamic world at the time, Morocco. There, his learnedness and religious conviction (and his hatred of their enemies, the Abbasides) so impressed the local Berbers of the Aouraba tribe that they elected him their leader, in 788, despite his foreignness. His rule was short-lived. Assassins sent by the Iraqi-based Abbaside caliph poisoned him in 792, two months before the birth of his soon-to-be-famous son, Idriss II.

Acclaimed at birth as the spiritual and political heir of the Prophet Muhammad, and crowned as king at the age of 11, Idriss II eventually moved his capital to the imperial city of Fez, which quickly defined itself as one of the world's Islamic strongholds and a center of culture and learning. It was during this period that Fez achieved glory, and the foundations were laid for the cultural splendor that would later make it the Islamic symbol of Morocco.

THE ALMORAVIDS

Spearheaded by a group of Mauretanians who converted rather late to Islam (around 800) and stayed aloof from the religious schisms tearing apart their rivals in Fez, these puritanical soldiers of Islam conquered, from their original base in southern Morocco, city after city. Their conquests included the relatively sophisticated desert trading empire of Sijilmassa, which fell to their attacks around 1053 or 1054.

The third-generation heir to the dynasty's founding father was the builder of Marrakesh, Youssef ben Tachfine. Establishing it in 1062, he later embellished it into one of the most glorious cities in the world. From Marrakesh over the next two decades, he conquered the by-now decadent city of Fez, Tangier, and Sebta (Ceuta), and within a few more years, the Rif mountains and most of the Algerian coastline. He was a rigid ascetic whose diet consisted exclusively of barley, meat, and camel's milk. His growing military power and the religious passion of his troops managed simultaneously to threaten both the Spanish Catholic monarch, Alfonso VI, and the Islamic caliphs ruling Andalusia from bases in Granada, Seville, and Badajoz.

IMPRESSIONS

Oh, traveller, if you come into our home, you will be the master of the house and we shall be your guests.
—OLD ARAB SAYING

THE ALMOHADS

Around 1125, a member of the Masmouda tribe named Ibn Toumert established a revolutionary military base for himself in the desert citadel of Tin Mal, where he rallied disaffected tribesmen to a new and severe interpretation of Islam. Well educated from rigid Koranic studies in faraway Egypt, and devoted to a purification of an Islam that he viewed as increasingly corrupted, he presented himself as a direct representative of Allah.

Organizing Morocco's desert tribes into a tightly controlled military unit, he laid seige to Marrakesh in 1130 and, after 40 days, seized it. (Although it was reconquered several days later by the Almoravid authorities, the government of Marrakesh collapsed finally 17 years later during a renewed assault.) After the brief period that followed the mountain rebel's death, his son Abd el Moumen subjugated the settlements within Morocco's Atlas mountains and, from a handful of mountainous guerrilla bases, demolished the Almoravid armies sent to destroy him.

Less ascetic than his father, Abd el Moumen insisted that his name be praised during daily prayers by each of the subjects throughout his empire. At its height, the Almohad holdings stretched from Tripoli to central Spain, a vast empire for that (or any) era.

THE MERENIDS

Their soldiers and leaders came from the dozens of nomadic tribes who roamed Morocco's sub-Sahara. Perhaps envious of the wealth and glory being amassed in Morocco's imperial cities, they established their headquarters in 1248 at Fez, whose glory had long ago been eclipsed by that of Marrakesh. Thirteen years later, after a bloody conquest, they moved their base to Marrakesh itself. Modeling themselves on the most advanced leaders of the western Muslim world, the caliphs of Granada, they fostered the arts, built many of the monuments that today grace Morocco, and steered the country into one of its wealthiest eras.

Simultaneously, they supported the corsairs that systematically terrorized the Christian world; subjugated all of central Algeria, organized the Berber tribes of central Morocco into carefully monitored military units, and continued the campaign of aggression against the Christian armies in Spain. Because the transit rights of caravans were protected, trade routes from the south flourished and the country grew wealthy from trade with the Sudan.

On the intellectual front, the Merenids fostered an era of Koranic and scientific studies. Fez earned a reputation for craftsmanship and the decorative arts that it still enjoys.

By the late 1400s, the dynasty had exhausted itself with squabbles, internal corruption, and the incessant revolts of mountain and desert tribesmen. When a series of treaties with Christian nations established European trading posts in such places as Agadir, the public outrage against the Merenids contributed to the complete collapse of their government in 1548.

THE SAADIAN REVIVAL

The humiliations of a suddenly potent Christendom, coupled with the establishment of Portuguese and Spanish trading colonies along the Moroccan coastline, led to a new form of Islamic fundamentalist rage. It defined itself in the 1500s and 1600s through the Saadian monarchs. Originating from a power base in the arid sub-Saharan Draa region, they conquered the two cities that by now symbolized imperial Morocco at its finest, first Marrakesh (in 1524) and then Fez (in 1548). They mounted a religious and military campaign to throw the Portuguese out of their trading posts at Agadir and El Jadida, succeeding at both tasks before 1578.

In 1590, the Saadian leader Ahmed el Mansour first sacked, and then arranged to have himself crowned at, the legendary Sudanese city-state of Timbuktu (which never recovered from his attack) in 1591. (Today, Timbuktu is located within Mali, but at the time it was considered part of the Sudan.) He later moved his capital to Marrakesh, perhaps to be close to his Saharan roots, but more important, to be as far removed as possible from the Turks who controlled Algeria and the Spanish who controlled Andalusia.

He adorned Marrakesh with elaborate buildings and monuments, the most visible of which remain the Saadian tombs.

Adding to his coffers were the huge ransoms he demanded from the Portuguese for the return of their aristocracy captured during an ill-conceived Portuguese crusade. Some of this wealth was exchanged by the sultan for blocks of fine Italian marble, which were carved into the monuments that make Marrakesh so intriguing today.

When the Moroccan ruler died, the quarrels of his many sons erupted into a series of blood feuds that effectively ended the dynasty and threw the country into anarchy. The lucrative caravan routes became controlled by local chieftains, who imposed whatever taxes they wanted upon the drivers. Commerce slowed and the country languished.

In the early 1600s, rich from its South American gold reserves, the Catholic regime of Spain forcibly evicted from Andalusia the remaining Muslims and Jews who refused under any circumstances to convert. Not particularly welcomed into positions of power by the Saadian establishment, many of the refugees established themselves in the maritime strongholds of Sale (near Rabat), in Tripoli, and along the Algerian coast. Without a strong central government to contain them, many of them quickly evolved into the fiercest of the corsairs who plagued Mediterranean shipping (especially Spanish but also English and French) for the next 200 years.

THE ALAOUITES

Around 1650, blowing out of the desert like a Saharan sirocco, the Alaouite dynasty rose to power in the person of Hassan Addakhil, an austere man convinced of his direct bloodlines to the Prophet Muhammad (through Fatima's daughter and her husband, Ali). He and his soldiers came from the region of Sijilmassa, the once-great trading city in Morocco's sub-Sahara.

His descendant was the dynasty's longest-reigning and most flamboyant monarch, Moulay Ismail, who ruled from 1672 to 1727. He established his capital at Meknes, where he redesigned the architectural landscape of the city.

In 1684, he took Tangier from the enraged English after a siege of five years, and threw the Spaniards out of their trading posts and military garrisons at Larache and Asilah (in 1681 and 1689, respectively).

His reign lasted longer (55 years) than that of any other Moroccan monarch before or since. During that time, Meknes was transformed from a mud-walled provincial village into one of the most glorious imperial cities of Morocco, an appropriate answer to the French capital being erected during the same period at Versailles by Louis XIV.

After Moulay Ismail's death, the empire was inherited by his son, Moulay Abdallah, whose grip on the empire was far less secure than his father's.

By the third generation of the dynasty's original founding, with the ascendency of Sidi Mohammed ben Abdallah, the dynasty's grip was more secure. The worst of the bickering elements were subdued, and the port of Essaouira was founded as a means of opening Morocco's interior to the commerce of Europe. The Portuguese were thrown out of El Jadida, and the Spanish were contained within their coastal sanctuaries at Ceuta and Melilla.

Meanwhile, the attacks by Moroccan-based corsairs became so frequent and expensive that Louis XV, rather than risk an all-out North African military campaign, established diplomatic relations with the Moroccan sultan, exchanged consuls, and in 1767 negotiated for a cessation of the attacks upon French shipping. Several years later, the Alaouite ruler of Morocco became one of the first heads of state to officially recognize the sovereignty of the United States, authorizing the sale of a plot of land in Tangier's casbah as the site for the first foreign embassy owned by the fledgling American government.

This act of generosity, however, wasn't performed within a vacuum. The same sultan was aggressively exchanging raw wool for finished textiles and guns from Britain. Also, although there existed trade agreements between Morocco and at least eight other European countries, more than 80% of Morocco's external commerce was with Spain during this era. Morocco was to an increasing degree opening its doors, perhaps unwittingly, to the types of economic imperialism for which the late 19th century was famous.

COLONIZATION BY EUROPE

The conquest of Algeria in 1830 by French forces, and the subsequent fascination on the part of France concerning its new territory, understandably threatened both the Moroccan regime and the rapidly evolving sense of Moroccan nationalism. An ill-conceived series of intrigues and an eventual war by the then-Moroccan sultan, Abd er Rahman, resulted in the bombardment by the French of Morocco's two most important ports, Tangier and Essaouira, and the bloody defeat of a body of Moroccan tribesmen at the battle of Isly in 1844.

What followed was a hugely complicated series of commercial expansions, with fortunes made and lost by French businessmen who—with the wholehearted support of their government—coveted the inexpensive labor pools and vast natural resources of Morocco.

In 1864, the entire Moroccan interior was opened to economic expansion by the European powers. (Until then, only the ports had been open to foreigners.)

The number of Europeans living in Morocco grew enormously during this period. In 1883 and 1884, a team of French geographers spearheaded by Charles de Foucauld (and accompanied by the rabbi Mardochee Abi Serour) embarked on a French-funded expedition to survey the surfaces of Morocco. The maps and statistics that emerged from this expedition were accepted as standard cartographical data for many years after.

Perhaps more important, their evaluations of the military preparedness of the Moroccan tribesmen, as well as their elegantly written, highly poetic descriptions of Moroccan customs, values, and art, raised forever the consciousness of France toward its Mediterranean neighbors. Almost immediately, a number of important French artists, including Delacroix, began painting Moroccan and Algerian landscapes and portraits of tribespeople in full native dress. The French romantic consciousness became enamored of North Africa.

Late in the 19th century, siding with the country he perceived as the least destructive of his many enemies, Sultan Moulay el Hassan (1873–94) entrusted the complete reorganization of the Moroccan armies to French advisors.

Although France's occupation, and later annexation, of Algeria was by this time a fait accompli, her designs upon Morocco deeply threatened the other European powers. The Entente Cordiale (1904), some of whose clauses led to the entangling alliances of World War I, contained provisions that more or less obliged France to pull out of Egypt if the British would pull out of Morocco. As part of the same series of agreements, Spain and France agreed secretly to divide and define their respective spheres of influence within Morocco. Spain would strengthen its influence in the far north of Morocco, and retain the vast mineral-rich desert known at the time as Spanish Mauritania (and later known as the Spanish Sahara and the Western Sahara), and France would retain its influence over the remaining bulk of the country.

This neatly defined arrangement was upset only by the envy of Germany's Kaiser Wilhelm II. In 1905, after a lavish and well-publicized arrival in Tangier, he succeeded in making his European competitors as uncomfortable as possible by delivering an impassioned speech on the feasibility of an independent and self-governing Morocco. Ecstatically applauded by thousands of Moroccans, his actions contributed to the international agreement, a year later, on the future of Morocco.

THE AGREEMENT OF ALGECIRAS

In 1906, representatives of (in alphabetical order) Austria-Hungary, Belgium, France, Germany, Great Britain, Italy, the Netherlands, Portugal, Russia, Spain, and the United States met at Algeciras, Spain, to decide the future of Morocco. All members agreed to a uniform and very low tariff on all goods imported and exported from Morocco. (This cut out, at a single stroke of the pen, a large part of the sultan's income.) They also agreed to open Morocco to the business enterprises of each of the signatories. They further agreed, perhaps to prevent any of their competitors from gaining the upper hand, to preserve (at least in theory) the integrity and the independence of the sultan and his subjects. Morocco was in effect relieved of any ability to decide its own destiny. The two principal players were France and Spain.

THE PROTECTORATE

The incursions of France and Spain into positions of privilege and profit enraged the local chieftains. In 1907, the construction of French-owned railway lines provoked the assassination first of a Frenchman in Marrakesh, then of nine French dockworkers in Casablanca. Using the murders as justification, France invaded through the frontier town of Oujda, on the Algerian border, eventually occupying the Atlantic coast and the main port of Casablanca, as well as part of the Moroccan hinterlands.

In 1911, France invaded Fez, the Islamic and intellectual stronghold of Morocco. Germany, presumably in an effort to aid the Moroccan nationalists, sent a gunboat to the Moroccan coastline, but quickly retreated when France agreed to a diplomatic barter granting Germany all economic rights within a section of the African Congo.

The cynicism and bitterness of the Moroccans deepened. In 1912, the Spanish pressured the French to officially note, by treaty, Spain's unrelenting claim to the extreme north and the extreme south of Morocco. Faced with hundreds of foreign troops, the sultan resigned in protest, signing as part of his safe departure an agreement (Le Protectorat) that divided Morocco's administration between French and Spanish zones of influence. Morocco ceased to function as a sovereign country. Within a few weeks, the capital of the French zone was transferred from Fez to the easier-to-control Rabat, and the capital of the Spanish zones became Tetuán.

Within the French zone, the task of subduing the dozens of insurrectionary tribes required more than 20 years, from 1912 until at least the mid-1930s. To their credit, the French made tremendous investments in Morocco, establishing schools and hospitals, and building an infrastructure of roads, railways, and ports (especially Casablanca) still largely in use today. They raised the educational level of the populace and ploughed back into Morocco most of the profits from what is still today the country's most profitable enterprise, phosphate mining. With ample justification, the French also claim the credit for introducing to Morocco the country's second language—French—which opened doors to the ideas and commerce of a far broader and more diverse world.

The French administration of Morocco during World War II fell into the hands of the collaborationist Vichy government. An officially neutral Spain, under the Fascist Franco government, imposed upon the residents of the Spanish zones of Morocco the same repressions witnessed in Spain. Neither European regime set any particularly exemplary moral example to their colonial subjects. Tangier, always an open and international city, became one of the war theater's centers for international intrigue and espionage. In 1942, the American army, led by Patton, liberated Morocco from the grip of the Vichy government and repelled the Nazis from North Africa. Before 1945, hundreds of Moroccan soldiers joined Patton's army, fighting with distinction on the American and Free French sides in Italy, France, and the Rhineland.

INDEPENDENCE

In 1947, Moroccan residents of the international city of Tangier became the most vocal supporters of independence from France.

The independence movement's principal spokesperson was the then-sultan of

Morocco, heir to the Alaouite dynasty, Sidi Mohammed ben Youssef (father of the present King Hassan II). He was dethroned in 1953 on French orders and exiled with his family to Madagascar. A few years later, on a wave of popular approval, Mohammed ben Youssef (Mohammed V) was recalled to the throne as a prelude to the granting by the French of Moroccan independence.

Independence was approved on March 2, 1956, by the French government, who relinquished all claims to the French section of Morocco. Less than six weeks later, the Spanish government of Franco gave up claims to most of the north of Morocco (with the exceptions of its colonies at Melilla and Ceuta, considered part of Spain). Spain, however, in a move that would have serious repercussions in the 1980s, retained its claim to the arid western deserts of the Spanish Sahara.

It took two years for the now-united Morocco to disassemble the French and Spanish infrastructures and the customs barriers that separated the two former territories. By 1958, both zones, plus the international city of Tangier, were united into the single sovereign state of Morocco.

With the retreat of the French, the two new nations of Morocco and Algeria entered almost immediately into an armed conflict regarding the exact position of the border that separated them. (This conflict was resolved by a United Nations agreement reached in 1963.)

Mohammed V worked to establish a modern definition for an ancient culture suddenly propelled into a new national consciousness, but his reign was short-lived. In 1961, he was succeeded by his 31-year-old son, Morocco's present king, Hassan II.

THE GREEN MARCH

The Spanish government's claim on Morocco's southwestern extremity had always been a matter of shame and a subject of endless diplomatic debate. In 1976, Hassan II organized the peaceful and amazingly effective Green March. Rallying 350,000 Moroccan volunteers—women, men, and children—from all parts of his country, he transported them in a makeshift and wildly diverse motorized caravan to the Western Sahara's border. After its conclusion, the Green March was regarded as one of the most successful, peaceful, and farsighted territorial campaigns in African history. In the face of the massive march, the Spanish government—embroiled in succession problems following Francisco Franco's recent death—withdrew its claim to the sparsely populated territory, leaving the field open to Moroccan expansionism.

Almost immediately a vague coalition of resistance fighters partially funded by Algeria identified itself and began a 10-year campaign of guerrilla resistance against Morocco.

By the late 1980s, this conflict, which had involved Morocco and its king in endless international embarrassments, became less prominent in the country's day-to-day life and eventually subsided. A period of Moroccan colonization followed with the importation of as many as 100,000 Moroccan nationalists into such cities as Laayoune.

Today, without renouncing either its Arabic or its African roots, Morocco has anchored its future and fortunes to the West. Because of its joint control with Spain of the enormously strategic Strait of Gibraltar, and because of the effective role it plays in negotiations between the Christian and Islamic worlds, Morocco is enormously important to the United States. It has officially asked to join the EEC, on the same footing as Greece, Spain, and Portugal, and to an increasing degree it has transformed the natural hospitality of its occupants into a vital and touristic allure.

POLITICS

Defined as a constitutional monarchy, Morocco is headed by King Hassan II, heir to the Alaouite dynasty. The country has a Chamber of Representatives, sited in the capital of Rabat, consisting of 306 deputies. One-third of its members are elected by an electoral college composed of representatives from municipal governments, artisans' guilds, labor unions, and the Chambers of Agriculture and Commerce. The remaining two-thirds are elected by popular vote. By some estimates, Morocco has more than a dozen political parties, some of them splinter groups. Six of these parties are represented in the Chamber of Representatives.

Morocco's present constitution, adopted in 1972 after a referendum and revised in 1980, is the second constitution since the country received independence from France in 1956. It provides for a "constitutional and presidential monarchy," together with a multiparty national assembly.

The king is considered both the political and the spiritual head of his country, bearing as one of his most prestigious titles, Commander of the Faithful (Amir al Mouminine). He is the ruler of Morocco's internal police and armed forces, and retains the right to appoint or dismiss the prime minister, his cabinet, and the national assembly. Although he is the leader of all aspects of Moroccan society, many of his decisions are adopted after consultations with Morocco's Chamber of Representatives. Despite his sweeping powers, the country remains a patchwork of ethnic and tribal groups whose strongest unifying force is Moroccan nationalism and an unswerving devotion to Islam.

Hassan's power has not gone unquestioned. There have been serious student disturbances, two attempted coups involving the armed forces, and two attempts on his life since he inherited the throne in 1961. At present, however, Hassan is without equal as the strongest and most reliable source of influence and power in Morocco.

Hassan is the father of five children, his designated heir being his oldest son, Prince Sidi Mohammed (born 1963). The prince is being carefully groomed for his eventual position as head of the Moroccan world.

Both the king and his heirs have vowed to remain faithful to the teachings of Islam, but not to endorse intolerant fanaticism in any of its variations. Simultaneously— while drawing upon the best aspects of the Western societies—they refuse to slavishly adopt Western values. This enlightened interpretation of Islamic teachings has traditionally cast Morocco in the role of a moderate intermediary between the Western and Arabic worlds.

Today, Morocco is considered at once strong, independent, and somewhat isolated from the whirlwinds of emotion surrounding it on every side. Because of its location at the western extremity of the Islamic world, its contacts with the West have been easier and perhaps more productive than those of the other Muslim societies.

2. ART, ARCHITECTURE, LITERATURE & LANGUAGE

ART

THE ISLAMIC INFLUENCE

The permeation of Islam into Moroccan society virtually erased distinctions between secular and religious art. In Morocco and throughout the Islamic world, the representation of any living being has always been viewed as a potentially dangerous temptation to idolatry, one that might distract viewers from the abstract concept of an all-encompassing One God. From the start, fully rounded sculpture and painting were expressly forbidden by Koranic law; they were (and still are) virtually nonexistent within Moroccan society. Because of these interdictions, the execution of increasingly sophisticated geometric and floral decorative motifs was soon elevated to a form of high art.

IMPRESSIONS

The whole Muslim world is practically controlled by music.
—WILLIAM S. BURROUGHS

The appeal of geometric decoration had probably always been present within pre-Islamic Berber society, and at least some of these ancient non-Islamic symbols were adapted for use within the newly imposed Islamic codes. Other symbols were borrowed from pre-Islamic Syrian and Egyptian sources, and passed westward with the Arab infiltration of Berber society.

Mathematically precise geometric decoration leads a worshipper from the confused muddle of this world to a recognition of "the Accuracy and Truth of the One God Allah." Rhythmic repetitions of motifs are soothing reminders that the universe is ordered, more perfect than the hodgepodge of present reality.

Geometric figures became artistic symbols of respect for the sacred harmony of mathematics. To the degree that builders could afford them, they covered the interior surfaces of religious structures. Geometric shapes derived from numbers took on mystical significance. Within 400 years of the death of Muhammad, the Arabs, from bases in Damascus and Andalusia, had become the premier mathematicians of the world. They expanded the theories of the ancient Greek metaphysician Phythagoras, created the system of Arabic numerals that is now used universally throughout the world, and developed advanced concepts of algebra, geometry, and calculus. Astronomy and its offshoot, astrology, were passionately studied, and the association of mystical or magical properties with numbers, as recorded in the Kabbala, became widely appreciated by many Islamic mystics.

At the same time, the art of calligraphy—decorative Arabic script, either written on parchment or incised into stone—became richly ornate. Arabic is the sacred language of Islam, believed by many Muslims to have been given to Muhammad directly from God as a vehicle for His wisdom as expressed by the Koran. Its script developed from the Nabato-Aramaic, which was itself a descendent of Phoenician.

The Malikite caliph, Abdel Malik (ruling from 685 to 705), ordered the standardization of Arabic calligraphy into two forms, the cursive and the kufic, whose basic forms—with regional variations—were adopted throughout the Islamic world. The form that was adopted as suitable for carving was the kufic, whose solid and angular forms could be legibly rendered into rock and plaster. In Morocco, the calligraphic form that later ornamented countless mosques and public buildings was the *maghrebi,* a combination of the cursive and the kufic, which developed in Andalusia in the 9th century.

As Morocco's dynasties evolved, artists vied with one another for the most elegant execution of Koranic verses. Depending on the artist's purpose, these were usually written with black ink on parchment using either a donkey-hair brush or a pen crafted from reed, silver, copper, stork's beak, or pomegranate slivers.

As architectural embellishments, calligraphic homages to Allah were carved into stone or plaster on public monuments, binding together the building's architectural elements as the Koran binds together the community of Islam.

Along with the appreciation of calligraphy as an art form, floral decoration also developed. Although in some Islamic sects and in some dynasties even the depiction of a flower or a vine was expressly forbidden, in others (notably in Persia) it was not. As Morocco grew more sophisticated, floral motifs were borrowed and appreciated, and used in geometrical arrangements to reflect the perfect garden of Paradise promised to the Faithful by Muhammad.

Adding extra passion to the artistic process was the belief that (according to the Koran) every artist on the Day of Judgment will be challenged to breathe life into the work he created during his lifetime, and upon failing, will be condemned. Understandably, artists worked feverishly.

The grandly ornate public buildings erected by the sultans were the most visible recipients of the art being executed in Morocco. The arts also flourished within Berber hamlets and villages, but in less grandiose forms than those ordained by Morocco's rulers. Developing some of the richest artistic traditions in the Maghreb, Morocco's rural craftsmen adopted geometric and calligraphic motifs as inspiration for their ceramics, jewelry, and carpet weaving. Although devout Muslims, the

Berbers nonetheless retained artistic motifs that predated the Islamic era, and whose exact origins remain a mystery.

Intensely regional in their interpretations, and often following motifs that were exclusive to their particular tribe, these artisans have produced some of the most charming and unusual handcrafts ever to come out of Africa. Examples of their work are widely available throughout Morocco today, in forms that have barely changed in thousands of years.

ARCHITECTURE
PRE-ISLAMIC ARCHITECTURE

It was in architecture that the arts in Morocco found their highest and most enduring expression.

The oldest structure remaining from the megalithic era is the cromlech of M'Soura, near Larache, where a circular arrangement of about 170 columns, the tallest of which measures about 18 feet, encircles a burial mound. Almost completely in ruins, the victim of endless looting over the eras, the site was probably built by a wealthy Phoenician centuries before the Romanization of Morocco. Despite lengthy excavations, the cromlech's exact purpose remains a mystery.

During the Roman era, hundreds of civic and domestic structures were erected, usually following the standardized examples in other Roman cities throughout the Mediterranean world—triumphal arches, forums, temples, theaters, and baths. The most impressive ruins can be found at the former capital of Roman Morocco, Volubilis, near Meknes, and at the coastal city of Lixus, near Larache.

Most of the columns were Corinthian, and the themes for most of the mosaics that ornamented the floors of buildings were conceived in Rome and executed from sketches by Berber laborers. Oddly, however, the colors used for Roman mosaics in Morocco tended to be more somber than their counterparts elsewhere in the Mediterranean world. Also, some of the geometrically patterned borders that served as frames for the mosaics showed some of the same patterns that later appeared prolifically during the Muslim period.

Some scholars credit the Romans with introducing to Morocco an interior design that was adapted in different variations throughout Moroccan history. It incorporated a rectangular series of rooms, each opening onto a central courtyard or atrium. A deliberately forbidding exterior had smallish (or no) windows.

After the Islamization of Morocco, the country's building styles diverged along two very different lines, Berber and Hispano-Moorish.

BERBER ARCHITECTURE

The most remarkable characteristic of the Berber style might be the way it survived with few adaptations over the centuries. It has never been significantly influenced, not even by the Arabic Muslims. Mostly confined to the countryside, the architecture adapted itself to the demands of mountain life, animal husbandry, and defense. The two most enduring examples of this architecture were fortified hilltop silos (*agadirs*), used for the storage of grain; and the larger and more evocative fortresses known as *kasbahs,* or *ksours* (singular: *ksar*).

Owing nothing to the elegance of Islamic Andalusia, and intended exclusively for shelter and fortification, a ksar's tall, crenellated walls were built from battered earth and sun-dried bricks cemented together with a mixture of mud and pulverized straw; the resulting colors blended perfectly into the landscape. Walls were almost always laid out along rectangular lines, always sloped upward and inward, and were accented at their corners with rectangular towers that, like the walls, sloped inward. "Believer is to Believer," said the Prophet Muhammad, "as the mutually upholding sections of a building." Access to a ksar was usually through a single monumental doorway, which closed tightly in case of attack.

The Islamic sense of community was reflected in the communal living arrangements inside these buildings. A labyrinth of dimly lit vaulted passageways and warrens opened onto an interior courtyard large enough to hold an entire clan with their domesticated animals, grain, and water supply. Vertical surfaces were incised with the carved repetitions of geometrical designs that included lozenges, chevrons, triangles, crosses, solar wheels . . . anything except a representation of some living thing (human, animal, or plant life). Individual rooms could (and can) be no bigger than the length of the trunk of a mature date palm, since that is what was usually used to support roofs and ceilings.

Despite the ksours' appearances of solidity, the inferior building materials used for their construction required constant maintenance. Some of the country's most elaborate examples of Berber architecture, when abandoned, usually fell into ruins within a half century, rarely leaving any worthwhile traces for archeologists. Southern Morocco is littered with their remains. Rainfall has been lethal to their well-being. But the fact that there are hundreds of Berber structures remaining today within Morocco attests to their continued use as homes by tribespeople, who carry on the endless process of maintaining them.

HISPANO-MOORISH ARCHITECTURE

The sweep of Islam from its origins in Saudi Arabia through the Middle East, across North Africa, and into central Spain created a melting pot of architectural elements. Distinctly different from the style that had evolved in Damascus, Persia, and India was the one developed during the 9th century in Andalusia by its newly arrived Islamic conquerers. The best remaining example is the cathedral of Córdoba, originally built during that period as a mosque. By the 10th and 11th centuries, the premises of this architectural style had permeated both sides of the Strait of Gibraltar, and Morocco had embarked on the construction of some of the finest buildings in the Muslim world.

Hispano-Moorish architecture aims to define an interior space—often succeeding with enviable theatricality—as something distinctly different from the hot and dusty wilderness that surrounds it. It tries to create a sheltered world, suitable for rest and contemplation, inside of which might be fountains, gardens, and expressions of reverence for Allah.

Some historians have noted that both the Christian and Islamic worlds drew their architectural inspiration from classical models of the ancient world, but while Europe frequently reached back to the pagan temples of ancient Greece, North Africa looked to the domes and arches of Christian Byzantium.

The name of a particular architect was never connected to any individual building. Construction depended on the desire of a sultan to make his capital equivalent to his glory. Thus, Morocco's four imperial cities (Fez, Meknes, Marrakesh, and Rabat) were each enlarged and ornamented in communal urban undertakings that depended more or less on the whims and caprices of their monarchs.

Some rulers impressed with the sheer scale of their building, recognizing the power of massive expanses of masonry. Especially noteworthy for this was the 17th-century Alaouite sultan Moulay Ismail, who ordered 16 miles of walls built around his capital at Meknes, and the creation within those walls of sumptuous palaces and mosques. At least some of the actual construction was performed by captive Christian and black Sudanese slaves.

The earliest Hispano-Moorish buildings derived from Berber architectural techniques, and the sun-dried bricks used in their construction fell rapidly into disrepair. Later, chiseled stone and kiln-baked bricks (an idea imported from the Muslim East) added to the life of the buildings.

Muslim architects in North Africa rejected the use of horizontal beams, perhaps because of the scarcity of suitable lumber, in favor of the horseshoe (broken) arch. Rarely rounded, as in Europe, columns were more usually square or rectangular. The capitals atop columns borrowed freely from Egyptian, Persian, and Roman traditions. In time, architects used columns as decorative pilasters rather than as freestanding structural necessities.

More and more, this trend emphasized the form (and philosophical unity) of the arch itself, rather than the embellishments that sometimes surrounded it. Throughout the Muslim world, arches were repeated rhythmically, as a meditational aid toward reaching an understanding of Allah and his Oneness. Arches were used in interlocking ways to support rounded domes rising from rectangular floor plans, to support the arcades ringing nearly every courtyard in the Maghreb, and to define and embellish every architecturally awkward corner of a public or religious building. The style of the arch varied greatly, and sometimes included dripping stalactites whose even spacings visually suggest the rippling sound of a musical scale.

Each dynasty approached the ornamentation of its architectural monuments differently. Common embellishments included the minarets (towers) added to mosques, as well as dozens of magnificently proportioned *babs* (monumental entryways) piercing the fortified walls ringing a city.

Communal colleges (*medersas*) were established for the instruction of Koranic studies. Other notable structures include *koubbas* (cupola-capped mausoleums for holy men). Even more impressive were the scores of palaces and aristocratic homes scattered across Morocco, many of which have today been converted into museums, hotels, restaurants, and administrative headquarters for the Moroccan government.

LITERATURE

The unbreakable links between the Moroccan identity and the precepts of Islam heavily influenced the country's literature.

Because the Arabic language was considered the direct gift of Allah, given to Muhammad when the wisdom of the Koran was unveiled, all medieval literature was penned in formal Arabic and intended for an erudite audience.

Morocco's earliest famous author was Ibn Rushd, who wrote under the name of Averroës. In the 1100s, he became celebrated for his Arabic-language commentary on the works of Aristotle, as well as for his writings on many of the aspects then known about science.

One of the most popular Arabic literary genres was, oddly, travel writing. Its greatest adherent was Ibn Batuta. Born in Tangier in 1304, he was without equal as the most prolific travel writer of his time, surpassing in fame and contemporary adulation the reputation of Marco Polo. The accounts that he left take readers to 14th-century Mecca, Samarkand, Peking, and Constantinople. When not traveling (which was rare), he lived in Fez.

Other writers, many of whom never received credit for their creations, chronicled the victories and achievements of the Moroccan dynasties, penned poetic adulations of important citizens, recorded the various miraculous acts of the Islamic saints, and reported on the specific rebellious activities of the Berber tribes. Certain of these works were written as poetry, some of it courtly, to flatter the sultans and amuse their harems. All of it consciously exploited the voluptuousness and expressiveness of the Arabic language.

One of Morocco's most respected medieval authors, credited with giving some of the most unbiased accounts of the events happening around him, was Ibn Khaldun. Born in Tunis in 1332, he was first a student, then a professor at the Koranic school of Fez. He compiled a highly erudite history of the Berber tribes of North Africa. Still highly regarded by Europeans and Arabs, it is considered one of the standard reference books for anyone seriously studying the ethnographies of North Africa. The same author's monumental examination and commentary on contemporary Islamic thought was called *Prolégomènes*.

As these examples show, Moroccan literature tended toward the erudite, the scientific, the philosophical, and the historical. Most of its intellectual stimulation came from the brilliant Muslim universities in Spanish Andalusia, although there was also literary interchange with the courts of the caliphs at Baghdad and Cairo.

From about 1930 onward, a new genre of Moroccan literature emerged— nationalistic appeal for decolonialization and self-determination. Although some pieces were written around the time of independence, the most noteworthy came after 1970. The most famous representatives of this movement include Tahar Ben Jalloun

(*The Scars of the Sun*, 1972; *Future Memory*, 1976), Ahmed Sefrioui (*The Tattooed Memory*, 1971; *The Wound of My Own Name*, 1974), Abdelhak Serhane (*Messaouda*, 1983; *The Children of the Narrow Streets*, 1986), and A. Laroui (*Contemporary Arabic Ideology*, 1970).

LANGUAGE

English is increasingly spoken in Morocco, even if grammar and syntax are not absolutely perfect. Despite the growing use of English, however, the three major languages of Morocco are Arabic, Berber, and French.

ARABIC

Imported from the Middle East by Muslim invaders in the 7th century, Arabic is divided into two streams of expression. These divisions are classical Arabic and dialectical Arabic.

Classical (literary) Arabic is the only form of the language that can be written and read. It is the official language of Morocco and of Islam. According to strict fundamentalists, it was revealed directly by Allah to His Prophet Muhammad as a vehicle for understanding the subtleties of the Koran. An innately religious, richly colored, highly nuanced language that translates clumsily, it is a source of endless poetic pleasure and wisdom. All of the correspondence of modern Morocco (government communications, legal documents, scientific journals, and newspapers) is published in classical Arabic.

Dialectical Arabic, also known as everyday (or vulgar) Arabic, is an oral language with no written equivalent whose expressions and pronunciation vary widely according to region. Its syntax and usage often vary widely from that of classical Arabic, and it is adapted according to the specific communication needs of the community speaking it at the time. (Oddly, the tribal dialect that most closely resembles the vocabulary and syntax of classical Arabic is *hassanya*, spoken by tribespeople deep in the arid sub-Sahara, and even that is densely peppered with local idioms.)

BERBER

It's the oldest living tongue of the Maghreb, and is usually spoken only by rural tribes of Morocco. Exclusively an oral language, it has no alphabet. Partly because of this, Berber has splintered into dozens of different dialects.

However, the lack of a written alphabet does not prevent the transmission from generation to generation of an evocative oral tradition. Legends, folk wisdom, and poetic epics of love, war, heroism, and sorrow are recited by tribespeople, with frequent elaborations and poetic repetitions adding to their charm.

3. FAMOUS MOROCCANS

The Blue Sultan (El Hiba) (1877–1919) Tracing his lineage directly to the Prophet Muhammad through Morocco's first Islamic monarch, Idriss I, he was born into a nomadic tribe of "blue men" from the region that is now the Western Sahara. Thanks partly to his illustrious ancestry and his fiercely imposing demeanor, and perhaps to some much-debated psychic abilities, he was quickly credited with a reputation for destroying the infidels and performing miracles for Muslims. His revolutionary efforts began in earnest in 1912, just after the partition of Morocco between the French and the Spanish. Thousands of partisans joined him from obscure regions of the Souss and the arid southern deserts. He established himself briefly as sultan of Marrakesh, retreated to the fortress at Taroudannt, and eventually died defeated by the power of the colonials.

Ibn Batuta (1304–77) Born in Tangier, he was the most prolific, most thoroughly acknowledged, and most widely read travel writer of his era, surpassing in his lifetime the fame even of his European counterpart Marco Polo. Ibn Batuta's accounts describe the sights and values of 14th-century Mecca, Samarkand, Peking, and Constantinople. When not traveling (which was rare), he recorded his experiences from a base in Fez.

Ibn Khaldun (1332–1406) Although born in Tunis, he came to the Koranic school at Fez early in his life and eventually was promoted to the rank of professor. He is the most consistently reliable historian of his era, recording events without the flattery and gloss characteristic of many of his contemporary colleagues. For his treatises on the history and mores of Berber tribes, he is considered the father of modern sociology. He died in Fez.

Juba II (reigned 25 B.C.–A.D. 44) A Romanized Berber, he became the puppet king of ancient Morocco, and as such imported into his capital at Volubilis the culture and values of ancient Rome. His reign was one of the longest and most architecturally prodigious of any Moroccan monarch. The woman he married was the child of Cleopatra and Mark Antony. The murder of Juba's son, Ptolemy, by Caligula sparked a bloody war between Morocco and Rome that eventually changed the social order of North Africa.

The "Rogui," Bou Hamara (ca. 1860–1909) Late in the 19th century, he was one of the Alaouite sultan's trusted henchmen. Accused of treachery, he was exiled from Morocco and settled in Algeria. Returning several years later disguised as an ascetic and itinerant imam, he quickly earned a reputation among the Berber tribes for piety and good deeds. Preaching revolt against taxation by the Alaouite sultans, he organized a potent rebellion, conquered the strategic mountain stronghold of Taza, and reigned as sultan there for six years. After one of the bloodiest military campaigns in Moroccan memory, the Alaouite sultan regained Taza in 1909, tortured its partisans, and carried Bou Hamara in a cage to Fez. There, after enduring prolonged torture and ridicule from crowds in the Medina, he was fed to the sultan's lions. A *rogui,* incidentally, is a derisive name for a pretender to a sultanate.

Yacoub el Mansour (reigned 1184–99) An Almohad sultan whose vision engendered construction of the ramparts of Rabat—an architectural infrastructure that the modern Moroccan government occupies today. Opposed by many of his advisers, who preferred to remain within the existing capital at Marrakesh, he partly derailed his own efforts by incessant campaigns to conquer Andalusia from the Christians. Construction on his hoped-for capital ended on the day of his death, and wasn't resumed until hundreds of years later by other dynasties.

4. RELIGION, MYTH & FOLKLORE

RELIGION
THE ISLAMIC BACKGROUND

Morocco is solidly anchored to the precepts of Islam, which permeate virtually every aspect of public and private life within the kingdom. The spiritual leader of the country is King Hassan II, who has publicly defined Islam as "a religion of order. More important even than its multiple benefits as a religion of prayer and meditation, it has revealed to humankind how to live within society, and how to promote and maintain good relations between different communities upon legislative bases."

Of the world's three great monotheistic religions, Islam has the greatest number of adherents—more than 900 million souls. Probably foremost among its many precepts is the concept of submission and obedience of the human soul to the will of the single Almighty, as clearly stated in the Koran.

The religion was established in Saudi Arabia by Muhammad ibn Abdallah, who is known variously throughout the world as the Prophet, Muhammad, Mohammed, or Mahomet. (Today, the name is without equal the most popular male name in Morocco, usually bestowed as a sign of honor on a family's firstborn son.) The Prophet was born around A.D. 570 into the influential Koreisch clan at Mecca, which was at the time an important stop along the caravan routes through the Arabian desert. Even then, Mecca was considered spiritually important, as the site of the Kaaba, a sanctuary established by Abraham, as well as a holy place to several pagan cults.

Orphaned early in life, and later raised and trained by a succession of relatives, the young Muhammad rose to positions of leadership in caravan expeditions into Syria. Many legends concerning his life discuss an eventual marriage to his employer, a wealthy widow 15 years his senior named Khadija. Devoted to him and his mission throughout her lifetime, she eventually bore him six children. The four who survived childhood were all girls, a fact that eventually contributed to passionate disputes among his followers regarding his spiritual legacy and succession.

Many of the names popular in modern Morocco are derived from Muhammad's immediate family. They include Anima (his mother), Abdallah (his father), Fatima (his oldest and most beloved daughter), Ali (his cousin and eventual son-in-law through a marriage to Fatima), Hassan and Hussein (his two sons, who did not survive childhood), Halima (his childhood wet nurse), and Omar (his best friend).

The successful father of a growing family, Muhammad and his wife joined a religious sect known as the Hanyfs, puritanical seekers of enlightenment who studiously respected the religious traditions of the Christians, the Jews, and the Zoroastrian Persians. He developed a meditational ritual of secluding himself in "a sterile valley" near Mecca for rest and meditation. During one of these visits, the Archangel Gabriel, revealed as the messenger of God, made the first of hundreds of subsequent appearances to Muhammad. These messages, which were eagerly recorded by the group of disciples that grew rapidly around Muhammad, were eventually accumulated and designated as the Koran.

The most threatening part of the Prophet's message for the polytheistic powermongers of Mecca was that in the eyes of the One God, masters and slaves are equal. Even Muhammad's powerful clansmen could not protect him from the wrath that such a doctrine aroused in the established civic and religious leaders.

In 622, fleeing for his life from Mecca with a band of disciples, he entered the city of Medina (whose name is literally translated as "town"), and was soon after elected as its ruler. The flight from Mecca, or the Hegira, is today accepted as the beginning of the Muslim era.

It was in Medina that Muhammad developed many of the practical moral and legal guidelines that at first ruled that city and later the Muslim world. As the numbers of his followers multiplied, he organized them, with the help of his devoted caliphs, into a fearsome army. His forces eventually occupied Mecca and all the rest of the Arabian Peninsula.

Muhammad died in Medina on June 8, 632, at the age of 60, a victim of pleurisy, and was buried with his head turned toward the sacred Kaaba of Mecca. He left a disputed inheritance that became the root cause of many of today's theological and ideological conflicts within the Islamic world.

The Sunni sect (to which Morocco officially adheres) believes in the hereditary legitimacy of three of the Prophet's caliphs. The Shiites, however, support the hereditary claims of Ali and Fatima, the Prophet's son-in-law and eldest daughter. Other sects, including the Druze, the Ismailis, and the Khajarites, maintain different beliefs concerning the beneficiaries of the inheritance of Muhammad.

The Sufis, a divisional offshoot of the Shiites, developed both a devotedly ascetic brotherhood and a series of rituals for mystical religious experiences. Sufism became extremely important in the development of Islamic doctrine in Morocco, with bases in such cities as Fez and Meknes and in the sub-Sahara.

Despite Islam's internal divisions, its armies rapidly conquered, in this order, Syria, Persia, Mesopotamia, parts of Armenia, and Egypt, converting the populace in the process. The conquest of Morocco was much more difficult (see "Geography, History, and Politics").

THE KORAN

Muslims believe its 114 chapters and 6,342 verses were dictated to Muhammad directly by God over a period of 20 years. Because Muhammad remained illiterate until the end of his life, the revelations were recited by him to scores of transcribers, who, the Muslims believe, recorded them verbatim. The accumulated verses, sermons, clarifications, and transcriptions of the Prophet were arranged and accumulated after his death by Caliph Omar (Muhammad's best friend) and Caliph Abu Bakr, who distributed them to different Islamic communities. A more precise accumulation was compiled several years later by the third caliph, Othman. He is reported to have been reading a copy of it at the moment of his death in 652.

Perhaps (but not necessarily) following the wishes of Muhammad himself, the verses were arranged not in the order of their revelation, but in order of their length—a decision that probably makes their memorization a bit easier.

The Koran is roughly divided into sections that concern: (1) the monotheistic nature of the One and All-Powerful Divinity, (2) the organization of the political structure of the Islamic community, and (3) guidelines for the Faithful on the choices of Good over Evil, and the mode in which a Believer should approach and consider God.

The Koran also stresses that God gives meaning to the collective and individual life of humankind, who will await the decisions of God on the eventual Day of Judgment. In Islam, charity and justice toward others are defined as an essential part of a daily schedule. Also inherent in Islam is a belief in the equality of all men and women in the eyes of Allah.

5. FOOD & DRINK

FOOD

Many experts consider Moroccan cuisine among the finest in the world, ranking with French and Chinese for subtlety and flavor. The cuisine was influenced by the invaders of the Maghreb (now Morocco, Tunisia, and Algeria).

The diet of the Berbers blended with that of the newcomers, who included the Phoenicians, the Carthaginians, the Romans, and the nomadic Arabs. Later, the Moors introduced the cooking of Andalusia, with its use of olives and olive oils. The latest and one of the most profound influences on Moroccan cuisine was from the French, who ruled the country for many years. Fine French cheeses and wines are sold in all major urban centers of Morocco.

MEALS & DINING CUSTOMS

The best food, everybody agrees, is served in Moroccan homes, where fresh ingredients are used and slow-cooking processes prevail. Perhaps you'll be lucky enough to get an invitation during your visit.

Moroccans eat with the fingers of their right hand, but spoons and forks are provided to visitors upon request. Don't worry about messy fingers. Small washbasins, sometimes perfumed with rose petals or lemon, are presented to each guest before and after a meal. The warm water is poured over the hands, which are held over the basin.

Rapid-fire conversation is not required at Moroccan meals—in fact, it may be resented. Long periods of silence are characteristic. This is not rude in any way. It means the diner is too busy enjoying the meal to indulge in much small talk. You can talk before or after eating.

TAKING TEA

The tea-making ceremony of Morocco is an ancient one. The tea-maker sits cross-legged on the preferred seat in a tea salon. There he is given a round tray, often one of the brass variety that you see in all the souks. On the tray rests a silver teapot, accompanied by glasses, some rather flamboyantly decorated. A box contains green tea; another, chunks of sugar; and a final one, sprigs of fresh mint.

From the kitchen emerges a copper kettle, the water still steaming inside. Sometimes the kettle rests on a charcoal brazier. The tea is put into the pot as boiling water is added. A very generous amount of sugar and plenty of mint sprays also go into the kettle. After the lid is put back on, the mixture stands for several minutes.

Then the tasting begins. A true taster brings all the style and grace of a customer sampling a $300 bottle of wine in a fancy restaurant. Sometimes the tea-maker doctors the tea after the first taste, perhaps adding one or more of the three ingredients cited above.

HEALTH CONCERNS

Most visitors to Morocco are concerned about sanitary conditions. A stroll through the markets, where meat hangs out in the open and is often fly-covered in hot months, only adds to the concerns. However, most Moroccan dishes are simmered endlessly in tight dishes or cauterized over a hot flame on an open-air brazier, so you can relax somewhat—only the toughest microbes can survive such heat.

Warning: Peel all fruit and eat only cooked vegetables.

(See also Section 3 of Chapter 2.)

THE CUISINE

The national soup is called *harira,* and usually contains diced mutton, saffron, and coriander. Served piping hot, it is often accompanied by dried dates and lemon slices with cinnamon sprinkled on top.

Other than soups, appetizers are sometimes omitted at meals in Morocco, although French restaurants offer them—everything from escargots in garlic butter to various pâtés. Moroccan appetizer salads are served, however. They are made with raw or cooked vegetables, and sometimes bits of cubed liver or brains are added for a more exotic touch. The most popular salad in Morocco is made with sliced oranges, dates, and lemons; sometimes this salad is kept on the table during the meal to "freshen the palate" between courses.

Kebabs and brochettes are also served as appetizers, although these could also be considered main courses for some. They are most often made with lamb, or sometimes beef. Many brochettes are offered at street stalls. Sometimes sheep's liver is skewered and grilled over charcoal; it is then sprinkled with cumin and served with a hot sauce for dipping.

Kefta is ground beef or lamb seasoned with herbs, skewered, and cooked over a charcoal fire. *Tajine* (or *tagine*), another common dish, is a stew made with almost anything, including camel's meat. A favorite version of this dish uses lamb and prunes; another variation, *hergma,* consists of lamb's trotters simmered with cracked wheat and chick peas. The word *tajine,* incidentally, refers both to the food itself and to the terra-cotta covered dish in which it is cooked and served. A tajine will traditionally have a conically shaped lid.

Couscous, steamed semolina (a wheat) with a stew ladled over it, is the national

IMPRESSIONS

Before coming here you should do three things: be inoculated for typhoid, withdraw your savings from the bank, and say good-bye to your friends—heaven knows you may never see them again.
—TRUMAN CAPOTE

dish. The stew portion is usually mutton, plus several vegetables, but beef or chicken is used too. It is served in a bowl with a matching cover, usually accompanied by two sauces: one to add spice and the other to moisten the semolina. Every feast, or *diffa,* in Morocco has couscous, but it's also a commonplace dish. Some Moroccans, in fact, eat it every day of their lives. Traditionally, it is presented at the end of a meal after the tajines have been served. The typical foreign diner is already full before the huge platter of couscous arrives.

The most famous Moroccan couscous is called *couscous aux sept légumes,* made with lamb shanks and lamb shoulder, and served with a bouillon flavored with onion, garlic, cinnamon sticks, salt, black pepper, hot red peppers, powdered saffron, olive oil, and chick peas. The vegetables are turnips, carrots, zucchini, eggplant, tomatoes, parsley, and pumpkin or some form of squash. Raisins can also be added.

In the Tafilalet, a sweet couscous is prepared with dates, almonds, raisins, and milk.

While you're in Morocco, do try the superb and time-honored lemon chicken, or chicken with olives. Both of these are cooked slowly in a tajine and served with rice and flat bread, and perhaps a glass of strong red or white Moroccan wine.

Mechoui is a dish for festivals, when lamb is heavily spiced and then cooked for many hours in a tight-fitting pot with raisins and almonds. Eaten with your fingers, mechoui is a delicious—and unavoidably messy—dinner. At its best, the meat literally falls off the bone. This dish (often spelled *m'choui*) is said to have originated in the campfires of the nomadic Bedouin tribes.

The famous *b'stilla,* which rivals couscous as the national dish of Morocco, consists of pounded pigeon, almonds, lemon-flavored eggs in a *mille-feuille* casing of delicate pastry. As a crowning touch, it's dusted with a fine layer of confectioner's sugar, which adds greatly to its flavor. Many purists prefer the pigeon cooked with the many tiny and pesky bones intact, supposedly because this gives the meat more flavor. Other chefs remove the bones. Sometimes, for foreigners, the dish is prepared with chicken, and although you might prefer it that way, it is not considered authentic.

Seafood is best enjoyed along the coast. From the Portuguese, the Moroccans learned the art of grilling sardines fresh from the ocean. Tuna, sea bass, sole, and bream appear on the menus at coastal resorts. You can also order prawns, mussels, crabs, and local lobsters.

The most popular vegetables are sweet peppers, onions, tomatoes (introduced perhaps from Andalusia), dried beans, zucchini, eggplant, artichokes, okra, and chick peas. These vegetables may be served as a separate side course or else blended with various combinations of meats. Butter, garlic, peppers, and onion flavor most vegetables, along with such spices as coriander, parsley, and cumin.

Fruits are used in many dishes, especially prunes, figs, and dates, but also apples, grapes, and quinces. These fruits are cooked with pigeon, lamb, and chicken. Mixed sometimes with ginger or cinnamon, they are transformed into flavorful desserts.

Bread is an important ingredient on any Moroccan table. "Give me bread in the name of Allah" is a cry heard throughout Morocco. Moroccan bread is unleavened, flat, and round.

Cornes de gazelle (kaab el ghzal) are horn-shaped pastries filled with almond paste and most often served with tea. Sometimes you may prefer to finish your meal with fresh fruit, as the melons and strawberries (especially those from Larache) are better than some of the sticky messes of sugar and water so popular at Ramadan.

DRINKS

WATER & NONALCOHOLIC BEVERAGES

Local custom dictates not drinking anything during your meal. However, you can get a glass of something if you feel you need it.

Although the water is said to be safe in the big cities and towns, I would drink only mineral water. (The mineral water from Sidi Harazem is said to cure kidney disorders—and it also tastes good.) In addition to the still water from Sidi Harazem, try the still mineral water from Sidi Ala. For sparkling water, the spring is at Oulmès, and produces what is said to be some of the best water in the world.

Coffee in Morocco is usually strong and black. The decaffeinated variety is available only in the most expensive hotels. Most Moroccans in cafés order *café-cassé*, which is coffee with milk, the French equivalent of *café au lait*. Women readers have reported that male waiters often ignore them when they enter a café alone or with another woman. If that should happen to you, go to the bar and order the coffee yourself.

In the soft-drink department, Coca-Cola is universal. It is much harder to find Diet Coke, except in the more expensive hotels. It is said that the Coca-Cola sold in Morocco contains a higher amount of sugar than that offered in Europe or North America, since Moroccans prefer their colas very sweet.

Apples and bananas are often blended with milk to form a Moroccan milkshake. Juices are popular in Morocco. What you are served—pomegranate, orange, black cherry, or grape—depends on the season.

A meal concludes with a refreshing mint tea, made with fresh young sprigs.

ALCOHOLIC BEVERAGES

Although the rule is often overlooked, in strict accordance with Koranic law it is illegal for a Muslim to consume liquor. Therefore, you should exercise caution in inviting someone for a drink. Never insist if you are politely turned down.

It's safest to confine your consumption of liquor to licensed establishments. Don't, however, expect to be served alcoholic beverages in certain local restaurants in the medinas of various towns and cities.

Moroccan wines are good, strong, and inexpensive, and should be better known. The wine-growing regions south of Meknes and Fez produce some excellent vintages, including an interesting *gris* that is lighter than a rosé but not clear enough to be white wine. The names to look for are Ksar and Château Toulal (the most popular reds), Guerrouane (my favorite), and Boulaouane. The few restaurants and hotels that offer imported French wines charge high prices.

Much of the local wine industry, cultivated so carefully by the French, is now dying out as production drops yearly. Many former wine-growing regions in this Islamic country are being converted to other forms of agriculture.

Moroccan beer might hit the spot on a hot day, but back in Munich, Germany, it wouldn't win any prizes for flavor. Try Flag Special, which is perhaps the best beer. Its rival is Stork, a lighter variety. If you don't like either of these, you'll have to settle for one of the imported brands, all at higher prices.

6. RECOMMENDED BOOKS, FILMS & RECORDINGS

BOOKS

Note: The years given in parentheses are the latest publication dates.

HISTORY

Neville Barbour's *Morocco* (1965) surveys the saga of Moroccan history from the arrival of the seafaring Phoenicians to the 1960s. *The Moors—Islam in the West* (1985), by Werner Forman and Michael Brett, traces the rise and expansion of Islam—not only in North Africa but in Andalusia. It documents the highlights of Moorish civilization in Europe, centering around Córdoba, and follows events through the reconquest of Granada by the Catholic monarchs. It's more than just history, as social, political, and economic issues are examined; and it's illustrated with photographs.

Maxwell Gavin's *Lords of the Atlas* (1983) profiles the Glaoui dynasty in the past two centuries, up to the granting of Moroccan independence in 1956. It is a fascinating story. *Lords of the Atlas* has been banned for sale in Morocco because of its political point of view. If you try to bring a copy in, it could be seized at the border.

GENERAL

Doing Daily Battle by Fatima Mernissi (translation by Mary Jo Lakeland), is a rare book by the same author who wrote *Beyond the Veil: Male-Female Dynamics in a Modern Muslim Society*. For the serious feminist who wants to know more about the daily life of women in a male-dominated society, this is perhaps the best voice. Nearly a dozen Moroccan women were interviewed.

Elias Canetti's *The Voices of Marrakesh* (1988) is the Bulgarian Nobel Prize winner's tale of the encounter between a European Jew and the Moroccan Jews of the *mellah* (Jewish quarter) during the last years of French rule.

Morocco That Was (1983) is a famous work by London *Times* correspondent Walter Harris, who originally published this account in 1921. An "instant classic" in its time, it tells of the country's feudal period and goes up to the beginning of French rule in 1912. The wealthy son of a British shipping family who settled in Morocco in 1886, Harris once owned the Kasbah (Tangier) home of Woolworth heiress Barbara Hutton. Other famous people who have lived in the Moroccan city are chronicled in "Bert and Mabel" Winter's *The Rogue's Guide to Tangier* (1986). Called "the funniest and most informative book ever written about Tangier," it's gossipy and amusing, and filled with witty anecdotes.

THE ARTS & ARCHITECTURE

Islamic Art (1981), by David Talbot Rice, surveys the entire spectrum of Islamic art, although two chapters specifically concern Morocco.

Architectural motifs and forms, along with handcraft traditions, are well documented in Richard Parker's carefully researched *A Practical Guide to Islamic Monuments in Morocco* (1986). It is available in some libraries and often at bookstores in Morocco.

If you can get a copy of André Paccard's *Traditional Islamic Craft in Moroccan Architecture* (1988), explore it for its photographs, not so much for the text. It contains rare pictures of royal palaces in Morocco never seen by the public. For one period of his life, Paccard worked as an interior designer for King Hassan II.

FICTION

The expatriate American novelist Paul Bowles's *The Sheltering Sky* was first published in 1949, and it remains his finest achievement. Considered a landmark in American fiction, and filmed in 1990 with Debra Winger, it takes as its theme the impact of Arab life on three Americans in a North African coastal city, and later in the Sahara. Bowles's *The Spider's House* (1953), a novel set against the daily life of Fez, revolves around the transformation and conflicts emerging during the last years of French rule.

In the Lap of Atlas (1977) is by Richard Hughes, author of *A High Wind in Jamaica*, who used to live in the Kasbah in Tangier. Here, he reworks Moroccan stories of wit and irony. He also writes of his visit to Telouet and the Atlas in 1928.

Tahar Ben Jalloun's *The Sand Child* (1984) is the work of the best-known fiction writer in Morocco. Although presently living in Paris, he remembers the country of his origin well, as recounted in this tale of a girl whose father reared her as a boy. A good read.

BIOGRAPHY

For Bread Alone (1987), by Mohammed Choukri, is the autobiography of a young man who was born poor and illiterate. It was translated from classic Arabic into English by expatriate novelist Paul Bowles. Bowles's own autobiography, *Without Stopping* (1972), begins with his early days in America. But later he writes of how he and his wife, the writer Jane Bowles, settled in Morocco after World War II and of the many visitors they encountered, including Tennessee Williams, Gore Vidal, and Truman Capote.

Jane Bowles is the subject of Millicent Dillon's *A Little Original Sin* (1981). Known for her novel *Two Serious Ladies* and her play *In the Summer House,* Bowles was called the "last great bohemian." She got deeply involved in Moroccan life, and although she and her husband went their separate ways in their marriage, they became virtual hostess and host to all the glamorous celebrities visiting Tangier.

Mohammed Choukri's *Jean Genet in Tangier* (1973) has been translated by Paul Bowles, with an introduction by William S. Burroughs. In just 82 pages, Choukri writes of his relationship with the French lion of postwar literature. Much of it reads like a conversation, set against the backdrop of Tangier in its heyday, when it was known as the "wicked city" of North Africa.

TRAVEL

Morocco—Its People and Places (1985), by Edmondo de Amicis, translated by C. Rollin-Tilton, was first published in Italy in 1882. It is one of the first travelogues written on Morocco, giving a fascinating account of "Arabian Nights" court life at the time. Edith Wharton's later and more famous *In Morocco,* first issued in 1920, offers a glimpse into harem life in the early 20th century. It's worth the effort to find it.

RECORDINGS

Here are some representative recordings of the major forms of Moroccan music. For sacred music, try *Musique réligieuse en Islam,* within the "Peoples of the World" collection by M. Louis, which includes calls to prayer and songs of the brotherhood of Aissaoua.

The traditional Arabic sound can be heard on *Morocco: Arabic Traditional Music* (Unesco Collection/Auvidis), with Abdeslam Cherkaoui; *Musique classique andalou-maghrébine* (Ocora), with the Fez Orchestra interpreting some of the oldest melodies in the Islamic-Andalusian repertoire; *Music of Morocco* (Folkways), funded by the U.S. Library of Congress, and assisted by longtime Morocco resident Paul Bowles; and *El Lebrijano and the Orchestra of Tangier* (Globestyle Recordings).

Berber music is represented on *Maroc/1* and *Maroc/2* (Ocora), compiled by Raïs Lhaj Aomer Ouahrouch, a two-record set containing music in the style of Tachelhit (Maroc/1), as well as both sacred and secular music from the Middle Atlas (Maroc/2). *Musique berbère du Haut-Atlas* (Disque Vogue) presents songs from marriage celebrations and folkloric music in the ahouach style, as recorded by B. Lortat-Jacob for the Musée de l'Homme in Paris. There is also *The Rwais, Moroccan Berber Musicians from the High Atlas* (Lyrichord).

For Sephardic music, there are *Judeo-Español Songs from Morocco* (Saga) and *Sephardic Jews—Ballads, Wedding Songs, Songs, and Dances* (Folkways).

Popular music is found on *Musique populaire marocaine* (Disque Bam), recordings of Jean Mazel from the Middle Atlas, the Anti-Atlas, and the south of Morocco.

CHAPTER 2

PLANNING A TRIP TO MOROCCO

1. **INFORMATION, ENTRY REQUIREMENTS, CUSTOMS & MONEY**
- **WHAT THINGS COST IN MARRAKESH**
2. **WHEN TO GO—CLIMATE, HOLIDAYS & EVENTS**
- **MOROCCO CALENDAR OF EVENTS**
- **MARRAKESH CALENDAR OF EVENTS**
3. **HEALTH, INSURANCE & OTHER CONCERNS**
4. **WHAT TO PACK**
5. **TIPS FOR THE DISABLED, SENIORS, SINGLES, FAMILIES & STUDENTS**
6. **ALTERNATIVE/ ADVENTURE TRAVEL**
7. **GETTING THERE**
- **FROMMER'S SMART TRAVELER: AIRFARES**
8. **GETTING AROUND**
- **SUGGESTED ITINERARIES**
- **FAST FACTS: MOROCCO**

This chapter is devoted to the where, when, and how of your trip—the advance-planning issues that are usually required to get it together and take it on the road.

After people decide where to go, most have two fundamental questions: What will it cost? and How do I get there? This chapter will answer those questions and then follow with additional practical information.

1. INFORMATION, ENTRY REQUIREMENTS, CUSTOMS & MONEY

SOURCES OF INFORMATION

For information before you go, in the **United States** get in touch with the **Moroccan Tourist Office,** 20 E. 46th St., Suite 1201, New York, NY 10017 (tel. 212/557-2520). There is another office at EPCOT Center, Walt Disney World, P.O. Box 40, Orlando FL 32830 (tel. 305/827-5337).

In **Canada,** the tourist office is at 2 Carlton St., Suite 1803, Toronto, Ontario M5B 1K2 (tel. 416/598-2208).

In **England,** a Moroccan National Tourist Office is at 174 Regent St., London, W1R 6HG (tel. 01/437-0073).

In **Australia, New Zealand,** and **Ireland,** citizens might find it more expedient to contact the London headquarters for information.

In **Morocco,** there are many English-speaking national and city tourist offices dispensing information to visitors. (See sections on individual cities.)

Other useful sources are, of course, newspapers and magazines. To find the latest articles that have been published on your destination, go to your library and ask for the *Reader's Guide to Periodical Literature* and look under the country/city for listings.

You may also want to contact the State Department for background bulletins. Write to Superintendent of Documents, **U.S. Government Printing Office,** Washington, DC 20402 (tel. 202/783-3238) for a list.

A good travel agent can also be a source of information. If you use one, make sure the agent is a member of the Society of Travel Agents (ASTA). If you get poor service from an agent, you can write to the **Consumer Affairs Department of ASTA,** P.O. Box 23922, Washington, DC 20006, for satisfaction.

And finally, we come to the best source of all—friends and other travelers who have just returned from your destination.

TRAVEL ADVISORIES

If you are concerned that travel to Morocco may at any time be dangerous, you can call the **Department of State Citizen's Emergency Center** (tel. 202/647-5226). If you have relatives already traveling there, the bureau is also helpful in providing news.

ENTRY REQUIREMENTS

DOCUMENTS

It's easy to enter Morocco: only a valid **passport** is required. For U.S., Canadian, United Kingdom, Australian, New Zealand, and Irish visitors, no visa is required, and tourists may stay in Morocco for up to three months. Those wishing to stay longer must apply to the local police for an extension.

A temporary passport, especially a "British visitor's pass," is not valid in Morocco.

If you're coming from a so-called disease-free country, such as the United States, Canada, Australia, New Zealand, or one of the countries of Western Europe, no vaccination is needed to enter Morocco.

Warning: You are not allowed to enter Morocco if your passport carries a stamp of either Israel or South Africa.

Document Protection

It is a good policy before leaving your country to make two copies of your most valuable documents. Make a copy of the inside page of your passport, the one with your photograph. You should also make copies of your regular driver's license, your international driver's license, your airline ticket, strategic hotel vouchers, and any additional identity card that might be pertinent, such as a youth-hostel card. If you're on medication, you should also make copies of prescriptions. Place one copy in your luggage and carry the original with you; leave the other copy at your home. The information on these documents will be extremely valuable should you encounter loss or theft abroad.

Securing/Renewing a Passport

In the **United States,** citizens 18 or older who meet the requirements are granted a 10-year passport. For an application, go to a U.S. post office or federal court office. In addition, there are federal passport agencies in 13 cities, which you can visit in person; these include New York, Washington, D.C., Stamford (Conn.), Seattle, Philadelphia, San Francisco, New Orleans, Boston, Honolulu, Chicago, Los Angeles, Miami, and Houston. Youths under 18 are granted a 5-year passport. Children under 13 must have their parents apply for their passport, and teenagers 13 to 16 must also have a parent's permission before applying. If your passport is 12 years old (or older), or was granted to you before your 16th year, you must apply in person at a passport agency, post office, or federal or state court office. Otherwise, you can renew it by mail for $42, or for $27 if you are under 18.

To apply for a passport, you'll need a complete government passport application form and you must provide proof of U.S. citizenship—a birth certificate or naturalization papers. An old passport (providing it's not more than a vintage 12 years) is also accepted. You should also have identification with your signature and photograph, such as a driver's license. You'll also need two identical passport-size photographs. You'll wait the longest to receive your passport between mid-March and mid-September; in winter it usually only takes about two weeks by mail. Passports can sometimes be issued in an emergency, providing you present a plane ticket with a confirmed seat.

In **Canada,** citizens seeking a passport may go to one of the nearly two dozen regional offices in such cities as Ottawa and Montreal. Alternatively, you may mail an application to the Passport Office, Section of External Affairs, Ottawa, K1A 0G3. Post offices have application forms. Passports cost $25 (Canadian), and proof of Canadian citizenship is required, along with two signed identical photographs. Passports are valid for 5 years.

In **Great Britain,** citizens may apply at one of the regional offices in Liverpool, Newport, Glasgow, Peterborough, and Belfast, or else in London if they reside there. You may also apply in person at a main post office. The fee is £15, and the passport is good for 10 years. Documents required include a marriage certificate or a birth certificate. Two photos must accompany the application.

In **Australia,** locals apply at the nearest post office. Provincial capitals and all big cities such as Sydney and Melbourne have passport offices. The fee is $76 (AUS). The passport is valid for 10 years. Those under 18 may apply for a 5-year passport for $31 (AUS).

New Zealand citizens may go to their nearest consulate or passport office to obtain an application, and they may file in person or via mail. Proof of citizenship is required, and the passport is good for 10 years. The fee is $55.50 (NZ).

In **Ireland,** you should write in advance to the Passport Office, Setanta Centre, Molesworth St. (without number), Dublin 2, Ireland (tel. 01/780-822). The cost is IR£35 Irish. Applications will be sent by mail outlining requirements and procedures to follow. Irish citizens living in North America may contact the Irish Embassy, 2234 Masschusetts Ave., NW, Washington, DC 20008 (tel. 202/462-3939). The embassy can issue a new passport or direct you to one of the three North American consulates that have jurisdiction over a particular region. The cost of an Irish passport, if arranged by mail through Irish consulates, is $65 (U.S.). If a citizen arrives in person, thereby avoiding mailing costs, there is a discount of $5 (U.S.).

CUSTOMS

ENTERING MOROCCO

Personal effects, including clothing, jewelry, and a camera with up to 10 rolls of film, can be brought into Morocco without restriction. Your baggage will usually be inspected, either at the airport of arrival or at the frontier. At least one suitcase will be opened, perhaps more if anything should strike an official as suspicious. All baggage must be cleared and stamped before you can enter the country. Likewise, upon leaving, your luggage may also be subjected to a customs inspection.

Morocco grants duty-free allowances for 400 grams of tobacco (or 200 cigarettes or 50 cigars), plus 1 liter of wine and 1 liter of liquor. You can also bring in ¼ liter of perfume and any personal medication you might need.

One hint that is endorsed by many frequent visitors to Morocco involves the assistance provided at airports by official (badge-toting) porters. With their carts, their understanding of Arabic, and their intuitive grasp of local customs procedures, they can make your passage through customs much easier and more graceful. Therefore, particularly if you have cumbersome luggage, the effort you'll expend to find a porter and the tip you'll eventually pay him are well worth it.

MONEY

To give you some idea of how much it's going to cost, see "What Things Cost in Marrakesh," below.

CASH/CURRENCY   The basic unit of Moroccan currency is the **dirham (DH).**

Currently there are 8 dirhams to $1 (U.S.). One dirham is worth about 13¢ (U.S.). You should confirm the official rate of exchange before you go to Morocco by checking with your bank at home.

The Moroccan dirham is divided into 100 **centimes.** Coins come in denominations of 1 and 5 dirhams; and 5, 10, 20, and 50 centimes. Bills come in denominations of 5, 10, 50, and 100 dirhams.

THE DIRHAM & THE DOLLAR

At this writing $1 = approximately 8 DH (or 1 DH = 13¢), and this was the rate of exchange used to calculate the dollar values given in this chapter. The rate might fluctuate from time to time and may not be the same when you travel to Morocco. Therefore, the following table should be used only as a guide.

DH	$U.S.	DH	$U.S.
1	.13	30	3.75
2	.25	35	4.38
3	.38	40	5.00
4	.50	45	5.63
5	.63	50	6.25
6	.75	60	7.50
7	.88	70	8.75
8	1.00	80	10.00
9	1.13	90	11.25
10	1.25	100	12.50
15	1.88	125	15.63
20	2.50	150	18.75
25	3.13	200	25.00

At the Moroccan border, foreign visitors must declare to Customs how much foreign currency and Moroccan money they have in their possession. Carrying Moroccan banknotes into the country is officially forbidden. Anyone bringing in Moroccan dirhams will have them confiscated upon entry.

You may convert foreign currencies or traveler's checks at any exchange office throughout Morocco. Exchange counters are found in hotels and at all ports of entry—the airports in Casablanca and Tangier, the port of Tangier—and some boats leaving Algeciras (Spain) for Morocco have exchange facilities right on board. It's important to keep a record of all your transactions with banks, as Morocco has very strict currency regulations.

Changing foreign currencies outside official exchange offices can be risky, and trading it with a resident of Morocco in exchange for goods or services is strictly prohibited. Payment must be in dirhams only.

Upon leaving Morocco, foreign nonresidents can reconvert dirhams up to 50% of the amount mentioned on their exchange statements if their stay exceeds 48 hours—and up to 100% if their stay does not exceed 48 hours. It is officially forbidden to export Moroccan banknotes.

TRAVELER'S CHECKS Before leaving home, purchase traveler's checks and arrange to carry some ready cash. (U.S. citizens should usually take about $200 in cash as a safeguard against unforeseen problems and inconveniences.) Purchase checks in a variety of denominations—$20, $50, and $100.

American Express (tel. toll free 800/221-7282 in the U.S. and Canada) is the most widely recognized traveler's check abroad. The agency imposes a 1% commission. Checks are free to members of the American Automobile Association.

Bank of America (tel. toll free 800/227-3460 in the U.S.; 415/624-5400, collect, in Canada) also issues checks in U.S. dollars for a 1% commission everywhere but California.

Citicorp (tel. toll free 800/645-6556 in the U.S.; 813/623-1709, collect, in Canada) issues checks in U.S. dollars, pounds, and German marks.

MasterCard International (tel. toll free 800/223-9920 in the U.S.; 212/974-5696, collect, in Canada) issues checks in about a dozen currencies.

Barclays Bank (tel. toll free 800/221-2426 in the U.S. and Canada) issues checks in both U.S. and Canadian dollars and in British pounds.

Thomas Cook (tel. toll free in the U.S. 800/223-7373; 212/974-5696, collect, in Canada) issues checks both in U.S. and Canadian dollars and in British pounds. It's affiliated with MasterCard.

Each of these agencies will refund your checks if they are lost or stolen, providing you can produce sufficient documentation of their serial numbers. Of course, your documentation should be carried in a safe place—never along with your checks.

When purchasing checks from one of the banks listed above, ask about refund hotlines. American Express and Bank of America have the greatest number of offices around the world.

Foreign banks may ask up to 5% to convert your checks into the local currency. Note, also, that you always get a better rate if you cash traveler's checks at the banks issuing them: VISA at Barclays, American Express at American Express, and so forth.

CREDIT CARDS Both **American Express** and **Diners Club** are widely recognized in Morocco. If you see the **Eurocard** sign or **Access** displayed at an establishment, it means it accepts **MasterCard.**

Credit cards can save your life when you're abroad, sparing your valuable cash and giving financial flexibility for large purchases or last-minute changes.

Of course, you may make a purchase with a credit card thinking that the amount in local currency will be converted into dollars at a certain rate, only to find that the dollar has declined by the time your bill arrives and you're actually paying more for an item than you bargained for. But those are rules of the game. It can also work in your favor if the dollar should unexpectedly rise after you make a purchase.

WHAT THINGS COST IN MARRAKESH	U.S. $
Taxi from the airport to the city center	6.25
Local telephone call	.25
Double room at Hotel Mamounia (deluxe)	225.00
Double room at Atlas Asni (moderate)	72.50
Double room at Chems (budget)	41.50
Continental breakfast at Chems	3.90
Lunch for one at Restaurant Bagatelle (moderate)	9.75
Lunch for one at Café de France (budget)	8.15
Dinner for one, without wine at La Trattoria de Gian Carlo (deluxe)	32.00
Dinner for one, without wine at Rôtisserie du Café de la Paix (moderate)	14.00
Dinner for one, without wine at Petit Poucet (budget)	7.00
Pint of beer	2.25
Coca-Cola in a café	1.25
Cup of coffee	.40
Roll of 100 ASA film, 36 exposures	5.95
Admission to a museum	1.25
A Moroccan pastry	.50
Guide for a day of sightseeing	12.50

2. WHEN TO GO — CLIMATE, HOLIDAYS & EVENTS

Claiming 350 days of sunshine a year, Morocco is by anyone's standards a year-round destination, with great allure in any season. Visitors, however, must take into account the various seasons that manifest themselves at different times of the year in different parts of the country.

Morocco has been called "a cold country with a hot sun." Many firsttime visitors arrive there expecting Sahara-like temperatures year round, only to discover cold winter winds. Still, it can be very, very hot, depending on where and when you go.

Certain months are considered ideal for certain regions. January and February are the most popular months for visiting the Deep South and Marrakesh. Then, hotels are likely to be filled with European visitors, especially the French, escaping the seasonal cold of their damp and foggy homeland. Midwinter is high (i.e., the most expensive) season for that region, although technically, high season there extends from November until Easter. During midwinter, the arid and sun-flooded southern beach resort of Agadir is extremely popular as well, because comfortable bathing temperatures prevail there year round.

In contrast to the south, the north of Morocco, including Tangier, can be quite chilly in winter, especially since there is an almost complete lack of heat in most buildings. The rainy season in the north usually lasts from December to February. In some parts of the country, sudden downpours can lead to flash floods.

Between December and April, while bathers cavort beside pools or on beaches in the Deep South, skiing is possible in the northern heights of the Rif mountains.

March, April, and May are ideal times for motor trips through the rest of the country. Native flowers, especially jasmine, are then at their best. Throughout the country, children stand beside roads selling massive bouquets of fresh wildflowers, and the land blossoms with color.

July and August are the driest and hottest months to visit Morocco. Many visitors, however, once they become accustomed to the temperatures, consider the dry heat away from the coast as both healthful and cleansing.

The summer—generally from late May to September—is the best time for enjoying north-coast resorts such as Tangier. As a year-round resort, Agadir is equally popular in summer and in winter, with thousands of families arriving from Europe to enjoy the constant sunshine and the somewhat lower prices. Even when traveling in Morocco during the summer heat, consider taking a sweater: you may find yourself a bit chilly on that High Atlas peak, or even in the nighttime chill of the desert, where drops in temperature always come as a surprise.

Many seasoned travelers like to visit Morocco during September and October, when the hot summer temperatures have dropped a bit, the olives and dates are ripening in the fields, and the landscape is rich in soft oranges and muted yellows. Driving around the country at that time is ideal, particularly if your itinerary includes a mixture of urban and rural views.

CLIMATE

Morocco's weather conditions vary widely depending on geographical and seasonal factors. They include everything from the freezing peaks of the Atlas mountains to the blistering heat of the Sahara desert. In winter, which is considered the rainy season, cities such as Tangier, Casablanca, Fez, Rabat, and Meknes have a climate similar to Southern California's, with occasional cold winds sweeping through Tangier and Casablanca. Summertime heat is much more intense as you move south to Marrakesh and the Sahara. To compensate, many people seek relief in the mountains.

Records show that among Morocco's major cities, Marrakesh has the greatest number of sunny days, Casablanca the fewest, with Tangier and Agadir somewhere in between.

The chart below lists average temperatures in degrees Fahrenheit.

Average Monthly Temperatures

	Jan	Feb	Mar	Apr	May	Jun	Jul	Aug	Sept	Oct	Nov	Dec
Agadir	69	70	72	74	76	77	80	80	79	78	76	69
Casablanca	63	63	66	68	72	75	81	81	82	77	68	64
Essaouira	64	64	64	66	68	68	72	70	70	70	68	66
Fez	61	63	66	72	79	88	97	97	90	81	66	61
Marrakesh	66	66	73	79	84	91	102	101	91	82	70	66
Meknes	59	61	64	70	77	84	93	93	86	79	66	61
Ouarzazate	63	67	73	80	86	96	102	100	91	80	70	62
Rabat	63	64	66	70	73	77	82	82	81	77	68	64
Tangier	59	61	62	66	72	77	80	82	79	73	64	61
Taroudannt	72	73	79	81	86	90	99	100	95	90	77	72

HOLIDAYS

Official holidays include March 3, the Fête du Trône, honoring the day of investiture of Mohammed V as king of Morocco, and independence (in 1956) from France; May 1, Worker's Holiday; May 23, National Holiday; July 9, the king's birthday; August 14, celebration of the reclamation of land from the desert; November 6, anniversary of the Green March, the peaceful conquest of the Western Sahara from Spain.

Religious holidays vary according to the Muslim calendar. Aid-es-Seghir is celebrated as ending the fast of Ramadan; Aid el Kebir commemorates Abraham's sacrifice; Mouloud honors the Prophet Muhammad's birth; and Achoura, the 10th day of the Muslim year, celebrates the beginning of the Hegiran year. All banks and shops are closed on these religious holidays. Check with the tourist office for actual dates in the year you plan to travel.

MOROCCO CALENDAR OF EVENTS

Partly because of their adherence to phases of the moon, the exact dates of many Islamic festivals change from year to year. Always check locally at the tourist office of the appropriate city, or at one of the national tourist offices abroad if you'd like to schedule your visit to coincide with a particular festival.

What follows is only a preview of Morocco's major festivals, each of which is subject, of course, to many changes.

FEBRUARY

☐ **Almond Blossom Festival,** Tafraoute. People, sometimes on camels, arrive from miles around to see the countryside "covered in snow" from the blossoms. Second week.

MARCH

☐ **Fête du Trône,** throughout Morocco. The entire country is caught up in this festival honoring the anniversary of King Hassan's accession to the throne. Festivals and celebrations take place in all cities, towns, and villages, including spectacular *fantasias*. In no way are any of these ceremonies aimed at tourists, but visitors are fascinated at some of the displays. March 2–4.

APRIL

✪ *Ramadan* This is the most holy and uncompromising religious holiday in Morocco. It was initiated by the Prophet Muhammad in commemoration of God's revelation to him of the Koran, and ordained to take place every year during the ninth lunar month of the Islamic calendar. It manifests itself as a nationwide ritual feast where neither solid nor liquid sustenance can be consumed, nor sexual activities of any kind carried on, during daylight hours. (It is considered impolite to eat, drink, or smoke in front of Muslims during the day, when they are fasting.) The fast is broken every evening after sunset, usually by partaking of a bowl of harira soup and then a family-oriented feast that continues for many hours. To compensate for the rigid restrictions of the daylight hours, nighttime activities are more frenetic during Ramadan than perhaps at any other time of year. The beginning and end of the monthlong ritual are marked with fireworks, cannon salvos, and nocturnal rejoicing in the streets.

   Where: Throughout Morocco. *When:* After April 8, but dates vary from year to year. (Although the festivities and the celebrations at night are of interest, hotel and restaurant services fall off considerably, and some travelers prefer to avoid Morocco during this period.) *How:* Best observed at Djemaa el Fna, the landmark marketplace of Marrakesh, after the sun goes down.

MAY

☐ **Rose Festival (Fête des Roses),** El Kelaa des M'Gouna, near Ouarzazate in the Dadès Valley. The roses in this valley are in their most spectacular bloom at this season. Occurs late in the month, but dates vary from year to year; ask at the tourist office in Marrakesh.

JUNE

☐ **Moussem of Goulimine,** Asrir. This is one of the main *moussems* of Morocco. (A moussem is a ritualized pilgrimage, similar to a fiesta in Spain, honoring an Islamic saint. It usually lasts 10 days.) The one at Goulimine is sometimes called "the camel's souk" because of the impressive number of dromedaries brought there by local tribesmen. Beginning of June.

JULY

☐ **Moussem of Tan Tan.** This festival is attended by the so-called blue men of the desert. After the prayer of the marabout, the traditional slaughtering of a she-camel takes place. It turns into an impressive show, involving both religious and secular themes, and visitors—both local and foreign—witness the *guedra* dance performed then. Sometime in July (dates vary).

AUGUST

✪ *Moussem of Moulay Idriss* *This is considered the country's grandest moussem. It commemorates Moulay Idriss, the founder of the first Islamic dynasty of Morocco. (Be discreet with your camera: the festivities aren't being staged for the benefit of tourists.)*
Where: *Zerhoun, considered a holy town, north of Meknes.* *When:* *Sometime in August or September (dates vary from year to year).* *How:* *Check with the tourist office in Meknes about any details you need to know.*

☐ **Moussem of Sidi Ahmed O Moussa,** Tiznit. This moussem has strong religious overtones, and is often a moving, fascinating event as the devout pay homage to Allah. Lasts five days, starting from the third Thursday of August.

SEPTEMBER

☐ **Festival of the Fantasia,** Meknes. This display of horsemanship uses as a backdrop a spectacular view of the ramparts of Meknes. Sometime in September (dates vary from year to year).
☐ **Moussem of Moulay Abdallah,** El Jadida. People journey here from throughout the province of El Jadida for this moussem, which is well known for its splendid fantasias. Dates vary.
☐ **Moussem of Moulay Idriss,** Fez. Tanners, coppersmiths, shoemakers, blacksmiths, and merchants slaughter oxen and offer huge decorated candles. This moussem, which involves participation by virtually the entire city, is held in homage of the patron saint of Fez. Mid-September.
☐ **Moussem of Engagements,** Imilchil, province of Er Rachidia. Imilchil is a small village in the Grand Atlas, lying 8,502 feet above sea level. For young people and their parents in the area, the tradition involves the signing of marriage contracts on the day of this moussem. Third week.

OCTOBER

☐ **Mouloud,** throughout Morocco. This Muslim holiday, one of the holiest, honors the Prophet's birthday. For the occasion, mosques stay open all night, homes are brightly lit and perfumed, and the feet of women and children are painted with henna. October 14–15.

MARRAKESH
CALENDAR OF EVENTS

JUNE

✪ *NATIONAL FOLKLORE FESTIVAL* *To many foreign visitors, this festival holds more interest than any of the dozens of other rituals held throughout Morocco. Staged as a showcase for uniquely Moroccan exhibitions of bravura, it is a virtual Arabian Nights fantasy of snake charmers, belly dancers, local musicians, horsemen, acrobats, and Berber*

dance troupes. *Performers come from all corners of Morocco to entertain and delight audiences.*
    Where: *On the grounds of El Badi Palace at Marrakesh.* **When:** *Ten days in June, beginning early in the month (dates vary).* **How:** *You can purchase tickets at many hotel desks or else at the tourist office in Marrakesh.*

JULY

☐ **Marrakesh International Music and Dance Festival,** Marrakesh. This festival includes dancers, singers, and musicians from Morocco and around the world, including black Africa, both North and South America, and Europe. July 4–12 (subject to change).

AUGUST

☐ **Moussem of Setti Fatma,** in the Ourika Valley, south of Marrakesh. One of the more fascinating pilgrimages in the area, which can be visited from a base in Marrakesh. Get details on the observance and the various sites from the tourist office at Marrakesh. Dates vary.

SEPTEMBER

☐ **Moussem of Sidi Moussa Quarquor,** near El Kelas du Straghna, north of Marrakesh. A moving event filled with colorfully attired people of the dessert. Get details from the tourist office in Marrakesh. Dates vary.

3. HEALTH, INSURANCE & OTHER CONCERNS

HEALTH CONCERNS

MEDICINES AND FIRST AID

Take along an adequate supply of any medication that you need—it's difficult to get prescriptions filled in certain parts of the country—and a written prescription that uses the generic name of the drug—not the American brand name. (French, not American, brands prevail.) Of course, carry all your vital medicines and drugs (the legal kind) with you in your carry-on luggage, in case your checked luggage is lost.

Consult your pharmacist about taking such over-the-counter drugs as Colace, a stool softener, or Metamucil. Also take your own personal medical kit. In it, you can include such useful items as first-aid cream, aspirin, nose drops, Band-Aids, hydrogen peroxide, and Mercurochrome. If you're subject to motion sickness on a plane or train, remember to bring along motion-sickness medicine as well.

You'll need a good insect repellent if you're going to tour, especially if you visit the Sahara in the summer. Also take a supply of salt tablets. Sun block lotion is essential too.

If you're in the desert, carry several bottles of mineral water with you in the backseat of your car. Not only are they useful in the event of an overheated radiator, but they're equally useful if your car breaks down and you find yourself alone in the desert. Increase your normal intake of water, even if you don't feel particularly thirsty—dehydration can creep up on you slowly in these climes. The extra water intake will only do you good. Sidi Harazem is an excellent brand of mineral water, available throughout Morocco. Its bubbly counterpart, Oulmès, is also sold almost everywhere.

VACCINATIONS & ANTIMALARIALS

As mentioned under "Entry Requirements," vaccinations aren't needed to enter Morocco if you're coming from a "disease-free" country such as the United States, Britain, or Canada.

Nevertheless, if you're planning to do extensive touring in the Maghreb, visiting some of the more remote outposts, many health authorities recommend preventive shots for cholera, typhoid, and tetanus. In such cases, it is prudent to have a stamped **International Health Card,** which can be obtained from your doctor after your inoculations.

If you have just visited a disease-affected country before coming to Morocco, you might be compelled, if you don't have your card, to have a vaccination at the border. One French newspaper reporter claimed he noted the "very same needle being used to vaccinate more than one person." Whether that is true or not, you would never want to risk your health in such a reckless way. So get the card if your travels mandate it.

If you're planning to travel extensively in the south of Morocco or the Western Sahara, you could be exposed to malaria, but this is extremely unlikely unless you are going to be there for an extended period. Most short visits don't require you to take antimalarials, although if you're continuing south along the west coast of Africa, you'll definitely need them. Consult your doctor. The greatest period of risk is from May to October.

MEDICAL SERVICES

They're fairly advanced in Morocco, but only in such major cities as Rabat, Casablanca, Tangier, and Marrakesh. Many Moroccan doctors train overseas, most often in France; nearly all of them speak French, and a large percentage speak English. If not, they at least employ an assistant who speaks English and can serve as an interpreter.

If a medical emergency arises, your hotel staff can usually put you in touch with a reliable doctor. If not, then contact one of the American embassies or consulates, as each one maintains a list of suitable English-speaking doctors.

Before you leave home, you can obtain a list of English-speaking doctors in Morocco from the **International Association for Medical Assistance to Travelers (IAMAT)** in the United States at 417 Center St., Lewiston, NY 14092 (tel. 716/754-4883); in Canada, at 188 Nicklin Rd., Guelph ON N1H 7LS (tel. 519/836-0102).

If your medical condition is chronic, always talk to your doctor before taking an international trip. He or she may have specific advice to give you, depending on your condition. For conditions such as epilepsy, a heart condition, and diabetes, wear a **Medic Alert Identification Tag,** which will immediately alert any doctor as to the nature of your trouble. It also provides the number of Medic Alert's 24-hour hotline so that a foreign doctor can obtain medical records for you. For a lifetime membership, the cost is a well-spent $25. Contact the Medic Alert Foundation, P.O. Box 1009, Turlock, CA 95381-1009 (tel. toll free 800/432-5378).

WATER & FOOD

Although tap water is considered safe to drink in the major cities, you'd be very wise to avoid it altogether and drink only mineral water. This applies even to iced drinks. Stick to beer, hot tea, or soft drinks, especially if you even suspect that you have a delicate stomach. Why risk an intestinal upset?

You can eat meat, but it should be thoroughly cooked. However, since meat is usually either grilled or baked in an intensely hot *tajine,* this should be no major obstacle. Save that rare steak until you return home.

Regarding fruits and vegetables, travel in Morocco the way you would in Mexico—that is, don't consume unpeeled fruit or raw vegetables. Always take extreme precautions here: there have been cases when contaminated water and food have led to all sorts of diseases, not only hepatitis A, typhoid, dysentery, and giardiasis, but cholera and polio.

Milk and milk products served in most tourist-oriented hotels and restaurants are considered safe, but it is prudent to drink and eat them sparingly. One problem you should guard against is the consumption of anything containing mayonnaise that has sat too long on a buffet table. Many hotels, catering mainly to European tastes, prepare salad buffets. Proceed with caution here. It's best to avoid the mussel salad in mayonnaise and go for the hearts of palm with vinaigrette instead. In any case, if you want to patronize buffets, go when they first open, as the food is fresh and safer.

In general, be selective about where you eat and avoid the grubby-looking street stalls. "Gourmet writers" often wax enthusiastic about the food served at such places, but refrigeration is nonexistent.

At some point in their journey, most visitors experience some form of diarrhea, even those who follow the usual precautions. This is primarily a result of a change in diet and eating habits, and doesn't necessarily mean you've had bad or contaminated food or water.

Mild forms of diarrhea usually pass quickly without medication. As a precaution, take along some antidiarrhea medicine, moderate your eating habits, and drink only mineral water until you recover. Always drink plenty of fluids during this period, as you can dehydrate rapidly. You must also consume more than your usual intake of salt, which will help your body retain water. Eat only simply prepared foods at such times, such as plain bread (no butter) and boiled vegetables or some broth; avoid dairy products, except perhaps yogurt.

If symptoms persist, you may have dysentery, especially if you notice blood or mucus in your stool. At this point you should consult a doctor.

Sometimes travelers find that a change in diet will lead to constipation. If this occurs, eat high-fiber food and drink plenty of mineral water. Avoid large meals and don't drink wine.

INSURANCE

Before purchasing any additional insurance, check your homeowner's, automobile, and medical insurance policies. Also check the membership contracts for any automobile and travel clubs you belong to and for any credit cards you have. If, after close examination, you feel you still need coverage, consider one or more of the following types of insurance:

1. Health and accident
2. Trip cancellation
3. Lost luggage

Many credit-card companies insure their users in case of a travel accident, providing that the travel cost was paid with their card. Sometimes fraternal organizations have policies that protect members in case of sickness or accidents abroad.

Incidentally, don't assume that Medicare is the answer to illness in Morocco. It covers U.S. citizens who travel south of the border to Mexico or north of the border to Canada. Canadians, however, are generally protected with health-insurance plans in their individual provinces.

Many homeowners' insurance policies cover theft of luggage during foreign travel and loss of such documents as your Eurailpass, your passport, and your airline ticket.

Coverage is usually limited to about $500 (U.S.). To submit a claim on your insurance, remember that you'll need police reports or a statement from a local medical authority that you did in fact suffer the loss or experience the illness for which you are seeking compensation. Such claims, by their very nature, can be filed only when you return from Morocco.

Some insurance policies (and this is the type you should have) provide advances in cash or else arrange transferrals of funds so that you won't have to dip into your precious travel funds to settle medical bills.

If you've booked a charter airfare, you will probably have to pay a cancellation fee if you cancel a trip suddenly, even if it is due to an unforeseen crisis. It's possible to get insurance against such a possibility; some travel agencies provide such coverage. Often flight insurance against a canceled trip is written into tickets paid for by credit cards from such companies as VISA and American Express. Many tour operators or insurance agents provide this type of insurance for a reasonable additional supplement.

Companies offering such policies are listed below.

Travel Guard International, 1100 Center Point Dr., Stevens Point, WI 54481 (tel. toll free 800/826-1300 outside Wisconsin, 800/634-0644 in Wisconsin), offers a comprehensive 7-day policy that covers basically everything, including lost luggage. The cost of the package is $52, including such categories as emergency assistance, accidental death, trip cancellation or interruption, medical coverage abroad, and lost luggage. There are restrictions, however, which you should understand before you accept the coverage.

Travel Insurance Pak, Travelers Insurance Co., 1 Tower Sq., 15 NB, Hartford, CT 06183-5040 (tel. 203/277-2318, or toll free 800/243-3174), offers illness and accident coverage, costing from $10 for 6 to 10 days. For lost or damaged luggage, $500 worth of coverage costs $20 for 6 to 10 days. You can also get trip-cancellation insurance for $5.50.

Mutual of Omaha (Tele-Trip), 3201 Farnam St., Omaha, NB 68131 (tel. 402/345-2400 or toll free 800/228-9792), will for $3 a day (with a 10-day minimum) provide foreign medical coverage up to $50,000. It also features global assistance and maintains a 24-hour hotline. The company also offers trip-cancellation insurance, lost- or stolen-luggage coverage, standard accident coverage, and other policies.

TRAVEL ASSISTANCE

A number of companies now offer policies and help in case you're stranded abroad in some emergency. Each maintains a toll-free 800 number for out-of-state callers.

HealthCare Abroad (MEDEX), 243 Church St. NW, Suite 100D, Vienna, VA 22180 (tel. 703/255-9800, or toll free 800/237-6615). One policy, good for 10 to 90 days, costs $3 a day, including accident and sickness coverage to the tune of $100,000. Medical evacuation is also included, along with $25,000 in accidental death or dismemberment compensation. Trip-cancellation and lost- or stolen-luggage clauses can also be written into this policy at a nominal cost.

WorldCare Travel Assistance Association, 605 Market St., Suite 1300, San Francisco, CA 94105 (tel. 415/541-4991, or toll free 800/666-4993), features a 9-to-15-day policy, costing $105, including trip cancellation, lost or stolen luggage, legal assistance, and medical coverage and evacuation.

Access America, 600 Third Ave., P.O. Box 807, New York, NY 10163-0807 (tel. 212/490-5345, or toll free 800/284-8300), has a 24-hour hotline in case of an emergency. This is a good company for those wanting family or individual policies. Medical coverage ($10,000) for 9 to 15 days costs $49. If you want medical plus trip-cancellation, the charge is $89 for 9 to 15 days. A comprehensive package for $111 grants 9-to-15-day blanket coverage, including $50,000 worth of death benefits.

4. WHAT TO PACK

CLOTHES

What you bring to wear in Morocco will obviously be subject to the specific destination and time of year that you go.

During the winter months in such cities as Tangier, Casablanca, Fez, Rabat, and Meknes, visitors can expect to wear typical summer attire and a jacket during the evenings. Visitors might need slightly heavier clothing in Tangier and Casablanca to fend off Atlantic winds. Swimsuits will also come in handy for the heated swimming pools, although it will probably be too cold for ocean bathing. Winter in the country's mountain resorts is, of course, a different story, and protective wool clothing should be worn.

During the summer months, cool, light materials are suitable for Casablanca and Tangier, but it gets unbearably hot the farther south you go, especially in Marrakesh and the Sahara.

SOME GENERAL TIPS

Always pack as light as possible. Airlines are increasingly strict about how much luggage you can bring abroad, not only carry-on items but checked suitcases as well. This is particularly true when flights are fully booked (or overbooked, as the case may be). Checked luggage should not measure more than a total of 62 inches (width plus length plus height); bags shouldn't weigh more than 70 pounds. Carry-on luggage shouldn't measure more than 45 inches (width plus length plus height), and the pieces must fit under your seat or in the overhead bin.

It almost goes without saying that you should take a wardrobe that "travels well." Sometimes it's possible to get pressing done at hotels, but don't count on it. Be prepared to wash your lightweights, such as underwear, in your bathroom and hang them up to dry overnight.

The general rule of packing is to bring four of everything. For men, that means four pairs of socks, four pairs of slacks, four shirts, and four pairs of underwear. At least two of these will always be either dirty or in the process of drying. Although garments dry quickly in the arid zones of Morocco, you'll occasionally have to wrap semiwet clothes in a plastic bag as you head for your next destination. Women could follow the same rule—four of each of the "basics," such as undergarments and stockings.

As a final rule, always take two comfortable pairs of shoes. You may get one pair soiled, and that extra pair will always come in handy.

DRESS CODE

If you're staying at deluxe hotels such as the Hyatt Regency in Rabat, the El Mansour or the Hyatt Regency in Casablanca, or the Mamounia in Marrakesh, you'll find that guests tend to dress more formally (especially during the midwinter high season) and perhaps you should too. If you plan to visit casinos and nightclubs, be casually chic, with women perhaps wearing a cocktail dress.

Dress codes, however, are rarely enforced in Morocco—that is, if you are "dressed." Obviously, you should never wear bikinis in the lobby of hotels or on the streets, or go into first-class or deluxe restaurants wearing a pair of shorts. Men should always wear trousers in such places, and women should be properly dressed (that is, not in a bathing suit).

Dress codes in resorts such as Agadir are more relaxed than in places like the capital city of Rabat, which tends to be more formal.

OTHER ITEMS

The smart traveler should take along toilet paper—it's a scarce commodity out in the hinterlands and within the medinas. You don't need to buy it to take with you, however. Toilet paper and tissues are readily available in Moroccan cities. Just make sure you have an adequate supply if you're planning a long trip through the desert or traveling overland from one city to the other.

A sun hat will come in handy many times, and sunglasses are vital in summer.

Make sure that you have warm clothing if traveling to the north of Morocco in winter. It's a common sight to see tourists who packed for Caribbean weather shivering in the cold and damp Atlantic winds.

5. TIPS FOR THE DISABLED, SENIORS, SINGLES, FAMILIES & STUDENTS

FOR THE DISABLED

Morocco has an unusually high number of disabled people, but few facilities are provided for them. Somehow they manage to cope. Traveling in Morocco is possible for the disabled, but it is not as easy as in parts of Western Europe and in the United States and Canada.

Many hotels are not at all suitable for wheelchair access, especially those that have been converted from former palaces. These criticisms aside, it should be pointed out that Moroccan hotel staffs are extremely solicitous in caring for the aged or infirm. For example, at La Gazelle d'Or at Taroudannt, a staff member, noting that an elderly American visitor had trouble walking, secured a wheelchair for her and took her on a tour of the hotel gardens. Sometimes disabled guests are literally carried from a bus or car to the hotel lobby, where a wheelchair and a staff member are waiting.

Before you go, there are many agencies that provide advance data to help you plan your trip. Unfortunately, since Morocco is not a prime tour target for most disabled travelers, some of these agencies have very sketchy information on touring in the country, but you can always try.

Travel Information Service, Moss Rehabilitation Hospital, 12th Street and Tabor Road, Philadelphia, PA 19141 (tel. 215/456-9600), is not a travel agent, but does supply information. It charges $5 per package, which contains names and addresses of accessible hotels, restaurants, and attractions—often based on firsthand reports of travelers who have been there.

You may also want to subscribe to *The Itinerary,* P.O. Box 2012, Bayonne, NJ 07002-2012 (tel. 201/858-3400), at $10 a year. A travel magazine, published bimonthly, it is filled with news about travel aids for the handicapped, special tours, information on accessibility, and other matters.

You can also obtain a copy of *Air Transportation of Handicapped Persons,* published by the U.S. Department of Transportation. The copy is sent free by writing for Free Advisory Circular No. AC12032, Distribution Unit, **U.S. Department of Transportation,** Publications Division, M-4332, Washington, DC 20590.

Many package-tour operators, particularly those in Great Britain, cater to the disabled traveler in Morocco. Names and addresses of such tour operators can be obtained by writing to the **Society for the Advancement of Travel for the Handicapped,** 26 Court St., Brooklyn, NY 11242 (tel. 718/858-5483). Annual membership dues are $40, or $25 for senior citizens and students; send a self-addressed, stamped envelope.

One such tour company is **Whole Person Tours,** P.O. Box 1084, Bayonne, NJ 07002-1084 (tel. 201/858-3400, or toll free 800/462-2237 outside New Jersey).

For the blind, the best source is the **American Foundation for the Blind,** 15 W. 16th St., New York, NY 10011 (tel. toll free 800/232-5463), which has much data to aid the blind person, including information on travel. For those legally blind, it also issues identification cards for $6.

FOR SENIORS

Many discounts are available for seniors—that is, men and women who have reached what the French call "the third age." Be advised, however, that you have to be a member of an association to obtain certain discounts.

For your initial source of information, write to *Travel Tips for Senior Citizens* (publication No. 8970), distributed for $1 by the Superintendent of Documents, **U.S. Government Printing Office,** Washington, DC 20402 (tel. 202/783-5238). Another booklet—and this one is distributed free—is called *101 Tips for the Mature Traveler.* Write or phone **Grand Circle Travel,** 347 Congress St., Suite 3A, Boston, MA 02210 (tel. 617/350-7500, or toll free 800/221-2610).

SAGA International Holidays is also well known for its all-inclusive tours for seniors. They prefer that joiners be at least 60 years old. Insurance is included in the net price of any of their tours, all of which encompass dozens of locations in Europe and usually last for an average of 17 nights. Contact SAGA International Holidays, 120 Boylston St., Boston, MA 02116 (tel. toll free 800/343-0273). Membership is $5 a year.

In the United States, the best organization to belong to is the **American Association of Retired Persons,** 1909 K St. NW, Washington, DC 20049 (tel. 202/872-4700). Members are offered discounts on car rentals, hotels, and airfares, even sightseeing in some cases. Its affiliate, **AARP Travel Service,** 100 N. Sepulveda Blvd., Suite 1020, El Segundo, CA 90024 (tel. toll free 800/227-7737), offers tours and, for those traveling independently, a list of discounts available on the road.

Information is also available from the **National Council of Senior Citizens,** 925 15th St. NW, Washington, DC 20005 (tel. 202/347-8800). A nonprofit organization, the council charges $12 per person to join (couples pay $16), for which you receive a monthly newsletter, part of which is devoted to travel tips. Discounts on hotel and auto rentals are previewed.

FOR SINGLES

A recent American census showed that 77 million Americans over 15 years of age are single. The travel industry, though, is far better geared for double occupancy of hotel rooms. One company that has made heroic efforts to match single travelers with like-minded companions is now the largest and best-listed company in the United States. Jens Jurgen, the German-born founder, charges $36 to $66 for a six-month listing in his well-publicized records. New applicants desiring a travel companion fill out a form stating their preferences and needs. They then receive a minilisting of the kinds of potential partners who might be suitable for travel. Companions of the same or opposite sex can be requested. Jurgen's listings are extensive, and it's very likely that you'll find a travel companion. For an application and more information, write to Jens Jurgen, **Travel Companion,** P.O. Box P-833, Amityville, NY 11701 (tel. 516/454-0880).

Singleworld, 401 Theodore Fremd Ave., Rye, NY 10580 (tel. 914/967-3334, or toll free 800/223-6490), is a travel agency that operates tours geared to solo travel. Two basic types of tours are available, either a youth-oriented tour for people under 35 or else jaunts for any age. Annual dues are $20.

FOR FAMILIES

If you take your family abroad, you'll need to do some advance planning. If you have very small children, you may want to discuss your vacation plans with your doctor and take along whatever you think the child will need, along with such standard supplies as children's aspirin, a thermometer, Band-Aids, and the like.

For $35, **Family Travel Services** will send you 10 issues of a newsletter about traveling with children. Subscribers can also call in with travel questions Monday through Friday, but only from 10am to noon Eastern Standard Time (later in the West). Contact TWYCH, which stands for Travel With Your Children, 80 Eighth Ave., New York, NY 10011 (tel. 212/206-0688).

You might also want to consider a Club Med vacation in Morocco for your children. The organization's most famous establishment is at the main square in Marrakesh, but they also operate vacation villages as well. For more information call **Club Méditerranée,** 3 E. 54th St., New York, NY 10022 (tel. toll free 800/258-2633).

FOR STUDENTS

Bona fide students can avail themselves of a number of discounts in travel. The most wide-ranging travel service for students is the **Council on International Educational Exchange (CIEE),** 205 E. 42nd St., New York, NY 10017 (tel. 212/661-1414). This outfit provides details about budget travel, study abroad, working permits, and insurance. It also sells a number of helpful publications, including the *Student Travel Catalogue* ($1). To bona fide students, it issues an International Student Identity Card for $10.

To keep costs bone-trimmed, membership in the **International Youth Hostel Federation (IYHF)** is recommended. Many countries have branch offices, including **American Youth Hostels (AYH),** P.O. Box 37613, Washington, DC 20013-7613 (tel. 202/783-6161). Membership costs $25 annually unless you're under 18 (then only $10).

6. ALTERNATIVE/ADVENTURE TRAVEL

Offbeat, alternative modes of travel often cost less, and yet they are a far more enriching way to travel. Some of the organizations arranging such ventures are listed below. Most of them concentrate on Europe, although occasional forays into Morocco are possible.

EDUCATIONAL TRAVEL

The best information is available at the **Council on International Educational Exchange (CIEE),** 205 E. 42nd St., New York, NY 10017 (tel. 212/661-1414). This outfit not only arranges low-cost travel opportunities, but offers information about working or studying abroad. It's best to request a copy of the 455-page *Work, Study, Travel Abroad: The Whole World Handbook* from them, costing $10.95 (plus $1 for postage and handling) if you'd like it mailed. Outlined are some 1,000 study opportunities abroad.

HOMESTAYS

Servas, 11 John St., Suite 706, New York, NY 10038 (tel. 212/267-0252), is a nonprofit, nongovernmental, international interfaith network of travelers and hosts whose goal is to help build world peace, goodwill, and understanding. They do this by providing opportunities for deeper, more personal contacts among people of diverse cultural and political backgrounds. Servas ("to serve" in Esperanto) travelers are invited to share living space in a privately owned home, normally staying without charge for visits lasting a maximum of two days. Visitors pay a $45 annual fee, fill out an application, and are interviewed for suitability by one of more than 200 Servas interviewers throughout the country. They then receive a directory listing the names and addresses of Servas hosts who will allow (and encourage) visitors in their homes. This program embraces 112 countries, including Morocco.

Friendship Force, 575 S. Tower, 1 CNN Center, Atlanta, GA 30303 (tel. 404/522-9490), is a nonprofit organization existing for the sole purpose of fostering and encouraging friendship among disparate people worldwide. Dozens of branch offices throughout North America arrange visits en masse, usually once a year. Because of group bookings, the airfare to the host country is usually less than you'd pay if you bought an individual APEX ticket. Each participant is required to spend two weeks in the host country, one full week of which will be as a guest in the home of a family. Most volunteers spend the second week traveling in the host country.

International Visitors Information Service, 733 15th St. NW, Suite 300, Washington, DC 20005 (tel. 202/783-6540), will send you a directory for $4.95 listing opportunities you might use for contact with local residents in foreign countries. It's called *Meet the People.*

ADVENTURE/WILDERNESS TRAVEL

Most Atlas summits can easily be climbed. Difficult itineraries have been designed in great numbers at Mount Toubkal, and to a lesser degree in the Central Grand Atlas. At Mount Toubkal, seven mountain resorts belong to the **Club Alpin,** which arranges excursions. Before you undertake an excursion or a climb in a remote area, it is recommended that you give your itinerary to the local authorities, who may offer special advice. You can also use mules as soon as you leave "carriageable courses." Information about mountaineering is available from Club Alpin, bd. Brahim Roudani (without number), Casablanca (tel. 2/26-76-41), or from its secondary office at bd. de Résistance, 13, Rabat (tel. 7/272-20).

7. GETTING THERE

BY PLANE

Of the many exotic lands of the Middle East or Africa, Morocco is by far the closest and most accessible. Although part of its allure stems from timeless customs and rituals, the methods of reaching it are among the most modern in the world.

FROM NORTH AMERICA

Established in 1946, and later endorsed as the official airline of the Kingdom of Morocco, **Royal Air Maroc** (tel. 212/750-6071, or toll free 800/344-6726) offers safe, well-monitored transatlantic flights on twice- or thrice-weekly departures from Montréal and from New York's JFK Airport. It is the only airline to fly nonstop between North America and Morocco, and the only one to connect the many far-flung cities of the country's diverse regions. Serving 60 destinations on four of the world's continents, and closely linking its computerized reservations systems to that of Air France, Royal Air Maroc is probably the most sophisticated airline in the Arab world.

Flights depart every Tuesday, every Saturday, and, depending on the season, every Thursday in both directions between North America and Casablanca. Flights originate in Montréal, and touch down at New York's JFK to pick up passengers before continuing on to Casablanca. Likewise, on westbound segments, flights originate in Casablanca, touch down in New York, then continue on to Montréal.

Flying time from New York to Morocco is 6 hours and 40 minutes, less than to many points of interest within Europe. The total flying time to Casablanca from Montréal is 9 hours and 40 minutes, which includes the time spent on the ground in New York.

APEX & Discount Fares

Fares to Morocco in any season usually cost less than equivalent fares to middle and central Europe on other airlines. Luckily, the least expensive fares are for flights that depart during the particular seasons that many visitors consider Morocco's most alluring. The most popular of these is the **Super APEX Magical Kingdom** fare between New York and Casablanca, available only during autumn, winter, and spring. Tickets must be reserved and paid for at least 14 days prior to departure, and no changes of any kind are permitted after 14 days prior to departure. An outright cancellation of this type of ticket is permitted, but only with the forfeiture of a $125 penalty. Your stay abroad with this type of ticket suits the amount of vacation time available to most travelers: between 7 and 30 days.

Despite these restrictions (which many passengers find they can easily live with), this ticket—priced at between $602 and $730, depending on the days you fly—is by far the best bargain available. Making it even more alluring for families is the 33% discount offered to children between the ages of 2 and 11, and the 90% discount offered to infants under 2.

If you absolutely want to fly during the heat of midsummer, you'll pay more for an APEX ticket with slightly different restrictions. For eastbound travel between June 1 and September 30 (and also for eastbound travel during the week before Christmas), you'll pay $1,154 round trip. Children and infants still receive the same discounts mentioned above. In case of any changes or alterations in your flight dates, the penalties are slightly less severe than with the Magical Kingdom fare. You can also arrange, with the regular APEX ticket, an additional air transfer to somewhere within Morocco for an extra $25.

Royal Air Maroc is one of the few international airlines that still offers a last-minute **youth fare.** Available to travelers aged 12 to 24 years (inclusive), it's designed for last-minute confirmations of flights that cannot be arranged more than 72 hours before departure. Depending on the season, they cost between $300 and $391 each way.

Royal Air Maroc also offers a fare exclusively for **senior citizens,** which RAM defines as all those over 60. Available only between November and March (when, once again, Morocco is beautiful and temperate), the round-trip fare is between $672 and $722. Fares must be booked 7 days prior to departure, with a $100 penalty for most cancellations or changes in scheduling. APEX fares from Montréal have slightly different restrictions than fares from New York. From Montréal, advance purchase of 14 days and a delay of 7 to 90 days before using the return ticket is required. For a round-trip ticket, you'll pay between $716 and $766 (Canadian) in winter, depending on the day of the flight, and between $1,010 and $1,060 (Canadian) for a flight in midsummer.

Regular Fares

If you want no restrictions of any kind regarding cancellation penalties or changes of flight dates, you might opt for a straight **economy** fare, costing $770 each way throughout the year. A **business-class** ticket, offering wider seating and upgraded food and beverage service, costs $1,303 each way. A **first-class** ticket, while much more expensive at $2,385 each way, offers the airline industry's ultimate in comfort (with seats that unfold into something approaching a bed) and prestige.

FROM EUROPE

Let's face it: many visitors may decide to visit Morocco as an extension of their holiday in Spain, France, or the rest of Europe. Madrid is an excellent transfer point into Morocco because both **Royal Air Maroc** and **Iberia** (tel. toll free 800/772-

FROMMER'S SMART TRAVELER: AIRFARES

1. Always ask for the lowest-priced fare—not just for a discount fare.
2. Keep calling the airline—availability of cheap seats changes daily. Airlines would rather sell a seat than fly empty. As the departure date nears, additional low-cost seats become available.
3. Ask about Royal Air Maroc's Super APEX Magical Kingdom fare: it's often the best bargain.
4. Travelers aged 12 to 24 can take advantage of RAM's last-minute youth fare.
5. Senior citizens (those over 60) can avail themselves of a heavily discounted fare between November and March on RAM.
6. Shop the airlines in Europe, as well as RAM, for the best bargain fare from a European capital, and add Morocco to a European holiday.
7. Try to fly in winter, spring, or fall (the best times to see Morocco), as fares are cheaper then than in midsummer.
8. If you go on a regular APEX ticket on RAM, get another city in Morocco included for only $25.

4642), the national airline of Spain, fly from there to such cities as Tangier, Casablanca, and Marrakesh.

Perhaps even more popular is Paris, as both Royal Air Maroc and **Air France** (tel. toll free 800/237-2747) fly from there to Tangier, Casablanca, and Marrakesh. The two airlines also have nonstop flights to Casablanca from such provincial French cities as Bordeaux, Marseille, and Nice, as well as from Geneva and Brussels. Iberia also flies to Casablanca from the Andalusian city of Málaga.

If you're in London, Royal Air Maroc offers six flights a week in midsummer from Heathrow to Casablanca, with easy connections to Agadir, Marrakesh, and Tangier; some seasonal bargains make these flights very economical. From Gatwick, a small airline called **Gibair** flies to Casablanca twice a week. Reservations within North America on Gibair are handled by British Airways (tel. toll free 800/247-9297).

You can reach Tangier on Gibair from Gibraltar, which itself is reached on regularly scheduled flights from London's Gatwick.

Charter flights are numerous from regional airports in both Britain and France, but you must check carefully with a competent travel agent about these, as their frequency varies and seats may not be available. Catering to the sun-worshipping yearnings of a European clientele, many of these charters are bound for the arid and constantly sunny beach resort of Agadir.

BY TRAIN

Even though Morocco lies across the sea from Europe, in North Africa, it is just 8 miles south of the Iberian Peninsula, so getting there by train—and then a final boat ride—is possible.

Many British travelers take a train leaving from London's Victoria Station for either Dover or Folkestone. There, they cross the English Channel and take the train to Paris.

In Paris, at the Gare de Lyon, a train departs daily at 10pm for Algeciras, the journey taking 36 hours. Algeciras is the ferry terminal port across from Gibraltar and has the most frequent connections to Tangier on the northern Moroccan coast. It is also possible to take an Intercity Express train running from Paris to Madrid, where rail connections can be made to Algeciras. For **SNCF** (rail) information in France, dial 45-82-50-50.

For possible discounted rail tickets to Morocco, inquire at the office of **Transalpino/European Rail,** 71 Buckingham Palace Rd., London, SW1 (tel. 071/834-9656).

BY BUS

From an embarkation point in Paris, it is possible to travel by bus to Morocco. **Eurolines** has departures from the Porte de la Villette station four days a week, heading for Casablanca. A morning bus departs Paris at 10:30am, and finally reaches Tiznit in the afternoon two days later, having made stopovers in all the major Atlantic coastal cities: Tangier, Rabat, Casablanca, and Agadir. On Wednesday and Saturday at 10:30am, a bus leaves from Paris with stopovers in Tangier, Meknes, Fez, Taza, and Oujda. To make reservations for this unusual form of travel, telephone Eurolines at Port de La Porte de la Villette at 42-05-12-10 in Paris.

Some British visitors take a bus from England, which is operated from April to September. About four buses a week leave Victoria Coach Station at this time, the drive south to Algeciras taking two days. For information about this mode of transport, telephone 071/430-0202 in London. Students are granted a 10% reduction.

BY CAR

If you're touring in Spain, crossing on a car ferry from Algeciras to Morocco is relatively easy. From other parts of Europe, it's a long haul. There are stories in England of people who have made the trip from London to Tangier in just two days, with one driver sleeping and the other behind the wheel. Four or even five days would be a more leisurely—and sane—pace.

If you're in Paris or anywhere in France, you can drive to Morocco by taking the coastal road the entire length of eastern Spain, going along the southern underbelly of Iberia—the Costa del Sol—until you reach the far frontier of that sun strip, Algeciras. Again, this is a three- or four-day drive, depending on what part of France you are in.

It is also possible to take a twice-weekly ferry from Plymouth (England), which will deliver you to Santander on the north coast of Spain. From there, you have to cross the entire peninsula by car until you reach Algeciras in the south.

The more usual crossing from England is to take one of the Brittany and **P&O** ferries from Dover to Folkestone to the north coast of France. From there, drive on one of the *autoroutes* through France and Spain until you reach Algeciras. For P&O information in England, call 071/734-4431; in France, call Paris 42-66-40-17.

PACKAGE TOURS

Many package-tour operators feature tours to Morocco. You'll need to do some shopping around to find which one is suitable for you.

One operator, **Le Soleil Tours,** 25 W. 39th St., Suite 902, New York, NY 10018 (tel. 212/869-1040, or toll free 800/225-4723), features at least three tours of the country. An Imperial Sahara tour of 14 days costs from $1,085 to $1,165; Le Soleil Imperial, 7 days, costs from $466 to $555; and the South and the Kasbah, 7 days, goes for $466 to $555. Prices are based on double occupancy and include four- or five-star accommodations, three meals, and escorted tours. Fly/drive packages can also be arranged. These tours—considered among the best offered in Morocco—are operated in cooperation with Royal Air Maroc. Prices given above are for land arrangements. Airfare is extra.

Other major operators include the following:

Flag Tours, 110 W. 40th St., Suite 701, New York, NY 10018 (tel. 212/921-3360), or 1960 West, Houston, TX 77069 (tel. 713/580-1700, or toll free 800/223-8889), is the oldest specialized tour operator to Morocco from the United States. It specializes in handling all types of arrangements, including incentive groups and special-interest tours. From the Sahara on camelback to dual-destination trips to Morocco and Egypt, this Houston-based agency offers individualized tours—tailored to your own needs—as well as packages.

On the West Coast, **Vista Travel,** 205 Arizona Ave., Santa Monica, CA 90401 (tel. 213/458-6950), is run by two experts on the Middle East who offer complete packages for individuals or groups contemplating visits to Morocco and Egypt.

8. GETTING AROUND

It's easier to travel around Morocco than you might imagine. Train connections, for example, between the major cities are good, and Royal Air Inter flies to most of the tourist areas. The best way to capture the essence of Morocco, however, is to travel by road.

Each city or town has many travel agents where you can pick up information and purchase bus, train, and plane tickets.

In Casablanca, I have always found the Anglo-Moroccan-owned **Olive Branch Tours,** rue de Foucauld, 35 (tel. 22-39-19), especially helpful. They can assist you with sightseeing tours, and will often cash traveler's checks as well. This company has been in business since 1958.

There's also an Olive Branch in Marrakesh at Palais El Badia (tel. 4/488-81); in Tangier, at rue Omar Ibnou el Aass, 11 (tel. 9/380-83); and in Agadir, at av. Hassan II, 125 (tel. 8/252-97).

BY PLANE

The domestic airline **Royal Air Inter** flies to Fez, Meknes, Tetuán, Oujda, Ouarzazate, Agadir, Marrakesh, and Rabat. Generally, you will arrive in Morocco either in Tangier or Casablanca. At both, you can rent cars, as well as make bus and train connections.

If Casablanca is not your final destination, **Royal Air Maroc** has connecting flights to Rabat (Salé) and Tangier. From here, many people fly to Gibraltar or Málaga, on Spain's Costa del Sol.

Domestic fares within Morocco tend to be very reasonable. Times are always changing, so don't rely on any published data; always ask a travel agent or call the airline for the last-minute information.

If you're in a hurry during your visit to Morocco, and don't have time to drive through the countryside, then the airplane can get you quickly and efficiently to all the major cities of tourist interest.

BY TRAIN

The **Moroccan State Railways (ONCF)** operates about 1,053 miles of rail lines, going from Tangier to Marrakesh, from Casablanca to Oujda. Train fares throughout Morocco are surprisingly reasonable, with children between the ages of 4 and 10 traveling for half price. The long hauls provide sleeper service, for which you pay extra. Otherwise, tickets are sold in first class, second class, and third class (the last is not recommended). Second-class seats tend to be about the same price as bus fares between cities.

If you're traveling in summer, first class is recommended because of air conditioning. Note that there are supplements for express trains with air-conditioned cars. Most major trains also have a restaurant and bar on board. In first- and second-class rail compartments, there are nonsmoking areas. To rent a couchette costs another 30 DH ($3.75), in addition to the price of a first- or second-class ticket.

To save 10% of the fare, purchase your ticket at the terminal before getting on the train. You can also buy tickets aboard the train, but must pay a surcharge for the convenience.

For more details about getting to a particular city, refer to the individual city or town listings.

The Eurailpass used in parts of Europe isn't valid in Morocco. However, if you're under 26 and qualify, you can avail yourself of an **InterRail Card.** This pass grants travelers under 26 one month of unlimited travel in 17 countries, including the countries affiliated with the Eurailpass, and also Great Britain (which is not affiliated), Romania, Hungary, Yugoslavia, and now Morocco—the only place outside Europe where the pass is valid.

An important consideration is that holders of the pass receive only a half-fare reduction on travel in the country where the pass is purchased, as opposed to unlimited travel outside the country where they purchased the pass. Unfortunately, this pass can be purchased only in a country where a student has resided for six months, and is therefore mainly of interest to American or Canadian students studying abroad. It is sold at all major rail terminals in Western Europe and through travel agents.

Otherwise, no special passes or discounts exist in Morocco. But even if you don't have a rail pass or discount, the fares are so low to begin with that you will feel you are traveling on the cheap.

In Morocco, the headquarters for ONCF are in Casablanca, at the **Casablanca Voyageurs Station,** bd. Ba-Hammad (without number) (tel. 24-58-01), with a branch office at the Casablanca-Port Station, bd. Al Hansali (without number) (tel. 22-30-11). Throughout all the other cities of Morocco, information, fares, and ticket sales can be arranged at the local railway stations, which are almost always in the center of town.

BY BUS

The major bus companies are **CTM** and **SATAS,** both operating out of the same offices and both employing an older Greyhound-type bus that is moderately comfortable. CTM operates all over Morocco, and SATAS operates between Casablanca, Agadir, and the section south of Agadir. Buses do get crowded at times. Be warned that you'll have meager toilet facilities in some of the smaller villages—a squat toilet only, if that. Bus fares are low, about 15 DH ($1.90) per 62 miles, but you pay a little bit extra for a reserved seat.

The CTM office in Casablanca is at rue Léon d'Africain, 23 (tel. 26-80-16); in Marrakesh, at bd. Zerktouni (without number) in Gueliz (tel. 344-02); and in Tangier, in the port area (tel. 324-15).

The best buses are operated by ONCF, the state rail system, but their runs are limited to linking major cities such as Tetuán and Agadir to the main rail system. You get much more comfort on these intercity express coaches, but pay about 50% more per ticket for the privilege.

BY TAXI

Even for the budget traveler, getting around Morocco by taxi is more feasible than it would be in such high-priced cities as Stockholm, London, Paris, and New York. In all Moroccan cities and towns, a vast battalion of small and peppy cars, each painted a different vivid color according to the particular city, roams the avenues and byways looking for fares. Known as *petits taxis,* they are strictly regulated, usually have working meters, and are legally forbidden to leave the perimeter of a city for jaunts into the countryside.

They can be hailed on the street without restrictions. Know in advance that your petit taxi has the right to carry up to a total of three passengers, who may not necessarily be traveling together. An attempt will be made by the driver to cluster different destinations into one more-or-less direct route. Traveling into neighborhoods you might otherwise not have seen is part of the fun. Fares run about 4 to 6 DH (50¢ to 75¢) per ride, usually not exceeding 8 DH ($1) for major hauls across towns.

The driver should always turn on his meter, if it's working. Otherwise, he may be tempted to assess you whatever fare he wishes. If there is no meter, you should arrange a fare in advance. If the meter has started running because of another passenger already in the car, *your* fare will begin adding up beyond whatever figure was shown on the meter when you initially entered the cab. Most of these petits taxis are legally authorized to impose a 50% surcharge for nighttime fares. A tip is always appreciated by the driver, and it's good form—if there hasn't been any major upset—to add several dirhams to whatever cost might have been agreed upon.

In this guide's reviews of hotels, restaurants, and urban attractions, the best mode of public transportation is always included as part of our recommendations. In many cities, it is almost invariably a petit taxi. They are cheap, convenient, and more dependable than any other form of urban transport within a Moroccan city.

Such large cities as Casablanca and Marrakesh have public buses, but most of them are not recommendable. Most of them tend to be unbearably overcrowded, and are used primarily to haul workers between the city center and the environs. Routes are not clearly marked, and delays are long between buses.

Charging about twice the price of the petits taxis are the **grands taxis,** which might be anything from an out-of-date, rather battered Mercedes to a new minivan. Legally authorized to go outside the city limits, they are still extremely reasonable in price, usually costing only about 40% more than the impossibly inconvenient public buses. Grands taxis are allowed to pack in as many as six unrelated passengers at a time; fares are assessed individually.

Whereas petits taxis can be hailed without restrictions on the street, you generally board grands taxis at a stand. They usually stick to the most traveled out-of-town routes. If you want a driver to deviate from a main route to take you to a particular destination, he will charge you more for his inconvenience. Agree on the price in advance, and maintain your sense of humor.

If you don't like to travel crowded in with others, you can also take a **taxi privé** (private taxi). Many of these can be hailed on the street, but the more usual method is to have a member of your hotel staff summon one to your hotel. Likewise, after a meal in virtually any restaurant in Morocco, the staff will (if requested) summon a private taxi for you. Most of these taxis have meters (Morocco has greatly improved in this regard in recent years), but if the meter doesn't work, agree on the price with the driver beforehand. If you don't know what a fair price is, ask a staff member at your hotel, or the waiter in the restaurant where you've just dined. Be polite, but don't suffer in ignorant silence. Even private-taxi fares, which change from city to city in Morocco, are still considered extremely reasonable by Western standards.

BY CAR

When two or more people travel together over long distances, renting a car often becomes the most exciting and cost-efficient way of seeing the countryside. The rural highways of Morocco are excellent, and the vistas are breathtaking.

Drivers, however, need to exercise caution, paying particular attention to pedestrians and such animals as goats, chickens, and sheep. In cities, too, streams of pedestrians and animals on the streets can present unnerving obstacles. Roads within the most congested urban centers, particularly within medinas, tend to be narrow, with sometimes open ditches on either side of very narrow streets; this encourages people to drive down the center of the street. Within cities, where you'll probably be searching for particular addresses, it's better to hire a petit taxi or, if you're sightseeing, to walk.

Don't be afraid to blast your horn while negotiating narrow mountain curves and blind corners.

A *final word of caution:* Drivers in unpopulated regions should never—repeat, never—allow their gas gauges to drop below the halfway mark if they can help it. You never know when the only gas station within 75 miles will be closed and locked (or, more disconcertingly, open but out of gasoline).

CAR RENTALS

Several North American car-rental companies are represented in Morocco, plus a host of local rental companies. Although at first glance the rates of the regional companies might appear cheaper than those of their U.S.-based counterparts, potential renters should exercise caution. Often you are given a badly maintained car and have to pay hidden "extras" when it comes time for the bill. You're probably better off renting a car, on an unlimited-mileage basis, from one of America's big three rental companies. These include **Hertz** (tel. toll free 800/654-3001 in the U.S.), **Avis** (tel. toll free 800/331-2112), and **Budget** (tel. toll free 800/527-0700).

Budget, for example, maintains offices not only in Casablanca, Marrakesh, Agadir,

Tangier, Fez, and Rabat, but also in the desert outpost of Ouarzazate and in the rarely visited Algerian-frontier town of Oujda. If it's reserved three business days in advance, a car can be waiting for you at an airport or delivered directly to your hotel. Budget charges around $258 weekly for its least expensive car (which it refers to as a "micro" car), a Renault 4. It theoretically seats four passengers, although I heartily recommend it for no more than two passengers and their luggage. Larger and more expensive cars from Budget's economy and compact categories rent for $271 and $385 per week, respectively. A very comfortable midsize car, a Renault 11, can comfortably seat five passengers and costs $440 per week, with unlimited mileage. Discounts are granted by Budget to renters who keep their cars for more than two weeks, and additional, less significant discounts are granted to renters who prepay in advance from North America. Remember, though, that all car rentals carry an additional 19% tax above and beyond the actual rental charges.

Collision-damage waivers cost between $3.75 and $5 per day, depending on the car's size. If you agree to accept the waiver, you'll be relieved of all responsibility for any damage inflicted upon your car during its rental. Otherwise, you'll be financially liable for all damage that the car sustains during your rental.

(Note that some U.S.-based credit-card companies, including gold and platinum American Express and gold VISA cards, sometimes offer to pay the cost of vehicle repair if the card is imprinted upon the contract at the time of rental. Such an arrangement gives cardholders the option of avoiding the cost of the collision-damage waiver. If you're considering this course of action, remember that each credit-card company makes different promises, and that enforcing them after your accident will require lots of paperwork. Some cardholders simply buy the extra insurance offered by the rental company to avoid the potential hassles this sometimes involves.)

All cars are equipped with safety belts (or should be), and luggage racks are available upon request. However, if you use one, you must take the same precautions you'd use in Italy, southern France, or most parts of North America—if there is luggage visible on top of (or within) your car, don't leave it unguarded at any time. (At parking lots throughout the country, an aged attendant—usually, but not always, with an official badge—will miraculously appear, offering to guard your car. This takes some getting used to, but the system usually works out happily. It's wise to acknowledge the guardian with a smile, and equally wise to offer a small tip—say, 3 DH (40¢)—when you return for your car.)

Despite the heat of Morocco, air conditioning is a rare luxury in a rental car, and difficult to arrange at any price through any company. Because the desert heat is dry—and, in my opinion, very healthful—an open window provides most of the ventilation you'll need, and a more immediate contact with the landscape outside.

Also considered unnecessary luxuries in Moroccan rental cars are automatic transmissions. Few companies offer them at any price, presumably because of the difficult-to-get spare parts needed for their repair.

Avis and Hertz both offer an almost identical array of well-maintained cars, in roughly the same cities covered by Budget. At least in Morocco, however, Avis and Hertz charge higher prices and offer less convenient terms than those offered by Budget. By the time of your visit, this situation could have changed, and you'd be wise to comparison-shop among all three companies before your trip.

GASOLINE

You'll spot such familiar signs as Mobil, at least in the main cities and towns. I've discovered that prices vary from day to day and that the farther south you go, the steeper the gasoline prices.

Be sure you know which type of gas your rented car needs. Only the cheapest, most primitive engines (often those in heavily polluting trucks or farming equipment) use the relatively inexpensive "pétrol mélangé," a mixture of gasoline and oil. If you're in doubt, ask for "super" or "pétrol super." This contains a lesser octane rating than its counterpart in North America, but it is suitable for most up-to-date rental cars in Morocco. Service-station attendants are usually helpful.

DRIVING RULES

Vehicles brought into Morocco, including motorcycles, can remain in the country for six months free of duty; after that, they are subject to the usual import restrictions.

In general, your valid hometown driver's license should be sufficient, particularly if you're dealing with a big car-rental company such as Budget, Hertz, or Avis. However, I have found that some of the smaller rental agencies insist on an international driving permit.

You must have adequate insurance to drive in Morocco. The **Carte Verte (Green Card)**, the international insurance certificate, is recognized and valid in Morocco. Your car-rental agency will arrange insurance for you as part of the rental agreement; otherwise, if you're bringing in that new car you just purchased in Europe, you can get local insurance at all ports of entry, such as Casablanca and Tangier. Third-party insurance is compulsory in case a driver doesn't possess a Carte Verte. This third-party insurance may be obtained at Customs upon arrival in Morocco.

Traffic drives on the right, and the French highway code is used. Inside Moroccan cities and towns, as well as on its national highways, signposts conform to international codes and standards.

Motorists will often be stopped for road checks by the traffic police, officers of the Sûreté Nationale patrol. Although their job is to watch for violations, they also aid motorists in distress. An officer is likely to ask to see your documents, including insurance certificate, driver's license, and car registration. For the most part, these checks are routine and you should not become unduly alarmed.

Do not drive at night. Because it is technically legal for a Moroccan motorist to drive at night if he or she doesn't exceed 12 miles per hour, the roads at dusk will have an occasional farm vehicle rumbling through the darkness. The roads will also be filled with mopeds and cyclists driving without lights, along with many black-robed figures, energetic children, and donkeys, sheep, and goats. Not to mention the potholes. Hire a taxi for short hauls instead.

And don't drink and drive.

INTERNATIONAL DRIVER'S LICENSE

Always useful, even if a car-rental company doesn't specifically require it, an international driver's license should be obtained before you leave home. It is available at any of the nationwide branches of the **American Automobile Association (AAA)**. To apply, you must be at least 18 years old, have a valid U.S. driver's license, pay a $10 fee, and submit two 2-by-2 photos of the passport variety.

If there isn't a branch of the AAA near you, send the photos (after signing them on the back) with a photocopy of the front and back of your valid U.S. license, plus the $10 fee, to AAA, 1000 AAA Dr., Heathrow, FL 32746-5063 (tel. 407/444-8000). The AAA will return the international license to you by mail. It will carry a one-year validity. However, you must bring your own license abroad as well. One does not replace the other.

ROAD MAPS

The best maps of Morocco are published by European cartographers, notably **Hallwag** and **RV Reise-und Verkehrsverlag. Michelin,** the tire people, also publish a map called *Maroc Nord et Centre.*

You can generally pick up city and town maps at tourist offices in various cities (see local listings for addresses). However, the medinas of Morocco remain unmapped, as there are virtually no street signs in many of them. If you're seeking a particular address or want to go on an escorted tour, or even if you plan to take one of our walking tours through the medinas, you'll need an official local guide (their prices are very reasonable).

Buy only maps of Morocco that include the Western Sahara. A map that shows a border between Morocco and the Western Sahara could be confiscated by Customs upon your entry into the country.

In the United States, you can order maps at **Michael Chessler Books,** P.O. Box 2436, Evergreen, CO 80439-2436. Write for details of what's available.

BREAKDOWNS/ASSISTANCE

If you break down along the highway, with no phone or other help, you can often wait for a member of the Sûreté Nationale (the patrolmen of the highway) to come by and provide assistance, which might include summoning aid from the nearest garage. Sometimes fellow motorists will stop and offer assistance; often the best they can do is to summon assistance once they reach a center that has a police station or other facilities. All the major towns have garages, and most of them have parts for standard European cars. Most garages are also accustomed to servicing Land Rovers.

BY FERRY

Morocco lies only 8 miles from the southern coast of Spain, to which it is linked by good ferry connections. Ferries to Tangier leave Monday through Saturday at the rate of four per day. On Sunday, service is curtailed to three per day. Frequency of service drops between November and March to two per day, Monday through Saturday only. Trip time is 2½ hours. Discounts granted are 50% for children, 20% for Eurailpass holders, and 30% for those with an InterRail Card. The cost is 3,440 pesetas ($34.90) per person in first class, 2,700 pesetas ($28.40) in second class, and 8,500 pesetas ($79.90) per car. Cars are not transported in stormy weather.

HITCHHIKING

Hitchhiking is not recommended in Morocco (or anywhere else). Buses and trains are so cheap that much of the financial incentive for hitchhiking simply doesn't exist—except in emergencies.

If you absolutely must hitch a ride, fellow tourists are probably your best bet, and even then, I'd suggest using great caution. Aside from any personal harm you might incur, you could be arrested. Morocco is a land of hashish and kef, and many Europeans purchase drugs here that they transport in their cars. If the police stop a car and drugs are discovered, the driver and everyone else in the car will go to jail!

If you disregard this advice and are picked up by Moroccans, you'll find that some of them will try to charge you for the ride anyway, at a rate higher than the bus.

Should *you* be the motorist, it is likewise dangerous to pick up hitchhikers. If the person you pick up is carrying drugs (and how are you going to know?), you could also be arrested for drug possession.

SUGGESTED ITINERARIES

In general interest and fascination, these are the most interesting cities or towns to visit in Morocco, ranked in order of importance: 1) Marrakesh, 2) Fez, 3) Tangier, 4) Meknes, and 5) Rabat.

IF YOU HAVE 1 WEEK

Day 1: Arrive in Casablanca and spend the night.

Day 2: Transfer north to Rabat for the night.

Day 3: Head west for Meknes, where you can stay overnight and still have time to visit Volubilis and Moulay Idriss.

Day 4: Continue west to Fez and spend the remaining time (and part of the next morning if needed) exploring its medina.

Days 5–7: Transfer south to Morocco's most fabled city, Marrakesh. One day will mainly be spent getting there; another day will be needed to explore the city, especially its medina; and a final day could be devoted to an excursion in its environs.

IF YOU HAVE 2 WEEKS

Day 1: From Casablanca, drive north to Rabat (for distances between cities, refer to the mileage chart). See the city and spend the night.

Day 2: Continue along the coast, bypassing Ksar el Kebir. Stop for lunch at the small Hotel Riad in Larache (part of the Diafa chain), which offers reliable food. Spend the night in Tangier. The trip to Tangier will take up most of your day.

Day 3: Explore Tangier.

Day 4: Drive south to Meknes, stopping to inspect Chechaouèn. This drive and stopover will take up most of your day.

Day 5: From Meknes, visit Volubilis and Moulay Idriss before making the relatively short journey east to Fez, where you can spend two nights.

Day 6: Explore Fez and its environs.

Day 7: Drive south through the Middle Atlas to Erfoud. Stop for lunch in Er Rachidia, providing you got an early start from Fez. Continue south to the desert oasis of Erfoud, which will put you at the gateway to the Sahara. Stay overnight in Erfoud, perhaps in a palm grove.

Day 8: From Erfoud (and to avoid returning on the same road to Er Rachidia), take the decent road that cuts northwest across a bleak countryside to Goulmima. However, once at Goulmima, head west for an overnight stopover in Tinerhir. There should still be enough daylight for you to drive the short distance through a lovely valley to the Gorges of Todra.

Day 9: From Tinerhir, continue west toward Ouarzazate, detouring, however, for a look at the Gorges of the Dadès. Stay overnight in Ouarzazate, which has several good, moderately priced hotels.

Day 10: Drive across the mountains to the fabled city of Marrakesh, where you can spend two nights.

Day 11: Marrakesh is a fascinating city, and you will want to allow this full day and night to take in its attractions.

Day 12: From Marrakesh, drive west to the coastal town of Essaouira. Once there, head south to Agadir, one of the beach-resort bargains of the world (you may want to spend a few days there relaxing if you have the time). Or if you're not interested in beaches, continue that same day on a road through a fertile valley going east to Taroudannt, which is much smaller, far more charming, and full of lots of local color and Moroccan flavor.

Day 13: While based in either Agadir or Taroudannt, you can make a swing south through the Anti-Atlas, along a narrow, sometimes dangerous, but still fascinating road to the little town of Tafraoute. After lunch there, head west again in the direction of Tiznit. From there, continue north to Agadir for the night.

Day 14: The next and final day, continue north along the coast, stopping for lunch either at Essaouira or El Jadida. Before dark you will reach Casablanca, where you can check into a hotel and be prepared for your return flight.

IF YOU HAVE 3 WEEKS

Days 1-2: Arrive in Tangier for two nights. Explore Tangier and its environs on the first day, and spend the following day making an easy excursion to the old city of Tetuán.

Day 3: Journey south along the coast, stopping for lunch at Larache and reaching the capital city of Rabat late in the afternoon. Explore Rabat with what time remains and finish with a morning sightseeing tour.

Day 4: Journey east to Meknes for the night. Explore the major attractions in the environs: Moulay Idriss and Volubilis. Head for Fez in the west for an overnight stopover.

Days 5-6: Spend this time in Fez, as the first day will have been spent reaching it after a late start from Meknes.

Days 7–10: Transfer to Marrakesh and divide your time between resting by the pool and exploring the souks of this ancient city of the desert. Spend one of the days making an excursion through the Ourika Valley.

Day 11: Leave Marrakesh for a visit to the deep south of Morocco. Head into *Beau Geste* country and plan to stay overnight in Ouarzazate.

Day 12: Continue to drive south to the Sahara for an overnight stop in the gazelle country around Zagora, the last major outpost before the desert. Spend the night there.

Day 13: Return north to Ouarzazate and this time head east along the Route of the Kasbahs for an overnight stop at El Kelâa des M'Gouna.

Day 14: The following day, visit Boumalne-Dadès and explore the Gorges du Dadès, spending the night in Tinerhir.

Day 15: Continue east toward the Algerian border, with an overnight stop planned at Erfoud, a town of oxblood-colored buildings that is the gateway to the Sahara.

Day 16: Transfer back to Marrakesh for an overnight stopover and rest.

Day 17: Leave Marrakesh, heading west into the Anti-Atlas, with an overnight stopover at Taroudannt, the capital of the Saadian dynasty.

Day 18: From Taroudannt, head west toward Agadir but take the spectacular winding mountain road south to Tafraoute, where you can stay overnight. Or else, if time remains, you can continue west to Tiznit, closer to the coast.

Days 19–20: Spend part of the day driving north to Agadir, one of Morocco's great resorts, where you may want to unwind before facing the stress of returning home.

Day 21: Drive north to Casablanca and a night's sleep before returning home or to your next destination.

 MOROCCO

American Express   Voyages Schwartz represents American Express in Morocco. Their offices are found in rue Mauritania (without number), Immeuble Moutaoukil, Marrakesh (tel. 33-022); bd. Pasteur, 54, Tangier (tel. 334-59); place du Marché Mucicipale, 87, Agadir (tel. 202-52); and rue du Prince Moulay Abdallah, 112, Casablanca (tel. 273-133).

Business Hours   Banks are generally open Monday through Friday from 8:30 to 11:30am and 2:30 to 4:30pm. **Stores** are generally open from 8:30am to noon and 2:30 until around 7pm (some stay open even later); many shops are closed on Sunday and Friday (the Muslim Sabbath). Most **offices** are open Monday through Friday from 8:30am to noon and from 2:30 to 6pm. **Bars** are not subject to licensing laws, and opening times depend on the whim of the management.

Camera/Film   Most film sold in France is available in Morocco as well, but only in the cities or big towns. Don't photograph anything of a military nature. You are free to take pictures of rural settings. Under no circumstances should you photograph a woman in the country without asking permission first. Sometimes if people allow you to photograph them and their animals, they'll ask you for money in return.

Since Morocco for most of the year is a hot, dry country, photographs are best taken in early morning or late in the afternoon. Otherwise, you are likely to get that "washed-out" look at midday, unless you're a very skilled photographer.

If you're photographing in the dark, dusty medinas even in midday, your picture can come out too dark unless you use fast film such as 400 to 800 ASA.

Camping   There are at least 30 camping sites throughout Morocco, including grounds outside the major cities, where you'll find adequate shower and toilet facilities. Contact the tourist offices for information and details.

Climate   See "When to Go," above.

Crime   See "Safety," below.

Currency   See "Information, Entry Requirements, Customs & Money," above.

Customs   The following items may be temporarily imported to Morocco duty free: still and movie cameras with two rolls of film for each; personal clothing and jewelry; binoculars; portable typewriters; camping and sports gear. Most foodstuffs are allowed, but in "reasonable quantities." Each visitor can bring in 400 grams of tobacco, or 200 cigarettes or 50 cigars, and one bottle of wine or spirits. Firearms and cartridges may be imported subject to a license issued by the police department in Rabat (Direction de la Sûreté Nationale).

Citizens of the United States who have been outside the country for 48 hours or more can bring home $400 worth of merchandise duty free—if they have claimed no similar exemption within the past 30 days. If you make purchases in Morocco, keep your receipts.

Documents   See "Information, Entry Requirements, Customs & Money," above.

Driving Laws   See "Getting Around," above.

Drug Laws   In recent years many young Americans and Canadians "went Moroccan" in Marrakesh—wearing djellabahs and *babouches* and sitting around Djemaa el-Fna square at night, eating a typical Moroccan meal and smoking kef. Most have disappeared after a crackdown by the police, who weren't too happy about their hash-smoking ways and their disruptive effect upon Moroccan society.

Kef, a raw-leaf marijuana, is often smoked in public in a clay pipe. Despite this rather blatant display, the sale of kef is illegal in Morocco. In one year alone, some 100 foreigners were arrested on drug charges. The maximum penalty has been raised from 5 to 10 years in jail, and the minimum from 3 months to 5 years for most offenses. Fines have been increased considerably, up to 500,000 DH ($62,500).

National law makes it a "major crime" to corrupt minors by inciting them to take drugs.

Warning: After a tour of Morocco, if you are returning to Spain by car, your vehicle will probably be searched thoroughly, as Spanish Customs look for hashish (kef). Sometimes it takes hours to gain clearance. And from what I hear, Spanish jails aren't the Hilton.

Drugstores   In an emergency, ask the concierge at your hotel to direct you to the nearest pharmacy. It would be wise to have him or her call ahead and explain your needs to the druggist in case there's a language problem.

Electricity   Generally, 220 volts, the same as that used within Europe, but you'll occasionally come across 110 volts. You will usually need an electrical converter before you can safely plug in your major American appliances.

Embassies and Consulates   In general, if you have business to transact, don't call; go in person during regular office hours Monday through Friday. See individual cities for addresses and phone numbers.

Emergencies   Dial 19 for police or an ambulance in Tangier, Rabat, Casablanca, Fez, Meknes, Agadir, and Marrakesh; call 15 for fire emergency.

Etiquette   Many North Americans and Europeans visit Morocco with the mistaken notion that they can go inside mosques or religious shrines as if they were sightseeing attractions. You can't, as frustrating as that revelation may be. Occasionally you'll come across some old medrassa that are no longer used for worship, and there you'll get a tantalizing hint of what a mosque looks like inside. When a functioning mosque is open, and Moroccans are at prayer inside, do not linger outside on the threshold peering in; it's considered very rude to gawk during people's personal, private moments.

Provincial Moroccans do not like to be photographed. It is considered very bad manners. Under no circumstance should you try to take a picture of a woman without asking permission. Marrakesh and Tangier are used to tourists, but exercise caution nevertheless.

Gasoline   See "Getting Around," above.

Guides   The sights in Morocco's medinas are best covered on foot, but if you want some help without taking an organized tour, hire an English-speaking guide for a half day of general orientation. Maps are usually inadequate, and many of the sights described really can't be found on your own, unless you have unlimited time.

City-licensed guides are available through your hotel or at the Syndicat d'Initiative (Chamber of Commerce) in every major city. Hiring an official guide is less expensive than you might think. Prices are regulated, but negotiate the rate and hours in advance; the cost varies from city to city.

In all the major cities, you will be pestered by characters wanting to guide you, and they will expect recompense for their trouble. On the whole, a firm "no" and complete disinterest will discourage the would-be "guides" and the "students of language."

Hairdressers Salons are found in all major cities and towns, but they vary in quality. Ask at your hotel for a recommendation if the hotel doesn't have its own.

Hitchhiking It is definitely not recommended. There is an element of physical danger involved, based on incidents in the past. You could also go to jail. If the police stop your car in this land of kef and hashish and search for drugs, and find some, everybody in the car, including driver and passengers, goes to jail.

Holidays See "When to Go," above.

Information See "Information, Entry Requirements, Customs & Money," above, and individual city chapters for the addresses of local offices.

Language Learning Arabic or Berber before going to Morocco is an almost hopeless undertaking. It is important to know some basic words in French, since a number of people will speak French if they don't speak English. Pick up a copy of the best phrase book on the market, *French for Travellers*, Berlitz ($5.95) or *French at a Glance*, Barron's ($5.95).

Laundry Pack easy-to-care-for clothing, as laundry and dry-cleaning facilities can be highly erratic. It's best to stick to the services of your hotel. In an emergency, I often tip the maid to launder and press a shirt.

Legal Aid There are no societies for this, as there are in the United States. You'll have to go to a consulate or embassy of your home country. These offices maintain a list of English-speaking lawyers who will come to your aid for a price.

Liquor Laws An Islamic nation, Morocco prohibits the sale of alcohol to Muslims. The law, however, doesn't appear to be strictly enforced except at Ramadan. Visitors are not affected by this ban on alcohol. Alcohol tends not to be sold in medinas, which are usually considered fundamentalist strongholds, but it is sold in "New Towns," in restaurants that cater to foreigners, and in hotel bars. There are no strict licensing laws.

Mail In the larger cities, post offices are generally open from 8:30am to 5pm Monday through Friday, and 8:30am to noon on Saturday. In smaller places, they are likely to shut down from noon to 3pm. Ask your hotel clerk.

It costs 2.50 DH (30¢) to send an airmail postcard to Canada or the United States, 3.50 DH (45¢) to send a letter (up to 20 grams). You won't find mailboxes along the streets; letters can be mailed through hotel reception desks, or else you can go yourself to the nearest post office. Stamps can be purchased at tobacconists, as in France, or at post offices. Allow at least 10 days for delivery. Even airmail postcards and letters can take up to two weeks (sometimes more, depending on where they were mailed in Morocco) to reach the United States. Parcels, both surface and airmail, are mailed at post offices, and you may be asked to fill out a declaration stating contents.

Morocco doesn't use postal or zip codes. In addressing mail to Morocco, just give the street address, then the name of the city and country, such as Casablanca, Morocco.

Maps City maps are usually available at tourist offices. These maps almost never include detailed depictions of city layouts. Street names often don't exist (and are certainly not signposted). You'll need a guide to get you through the medinas, especially the labyrinths of Fez and Marrakesh. For touring in the country, the best road maps are published by **Hallwag; RV Reise-und Verkehrsverlag;** and **Michelin.** These maps are sold in bookstores throughout Morocco; they can also be purchased before you go at many big bookstores in American cities that have large map and travel-guide departments. Otherwise, write **Michael Chessler Books,** P.O. Box 2436, Evergreen, CO 80439-2436, to see what Moroccan maps this store has in stock.

Newspapers/Magazines   The *International Herald Tribune* is flown to Casablanca and Rabat from Paris, but it's not available until late afternoon. Some English newspapers filter in through Gibraltar. Copies of *Time* and *Newsweek* are sold at news kiosks and in hotels.

Passports   See "Information, Entry Requirements, Customs & Money," above.

Pets   An international health and inoculation certificate is required for pets entering Morocco.

Police   Dial 19 for police in Tangier, Rabat, Casablanca, Fez, Meknes, Agadir, and Marrakesh.

Radio/TV   Broadcasts on Moroccan radio and television are in either French or Arabic. However, in the north of Morocco, owing to its close proximity to Gibraltar and Spain, you can often tune in to either English- or Spanish-language broadcasts on both radio and TV. Morocco has two television channels, but some hotels receive satellite TV such as the English-language Sky. It is also possible to listen to BBC World Service on 9.41 and 5.975 mhz (31.88 and 50.21 m).

Religious Services   You'll find facilities for most religious denominations in big cities. As for smaller towns, only those with a European population will have non-Muslim religious facilities (most often Roman Catholic churches).

Rest Rooms   All modern airports and rail and bus terminals have toilets, which may or may not be well maintained. Public toilets in the major cities and towns are often cesspools, and I'd recommend that you avoid them except in dire emergencies. Instead, use the rest rooms of major hotels and restaurants. The squat toilet, a porcelain or metal square with a hole in the middle, is still common in Morocco. Bring toilet paper. Be brave.

Safety   Don't leave luggage in your car, even when it is locked, and don't examine the contents of your wallet in the street. This is just asking to have it lifted. One possible solution is to have wallets and passports firmly pinned inside a money belt or inside pocket, leaving only a handful of dirhams readily available in a side pocket for tips, small purchases, and taxi fares.

Similarly, don't distribute money grandly in the streets, except perhaps for a photograph, unless you want to be mobbed. Official guides, who display badges, can usually be relied on to protect your interests. (See "Guides," above.) Still, there are clip joints and nightclubs where you will be shamelessly ripped off, and you will have to learn to spot them.

Taxes   Depending on the hotel, a government tax of 17% to 19% is added to all hotel and restaurant bills.

Telephone, Telex, Fax   Telephone service is operated by the post office. Local calls in such cities as Tangier and Casablanca can be made at public phone booths, but international phone calls are routed through Rabat. The large cities are linked by automatic telephone and all you have to do is dial the area code (see the directories of the *Postes Chérifiennes*) and the number. However, some small places require operator assistance.

Chances are your hotel will be able to send a telex or fax for you. However, smaller inns and hotels, most likely, won't be equipped to send one. These can also be sent from the larger post offices.

Time   Greenwich Mean Time (GMT) is in force all year in Morocco. The country is 5 hours ahead of Eastern Standard Time (6 hours in summer).

Tipping   Everyone seems to have a hand out and this can become annoying. Nevertheless, certain tips are expected—and rightly so. Here are the guidelines. Take every opportunity to fill your pocket with 1-DH (15¢) pieces. They'll go quickly enough. Most restaurants and hotels include a service charge, often 17% to 19%—but don't take that too seriously. The waiter expects at least another 7%. Give 5 DH (65¢) per bag to the porter for taking your luggage to your room, 5 DH (65¢) to the taxi driver unless the ride has been unusually long. Guides who show you through museums expect at least 5 DH (65¢). Train and boat porters expect 10 to 15 DH ($1.25 to $1.90). If you've required the assistance of a hotel concierge for a stay of at least three days, then about 50 DH ($6.25) is adequate.

Tobacco American and British cigarettes are sold in major cities, along with such Moroccan brands as Gauloises and the popular Casa Sports. Tobacco can be purchased in food markets and cafés as well as tobacco shops.

Tourist Offices See "Information, Entry Requirements, Customs & Money," above, and individual city chapters.

Visas See "Information, Entry Requirements, Customs & Money," above.

Water Water is considered safe to drink in the big cities, not in rural areas. Even so, if you have a delicate stomach, you should stick to mineral water. You may be glad you did.

Yellow Pages If you're in a town where the directories are in Arabic, forget it. In larger cities, such as Casablanca, you'll find listings in French but, even so, you'll have to know that language well enough to know what heading to look under. It's usually faster to ask someone at your hotel to look up a particular establishment, and perhaps even make a strategic call for you.

CHAPTER 3

T TANGIER

- **WHAT'S SPECIAL ABOUT TANGIER**
1. **A BRIEF HISTORY**
2. **ORIENTATION & GETTING AROUND**
- **FAST FACTS: TANGIER**
3. **ACCOMMODATIONS**
- **FROMMER'S SMART TRAVELER: HOTELS**
- **FROMMER'S COOL FOR KIDS: HOTELS**
4. **DINING**
- **FROMMER'S SMART TRAVELER: RESTAURANTS**
- **FROMMER'S COOL FOR KIDS: RESTAURANTS**
5. **ATTRACTIONS**
- **SUGGESTED ITINERARIES**
- **DID YOU KNOW . . . ?**
- **FROMMER'S FAVORITE TANGIER EXPERIENCES**
6. **SAVVY SHOPPING**
7. **EVENING ENTERTAINMENT**
8. **EASY EXCURSIONS**

As with most parts of Morocco, each time Tangier was conquered, a new leader presided over its Kasbah, bringing new cultural and religious influences to Moroccan life.

With golden sandy beaches at its feet and the Rif mountains in the background, Tangier is a modern Mediterranean resort, although its legendary memories as the "wicked city" of North Africa live on.

Only the narrow Strait of Gibraltar separates it from the southern coast of Spain and Europe itself. The city deserves a description of its own history, because from 1923 until Morocco was granted independence in 1956, Tangier was an international tax-free city, making its own laws through a committee composed mostly of Europeans. Its reputation for decadence and intrigue, which figured in the plot of countless books and films, comes from those days when it was notorious as a haven for spies, rogues, and "most unforgettable characters" in general.

The frequent arrivals of such Hollywood film stars as Marlene Dietrich and Errol Flynn, of literary expatriates such as Paul Bowles (author of *The Sheltering Sky*), and of visiting celebrities such as playwright Tennessee Williams only fanned media interest in Tangier. No one gave the city more publicity than the fabulously wealthy and ultimately tragic former resident, the Woolworth heiress Barbara Hutton, the "poor little rich girl" who lived in the Kasbah.

Although the international headliners captured the world's attention, Tangier was (and is) a Moroccan city with many characteristics of the rest of the country. The streets of the Medina are narrow and steep, often no more than stairs, as they make their way to the legendary Kasbah.

For many, especially those coming from Europe, Tangier will be their gateway to Morocco. A city with about 200,000 permanent residents, it is built like an amphitheater, with houses painted white and pale blue or purple, stretching up the hill to the Kasbah. Colorful minarets still fill the city, although the Ville Nouvelle (New Town) is modern.

Tangier, with its dazzling light, has long been attractive to artists. The Frenchman Eugène Delacroix (1798–1863) was the first major painter to be attracted to the play of color against the local buildings. He came here in 1832, finding many subjects that fascinated him.

Following much later in his footsteps was Henri Matisse, who spent three months here in 1912, completing 23 paintings in Morocco and five dozen small drawings. Of

WHAT'S SPECIAL ABOUT TANGIER

Beaches
☐ Tangier's beach is considered one of the best along the Mediterranean. Dotted with restaurants and cafés, it's a playground for both the Muslim and the European worlds.

Historic Districts
☐ The Kasbah, former stronghold of the sultans, the "crown" of Tangier, and later the villa-studded quarter of the internationally wealthy.
☐ The Medina, a narrow, labyrinthine maze—filled with shops, restaurants, cafés, and enough carpets to pave a road to the moon.

Buildings
☐ Grand Mosque, constructed by Sultan Moulay Ismail in the late 17th century. Non-Muslims can't go inside.

☐ The Old American Legation, a palatial gift of the sultan to the American people.

Parks/Gardens
☐ The Gardens of the Sultan, within the walls of Dar el Makhzen (the former palace), designed in the Andalusian style.

Museums
☐ The late publisher Malcom Forbes's Museum of Military Miniatures, with some of the rarest model soldiers in the world. But mainly a look inside the house of one of the world's richest and most famous.

Film Locations
☐ Scenes from *The Sheltering Sky* (after Paul Bowles's novel) were shot at the Kasbah.

---

course, he could not paint women, one of his favorite subjects, because the "law of the veil" prevailed at the time of his visit. Only prostitutes and Jews were exempt from this restriction. Long after Matisse left Morocco, he painted one of his masterpieces, *The Moroccans*, in Paris in 1915, and over the next 40 years his paintings would frequently evoke memories of Tangier.

The play of the sun on Tangier's white buildings was said to be so bright and exceptional that in the 1930s Pinkerton's detective agency sent its trainees to the city to teach them how to trail someone under difficult circumstances, especially when they escaped suddenly from the bright into the lengthening shadows of the Medina.

Quite frankly, Tangier is no longer the gilded, glamorous mecca that it once was in the golden age before and after World War II. Increasingly, it is viewed as a mass passenger port and a modern summer resort, popular with the Moroccans themselves. Tangier, in fact, is more or less officially designated as the "summer capital" of Morocco by King Hassan II, who has a palace there. Once some 60,000 expatriates lived in the city. Now it is estimated that the number has dwindled to about 175 Americans and Britons, about 850 Spaniards, "and a few French."

1. A BRIEF HISTORY

By everyone's estimate, Tangier is the oldest city in Morocco, with an active commerce established as early as 1600 B.C. Roman mythology attributes its founding to the Greek giant Anteus, who was produced through the union of Poseidon, god of the sea, and Gaia, goddess of the earth.

The city was known by the ancient Berbers, the Phoenicians, and the Romans. At least for a short period of their control, the Romans considered Tangier an administrative part of their colonies in Spain rather than associating it with the rest of North Africa.

IMPRESSIONS

In Tangier everything is possible—and everything that isn't possible is possible, too.
—JACK KEROUAC

During the 1300s, Tangier—with Barcelona, Genoa, Venice, and Marseilles—was one of the five major trading cities of the western Mediterranean world. Major exports included carpets, leather goods, raw wool, grain, and sugar. Imports consisted of spices, metal, finished cloth, and caged birds of prey for falconry.

In 1471, Tangier was conquered by the Portuguese, who retained it as a trading post and strategic military garrison. Between 1578 and 1640, thanks to a complicated alliance between the royal houses of Europe, the city became Spanish, then reverted back to the Portuguese. In 1661, Tangier was part of the dowry received by the English King Charles II for his marriage to the Portuguese royal heiress Catherine of Braganza.

The English departed in 1684, and the sultan's Sudanese troops immediately dismantled most of the English fortifications before turning their attention elsewhere.

The commercial fortunes of the city went into a decline that persisted into the 19th century. In the 19th century, Tangier became recognized as a beautiful and convenient city with a desirable climate and a bountiful labor pool where European merchants and businessmen could profitably establish their headquarters. As Spain, France, and Britain became less discreet about their thirst for colonial expansion in Morocco, Tangier housed a thriving and politically acquisitive European colony with a legendary social life.

The designation of Tangier as an "international concession" (1923) launched the city's golden age. Although the sultan retained nominal control of Tangier's government, most decisions were made by a 30-member committee whose bylaws were established by the European powers and 21 of whose 30 members came from a carefully balanced assortment of European representatives. The city adopted French, Spanish, and Arabic as its official languages, and tax-free status was granted to all imports, exports, and income. The colonial merchants, and some of their Moroccan middlemen, thrived.

Preoccupied with the need to forge an administrative unity from the remnants of the colonial bureaucracies, Morocco allowed Tangier to retain its independence and tax-free status until 1960. Then, politically united with the rest of Morocco, the city adopted all the fiscal and civil laws of the newly formed country.

Before 1960, however, a flight of capital had begun, and within a few years, Tangier had stagnated. Civil unrest, fiscal uncertainty, and the tensions of the Arab-Israeli feuds made life for foreigners extremely uncomfortable. The commerce in drugs and contraband increased. Although the rate of violent crimes was lower in Morocco than throughout most of Western Europe, within Tangier it was higher than anywhere else in Morocco.

Today, the major legal industry of Tangier is tourism. This includes huge numbers of visitors from Europe. A new phenomenon, however, involves a growing number of

---

IMPRESSIONS

Sodom was a church picnic and Gomorrah a convention of Girl Scouts compared to Tangier which contained more thieves, black marketeers, spies, thugs, phonies, beachcombers, expatriates, degenerates, characters, operators, bandits, bums, tramps, politicians, and charlatans than any place I've ever visited.
—ROBERT RUARK, AS I WAS SAYING, 1950

visitors from other parts of Morocco, each of whom appreciates the unique history of the country's oldest—and perhaps its most unusual—city.

2. ORIENTATION & GETTING AROUND

Tangier is a major port and gateway not only to Morocco but to the Mediterranean. As you enter the city, particularly at the port, you are likely to be besieged by prospective **guides,** who aggressively sell their services. In a land of some 80% male unemployment, with nearly half the population under 21, unofficial guides will assault you at every turn.

You will not be left alone, and you might as well accept this as a fact of life. Wherever you try to go alone, you will be approached by young men offering to guide you somewhere. Under no circumstances should you accept one of the wads of chocolate-colored hashish that is a legendary product of the Rif mountains; nor should you accept illegal drugs of any kind. The consequences could be more horrible than you ever dreamed, the most obvious being that your dealer is also an informant for the police. You may legitimately want someone to show you around. But it is best to go to the Tangier Tourist Office (see below) and arrange for one of the official guides, as these are regulated by the government and have to meet certain linguistic and ethical requirements.

Even if you don't really want a guide, an official guide will keep the hustlers away from you and let you sightsee with a modicum of peace. Agree on the price before setting out. The rates, as fixed by the tourist office, tend to be reasonable: 50 DH ($6.25) per half day, 100 DH ($12.50) per full day. Of course, the guide will be most happy to accept a tip. Get used to tipping a lot in Morocco. It is always wise, as soon as possible, to acquire small change in dirhams. Technically, you're not supposed to dispense dollars or European currencies for services rendered, even though guides may specifically request that you pay them in dollars, German marks, or whatever.

Even with an official guide, purchases made in shops, even meals consumed at restaurants, may carry a small hidden surcharge. Many of the guides return later to the store in which you bought something—perhaps a small Moroccan carpet—to demand their commission. They even go to restaurants and demand a commission for having enticed you to eat there. Well used to this practice, the shopkeeper or restaurant owner simply adds the "commission" to your purchases.

This information is presented not to deter a visit or to discourage or disappoint you. It's just an accepted fact of life in Morocco, and you should be forewarned about what to expect so as to avoid problems later. Always remember, however, that most encounters in Morocco—as anywhere—can be handled with humor and grace, and you may quickly surprise yourself with the breadth of your interpersonal skills.

ARRIVING

BY PLANE

Boukhalf-Souahel, the airport of Tangier, lies 9 miles southwest of the city center on the P2 road to Rabat. There are flights from Agadir, Marrakesh, Rabat, and Casablanca, and also from many of the capitals of Europe. Flights also come across the strait from Gibraltar, taking only 1 hour and 20 minutes. In addition to Royal Air Maroc flights, British Airways arrives from London, Air France from Paris, Lufthansa from Germany, and Iberia from Madrid.

The only **airport buses** that might be waiting to take travelers into the city are those that have been especially chartered for members of a tour group. If you're participating in an organized tour, you'll be met by a bus and a guide, and your luggage will be safely transferred to your hotel.

Backpackers, to save money, walk just over a mile from the airport to the main highway, where they can wait for bus no. 17 or 70 to take them into the center of Tangier. The bus will deposit them at the Grand Socco.

If you are an individual traveler, you'll have to negotiate with a **taxi** driver to take you into the center of the city. The charge is at least 100 DH ($12.50) for up to six passengers. You might consider this price a bargain, considering the hassle of negotiating a public bus with your luggage.

Likewise, to return to the airport, you can arrange to have a taxi come by your hotel (the receptionist can arrange this for you). Because of security checks and any possible traffic delays, always head for the airport at least 1½ hours in advance of any flight you might have.

Warning: To be absolutely on the safe side, try to arrive 2 hours earlier. Overbooking of planes is common here, so those who show up earlier get the seat.

BY TRAIN

Tangier's main railway station, known as **Gare Tanger-Port,** av. d'Espagne (without number) (tel. 312-01), lies just 55 yards beyond the gates leading to the port of Tangier. Passengers can disembark from European ferryboats and step almost immediately onto trains bound for the countryside. Some experienced visitors prefer to disembark and embark at Tangier's second, less overwhelming railway station, **Gare Tanger-Ville,** av. des F.A.R. (without number) (tel. 312-01), which lies about a half mile before the port, directly in front of Tangier's strip of beachfront hotels. Both stations are literally in the center of town, so getting from them to your hotel usually means just a short and inexpensive taxi ride.

Trains pull in and out of Tangier from all the major cities of Morocco, including Rabat, Casablanca, Meknes, Fez, and Marrakesh. If you're going to Marrakesh from Tangier, you must change trains in Casablanca or else take the *Midnight Express* sleeper that departs from Tangier nightly at 8:15pm.

There is a **luggage storage** office at the Tangier railway station, but it will accept your baggage only if it is securely locked. You are charged about 3 DH (40¢) per bag per day.

You might easily decide to begin an all-rail excursion through Morocco, since trains provide one of the country's most comfortable and reasonably priced forms of long-distance travel. Pick up a schedule of train departures at the railway station. To indicate some price levels, a one-way ticket from Tangier to Rabat costs 57 DH ($7.15); to Casablanca, 75 DH ($9.40); and to Marrakesh, 140 DH ($17.50). Direct service is provided to Fez for 62 DH ($7.75), and to Meknes for 52 DH ($6.50).

BY BUS

The **Tangier Bus Station,** rue de Fès (without number) (tel. 324-15), lies 2 miles from the port. Buses operated by CTM pull in here from all parts of Morocco. Five buses a day, for example, run to Rabat, the trip taking 6½ hours and costing 60 DH ($7.50), with continuing service from Rabat to Casablanca taking 1½ hours. The price of a ticket from Tangier to Casablanca costs 80 DH ($10). Two buses a day leave for Fez, taking 6 hours and costing 55 DH ($6.90) one way. CTM buses also depart on the hour for Tetuán (see Chapter 4) and for the Spanish enclave of Ceuta.

BY CAR

You can take the P2 highway from Rabat to Tangier in about 3 hours, a distance of some 175 miles. If you're arriving by car from Europe, **car-ferry** services are operated by **Trasmediterránea** from Algeciras. If the weather is stormy, cars are not transported.

If you're bringing in a car from Spain, always—but always—get the permission of the car-rental company before attempting such a crossing. Hertz and Avis usually refuse permission, although Budget will sometimes allow it, but only if it is arranged in advance.

Upon arrival in Tangier with your own car, you must have the vehicle logged into your passport. *If you don't, you could be liable for 50% duty when you take it out of Morocco.* On leaving the dock area, you will also be pulled over, usually by the police, and required to purchase insurance that will cover the car while you are in Morocco.

Frankly, it's probably better to begin a new rental agreement on Moroccan soil with a Moroccan-based rental company. (Budget, Hertz, and Avis are all represented in Tangier.)

BY FERRY & HYDROFOIL

The major mode of transportation for arrival in Tangier is the ferry operated by **Trasmediterránea** (tel. 956/66-38-62), leaving from Algeciras, a port city on Spain's Costa del Sol at its far western extremity. Times have changed, however, and no longer are you carried ashore on the bare shoulders of a local stevedore, as arriving French passengers were in the heyday of the Belle Epoque.

From Algeciras, ferries leave at the rate of 4 per day Monday through Saturday, with 3 departures on Sunday. From November to March, the winter schedule is twice daily, Monday through Saturday only. The trip takes 2½ hours. Class A tickets sell for 3,400 pesetas ($31.95), with Class B tickets costing 2,700 pesetas ($25.40). Standard-size cars are transported for 8,500 pesetas ($79.90). Certain discounts are granted: 50% for children, 20% for Eurailpass holders, and 30% for InterRail pass holders. From Tarifa to Tangier, a hydrofoil leaves daily at 9am, the trip taking 1 hour and costing 2,550 pesetas ($24).

It is also possible to go back and forth between Tangier and Gibraltar on a **Gibline catamaran.** The trip is on Monday, Wednesday, Friday, and Sunday, with about 2 departures daily (check for the changing schedules). The trip takes 2½ hours and costs 210 DH ($26.25) one way, with a same-day return selling for 310 DH ($38.75).

TOURIST INFORMATION

The **Tangier Tourist Office,** bd. Pasteur, 29 (tel. 09/329-96), lies about a 15-minute walk up from the port. July to August, it's open Monday through Friday from 9am to 3pm; September to June, Monday through Friday from 8:30am to noon and 2:30 to 6:30pm. A not very detailed map of Tangier is distributed free here.

CITY LAYOUT

MAIN ARTERIES & STREETS

All streets in Tangier have two names, one European, such as rue des Vignes or rue du Prince Héritier; and one Moroccan, such as El Mansour Dahabi.

The **port** area of Tangier lies below the **Medina.** The main streets of the **Ville Nouvelle (New Town)** radiate from the **Grand Socco.** Rue Semmarine leads to the **Petit Socco,** the café-surrounded plaza that is safely visited only during the day (don't go into this area at night).

Rue de la Liberté connects the Grand Socco to **place de France,** which, as much as anything else, might be called the heart and soul of Tangier. Sitting and enjoying a coffee on this square at the Café de Paris is considered one of the sightseeing events of Tangier. To the east of place de France, **boulevard Pasteur** is one of the main streets of the New Town. It becomes boulevard Mohammed V before running into place des Nations.

FINDING AN ADDRESS

Buildings that have numbers (some do not) are even on one side of the street and odd on the other, running in consecutive order. That's not the problem. The actual names of the streets themselves are confusing.

In a surge of nationalist pride, Morocco officially decided to remove each of the long-entrenched French names of its streets, such as rue de la Plage, rue Rembrandt, and rue Goya, and change them to Arabic names such as Zankat Salah Eddine El Ayoubi, Zankat El Jabha El Quatania, and Zankat Moulay Al Abdallah, respectively. Place de France was changed to place de Faro, but nearly every Moroccan citizen still refers to it as place de France.

Legally, maps—at least those printed in Morocco—must use the Arabic names. In general, those printed in Europe still use the more familiar French names. Most street signs still carry the old French names, even though the map you may be reading gives the new Arabic names. Sometimes the old Spanish colonial names are still on the streets. **In this guidebook we have attempted to use the new names only when the street signs themselves have been changed.**

Because of the confusion, you may want to use an official guide, as previously recommended.

Exploring Tangier on your own as a first-time visitor is a bit tricky. The New Town at least is mapped, but not the Medina and the Kasbah.

NEIGHBORHOODS IN BRIEF

The Kasbah Towering over Tangier, the Kasbah is walled off from the Medina and constructed on the highest point of the city. Traditionally, this was the home of the sultan and his harem. A palace has stood here since Roman days. In the 1920s, this was one of the most luxurious addresses along the Mediterranean, especially if you owned one of the grand villas, as did Richard Hughes, author of *High Wind in Jamaica*. The Kasbah contains the former Sultanate Palace, now the Dar el Makhzen, a museum of crafts and antiquities.

The Medina Following the outlines of the ancient Roman city plan, the Medina contains the two principal squares of Tangier, the Grand Socco and the Petit Socco. It is filled with labyrinthine alleys that are flanked with houses made with thick walls to keep out both the heat and the cold. Its main entrance is rue es Siaghin, leading off the Grand Socco. Rue es Siaghin (Street of the Silversmiths) was the main street of Tangier in the 1930s. The most adventurous travelers rent rooms in the Medina. Though they are invariably cheap, they are not safe at night, and hotels here are recommended only for the most seasoned North African habitués.

Ville Nouvelle The New Town was the traditional French, and later the international, quarter. Rue de la Liberté slopes up to the landmark place de France (technically place de Faro), which is the center of the New Town and the seat of its most frequented cafés. Most of the tourist hotels are located in the Ville Nouvelle. Boulevard Pasteur, traversing this section, is the major shopping street of Tangier. The Ville Nouvelle stretches all the way to the Grand Socco. As late as the 1930s, so the locals tell you, camels used to bring wares from the desert to this ancient trading post in the center of town.

La Plage The Tangier beach strip is a tourist mecca. Long patronized almost exclusively by the expatriate colony, which earned a reputation for sexual excesses, the beach today is increasingly Moroccan, frequented by families from nearby regions who visit in July and August to escape the intense inland heat. Filled with cafés and restaurants, the beach is most often visited during the day. At night, you might have a taxi take you to one of the popular restaurants, such as the Windmill. However, you should avoid walking on the actual beach at night. Many hotels—a few good ones, many bad ones—stretch along the major boulevard flanking the beach. They begin near Gare Tanger-Ville and stretch along avenue des Forces Armées Royales, better known as avenue des F.A.R.

The Port of Tangier This commercial port lies at the foot of the city, which is reached by heading down rue de la Plage and going left at avenue d'Espagne. The port is where the typical one-day "tripper" is introduced not only to Tangier, but to Morocco. What an unfortunate choice! Neither the city nor the country puts its best foot forward in this sleazy area, filled with con artists and dubious would-be guides. Women traveling alone should get through the area as quickly as possible, and never venture there at night. If you're curious and want to see the port, having perhaps arrived by airplane, it is best viewed in the early morning, when you can see the fishing fleet preparing to sail. The safest haven here is the Tangier Yacht Club, which allows "suitably dressed" foreigners to visit, although technically it is a private club.

STREET MAPS

As mentioned before, confusion exists in street maps, because of the changeover in names from French or Spanish to Arabic. You may be looking for a French name on your map, only to see an Arabic one, or vice versa.

What you should look for—assuming it is available—is a map of Tangier that will handle the street problem by listing in its index the *ancien* name of the street (usually in French) and the *actuel* name of the street (the modern Arabic version). That way, you can learn that the rue d'Etroit's new name is Zankat Boughaz.

Before setting out—assuming that you are walking—it is always best to have a hotel staff member trace the route on your map.

You can get a free map from the **Tangier Tourist Office** (see above), but it lists only the major arteries. Check at the local bookstores to see if a good map has been issued at the time of your visit. The best place to look is the **Librairie des Colonnes,** bd. Pasteur, 54 (tel. 369-55), the most widely respected bookstore in Tangier.

Invariably, detailed street maps of the medinas in Moroccan cities, including Tangier, don't exist. Even if they did, many of these narrow streets don't have names signposted anyway.

GETTING AROUND

The options are by bus, by taxi or car, by bicycle (often impractical), and on foot. There are no discount passes: everybody pays the same fare.

BY BUS

Buses aren't really needed within the heart of Tangier. Most of the major places along the beach or in the New Town are within walking distance. The streets of the Medina are too narrow for buses. Tour buses can reach a point in the center of the Kasbah, although the rest of the area must be explored on foot. Buses are used mainly by Moroccans, most of whom are going to distant points in the environs of Tangier.

Local buses depart from the Grand Socco, at the entranceway to the Medina. Other bus routes fan out to the suburbs from place de la Marche-Verte, which lies outside the gates that define the perimeter of the port of Tangier.

BY TAXI

This is the most popular means of transportation. *Grands taxis* are usually large black Mercedeses, each of which can carry up to six passengers according to the law. Agree to the price when you get in. Most foreigners on a typical trip within the city pay 10 DH ($1.25), but check first. A tip is expected. Grands taxis are easily found at the Grand Socco.

Petits taxis, as their name suggests, are very small and cramped, and are usually painted a vivid blue/green. They carry just three passengers. Technically, they are supposed to be metered, but often the meter "doesn't work, monsieur/madame"; in that case, agree on the fare. The standard rate (subject to change, of course) is about 6 DH (75¢). Petits taxis don't have taxi ranks, but can be flagged down as they make their way around the city. Though harder to find than grands taxis, they can usually be hailed at the gateway to the port, at the Grand Socco, and along boulevard Pasteur.

Since even *taxis privés* (private taxis) are inexpensive for most city visits, most foreigners will want to flag down a regular passenger taxi in the street. In that case, you pay the full fare if the driver doesn't pick up any other passengers along the way.

To call a taxi, dial 355-17.

BY CAR

See "Car Rentals" under "Fast Facts: Tangier," below.

Parking

Extremely difficult—especially in the traffic-clogged summer months, with the beach area virtually impossible. If you want to look for a parking place, go to the Medina side of the Grand Socco and search for a spot on one of the branches leading off from boulevard Mohammed V. Usually an old man will identify himself as the guardian of your car. Tip him 2 or 3 DH (25¢ or 40¢) and thank him for his help. A recommended garage is **Tanjah Auto,** av. de Rabat, 2 (tel. 369-38) and costs around 7 DH (90¢) per hour.

BY BICYCLE

In Tangier, you can rent bicycles and motorbikes from **Meshbahi et Cie.,** rue Ibn Tachfine, 7 (tel. 409-74). This is a small office on a street leading up from the avenue des F.A.R., where Abdullah Scullion, a quiet American from Ohio, rents bikes for 60 DH ($7.50) per day. Motorobikes cost from 150 DH ($18.75) for a 50-cc vehicle for one person to 400 DH ($50) for a 125-cc bike. Three-day and weekly prices are available too. The prices include insurance and tax. You must pay a refundable deposit of 1,000 DH ($125) for a rental of three days or more. Helmets are not compulsory, and it is unlikely that you will be able to rent one.

Bicycles are not practical for traveling up and down the hilly streets of the New Town, the Medina, or the Kasbah, but you may want to bicycle along the beach area into the coastal environs of Tangier.

ON FOOT

This is the ancient way to explore Tangier, and no one has improved on the system yet. Here is a potential course for an invigorating walk through Tangier: As you emerge from the port, you can take either rue du Portugal or rue Salah Eddine El Ayoubi and follow it uphill to the Grand Socco (the central square of Tangier and the gateway to the Medina). The Medina can be traversed only on foot. Some of its lanes are so narrow that they are hardly suitable for people—much less cars.

At the southern edge of the Grand Socco, take rue de la Liberté uphill to place de France (place de Faro), which, as mentioned, is the heart of the New Town. To the east of this square, you can walk along boulevard Pasteur, the main shopping artery, until you arrive at another landmark street, boulevard Mohammed V, named for the former king.

Remember as you walk along, that the words *rue, calle,* and *zankat* all mean street.

 TANGIER

American Express   The local representative is **Voyages Schwartz,** bd. Pasteur, 54 (tel. 9/334-59). Since this is a branch office of American Express, it does not accept wired funds. However, cardholders can purchase traveler's checks with personal checks if they present a passport. Open Monday through Friday from 9am to 12:30pm and 3 to 7pm; on Saturday from 9am to 12:30pm.

Area Code   09.

Baby-sitters   There is no local agency that specializes in baby-sitting. Arrangements can be made—as far in advance as possible—through the various hotels. Usually a staff member will shoulder this responsibility for a fee to be agreed upon in advance. It is difficult to find a baby-sitter who speaks English, which might be a problem for your child.

Bookstore   Librairie des Colonnes, bd. Pasteur, 54 (tel. 369-55), is the best-stocked and most respected bookstore in Tangier, lying a few steps from the Hotel Rembrandt. Established in 1949, it offers French, Spanish, and English-language titles. Travel guides and maps are also sold here. It is open Monday through Friday from 9am to 1pm and 4 to 7pm; on Saturday from 9am to 1pm.

Business Hours   See "Fast Facts: Morocco," in Chapter 2.

Car Rentals   It would be difficult to see the sights of Tangier by car, as many of the most interesting streets are for pedestrians only. But if you're exploring the city's environs, a car is the only way other than a grand taxi. The offices of **Budget Rent-a-Car** are at rue Prince Moulay Abdallah, 7 (tel. 379-94). This company rents everything from "super economy" specials to luxury Renaults and minivans. **Hertz** has offices in Tangier at av. Mohammed V, 36 (tel. 333-22), and **Avis** is at bd. Pasteur, 54 (tel. 330-31). Budget, Hertz, and Avis also have offices at the Tangier airport. If you'd like to deal with a local company instead of one of the American chains, try **Amine Car,** bd. Mohammed V, 43 (tel. 440-50).

Climate   See "When to Go" in Chapter 2.

Currency   See "Information, Entry Requirements, Customs & Money" in Chapter 2.

Currency Exchange   For the convenience of their guests, hotels will gladly exchange dollars, pounds, pesetas, or francs into dirhams, but they take a good commission. Most of the travel agencies along the port area will also exchange money. Legally, they are supposed to convert your currency at the official rate, but sometimes cheating occurs. Know what the official rate is and ask for a receipt. Many hustlers along the port will approach you offering to exchange money on the black market. Beware. Such transactions are against the law in Morocco and could get you in trouble with the police. Whenever possible, it is best to exchange money at banks. Two centrally located ones include **Banque du Maroc,** av. Mohammed V, 78 (tel. 356-00), and B.M.C.I, place de France, 8 (tel. 355-53).

Dentist   Contact **Dr. Ibrahim Filali,** rue Prince Moulay Abdallah, 53 (tel. 312-68), who speaks English.

Doctor   **Dr. Joseph Hirt,** rue Sorolla, 8 (tel. 357-29), is a well-known English-speaking doctor who has catered to the medical needs of the tourist community for many years. A routine visit by him to your hotel room, if it's necessary, usually costs 200 DH ($25).

Drugstores   **Pharmacie Razi,** rue Hassan, 80 (tel. 355-09), is the place to go, or else **Pharmacie Pasteur,** place de France (without number) (tel. 324-22). The government-owned **Pharmacie de Fez,** rue de Fez (without number) (tel. 326-190), is open 24 hours a day.

Electricity   See "Fast Facts: Morocco" in Chapter 2.

Embassies/Consulates   The **United States Consulate** is at rue El Achouak, 29 (tel. 359-04), and it is open Monday through Friday from 7am to noon and 1:30 to 5:30pm. The **United Kingdom Consulate** is at rue d'Amérique du Sud, 9 (tel. 358-95), keeping the same hours.

Emergencies   For the police, dial 19. To report a fire or call for an ambulance, dial 15 in both emergencies.

Eyeglasses   A good optician is **Lux Optica,** rue de la Liberté, 91 (tel. 340-31), next door to the Hotel El Minzah.

Hairdresser/Barber   For men or women, one of the best places is **Coiffeur Aziz,** Hotel Les Almohades, av. des F.A.R. (without number) (tel. 401-27). Average prices range from 50 DH ($6.50) to 70 DH ($9).

Holidays   See "When to Go" in Chapter 2.

Hospital   Call the **Hôpital Al Kortobi,** rue Garibaldi (without number) (tel. 310-73), which is open 24 hours a day, for medical emergencies. It lies midway between the Medina and the port.

Information   See "Information, Entry Requirements, Customs & Money" in Chapter 2.

Laundry/Dry Cleaning   Laundry is usually arranged through hotels. Even at small hotels, someone on the staff often washes and irons your clothes. Dry-cleaning establishments are difficult to find. Try **D'Etroit Pressing,** rue El

Jaraoui, 10 (no phone), which is across from the Café de Paris in the center of town. Discuss the prices in advance.

Library   Expatriates often join the **Tangier Book Club.** Visitors can take out books if they join and post a small deposit that is refunded when the books are returned. The library is housed in the Old American Legation, Zankat/rue d'Amérique, 8 (tel. 353-17) in the Medina. Go only from 9:30am to noon Tuesday through Saturday.

Lost Property   Usually, this is a lost cause in Tangier. Call the police at 19 and report the loss, providing you can find someone who speaks English. Give the name of your hotel and the date of your departure from Tangier. You can also leave a forwarding address. But don't spend too much time waiting for a reply.

Newspapers/Magazines   Copies of London papers and the *International Herald Tribune* are sold at news kiosks throughout Tangier and at hotel gift shops. Copies of *Newsweek* and *Time* are also on sale. The French-language *Matin du Sahara*, a local paper, is widely available.

Photographic Needs   A good place to purchase film or get it developed is **Studio Flash**, rue de la Liberté, 79 (tel. 313-99).

Police   See "Emergencies," above. The main station is at rue Ibn Toumert (without number) (tel. 19).

Post Office   The **Tangier Post Office** is at bd. Mohammed V, 33 (tel. 356-57), and is open Monday through Friday from 8:30am to 12:15pm and 2:30 to 5:45pm.

Radio/TV   Radio and television broadcasts are in French or Arabic. However, in Tangier, you can often get broadcasts from Spain or English-speaking Gibraltar. Some of the better hotels receive satellite TV programs, such as the English-language Sky Channel. It is also possible to listen to BBC World Service on 9.41 and 5.975 mhz (31.88 and 50.2 m).

Religious Services   Services are held at the **American Church,** rue Hassan Ibn Ouezzane, 34 (tel. 327-55), sometimes still known as rue Léon l'Africain, at 11:30am on Sunday. It is an interdenominational Protestant organization, established in the 1970s. **St. Andrew's Episcopal Church,** rue d'Angleterre, 50 (tel. 346-33), also has services each Sunday at 11am. It is an interesting mix of European and Arabic architecture, with a pleasant churchyard where you can sit in peace away from the noise of the city.

Rest Rooms   Hotels, cafés, terminals, restaurants, and bars all have toilets, some of them not as well maintained as they should be. Public toilets in central squares in Tangier—always of the squat variety—tend to be unclean and should be used only in emergencies. All the restaurants and cafés along the beach strip have working toilets, although technically you should order a soft drink or something if you patronize them, as they are designated for customers only, not for the beach public at large.

Safety   Some areas of the city are very dangerous at night, and they are mentioned in the appropriate section. Make it a policy not to engage one of the guides who will solicit you on the street; only use official Tangier Tourist Office personnel or someone recommended by that office. Likewise, it is not advisable to exchange money outside a bank or hotel—and always get a receipt. Avoid the Medina after dark and don't wander at night on the streets. After dark, it's best to use a taxi. Taxis are cheap and will get you where you're going safely.

Shoe Repair   Itinerant cobblers come into the city every day, setting up little stands along the street. You'll see them in the port area. You can get your shoes repaired while you wait, or else a shine.

Taxes   Tangier imposes no special city taxes other than the 17% or 19% government tax added to hotel and restaurant bills.

Taxis   Cars line up at Tanger-Ville, Tanger-Port, and place du 9 Avril. See "Getting Around," above.

Telegrams/Telex/Fax   Telexes and faxes can often be sent from your hotel if it is big enough. Or else all three services are provided at the Tangier Post Office (see "Post Office," above).

Transit Information   For airline information, call 370-52; for train information, 312-01; and for bus information, 324-15. But don't count on the person at the other end of the phone speaking English.

Weather   Most visitors describe the climate in Tangier as extremely mild. It is a year-round tourist destination, although swimming is feasible mainly from May to early October. Tangier experiences an average of 77 rainy days per year. The climate is agreeable, except when the East wind blows for several days in a row. See the temperature chart in Chapter 2 for monthly temperature averages.

3. ACCOMMODATIONS

Tangier offers a number of hotels within several price ranges, most of them somewhere between boulevard Pasteur (the main shopping and business street of the Ville Nouvelle) and the beach; many are within easy walking distance of either area. Some are built on sloping streets, affording views of the bay.

I used to recommend budget hotels in the Medina in the 1960s. However, the hotels here, including those that guides will steer you to along rue Mokhtar Ahardan (formerly rue des Postes), are no longer recommendable to an average client. The Hotel Continental, on a hilltop above the Medina, is an exception. Although some of these hotels, once you're inside, are adequate in cleanliness and amenities, getting to them at night can be unsafe. It is best to look for a hotel in the former European quarter, the Ville Nouvelle (New Town). Several are found along rue Salah Eddine El Ayoubi.

Nevertheless, the hotels of the Medina form an enduring legend of the Tangier that used to be. The rundown hotels are exemplified by the Hotel Fuentis, rue Arfaoui, which once housed French composer Camille Saint-Saëns, or the Hotel Mamora, rue des Postes, that once sheltered James Leo Herlihy, author of *Midnight Cowboy*.

New glamour came to the 17th-century relic, the Hotel Palace, rue des Postes, when the *The Sheltering Sky* crew stayed here. Many of the famous old properties are but memories now, best confined to memoir reading. Take the Hotel Farhar, where Tennessee Williams used to stay. Of El Farhar, Williams wrote, "Rhymes with horror. Spectacular view—every possible discomfort." Truman Capote also stayed here with his lover Jack Dunphy, as did Cecil Beaton.

Each year—memoirs in hand—literary fans arrive in Tangier hoping to stay where their favorite authors did, only to find it impossible in most cases.

RATES & RESERVATIONS

Technically, rates quoted should include taxes and service, but when checking into a hotel, especially the smaller, owner-managed places, it is always wise to determine that in advance. At the time, it should also be determined whether the price includes breakfast or whether you will be charged extra for it. Invariably, breakfast will be the Continental variety. Some of the major hotels will serve you an American or English breakfast, but you'll always pay extra for it.

Reservations are difficult to arrange on your own. Mail takes a long time to get through, and many hotels, already filled with clients in summer, don't bother to answer your inquiries, particularly if they are from far away and your arrival date is imminent. And there are virtually no toll-free numbers to call, as Tangier doesn't have

Africa **11**
Bristol **7**
Chellah **5**
Continental **1**
D'Anjou **4**
El Minzah **3**
El Oumnia **15**
Grand Hotel Villa
de France **2**
Les Almohades **14**
Madrid **8**
Panoramic Massilia **9**
Rembrandt **10**
Rif **12**
Shéhérazade **13**
Solazur **16**
Tarik **17**
Valencia **6**

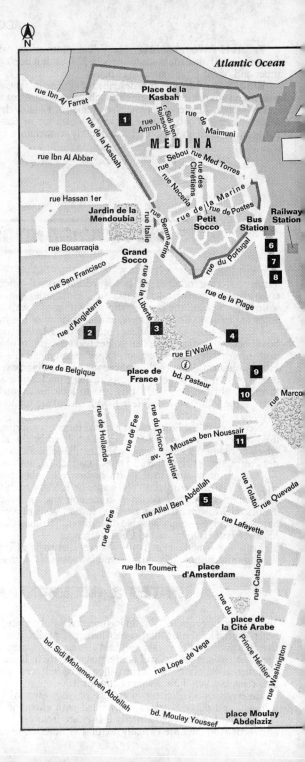

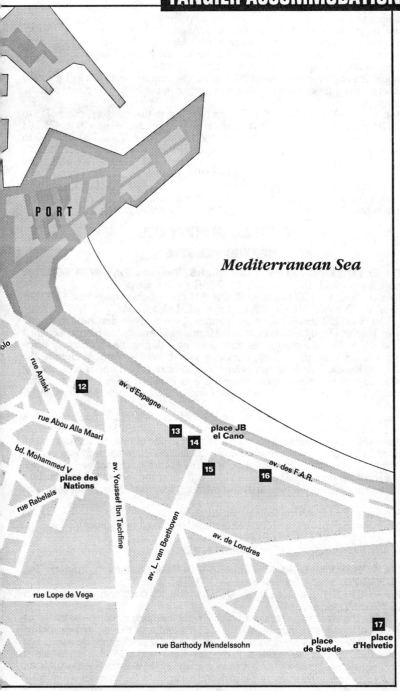

PORT

Mediterranean Sea

olo

rue Antaki

12

av. d'Espagne

rue Abou Alla Maari

13

14

place JB
el Cano

bd. Mohammed V

place des
Nations

av. Youssef Ibn Tachfine

15

av. des F.A.R.

16

rue Rabelais

av. L. van Beethoven

av. de Londres

rue Lope de Vega

17

place
d'Helvetie

rue Barthody Mendelssohn

place
de Suede

City Walls

Information

representatives of such chains as Hyatt, as Casablanca and Rabat do. It is best to use travel agents.

The most crowded times are July and August, when many of the visiting Moroccans themselves tend to fill the hotels. Also, the heaviest bookings from European tour groups, notably those from France and England, arrive at this time. Always nail down a reservation before arriving in Tangier.

Should you appear in off-season (any time but the months cited), you will generally find a room. Since Tangier is primarily a summer resort, there is always plenty of room in winter.

Hotels rated "Very Expensive" in Tangier (very few in that category) charge 715 to 1,020 DH ($89.40 to $127.50); those ranked "Expensive" are in the 410 to 475 DH ($51.25 to $59.40) range; and hotels called "Moderate" cost 320 to 390 DH ($40 to $48.75)—all doubles. Hotels listed as "Inexpensive" are those charging 215 to 240 DH ($26.90 to $30.00) a night for a double. Those rated "Budget" are a specialty category, not for every visitor, but for those willing to settle for a clean, safe nest with few amenities. Hotels in this classification charge 100 to 160 DH ($12.50 to $20) a night for a double room, and you can come out even cheaper if you request a room without private bath, but with shared facilities in the hallway.

IN VILLE NOUVELLE
VERY EXPENSIVE

HOTEL EL MINZAH, rue de la Liberté, 85, Tangier. Tel. 09/358-85. 100 rms (all with bath), 10 suites. A/C MINIBAR TV TEL **Bus:** 15.

$ Rates: 800 DH ($100) single; 1,020 DH ($127.50) double; suites from 1,500 DH ($187.50). Breakfast 70 DH ($8.75) extra. AE, DC, MC, V.

The Hotel El Minzah is the most glamorous, legendary, and sophisticated hotel in Tangier. Highly ornamented with Moorish and Andalusian motifs, it opened in the 1930s and enjoyed its greatest renown during the chic heyday when Tangier was an international city, attracting such clients as Barbara Hutton, the Woolworth heiress. The hotel sits behind an elaborate carved portal on a sloping street leading to the New Town. Its center is a blue-and-white-tiled Andalusian courtyard, where breakfast is served beside one of the most beautiful fountains in Tangier.

Classified as a Relais & Châteaux, the hotel offers comfortable bedrooms, each reached via Sahara-inspired hallways covered with straw-colored Moroccan weavings.

Dining/Entertainment: You can have dinner in one of two elegant restaurants, El Erz or El Korsan, serving French and Moroccan cuisine, respectively (see below). The richly ornamental Patio Wine Bar, which is both a restaurant and a bar (see below), is set up near the Andalusian courtyard, as is the tearoom, Yasmina. Live Moroccan entertainment is provided most evenings; there is also piano-bar entertainment.

Services: Room service, laundry facilities.
Facilities: Swimming pool (behind the hotel, enclosed in a garden).

EXPENSIVE

HOTEL REMBRANDT, bd. Mohammed V (without number), Tangier. Tel. 09/378-70. 80 rms (all with bath). A/C TV TEL **Bus:** 7.

$ Rates: 375 DH ($46.90) single; 475 DH ($59.40) double. Breakfast 30 DH ($3.75) extra. AE, DC, MC, V.

Set in the commercial center of Tangier, the Rembrandt compensates for its lack of beachfront with a walled-in garden and an oasis-inspired swimming pool. The six-story hotel was built in 1951 in a marble-sheathed design; its first guest was the then Tunisian president, Bourguiba. Renovated in 1988, it is now one of the most prestigious hotels in Tangier. In fact, many regard it as the finest small hotel in the city for those seeking discreet charm and luxury. On the premises is a sparsely decorated dining room, Le Restaurant, with a *menu touristique* costing 120 DH

($15). Le Bar, vaguely evocative of a middle-class Italian hotel along the Adriatic, is a favorite international watering hole.

MODERATE

AFRICA HOTEL, rue Moussa Ben Noussair, 17, Tangier. Tel. 09/355-11.
86 rms (all with bath). TEL **Bus:** 15.
$ Rates: 253 DH ($31.65) single; 320 DH ($40) double. Breakfast 31 DH ($3.90) extra. AE, DC, MC, V.
The Africa Hotel lies in the crowded commercial center of the New Town, not far from place de France and boulevard Pasteur. Built in the early 1970s, it offers simple but clean and comfortable bedrooms, each with a well-scrubbed tile bath and a collection of modern angular furniture. The hotel's lively bar is often filled with tour groups. Facilities include a rooftop swimming pool, a fifth-floor restaurant, and a basement-level nightclub. Both Moroccan and international food is served, with meals costing from 100 DH ($12.50).

HOTEL EL OUMNIA, av. Beethoven (without number), Tangier. Tel. 09/403-66. 100 rms (all with bath). TEL **Bus:** 15.
$ Rates: 295 DH ($37.90) single; 386 DH ($48.25) double. Breakfast 31 DH ($3.90) extra. No credit cards.
Opened in 1971 and renovated since then, this hotel rises above the New Town's urban flatlands about a block from the seaside promenade. Each bedroom has a balcony and comfortable warm-weather furniture. A swimming pool is set within a garden at the rear of the hotel.

INEXPENSIVE

CHELLAH HOTEL, rue Allal Ben Abdallah, 47-49, Tangier. Tel. 09/420-03. Fax 09/455-36. 172 rms (all with bath), 10 suites. TEL **Bus:** 12.
$ Rates: 191 DH ($23.90) single; 234 DH ($29.25) double; suites from 600 DH ($75). Breakfast 23 DH ($2.90) extra. AE, DC, MC, V.
Built in the early 1970s, it has comfortable, well-furnished bedrooms, many of them occupied by tour groups in summer. Set on a residential street in the Ville Nouvelle, it provides air conditioning (not very powerful) in about half of the rooms and TV in the other half. There's no price difference for these amenities. The hotel contains one of the most elaborate discos and tearooms in town. The dining room serves both Moroccan and international dishes.

GRAND HOTEL VILLA DE FRANCE, rue de Hollande, 143, Tangier. Tel. 09/314-75. 60 rms (40 with bath). **Bus:** 12.
$ Rates: 90 DH ($11.25) single without bath, 175 DH ($21.90) single with bath; 142 DH ($17.75) double without bath, 215 DH ($26.90) double with bath. Breakfast 21 DH ($2.65) extra. AE, MC, V.
Built in 1902 between the Medina and the New Town, this is a landmark hotel. Gertrude Stein used to recommend this hotel to her friends, and one of those friends, Henri Matisse, became the hotel's most famous guest. Matisse painted *View of Tangier Bay* from Room 35. Some consider this hotel a bit threadbare and rundown today, but for the traditionalist it still exerts a powerful attraction. Half of the rooms open onto views of the sea, and the other half have views of the Medina. Most of the rooms offer a telephone. Bedroom furnishings are a bit shabby, but the whole place exudes an atmosphere that the bandbox modern hotels along the waterfront will never duplicate. Facilities include a patio, a swimming pool, and an old-fashioned dining room, serving meals for 65 DH ($8.15) to 75 DH ($9.40).

BUDGET

HOTEL PANORAMIC MASSILIA, rue Targha, 11, Tangier. Tel. 09/350-15. 20 rms (15 with shower and toilet, 5 with shower but no toilet). TEL **Bus:** 7.
$ Rates (including breakfast): 98–116 DH ($12.25–$14.50) single with shower and

with or without toilet; 150 DH ($18.75) double with shower and toilet. No credit cards.

Located between the beach and boulevard Pasteur, this hotel in the New Town is built on a hillside, giving many of the bedrooms a view of the sea. The furnishings are not so new, but the beds adequately comfortable. Built in 1966, the Massilia offers modest amenities and good service, and has one of the best and most scenic locations among the low-cost hotels in Tangier.

ALONG THE BEACH

VERY EXPENSIVE

HOTEL LES ALMOHADES, av. de l'Armée Royale (without number), **Tangier. Tel. 09/404-31.** Fax 09/463-17. 150 rms (all with bath), 10 suites. A/C MINIBAR TV TEL **Bus:** 7 and 12.
$ Rates (including breakfast): 480 DH ($60) single; 715 DH ($89.40) double; suites 900 DH ($112.50). AE, DC, MC, V.

Originally built in 1970 and renovated many times since, this is considered the best-equipped and the most stylish modern hotel in town. Its public rooms are well-designed re-creations of traditional Moroccan salons, with carved plaster ornamentation and geometric patterns. Each of the spacious bedrooms contains a marble-covered bathroom, wood paneling, a balcony, and much comfort. All but 30 of the rooms have a view of the sea.

Dining/Entertainment: Moroccan entertainment is frequently provided in one of four different restaurants. There's also a choice of drinking areas, including Bar Imlil. On the seventh floor, there is a popular nightclub, Up 2000 (see below).

Services: Laundry, room service, massage.
Facilities: Outdoor pool, garden, sauna.

EXPENSIVE

RIF HOTEL, av. d'Espagne, 152, Tangier. Tel. 09/359-10. 130 rms (all with bath). TEL **Bus:** 7.
$ Rates: 350 DH ($43.75) single; 410 DH ($51.25) double. Breakfast 35 DH ($4.40) extra. AE, DC, MC, V.

The Rif maintains its position as the doyen of Tangier hotels, a position enjoyed since 1936. With its well-trained staff and Moorish flair, this lavishly decorated six-story establishment is the place for visitors who require comfort and elegance. Facing the beach and the waters of Tangier Bay, the hotel welcomes you into a cool marbled lobby with deep, comfortable leather armchairs. The lounges and public rooms overlook the sea and are decorated in extravagant Moorish style. Modern furnishings blend well with the traditional.

All bedrooms overlooking the bay are in the traditional style, with Moorish filigree woodwork on the cupboards and friezes. Good beds and balconies are another plus, and baths are efficient. At the back, overlooking the garden, the rooms are furnished in a contemporary style.

Dining/Entertainment: The dining room and the leather-covered bar look out onto the sheltered patio and pool area. If you prefer to skip the 120-DH ($15) dining room meal, lunchtime salads and sandwiches are available poolside. On most evenings, live Moroccan entertainment is provided.

Services: Massage, room service, laundry.
Facilities: Swimming pool, popular tourist bar, tennis courts, sauna.

MODERATE

HOTEL SHEHERAZADE, av. de l'Armée Royale (without number), Tangier. Tel. 09/405-00. 146 rms (all with bath). TEL **Bus:** 7 and 12.

$ Rates: 253 DH ($31.65) single; 320 DH ($40) double. Breakfast 22 DH ($2.75) extra. AE, DC, MC, V.

Originally built in 1970, and renovated several times since then, this comfortable three-star hotel is set beside the seaside promenade, a short walk west of Gare Tanger-Ville. It was designed in a white-fronted rectangular style, with big sun-flooded windows. Bedrooms are well furnished, although relatively simple, in a comfortable style with modern Moroccan furnishings. The bedrooms are ventilated, not air-conditioned.

Dining/Entertainment: There is a pleasant modern restaurant serving both international and regional dishes, as well as a lobby-level bar and café. Across the busy boulevard, set within its own courtyard on the sands of the beach, the hotel has its own beach bar and semiprivate sun terrace, open mid-May to October, daily from 8am to 8:30pm. The Sheherazade also has a disco, Les Grottes.

Services: Room service, laundry.

Facilities: Courtyard-enclosed swimming pool, private beach bar, and sun terrace.

AT TANGER-PORT

INEXPENSIVE

HOTEL BRISTOL, rue El Antaki, 14, Tangier. Tel. 09/310-70. 33 rms (29 with bath). TEL **Bus:** 7.

$ Rates: 96 DH ($12) single without bath; 173–208 DH ($21.65–$26) double with bath; 280 DH ($35) triple with bath. Breakfast 13 DH ($1.65) extra. No credit cards.

Ⓕ FROMMER'S SMART TRAVELER: HOTELS

VALUE-CONSCIOUS TRAVELERS SHOULD TAKE ADVANTAGE OF THE FOLLOWING:

1. Nearly all hotels grant off-season reductions, usually from November through March, often at least 20%. But you have to ask.
2. The price you pay in cheaper hotels depends on the plumbing. Rooms with showers are cheaper than those with private bath. Even cheaper are rooms with hot and cold running water (with use of the corridor bath).
3. Parents should ask if their children can stay free in the same room or at a greatly reduced rate.
4. At the cheaper hotels that take credit cards, ask if payment by cash will get you a reduction.
5. If you're going to spend a week in Tangier, ask about any special "long-term" discounts.

QUESTIONS TO ASK IF YOU'RE ON A BUDGET

1. Is there a surcharge for either local or long-distance phone calls? Usually there is. In some hotels, it is an astonishing 40%. Better to know beforehand, so you can make your calls at the nearest post office.
2. Are service and the government tax of 17% to 19% included? In other words, does the hotel include the service charge and tax in the price of a room, or will they be added later? It makes a big difference in the final tally.
3. Is breakfast included in the rate? Sometimes it isn't and you pay extra for either a Continental or an American breakfast. If it is included, it's strictly Continental. Watch ordering any extras, as they are strictly à la carte.

Built in 1936 near Gare Tanger-Port, this is one of Tangier's oldest hotels. Spread across four floors, it is reached by a "historic" and creaking elevator. Some rooms overlook the street, others open onto other buildings, and some have a glimpse of the sea. Single rooms here are very basic, with only a sink, but the doubles are a little more comfortable, furnished in functional modern style. There's a bar, but no restaurant.

BUDGET

HOTEL D'ANJOU, rue Ibn Al Bana, 3, Tangier. Tel. 09/342-44. 20 rms (16 with bath). TEL **Bus:** 7.

$ **Rates:** 95 DH ($11.90) single without bath, 132 DH ($16.50) single with bath; 126 DH ($15.75) double without bath; 154 DH ($19.25) double with bath. Breakfast 15 DH ($1.90) extra. No credit cards.

Built in 1949, with its location near the port, this place is one of the best bargains in Tangier. It's down a steep road beside the Hotel Rembrandt, with views of the harbor and the strait. It has hot water and, in the cooler months, central heating. A Continental breakfast, French style, is the only meal served, but the hotel is clean, well furnished, and quiet.

 FROMMER'S COOL FOR KIDS

HOTELS

Hotel Shéhérazade   *(see p. 80)* A secure haven for children, and one of the more reasonably priced hotels suitable for families. There's a courtyard-style swimming pool safe for children, and if they want to enjoy the beach, they can do so from the relative comfort of the hotel's own private beach bar and terrace.

IN THE MEDINA
BUDGET

HOTEL CONTINENTAL, rue Dar Baroud, 36, Tangier. Tel. 09/310-24. 70 rms (all with bath). TEL **Bus:** 11 or else a taxi from the port.

$ **Rates:** 105 DH ($13.15) single; 125 DH ($15.65) double. Breakfast 15 DH ($1.90) extra. AE, DC, MC, V.

The Hotel Continental was originally built in 1885, with the Duke of Edinburgh as its first official visitor. Today it's a well-directed hotel on a steep bluff above the sea whose main entrance is an iron gate opening directly into an impossibly narrow street in the Medina. A flowering forecourt, where breakfast is often served, leads to a series of Moroccan salons, once filled with English tourists. Most of the bedrooms have a sweeping view of either the sea or the Medina. Soussi Mohammed, the director, has employed a helpful staff. It's a good, safe place to dine in the Medina or to drop in for afternoon tea.

4. DINING

The heyday of foreign restaurants declined dramatically after the collapse of Tangier's status as an international city. Many of the great French chefs have died and have never been replaced. The city, however, continues to offer an assortment of international food, ranging from American to French, from Spanish to Moroccan.

Many of the hotels serve blandly insipid international food, such as spaghetti and veal cutlet. Half board in most hotels is disappointing, although relatively cheap and a good bargain if your idea of dining is to eat quickly and then rush off to see the sights. But if your palate demands more, try to visit some of the independently run restaurants that offer a reasonably good cuisine, usually at moderate prices.

In Tangier, you'll pass many little restaurants catering strictly to the local trade. While many of these places have lots of atmosphere and exotic aromas coming from their kitchens, make sure your digestive system is up to meet the challenge of their cuisine.

Restaurants rated "Very Expensive" charge 220 to 240 DH ($27.50 to $30) per person for a meal (without wine). Those rated "Expensive" charge 160 to 210 DH ($20 to $26.25), and "Moderate" suggests about 100 DH ($12.50). Anything under 60 DH ($7.50) for a meal is considered "Inexpensive."

IN VILLE NOUVELLE
VERY EXPENSIVE

EL ERZ, Hotel El Minzah, rue de la Liberté, 85. Tel. 358-85.
Cuisine: FRENCH. **Reservations:** Recommended. **Bus:** 15.
$ **Prices:** Appetizers 55–180 DH ($6.90–$22.50); main dishes 110–150 DH ($13.75–$18.75). AE, DC, MC, V.
Open: Lunch daily 1–3pm; dinner daily 8–10:30pm.

Everything about El Erz hints at the kind of life enjoyed by Morocco's Muslim and European aristocracy before independence. Considered a staple of Tangier's dining scene, it lies adjacent to a charming bar, where you might want to enjoy a drink before your meal. Menu items here are unashamedly European, and include such French-inspired dishes as lobster in puff pastry with spinach and white-wine sauce; asparagus with a fricassee of fresh *cèpe* mushrooms; poached turbot with hollandaise sauce; and a casserole of chicken *bonne femme,* prepared with lardoons and pearl onions in the classic French style. Dessert might be a flambéed crêpes Suzettes. There's usually a pianist in the evenings.

EL KORSAN, Hotel El Minzah, rue de la Liberté, 85. Tel. 358-85.
Cuisine: MOROCCAN. **Reservations:** Recommended. **Bus:** 15.
$ **Prices:** Appetizers 60–110 DH ($7.50–$13.75); main dishes 120–140 DH ($15–$17.50). AE, DC, MC, V.
Open: Tues–Sun 8–11pm.

This most formal of Moroccan restaurants is found within one of Tangier's most elegant hotels. Within a voluptuously ornate decor, surrounded with fine examples of indigenous handcrafts, you can enjoy traditional Moroccan specialties, beautifully served and accompanied by Moroccan music. There are six kinds of *tajine,* including a preparation of sea bream cooked with green peppers and tomatoes in the style of Safi; sea bass or bream stuffed with dates (for two); pigeon roasted with pears and plums; and a delectable version of *mechoui,* or slow-cooked lamb (for two).

EXPENSIVE

PATIO WINE BAR, Hotel El Minzah, rue de la Liberté, 85. Tel. 358-85.
Cuisine: FRENCH. **Reservations:** Recommended. **Bus:** 15.
$ **Prices:** Appetizers 12–150 DH ($1.50–$18.75); main dishes 80–110 DH ($10–$13.75); 4-course fixed-priced menu 78 DH ($9.75). AE, DC, MC, V.
Open: Mon–Sat 8–11pm.
On the ground floor of the most famous and historic hotel of Tangier, it's a dinner-only restaurant as well as a wine bar. Much of its allure derives from its status as the first establishment in Morocco to showcase the country's oenophilic bounty. Within a cramped, fully paneled, and intimate dining room, surrounded by paintings by local artists, you dine at tables whose former occupants included Rock Hudson,

MOROCCO

Tangier
★ Rabat

Africa 6
Big Mac 8
Damascus 15
Detroit 1
El Erz 7
El Korsan 7
Emma's B.B.C. 21
Fenecia 22
Granada 5
Hamadi 3
Hotel Continental 2
La Grenouille 9
La Pagode 10
Laiterie M. Ibn Abbad 18
Mamounia Palace 4
Miami Beach 20
Number One 11
Osso-Bucco 17
Patio Wine Bar 7
Raihana 12
Romero 16
San Remo 14
Sun Beach 19
Vienne 13
Windmill 23

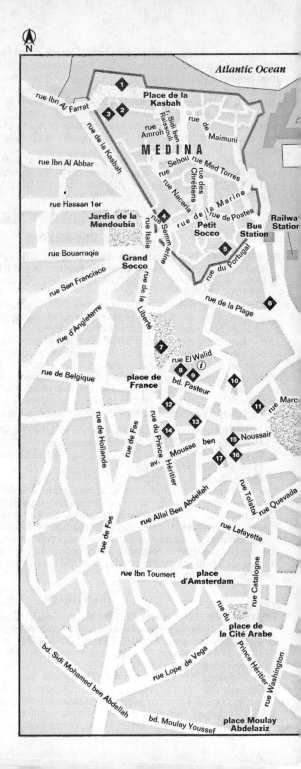

PORT

Mediterranean Sea

olo

rue Antaki

19 **20** **21**

av. d'Espagne

rue Abou Alla Maari

18

bd. Mohammed V

place des Nations

place JB el Cano

22

23

av. des F.A.R.

av. Youssef Ibn Tachfine

rue Rabelais

rue Lope de Vega

av. L. van Beethoven

av. de Londres

rue Barthody Mendelssohn

place de Suede

place d'Helvetie

City Walls ——— Information ⑦

Timothy Dalton, Farrah Fawcett-Majors, Ryan O'Neal, and Jacques Cousteau. Naturally, the wine accompanying the meal will be Moroccan. You can try the deceptively strong red or rose Guerrouane or a Ksar Blanc. Menu items are derived from the classic repertoire of France. Dishes include smoked swordfish in a Provençale style, freshly made noodles with ham and mushrooms, chicken casserole "in the style of the farmer's wife," and a *blanquette* of shrimp with mushrooms.

MODERATE

DAMASCUS, rue Prince Moulay Abdallah, 2 bis. Tel. 347-30.
Cuisine: MOROCCAN. **Reservations:** Not required. **Bus:** 7.
$ Prices: Appetizers 15–20 DH ($1.90–$2.50); main dishes 45–65 DH ($5.65–$8.15). DC, MC, V.
Open: Lunch daily 11:30am–3pm; dinner daily 7–11:45pm.

Decorated in a typical Moroccan style, Damascus contains two different dining rooms, both richly ornate. Menu specialties include tajine of fish, beef, lamb, or chicken. You might begin with *harira* soup. Other specialties include couscous and *pastilla* (or *b'stilla*—pigeon pie). The restaurant also has a bar and tearoom.

LA GRENOUILLE, rue El Jaba El Quatania, 3. Tel. 362-42.
Cuisine: FRENCH. **Reservations:** Recommended. **Bus:** 15.
$ Prices: Appetizers 12–18 DH ($1.50–$2.25); main dishes 45–60 DH ($5.65–$7.50); fixed-priced menu 50 DH ($6.25). AE, DC, MC, V.
Open: Lunch Tues–Sun noon–2:30pm; dinner Tues–Sun 8pm–midnight.

Situated on a small side street off the boulevard Pasteur, this air-conditioned restaurant is one of the best gastronomic bargains in Morocco. It's on two levels, and decor includes soft lighting, rattan chairs, upholstered divans along the walls, plus a cozy bar at one end. Service is courteous and efficient, with a wide choice of dishes available. Begin with a *salade niçoise* or escargots, then order sole meuniere, grilled filet mignon, or even grilled kidneys in sherry. For dessert, try peach Melba, a special cake, or cheese.

OSSO-BUCCO, rue Prince Moulay Abdallah, 1. Tel. 318-13.
Cuisine: INTERNATIONAL. **Reservations:** Recommended. **Bus:** 7.
$ Prices: Appetizers 15–35 DH ($1.90–$4.40); main dishes 50–70 DH ($6.25–$8.75). MC, V.
Open: Lunch Mon–Sat noon–3pm; dinner Mon–Sat 7pm–midnight.

Located on the street level of a two-star hotel (the Hotel Maroc) not recommended in this guide, it's stylishly decorated with postmodern Italian flair and staffed by one of the most charming battalions of waiters in town. In addition to different daily specials, you'll find such dishes as the trademark osso buco, as well as roasted veal, prawns, oysters, filet of sole (either grilled or *à la normande*), and whenever it's in season, fresh lobster.

SAN REMO, rue Ahmed Chaouki, 15. Tel. 384-51.
Cuisine: ITALIAN. **Reservations:** Not required. **Transportation:** Petit taxi.
$ Prices: Appetizers 16–50 DH ($2–$6.25); main dishes 40–60 DH ($5–$7.50). AE, DC, MC, V.
Open: Lunch Mon–Sat 12:30–3pm; dinner Mon–Sat 7:30pm–midnight.

Despite its lack of pretension and unpromising decor, this is one of the city's most convivial dining spots. In its own understated way, it's probably one of the most fashionable places in town, much appreciated by a sophisticated crowd of Moroccan and European diners. Although the menu lists food that is almost exclusively Italian, the ambience is like that of a crowded and bustling French bistro. Three of what might be the most desirable tables are set upon a balcony. Many of the day's best dishes depend on the load of fish brought in that morning, shown in a display case near the staircase leading upstairs. Menu items include fish in all its variety—brochettes of fish, mixed fish fries, shrimp and crayfish, coq au vin, soups, swordfish meunière, grilled meats, and pastas.

INEXPENSIVE

RAIHANA, rue Ahmed Chaouki, 10. Tel. 348-66.
Cuisine: MOROCCAN. **Reservations:** Not required. **Transportation:** Petit taxi.
$ Prices: Appetizers 15–40 DH ($1.90–$5); main dishes 36–65 DH ($4.50–$8.15); 4-course fixed-priced menu 50 DH ($6.25). AE, DC, MC, V.
Open: Lunch daily noon–3pm; dinner daily 7–11pm.

Established 20 years ago by a Moroccan family wishing to retain Moroccan traditions, this restaurant contains two warmly decorated dining rooms, each paneled in carved slats of burnished pinewood. One of the most popular nights is Monday, when a Moroccan spectacle accompanies the food after 8pm. Menu items include six different preparations of lamb, plus couscous, a spicy version of lamb liver, and roast chicken.

RESTAURANT ROMERO, rue Prince Moulay Abdallah, 12. Tel. 322-77.
Cuisine: SPANISH/MOROCCAN. **Reservations:** Recommended. **Bus:** 7.
$ Prices: Appetizers 15–40 DH ($1.90–$5); main dishes 35–50 DH ($4.40–$6.25). No credit cards.
Open: Lunch daily noon–3pm; dinner daily 6:15pm–11:30pm.

If you're nostalgic for hearty Spanish food, this budget restaurant is the place to go. It's crowded with small tables with fresh paper cloths set for each party. A cold chest displays the day's catch from the sea, and during your meal a couple of fishermen may arrive with very fierce-looking fresh lobsters to be added to the selection. Both lunch and dinner are à la carte. Among the appetizers are *chanquettes* (small seasonal whitebait), squid, shrimp mayonnaise, fish soup, monkfish à la romano, and salade niçoise. Many low-priced omelets are offered, and meat dishes include pork chops, grilled kidneys, and *tajine marocaine*. If you insist on eating Moroccan, a bowl of couscous will be served along with brochettes of meat, liver, kefta, and fish. Try a bottle of Toulai red wine or a half bottle of Valpierre. The restaurant lies in the center of the New Town, across from a cabaret called The Morocco Palace.

ALONG THE BEACH
MODERATE

EMMA'S B.B.C., av. d'Espagne (without number). No phone.
Cuisine: INTERNATIONAL. **Reservations:** Not required. **Bus:** 7 or 20.
$ Prices: Appetizers 10–25 DH ($1.25–$3.15); main dishes 30–150 DH ($3.75–$18.75). No credit cards.
Open: Daily 8am–2am. **Closed:** Nov–Apr.

One of the most famous beach bars along the whole coast of North Africa, Emma's was established by Emma Bodenz, a Dutch-born expatriate who actually came to Tangier in 1951 to open a pickled-herring factory. Before founding this bar, Emma was the first woman taxi driver ever to qualify in Morocco. Her place, opposite the Hotel Miramar, is set directly on the beach. There's a wide menu selection, including steaks, filet of sole, spaghetti, fried fish (including fresh sardines), hamburgers, and sandwiches. Try the "dream plate" prawn curry. B.B.C, by the way, stands for Beach Bar Carrousel.

MIAMI BEACH, av. des F.A.R. (without number). Tel. 434-01.
Cuisine: INTERNATIONAL. **Reservations:** Not required. **Bus:** 7 or 20.
$ Prices: Appetizers 8–25 DH ($1–$3.15); main dishes 30–45 DH ($3.75–$5.65). No credit cards.
Open: Daily 10am–6pm. Closed: Nov–Apr.

Its decor is one of the most alluring of the highly competitive restaurants strung along Tangier's beach. There is a long stand-up bar, as well as an outdoor patio and a terrace with sun parasols. From late morning until dusk, lunch is served. Choices include cream of vegetable soup, roast chicken, spaghetti with meatballs, hamburgers, grilled steaks, and daily specials. If you call in advance, the chef will prepare a paella for you. At night, when the bar is open, the place becomes a gay bar and disco.

SUN BEACH, av. des F.A.R. (without number). Tel. 434-01.
   Cuisine: INTERNATIONAL. **Reservations:** Not required. **Bus:** 7 or 20.
$ **Prices:** Appetizers 15–30 DH ($1.90–$3.75); salads 8–12 DH ($1–$1.50); main dishes 25–45 DH ($3.15–$5.65). No credit cards.
   Open: Daily 9am–1am.
Set within a low-slung concrete building directly on the beach, this popular bar/restaurant stands across the busy avenue from the Hotel Miramar. It is one of the few beachfront places to remain open all year, the other two being Neptuno and Chellah Beach. Sun Beach makes a suitable luncheon stopover, and a good choice for a cool-me-down drink. Menu items include an array of fish dishes, tajines, brochettes, escalopes, and salads. Tennessee Williams made this his favorite watering hole during the days when he was writing *Suddenly Last Summer*.

WINDMILL, av. F.A.R. (without number). Tel. 409-07.
   Cuisine: INTERNATIONAL. **Reservations:** Not required. **Bus:** 7 or 20.
$ **Prices:** Appetizers 25–40 DH ($3.15–$5); main dishes 60–70 DH ($7.50–$8.75). V.
   Open: Daily 10am–2am. **Closed:** Nov–Apr.
This is the oldest of the harborfront restaurants, established in the 1920s and long a favorite of expatriate Englishmen. It has large windows overlooking the beach, and a vaguely English or European decor. Opposite the Hotel Solazur, it offers a wide variety of snacks, fresh fish, seafood, and sometimes couscous. You can order crayfish *pil pil* (in a hot sauce), fish soup, tournedos, a tajine of fish, and often paella. For dessert, the spectacular choice is crêpes Suzette. This was once the hangout of the famous British writer Joe Orton, who wrote *Entertaining Mr. Sloane*.

AT TANGER-PORT

INEXPENSIVE

RESTAURANT AFRICA, Zankat Salah Eddine El Ayoubi, 83. Tel. 354-36.
   Cuisine: INTERNATIONAL. **Reservations:** Not required. **Bus:** 7, 8, or 12.
$ **Prices:** Appetizers 7–15 DH (90¢–$1.90); main dishes 16–40 DH ($2–$5); fixed-priced menu 40 DH ($5). No credit cards.
   Open: Daily 10:30am–midnight.
Opposite Gare Tanger-Ville, this is a clean, well-managed, and appealing cost-conscious bistro, set a few paces from the seaside promenade of the New Town. It was purchased several years ago by the Bennani family, who once worked in the most famous brasserie in Paris, La Coupole. Specialties include four kinds of omelets, fresh salads, gazpacho, and spicy versions of Tunisian brochettes. You can also order a mixed fish fry and—only if you call in advance—paella.

IN THE MEDINA

MODERATE

RESTAURANT GRANADA, rue Dar Dbagh (without number) Escalier des Tanneurs–Escalier Américain). Tel. 475-60.
   Cuisine: SPANISH/MOROCCAN. **Reservations:** Not required. **Transportation:** Petit taxi.
$ **Prices:** Appetizers 25–55 DH ($3.15–$6.90); main dishes 55–65 DH ($6.90–$8.15); fixed-priced menu 100 DH ($12.50). MC, V.

FROMMER'S SMART TRAVELER: RESTAURANTS

1. Look for the daily special, which is often cheaper in price than the regular fare on the à la carte menu.
2. Watch the booze. Liquor and wine are very expensive in Morocco, and your tab will mount rapidly.
3. Patronize the Moroccan restaurants, as they are invariably cheaper than the international ones, especially the French ones.
4. Have a light lunch of sandwiches or hamburgers at one of the many beach bars and cafés during the day and save your big meal for the evening.
5. Go to places that feature a set menu for a fixed price. Almost always more economical than ordering from the à la carte menu.
6. Make sure that tax is included in the prices quoted. It's another 19% and could make a big difference when it comes time to pay your bill.

Open: Lunch daily 11am–3pm; dinner daily 7–11pm.

The original building, dating from the 1930s, was the American Cinema, once the city's headquarters for the projection of French and Arabic translations of U.S.-made films. It has been renovated with thousands of blue and white tiles, a beautifully ornate ceiling of intricately carved plaster, comfortable banquettes, and a small stage for musical entertainment. One of the most charming restaurants of the Medina, and one of the only ones consciously to celebrate the memory of Muslim Andalusia, it offers simultaneous menus: one Moroccan, one Spanish. Depending on your mood, you can order either paella or couscous with lamb, gazpacho or harira soup, or perhaps chicken pickled in olives and lemon, stewed lamb with prunes, fish soup or a mixed fish fry, or a very good adaptation of pastilla made with boneless chicken.

INEXPENSIVE

RESTAURANT HAMADI, rue de la Kasbah, 2. Tel. 345-14.
 Cuisine: MOROCCAN. **Reservations:** Recommended. **Bus:** 20.
$ **Prices:** Appetizers 10–15 DH ($1.25–$1.90); main dishes 25–45 DH ($3.15–$5.65). MC, V.
 Open: Lunch daily noon–3pm; dinner daily 8–11pm.

A short walk from the Grand Socco at the edge of the Kasbah, across from the Capital Cinema, this restaurant was established in the 1950s in a 1920s building, and is still run by the descendants of the original owner. Serving some of the best Moroccan food in the city, it is a good place for a traditional Moroccan evening, with harira soup, lamb couscous, and lemon chicken or chicken with olives. Mechoui, a dish often reserved for festivals, is a specialty here.

SPECIALTY DINING

DINING WITH A VIEW

LE DETROIT, Riad Sultan, Kasbah. Tel. 380-80.
 Cuisine: MOROCCAN. **Reservations:** Not required. **Transportation:** Petit taxi.
$ **Prices:** Appetizers 15–40 DH ($1.90–$5); main dishes 35–50 DH ($4.40–$6.25); fixed-priced lunch 100 DH ($12.50). No credit cards.
 Open: Daily 9am–6:30pm.

FROMMER'S COOL FOR KIDS
RESTAURANTS

Ralhana *(see p. 87)* A nice, safe family-run place that will give your child a chance to sample typical Moroccan food. If it's a Monday night, stick around for the 8pm Moroccan folkloric special.

Emma's B.B.C *(see p. 87)* A good choice if your child would like to eat along the beach in a bathing suit. Sandwiches and hamburgers are good midday selections.

Restaurant Granada *(see p. 88)*. An enjoyable restaurant to visit with your children during a tour of the Medina. Here, children can enjoy a more "sanitized" version of Morocco's famous pastilla—made with boneless chicken rather than the richly ethnic version concocted from pigeon meat laced with tiny and pesky bones. With its sugar-coated pastry topping, kids at first think it's a dessert.

Big Mac *(see p. 90)* Not affiliated with the famous McDonald's chain, but similar in almost every way. Let your child do a taste test.

Set near the pinnacle of the Kasbah, this restaurant and tearoom offers one of the most sweeping views of Tangier. You climb to a second-floor aerie near the Museum of the Riad Sultan. A sprawling room is capped with an ornate filigree-plaster ceiling, with wraparound windows overlooking the Strait of Gibraltar and the faraway Spanish coastline. The Detroit was established in the 1960s by Brion Gysin, the Beat writer, who turned it into a venue for his drummers and pipe players, the Trance Musicians of Jakouka. Today, tour groups pour in here to order set lunches—a predictable array of brochettes, tajines, and grilled meats. You can also order *soupe de poissons* (fish soup), salade niçoise, and Russian salad. Since no commercial buses (other than tour buses) run to this part of the Kasbah, you can take a taxi or include a stop here as part of your walking tour.

LIGHT, CASUAL & FAST FOOD

BIG MAC, bd. Pasteur, 2. Tel. 384-80.
   Cuisine: HAMBURGERS. **Reservations:** None. **Bus:** 7.
$ **Prices:** Burgers 15–18 DH ($1.90–$2.25); steak with fries 18 DH ($2.25).
   Open: Daily in summer 7:30am–2am; daily in winter 7:30am–midnight.
Technically, it's not associated in any way with the famous American hamburger chain, McDonald's. But it's a clone nevertheless, occupying a clean, modern corner storefront whose counters are made of marble. It serves some of the best fast food in town, with a particularly helpful staff. Eggburgers and cheeseburgers appear on the menu along with a so-called Big Mac, as well as a *steak minute* and *pommes frites* (french fries).

5. ATTRACTIONS

The number of Tangier's attractions suitable for specifically targeted visits are surprisingly few. It is the city as a whole—its beaches, its environs, its souks, and its Kasbah—that combines into the most compelling reason to visit. For the best overall preview of the city, if your time is limited, take the walking tour (see below).

SUGGESTED ITINERARIES

IF YOU HAVE 1 DAY

Day 1: Accompanied by a guide, visit the Kasbah. Take in its spectacular view and spend some time wandering its narrow streets. Explore the museum in the former sultan's palace at the top of the Kasbah, going on a shopping tour of the Medina in the afternoon. Promise yourself a return visit when you have more time, and then have a mint tea at Le Detroit (next to the sultan's palace).

IF YOU HAVE 2 DAYS

Day 1: Explore the Kasbah, including the former sultan's palace, Dar el Makhzen. Visit the Gardens of the Sultan and wander around (accompanied by a guide) through the narrow streets of the Kasbah. In the afternoon, visit the Forbes Museum of Military Miniatures and later have a coffee or drink at the Café de Paris in the Ville Nouvelle. In the evening, go to a Moroccan restaurant that features typical folkloric entertainment.
Day 2: Spend a leisurely day exploring the Medina, browsing through the souks, visiting the Grand Socco and the Petit Socco. At the latter, have a coffee in the Café Central, the legendary Beat location made famous by Allen Ginsberg and William Burroughs. In the afternoon, explore the Old American Legation. Have dinner and see the show at the Morocco Palace.

IF YOU HAVE 3 DAYS

Days 1–2: Spend these days as outlined above.
Day 3: Take an excursion to the lighthouse at Cape Spartel, 9 miles from Tangier, at the most northwesterly tip of Africa, and visit the Caves of Hercules. You can go swimming here and make a day of it.

IF YOU HAVE 5 DAYS OR MORE

Days 1–3: Spend these days as outlined above.
Day 4: Take a day trip, visiting Tetuán and Ceuta (the Spanish enclave—see Chapter 4).
Day 5: With Tangier as a base, visit the town of Chaouen, nestled in the Rif mountains, about 100 miles from Tangier but reached by a good highway. Get an early-morning start so you can be back in Tangier before dark.

THE TOP ATTRACTIONS

THE KASBAH QUARTER

Although a number of expatriates have moved in, the Kasbah is still the old Arab residential quarter of the city. It sits on a hill overlooking the bay and the streets of the Medina, another residential and commercial area.

For thousands of years, the uppermost part of Tangier, the Kasbah (also spelled Casbah) has been the home of the sultans, filled with castles and palaces. Everyone from Byzantine rulers to Roman governors made the Kasbah their headquarters. Portuguese crusaders lived here, as did Arab princes. It was the citadel of Tangier: the person in control here was in control of the city.

An ancient medieval fortress stood here, but the departing English burned it to the ground in 1685. Samuel Pepys, the famous English diarist, the overseer of the retreat, seemed all too glad to leave, claiming the place was "a nest of papacy where Irish troops and Roman bastards could desport themselves unchecked." He considered the

Café Central **11**
Dar el Makhzen **1**
Garden of the Sultan **1A**
Grand Mosque **9**
Grand Socco **12**
The Kasbah Quarter **3**
The Medina **4**
Mellah **7**
Mendoubia Gardens **6**
Mendoubia Palace **5**
Musée des Antiquités **1B**
Old American Legation **8**
Petit Socco **10**
Place de la Kasbah **2**
Sisi Bou Abib Mosque **13**

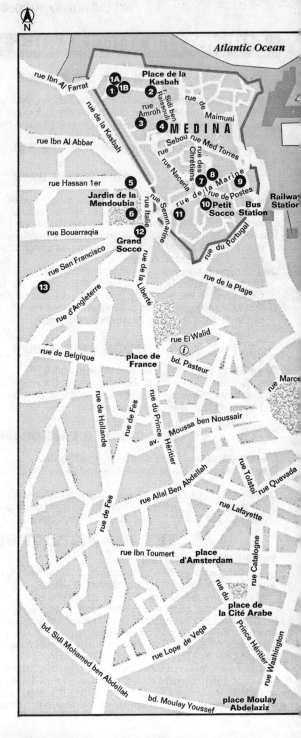

PORT

Mediterranean Sea

Polo

rue Antaki

av. d'Espagne

rue Abou Alla Maari

**place JB
el Cano**

bd. Mohammed V

av. des F.A.R.

**place des
Nations**

av. Youssef Ibn Tachfine

rue Rabelais

av. L. van Beethoven

av. de Londres

rue Lope de Vega

rue Barthody Mendelssohn

**place
de Suede**

**place
d'Helvetie**

City Walls

Information ①

?DID YOU KNOW . . . ?

- Tangier and Ceuta are the only towns in Morocco to have been occupied by the Byzantines.
- Woolworth heiress Barbara Hutton outbid General Franco, the dicator of Spain, to acquire her famous palace in the Kasbah.
- The old American Legation is the first real estate the U.S. government ever acquired abroad.
- The tiny rue es Siaghin (Street of the Silversmiths) was Tangier's main street, and also its richest, in the 1930s.
- The overseer of the British garrison's final withdrawal from the Kasbah in 1685 was none other than Samuel Pepys, the great English diarist, who also reorganized the British navy.
- In the 1920s a pre-Neolithic hall containing hundreds of phalluses carved from rock and used in ancient rituals was discovered at the Caves of Hercules.

women of the town "whores," being particularly shocked at the governor's pastime of cavorting with prostitutes.

Most of the sultan's palace you see today was constructed by Moulay Ismail in the 18th century. The palace was last used by Islamic royalty in 1912.

The Kasbah became famous as a place of residence for foreigners. The parties, orgies, and debaucheries that transpired here are the stuff of legend.

Walter Harris, a noted homosexual and author of the landmark Moroccan guidebook, *Morocco That Was,* was the much-respected London *Times* correspondent in Tangier from the 1890s until his death in 1933. In 1903, Harris was kidnapped by Ahmed Raisuli, called "the sultan of the mountains," and was later freed when the city of Tangier agreed to release some of Raisuli's captured men. Harris was the original owner of the palace later purchased by Woolworth heiress Barbara Hutton.

Hutton did a little architectural rearranging of the Kasbah. When she learned the streets were too narrow for her Rolls-Royce, she had them widened. For some mysterious reason, young Moroccan guides, born long after the death of the heiress, call her "Barbara Button." One told me that Ms. Button "owned all the buttons made in the world."

Another famous resident was Richard Hughes, author of *A High Wind in Jamaica.* His address became legendary: "Numero Zero, La Kasbah, Tangier."

To reach the Kasbah, enter the Bab el Assa at the end of rue Sidi ben Raissouli in the Medina. From the Medina, the narrow rue des Chrétiens will take you here. From the Grand Socco, follow rue d'Italie north to Bab Fahs, the Moorish gateway. Go up the steep incline of rue de la Kasbah until you reach Porte de la Kasbah. You will have to go on foot or else take a taxi from the port.

Specific attractions to visit in the Kasbah include the three mentioned in the following paragraphs.

Dar el Makhzen, place de la Kasbah (tel. 320-97), stands in the center of the Kasbah, near the main gateway to the Medina, Bab el Assa. This complex of buildings filled with museums was the former home of the sultans. When it was constructed in the late 17th century, the English had just evacuated Tangier. To celebrate his reconquest of the city, Sultan Moulay Ismail erected this palace, which was enlarged and embellished around 1750. Later it became the residence of the city pashas before it became a museum. It's located around the corner from the Garden of the Sultan.

The museum sections include **Le Musée des Arts marocains** and **Le Musée des Antiquités.** The former, centered around a tile patio, contains six rooms filled

---

IMPRESSIONS

Tangier . . . a madhouse.
—Aaron Copland

IMPRESSIONS

The African perdition called Tangier.
—MARK TWAIN

---

with antique Moroccan carpets, jewels, Hispano-Moorish artifacts, Bedouin crafts, wrought iron, antique furniture, and silk embroideries. The antiquities museum has a courtyard with a Roman mosaic, rooms with prehistoric carvings found throughout the countryside around Tangier, plus artifacts from the Portuguese and English occupations. An annex contains the Bit et Mal, a noteworthy piece of Moorish architecture that once contained the sultan's treasures. Admission is 10 DH ($1.25), plus a tip for the guide, and guided tours are available on Monday, Wednesday, Thursday, Saturday, and Sunday between 9am and noon and between 3 and 7pm, on Friday between 9am and 11:30am. The museum is closed on Tuesday. You can reach it either by taxi or on foot.

Enclosed within the walls of Dar el Makhzen (see above) is the **Garden of the Sultan,** Place de la Kasbah, a beautiful, rather formal Andalusian garden with orange and lemon trees, some palms, and other shrubbery. The smell of the jacaranda permeates the atmosphere, as it must have for the sultan and his harem centuries ago. Sometimes you can see carpets being woven along the northern perimeter of the garden within its artisan halls. The gardens are a welcome respite from the confusion of the Kasbah. As you leave, you'll pass the Le Detroit, established by Beat writer Brion Gysin in the 1960s. From its windows, a dramatic view of the city and the bay unfold, although the place is very touristy and often filled with one-day tour groups from Spain. Admission to the gardens is 10 DH ($1.25), and they are open Monday through Saturday from 8am to 2pm. Reached by taxi or on foot from the Medina.

The **Place de la Kasbah,** the central square of the Kasbah, is sometimes called Mechouar. It's near the gate, Bab el Assa, and is the point where you enter Dar el Makhzen. Traditionally, this was the place where criminals were either punished or executed. The former law courts, notorious for their "justice," were in a wing of Dar el Makhzen called Dar ech Chera. You'll see the minaret of the Mosque of the Kasbah rising from here. If you take one of the gates, Bab er Raha, you will come to a belvedere with a panoramic view of the Strait of Gibraltar. Even as late as the early part of the 20th century, the pashas of Tangier held public audiences here.

THE MEDINA

⭐ Built to follow the architecural outline of the old Roman city, the walls of the Medina stretch along ancient fortifications built centuries ago, with the Kasbah, the "crown" of the Medina, looming overhead. The two principal sightseeing attractions of the Medina are the Grand Socco and the Petit Socco.

The teeming life of old Tangier took place in the Medina. The allure of the place was best captured by Paul Bowles: "Its topography is rich in prototypical dream scenes: covered streets like corridors with doors opening onto rooms on either side, hidden terraces high above the sea, streets consisting only of steps, dark impasses, small squares built on sloping terrain so that they looked like ballet sets designed in false perspective, with alleys leading off in several directions; as well as the classical dream equivalent of tunnels, ramparts, ruins, dungeons, and cliffs."

IMPRESSIONS

Tangier at long last! At this moment I feel like a man who is dreaming and fears that what he sees will escape him.
—DELACROIX, 1832

The Medina today is home to many Arabs and Berbers, plus a dwindling number of expatriates. It is dangerous, particularly at night, when it is not advisable to walk its streets.

In and around the two Soccos, you'll find the carpet shops, the bazaars, and the vegetable markets for which the city is well known. For a flavor of the markets during the day, have a cup of mint tea amid the smell of exotic spices.

You can take a petit or grand taxi to the Grand Socco, but the rest of the Medina will have to be explored on foot. The walking tour (see below) cuts through its most interesting streets. To approach the Medina from the Grand Socco, head down rue Semmarine to the left of the entrance to the Grand Socco. Turn to the right and continue downhill along rue es Siaghin until you reach the Petit Socco. From the port, head west along rue de Cadiz. Eventually you come to a series of stairs (they'll be on your left). Take them to rue des Postes (also called Mokhtar Ahardan).

Principal sites to visit in the Medina include those mentioned just below.

The **Grand Socco,** a busy square and traffic circle, is the commercial heart of the Medina. It stands where rue d'Angleterre and rue de la Liberté converge. Tennessee Williams once confided that he got the idea for one of his most sensitive plays, *Camino Real,* by watching the hustle and bustle of this market square.

Camels carrying tradesmen and their wares from the desert and the Rif mountains used to "park" here, but now motor vehicles have taken over. Herb stands, fruit peddlers, and stalls cooking lamb kebabs cluster around the square. You can visit the Central Market, a bewildering and not always pleasant experience, with a variety of aromas assailing your nostrils. Adjacent to the fruit and vegetable section is a fish market, selling everything from eels to sharks.

Thursday and Sunday are particularly busy days for exploring the Grand Socco. It is then that Berber women from the Rif mountains come into the city. You'll spot them by their characteristic wide-brimmed hats, folded blankets draped around their waist, and red-and-white-striped aprons. They wear leather shin guards to protect their legs from thorns. Walk along rue Salah Eddine El Ayoubi, which leads to the port, for a glimpse of some Berber trading. You can also visit various covered markets along the way. Everything from car radios (often either stolen or nonfunctioning) to live chickens and ducks are sold here.

It is believed that the Grand Socco grew up on the site of what had been a Roman forum. Strategically, it divides the Old Town, or the Medina, from the New Town (Ville Nouvelle), which used to be known as the French quarter or the international quarter.

Flanking the Grand Socco are the **Mendoubia Gardens,** the former stomping ground for the Mendoub, or sultan's representative. Today, they are the grounds of the law courts of Tangier, and not officially open to the public. The gardens are somewhat neglected, but they are a historic place. A low, green-painted door is left open, and perhaps you can sneak in to take a peek at the most famous tree in Tangier, a banyan tree believed to be eight centuries old. Sometimes on a Sunday, when the law courts are closed, groups are given a short tour of the gardens, where there are several ornamented cannons used in former sieges of Tangier; some of these cannons date from the 17th century. Ring the bell if the door is closed and tip generously. From the gardens you can see the former **Mendoubia Palace,** where the sultan's representative lived before tribunal judges took it over. It is definitely off limits unless you're on trial.

On the opposite side of the Grand Socco stands the **Sidi Bouabid Mosque,** remarkable for its minaret covered with tiles. Entrance is forbidden to non-Muslims.

From the Grand Socco, continue along **rue es Siaghin,** the old silversmiths' street, to the Petit Socco. However, you'll see two alleyways on your right that will take you into the **Mellah,** the ancient Jewish quarter of Tangier, which had nearly a dozen synagogues, most of them minor.

Two narrow streets of the Medina, rue de la Marine and rue des Postes (also called Mokhtar Ahardan), skirt the **Grand Mosque,** place El Koweit, a gift from the Emir of Kuwait. Built along traditional Islamic lines in the 1970s, it occupies one of the largest sites of any house of worship in North Africa, and entrance to it is forbidden to non-Muslims. The site has had an interesting history. It was originally constructed as a mosque over the ruins of a Portuguese cathedral, although some Muslims feared that Allah would be offended by building a house of worship over a Christian site. Actually, the cathedral had been constructed on the site of an even earlier mosque, which, it is believed, was built on the foundation of a Roman temple. So the gods kept changing at this site until it finally settled into its present role. Across from the Grand Mosque are the gates to a 14th-century **Medersa** (Koranic school) founded by the Merenids.

The **Petit Socco** (Little Market), at the end of rue es Siaghin, is amazingly small to be as famous as it is. If you blink, you'll pass it by. Historically it was at least twice as big, as old maps of the city reveal. At the turn of the century, Europeans started erecting hotels and cafés here, thus absorbing much of the market. But it was this congestion that led to the opening of various sin-and-sleaze businesses, such as hash centers and brothels. The Petit Socco appears in some of the stories of a Moroccan author named Mohammed Mrabet, whose works have been translated into English by Paul Bowles.

The **Café Central** was the heartbeat of the expatriate generation, attracting such diehards as William Burroughs, who'd originally come to Morocco, as he himself has said, to purchase drugs and live cheaply. Occasional tourist friends such as Allen Ginsberg and Jack Kerouac passed through too. After the sale of alcohol in the Medina was banned, following the Moroccan takeover of Tangier, the old cafés lost most of their appeal.

From the little square, the narrow turning on your left, rue des Chrétiens, will lead to the Kasbah district. Along the way, hustlers will entice you with offers: "Something special, *mi amigo*." The sleaze factor of yesterday still exists, but in a much tamer version. Hashish is still hustled, and "Arabian Nights" pleasures are touted in rooms upstairs.

FORBES MUSEUM OF MILITARY MINIATURES, rue Shakespeare (without number). Tel. 396-06.

A short distance from the Kasbah, in the inner suburb of Marsham, the late American magazine tycoon Malcolm Forbes turned the Palais Mendoub, the former residence of the sultan of Morocco, into a museum filled with the world's rarest toy soldiers. The exhibit includes a representative collection of Arab models, along with British, German, Russian, and French toy figures. Among the large exhibits is a detailed model of the 15,200-ton battleship *Asahi,* built in the early 20th century for Japan by a British firm. More exhibits are displayed in a garden extension, including an entire battalion of the London Scottish Regiment, which saw active service in France in 1916. There's a fascinating display of wartime propaganda posters as well. Visitors can also get a view of the port of Tangier and the Strait of Gibraltar.

Admission: Free.
Open: Daily 10am–5pm. **Transportation:** 8-minute taxi ride from the center.

OLD AMERICAN LEGATION, Zankat d'Amérique, 8. Tel. 359-04.

The Tangier legation building, now a museum and study center, is the oldest diplomatic property continuously owned by the United States. In the Medina of Tangier, south of place de la Kasbah, it is believed to be the first real estate the U.S. government ever acquired abroad. In 1821, Sultan Sidi Moulay Suliman gave it to the

---

IMPRESSIONS

Ah, Tangier, Tangier! I wish I had the courage to get the hell out.
—HENRI MATISSE, 1912

American people. The building housed the U.S. Consulate till 1961. The legation is maintained by the staff of the American consul-general through their voluntary efforts and through contributions. It offers one of the finest lithographic collections I've seen. And a notable addition is a Moorish pavilion overlooking a courtyard. Note in particular the carved doors leading from the terrace into the pavilion; they are more than 400 years old. The antique doors, shutters, ceilings, and tiles within the pavilion were found in Fez and other parts of Morocco.

Admission: Free.

Open: Mon–Fri 10am–5pm. **Transportation:** Taxi to Petit Socco, then walk south through the Medina.

NEW TOWN (VILLE NOUVELLE)

Head down rue de Belgique to **place de France** and have a coffee at the Café de Paris, and you will be in the heartbeat of the New Town, the traditional quarter of the international set when Tangier was a free port. Go here to observe the pulsating life of the new Tangier. Many shoppers prefer to look for Moroccan handcrafts here if they feel intimidated by the shops of the Medina. Boulevard Pasteur is the main shopping street. It leads east from place de France into boulevard Mohammed V.

Although the New Town is lean in terms of sightseeing, it does contain the **Museum of Modern Art (Musée D'Art Contemporain de Tanger), rue d'Angleterre, 52 (tel. 384-36).** Located within the white-walled villa that originally served as the English consulate, it is exclusively devoted to the exposition of works by contemporary Moroccan artists, and to educational programs about modern art, given in Arabic. Admission costs 10 DH ($1.25). The museum, best reached by petit taxi, is open Wednesday through Monday from 9am to noon and 3 to 6pm.

COOL FOR KIDS

Look under "The Top Attractions" (above) and "Easy Excursions" (below) for the following Tangier area attractions that have major appeal to kids of all ages.

Forbes Museum of Military Miniatures   *(see p. 97)* The late billionaire publisher Malcolm Forbes was called "still a boy" when he died at 70, and in his private home he assembled "Africa's largest private army"—all in miniature, of course. It's been called a "giant toy box."

The Caves of Hercules   *(see p. 110)* An ancient site, where millstones were quarried for centuries, creating a shape like a mammoth scallop shell. The turbulent sea thunders and roars into a lower rock. The effect is dramatic and eerie.

The Kasbah   *(see p. 91)* Some kids think a movie director built the quarter as a background for a film. Children delight in exploring the walled compounds, gates, colonnades, and occasional belvederes where cannons stood guard.

Finally, the one souvenir all kids want from a visit to Tangier is a picture of themselves on top of a **camel.** Stroll along the beach and you'll see an occasional camel brought in from the desert waiting to have his picture taken with your kids. Posing keeps the camels in food.

SPECIAL-INTEREST SIGHTSEEING
FOR THE LITERARY ENTHUSIAST

The **English Church,** on rue d'Angleterre near the Grand Socco, is the resting place of the flamboyant journalist Water Harris. The correspondent for the London *Times* in Tangier from the 1890s until his death in 1933 wrote the classic travel book on the country, *Morocco That Was;* originally published in 1921, it is still widely read. The church itself contains Moorish decoration, and if the caretaker is there, he will show you around.

Also buried in the graveyard is Emily Keane, another Briton considered eccentric. *Her Life Story,* out of print now, is considered a classic of expatriate literature about

Morocco. The Shereef of Ouezzane fell in love with her as he watched her combing her hair, or so it is said. Although filled with contradictions, her book tells of her 1873 marriage to the famous figure and their eventual separation. She lived out her days in Tangier, giving vast amounts of candy to children on the street.

A WALKING TOUR —— TANGIER

Start: Praça de Faro
Finish: Place de la Kasbah
Time: 4 hours
Best Time: Any day from 9am to 5pm

(Because of the absence of street maps of the Medina and Kasbah, this tour will need to be taken with a guide. Tell him rather firmly where you want to be taken, although he will probably have suggestions of his own where you should shop.)

Begin your tour at the point where Tangier's New Town adjoins its Old Town:

1. **Praça de Faro/place El Maguise.** (The dual Portuguese/Arabic names for this square translate as Place of the Lighthouse or Place of the Lazy Workmen, depending on which language you prefer.) The four cannons overlook a sweeping view of the faraway port of Tangier, which they were long ago commissioned to protect. Look for the date 1692 amid the cannons' rococo ornamentation.

    Walk down the gentle slope toward:

2. **place de France,** center of the New Town, which the French call Ville Nouvelle. Along the way pass the well-known Pharmacie Pasteur, perhaps stopping for coffee at the most famous café of Tangier, the Café de Paris.

    Facing you, from the corner of place de France and rue de la Liberté, is the Consulat de France, whose Moorish loggia is set behind a private garden.

    Turn right onto rue de la Liberté, which will slope downhill. The first building on your left is the:

3. **Centre Culturel Français,** site of the Galerie Delacroix, well known for its changing series of art exhibitions. Because of the lack of any publicly funded museums of modern art, this and a handful of other private galleries have traditionally fulfilled the role occupied in other countries by government or municipal art museums.

    Continuing your descent of rue de la Liberté, you'll pass the Andalusian-inspired facade of the most famous hotel in Tangier:

4. **El Minzah.** Since its construction in the early 1900s, it has been famous for convoluted episodes of espionage and intrigue, and for the sybaritic luxury offered to some of the 20th century's most colorful and famous artists and politicians. Today, with four or five unusual bars and restaurants, it is acknowledged as one of the best and most interesting hotels in Tangier.

    Continue walking downhill, past a small square whose boundaries mark the beginning of a fork in the street. Gently bear right onto the continuation of rue de la Liberté. If you don't notice a street sign, your landmark is a jewelry store called Dar Bennan, famous since the days of the French Protectorate. Continue to walk another three blocks downhill to where rue de la Liberté opens onto one of Tangier's most famous squares:

5. **place du Grand Socco** (also known as the place du 9 Avril). At its center is a series of black and white concentric circles, laid like mosaics in the Portuguese style, with pebbles. In many ways, these concentric circles mark the geographic and spiritual center of Tangier, and the site of some of the 19th century's most vigorous mercantile negotiations. From your position at the square's mosaic centerpiece, with your back to rue de la Liberté, you can admire—from afar—the ornate minaret of the old mosque, Sidi Bouabid. Flanking the Grand Socco are the:

6. **Mendoubia Gardens,** the former private gardens of the sultan's representa-

FROMMER'S FAVORITE
TANGIER EXPERIENCES

Seeing the Grand Socco from a Café Donkeys laden with goods from the Rif mountains arrive on Thursday and Sunday at the Grand Socco. From a table at the Café Orient, you can see this parade of water sellers, beggars, carpet merchants, snake charmers, and the like.

A Cup of Coffee at the Café de Paris You'll feel trapped in an old movie at place de France, and will expect Errol Flynn or Hedy Lamarr to arrive at any moment at this landmark café. This was "the hangout" during the heyday of the international administration, when everybody was either a spy or a sybarite, or both. Today you see a cross section of the new Morocco passing by on the sidewalk outside.

Shopping the Medina Wander leisurely through the alleyways, shops, and souks that make up this labyrinthine quarter of the Old Town. The dusty old shops sell everything—from the carpet you can't live without to a pair of silk underwear allegedly worn by the late heiress Barbara Hutton.

A Day at the Beach Despite the aggressive hucksters (they'll even follow you into the water to sell fresh fish), the beach of Tangier is still its most enduring summertime amusement. It's where the Islamic world meets the West on the sands. Later you can patronize one of the beach bars made famous by such writers as Tennessee Williams and Joe Orton.

tives. Today the site is used by the Tribunal de Justice. Visitors are permitted to enter only on rare occasions (often on Sunday, when justices are gone). It depends on the whim of the guards at the gate. If you are allowed to enter, look at the 800-year-old banyan tree in the center. The former palace of the sultan is off-limits.

You are about to enter the congestion and confusion of:

7. The Medina. From your position in the center of the Grand Socco, still with your back to rue de la Liberté, notice the many passageways that pierce the wall of buildings at the edge of place du Grand Socco. Each leads into the Medina, but for the purposes of this walking tour, identify from afar the only two passageways whose entrances are capped with masonry arches. Midway between those two arched passageways is the entrance to:

8. rue Semmarine. Take a deep breath and plunge into the Medina. Follow rue Semmarine to its first fork, where you'll turn right. At this point, almost every semblance of a street sign will have been obscured by the mountains of objects for sale that make a souk so fascinating. Often, your only landmarks, other than the knowledge provided by your guide, will be the names of specific shops or restaurants that lie along your path.

Pass the Mamounia Palace restaurant. Continue your descent of rue Semmarine. Next pass the massive inventory of artifacts within a store called Marrakech La Rouge (see "Savvy Shopping," below). A few steps downhill from the well-marked entrance to Marrakech La Rouge is the unmarked Hispano-Moorish façade of the:

9. Spanish Cathedral. Now boarded up and decaying, this famous old church is but a relic of its former self in its colonial heyday. Continuing downhill (don't even hope for a street sign at this point), notice, on the right side of the street, the Doric columns of the Medina's *Préfecture de Police*, where most of the district's marriages, divorces, and arrests are made more or less official.

WALKING TOUR — TANGIER

200 m
220 y

N

finish here
KASBAH

Bab Haha

Bab
el Aca

Bab el
Marsa

M E D I N A

rue. Assad Ibn Al Farrat

rue de la Kasbah

rue Ibn Al Abbar

rue de Maimuni

rue ben Raissouli

rue Seboui

rue Med Torrès

rue du Commerce

rue des Chrétiens

rue Naceria

rue de la Marine

rue Hassan 1er

Jardin de
la Mendoubia

Petit
Socco

rue des Postes

rue Italie

rue Semmarine

Grand
Socco

rue Bouarraqia

rue du Portugal

rue San Francisco

rue de la Liberté

rue d'Angleterre

rue de Hollande

rue de la Plage

start here

place
de
France

rue El Walid

ONMT

bd. Pasteur

rue de Belgique

City Walls

1 Praça de Faro/ place El Maguise	**11** Petit Socco	**21** Place Amrah
2 Place de France	**12** Café Central	**22** Place de la Kasbah
3 Centre Culturel Français	**13** Rue Mokhtar Ahardan/ rue des Postes	**23** Dar el Makhzen
4 Mendoubia Gardens	**14** Rue Iskiredj	**24** Museum of Ethnography and Archaeology
5 Place du Grand Socco	**15** Old American Legation	**25** Rue Riad Sultan
6 El Minzah	**16** Rue Dar Dbagh	**26** Le Detroit
7 The Medina	**17** Rue des Almouades	
8 Rue Semmarine	**18** Rue Sidi ben Raissouli	
9 Spanish Cathedral	**19** Kasbah of Tangier	
10 Rue es Siaghin	**20** Villa "Sidi Hosni"	

The street will now have changed its name to:

10. rue es Siaghin. In the 1930s, this was the richest street of the town, filled with jewelry stores. Back then it was actually considered "main street," regardless of how unlikely that appears today. Now it is flanked with shops selling everything from fruit to cheap clothing. Its illustrious jewelry stores are long gone. The street opens suddenly onto the:

11. Petit Socco (aka place Souk Dakhil), a square that has witnessed the greatest number of unprintable interpersonal arrangements and agreements in the history of Morocco. Opening onto one side of it, behind an earth-toned tile facade, is a:

REFUELING STOP   12. Café Central, Petit Socco. It does not have a sign posted on its facade, nor does it even have a telephone. But management accurately assumes that everyone in Tangier will know of the allure of this café. During the city's golden age, it was famed as a night haunt of the Beat Generation. It was the scene of countless trysts and other colorful confrontations. Amid its seedy charm, have a coffee, try to imagine Errol Flynn getting drunk here back when alcohol was served in the Medina, and then continue on your way.

Exit from the café and turn left. Within 20 paces, fork right onto a very narrow alleyway whose sign identifies it as either:

13. rue Mokhtar Ahardan or rue des Postes. If there's no sign, identify the street by its most prominent hotel, the Pension Palace. This was the hotel that so intrigued Bernardo Bertolucci for his film *The Sheltering Sky*. It's hard to imagine Debra Winger and John Malkovich here, but they were. Across the street from the Pension Palace is an obscure and architecturally undistinguished mosque whose barred windows will be on your right.

Walk along this street, pass several small restaurants, and just before the overpass belonging to the Hotel Mamora, turn right onto the very narrow:

14. rue Iskiredj. You will now walk in a more or less straight line along rue Iskiredj for five or six blocks. The names of some of the alleyways that will intersect your path include rue Ben Charki, rue Ben Slimane, rue de l'Ombre, and several alleyways without markings. Rue Iskiredj will fork right, then make an immediate jog left. Continue along this increasingly claustrophobic "street." You are in the heart of the Medina. Soon, gables and overhead passages will block even the direct sunlight, and a strong sense of the Middle Ages will close in upon you.

The street changes its name to rue du Four, and will jog to the right before dead-ending at rue Haybender, although there may not, at this point, be a sign. Before the end of the block, turn left onto rue d'Amérique. Within 40 paces, you will arrive at the:

15. Old American Legation, composed of four different Arabic-style houses, containing a total of 44 rooms. The most recent of the houses is 200 years old, and each is interconnected with a series of inner passageways and covered overhead bridges. Ring a bell and a guardian will show you the interior. The building's power and prestige was highest between 1912 and 1955 during the rule of Tangier by an international committee of foreign powers. Since Morocco was granted independence in 1956, all official transactions have been transferred to Rabat.

After your visit to the legation, turn right after exiting from its main entrance. At the next junction, go left, then descend a flight of steps. These steps, after passing beneath an archway, will deposit you onto the impossibly narrow sidewalk of a modern asphalt street whose cars and traffic might come as a shock after the narrow pedestrian walkways of the Medina. Although you won't see a street sign here, turn left and descend the steeply inclined street. (Later, the street will be identified as rue du Portugal.) Notice the Jewish cemetery's encircling wall on your right, and the steep perimeter of the Medina on your left.

As you continue to descend, admire the sweeping and historic panorama of the port of Tangier that unfolds in front of you.

At the bottom of the hill, take the first major left-hand turn onto:

16. rue Dar Dbagh. There may not be a sign there, but its wide boundaries present the first realistic opportunity to enter once again the narrow streets of the Medina. Within about a half block, notice the Restaurant Granada on your left.

Climb the tall and imposing stairs of the Escalier Americain, passing the entrance to the restaurant. Near the top, as you pass beneath an overhead archway, you'll traverse (but not turn onto) avenue Faquih Haouari. Continue walking straight along the flat street at the top of the stairs. Its name will be identified eventually as rue des Postes (Mokhtar Ahardan).

Pass beneath the archway containing the overpass belonging to the Hotel Mamora (you're suddenly on familiar ground) and continue walking until you reach the perimeter of a square you have already visited, Petit Socco.

Backtrack to a point beyond the Café Central, to the beginning of a very narrow street called:

17. rue des Almouades, which will turn right from a point that originates on the left-hand side (as you face it) of the Café Central. Turn right onto rue des Almouades (which is sometimes, depending on the context, spelled rue des Almouahidine) and walk downhill beneath an overpass, entering once again the filtered sunlight and surrealistic visuals of the Medina. As you walk along this street, you'll pass dozens of shops selling artifacts and crafts.

Eventually, the street will lead to place Quad Ahardan, actually no more than a small opening in the congestion of the Medina. Walk through it. At its end, fork right onto the small alleyway that will eventually identify itself as:

18. rue Sidi ben Raissouli. Walk uphill along its narrow confines, some of which are extremely steep. The longest of these flights of stairs will mark the entrance to the fortress known for centuries throughout the European and Muslim worlds as the:

19. Kasbah of Tangier. Within a few paces, the stairs will fork. Go right and continue to climb. Halfway up this second long flight of steps, you'll notice an iron gate guarding the entrance to the almost concealed:

20. Villa "Sidi Hosni." This is the villa that once belonged to (and housed) the tragic and legendary American heiress Barbara Hutton. Her parties here were the talk (and scandal) of contemporary Tangier. At press time, the villa belonged to residents of Paris.

Continue walking uphill, pass beneath the covered passageway into the:

21. place Amrah, whose pavement continues to slope uphill. Pass beneath a brick-and-stucco pointed archway, and find yourself within the monumental and irregularly shaped square known as:

22. place de la Kasbah. Almost immediately after you enter it, notice the pair of tall arched doors to your right near the lowest point of the square. They mark the entrance to a once-secret tunnel built by the Kasbah's 17th-century English occupants to connect their hilltop fortress with the port of Tangier.

Massive and sometimes crumbling ramparts will surround you on all sides. Despite the Kasbah's original role as a military garrison, it still has some desirable real estate and houses within its walls. Continue to ascend the pavement of place de la Kasbah, imagining the bloody wars for possession that have dominated the collective lives of this strategic site's many occupants.

Facing you as you climb, one of the highest buildings that you'll now be able to see is the residence of the former sultans of Tangier:

23. Dar el Makhzen. Oddly, the only sign indicating the location of this famous palace is a street sign, in both French and Spanish, saying, PLACE DE LA KASBAH/ PLAZA DE ALCAZABA.

To the left of the palace, within a low white building devoid of any architectural adornment, is the:

24. Museum of Ethnography and Archeology. At this point, look across the street for the solidly rectangular façade of a building marked "0." Although the numeration of this building might oppose everything you've ever believed about the organization of street numbers within cities, "Number Zero," place de la Kasbah, was once the home of Richard Hughes, author of *A High Wind in Jamaica*.

Retrace your steps to the front of Dar el Makhzen and swing around the palace's most distant side (i.e., the right-hand side, as you face its façade). The name of the street to the palace's side is:

25. rue Riad Sultan. Climb it. (The crenellated ramparts that define the perimeter of the Kasbah will be on your right.) An ornate passageway soars overhead. Pass beneath it, and notice the flight of stairs that pierces a hole in the forbidding-looking high wall on your left. Climb these stairs to reach the sweeping views and sun-flooded vistas of your final:

REFUELING STOP 26. Le Detroit, Riad Sultan, Kasbah, an extension of Dar el Makhzen. The café contains a labyrinth of ornate rooms lavishly decorated in the Moroccan style. But visitors prefer the big room because of the picture windows overlooking the Strait of Gibraltar and the coastline of Spain. The lavishly ornate plaster-filigree ceiling was re-created from original models in 1967. This is the best place in the Kasbah for mint tea and Moroccan pastries.

---

6. SAVVY SHOPPING

THE SHOPPING SCENE

Shoppers, beware. Many of the "authentic" Moroccan crafts sold in the Medina were made in Turkey or in factories in Spain. They are often "chemically distressed" to make them look old. "Silver" is often pewter.

Everything is for sale in Tangier, and we do mean everything, including the redoubtable Spanish fly available in local apothecaries. You don't even have to go find the merchandise: the mountain will come to Muhammad, so to speak. If you're sitting on the beach, salespeople peddling various crafts, even carpets, will approach you. If you're having coffee at a café, someone will approach you. That doesn't mean you need to be terribly interested in the merchandise, unless it appeals to you.

Exercise caution with what you buy, and don't take any shopowner's "guarantee" that merchandise will be shipped back to your home. Take the merchandise with you. Buy only what you like—never for "investment purposes"—and you should do well.

There is no refund of the government tax of 17% to 19% added to goods and services in Morocco. Bargaining (see Chapter 2) is acceptable in all stores that don't have fixed prices. Stores that publicize fixed prices usually include various government-operated artisan centers.

SHOPPING AREAS

The souks are found in the **Medina,** and most of the major Moroccan handcrafts are sold here, including in store after store devoted to Moroccan carpets. Most of the shops and stores in the Ville Nouvelle (New Town) are found along **boulevard Pasteur** or in the streets branching off this major artery.

BEST BUYS

There are many good shops and much wonderful merchandise in Tangier, but a huge amount of it is made in other parts of Morocco, where there might be a greater variety of choice and perhaps more reasonable prices.

For example, many handmade **leather products** find their way to Tangier, but if you're going to either Fez or Marrakesh, you should delay your leather purchases until you reach those cities.

Certain **copper utensils** are considered good buys, and **wrought iron,** drawing upon the Spanish traditions so long ago established in the north of Morocco, is also tempting. **Carpets** from the Middle Atlas, which originated in such centers of Berber tradition as Azrou, are sold in the souks of Tangier. **Silver,** if you can be sure it's silver, is also worked into intricate designs in the villages of the plateaus and in the nearby Rif mountains, and it is often combined with coral and amber to make interesting bracelets, ankle ornaments, and pendants.

Embroideries, including the famous dark-blue Fez variety, are also sold in Tangier, along with embroideries from Tetuán. **Ceramics,** too, are found, the most famous of which are made in Fez and Safi.

Though Tangier has a selection of merchandise from throughout the country, Marrakesh is frankly a more interesting center for handcrafts. If you're going to Marrakesh, save your most serious shopping until you reach that city's medina.

Several buyers who return yearly to Morocco to resupply their commercial outlets confided to me that "merchandise that can't be sold anywhere else in Morocco is brought to Tangier and offered for sale." There is a bit of truth in this cynical view, because Tangier attracts the day trippers who come over from the coast of Spain, and many of them are interested only in acquiring some souvenir of their all-too-quick Moroccan sojourn.

SHOPPING A TO Z
ANTIQUES

GALERIE TINDOUF, rue de la Liberté, 64. Tel. 93-15-25.
In the opinion of dozens of professional decorators from Madrid and Paris, this is the finest and most exclusive antiques store in Tangier, filled to the rafters with the decorative wealth of many different dynasties. Especially beautiful are the inlaid mother-of-pearl mirrors, which require special crating and packaging. Known for its reliability and fairness, the shop is the domain of Mr. Bouker Abdelmalek, and is located across the street from the Hotel El Minzah. (The other Tindouf, recommended below, is not to be confused with the more upscale establishment just described. They are run by the same family.) Open Monday through Saturday from 9am to 1pm and 4 to 9pm. Major credit cards are accepted.

HANDCRAFTS

COOPARTIM, Ensemble Artisanal, rue de Belgique (without number). Tel. 325-80.
Government-controlled and -supervised, this is Tangier's officially sponsored showcase for Moroccan arts and handcrafts. Within an interconnected complex of shops and studios, you'll find a large inventory collected from around the country. You won't have the fun here you might have had bartering with individual merchants within a souk, partly because of the sense of bureaucracy that prevails and partly because of the policy of rigidly fixing fair prices on everything sold. Despite that, it's a good place to learn a smattering of what's available and what general costs are.

In addition to the sales outlet here, the government maintains about a half dozen workshops as an exposition of the craftsmanship of Morocco. Among the most successful of these boutiques is **Mohamed Lymouri,** Ensemble Artisanal, rue de Belgique (tel. 315-89), a bookbinder who sends many of his elegant leather-bound volumes to libraries and collectors in France. He also sells wallets, purses, handbags, and leather desk blotters, each embossed with gold detailing.

MARRAKECH LA ROUGE, rue es Siaghin, 50. Tel. 311-17.
Sprawling over two very large floors packed with examples of recently produced Moroccan handcrafts, this is one of the Medina's largest collections. A visit to its well-illuminated supermarket-style shelves gives an insight into the breadth and astonishing quantity available in the surrounding bazaars. The upstairs is devoted almost exclusively to carpets. It is open daily from 9am to 7pm.

SAHARA, rue des Almouahidine, 30. No phone.

Although it's surrounded by dozens of other shops, the small, family-managed Sahara is charming and usually reliable. For over 20 years, members of the Abdessalam family have stocked it with carpets and artifacts from throughout Morocco. Look for the decorative brassware, leather goods, and carpets that hang in tempting displays out on the street.

TINDOUF, rue de la Liberté, 64. Tel. 315-25.

This shop contains one of Tangier's most highly collectible collections of hand-me-downs. Dear to the hearts of any visiting historian are the thousands of old-time postcards, as well as an array of objects best described as Arabic kitsch. Don't overlook the many objects of beauty and value, such as the most charming inkstands in town, scattered amid all the dusty relics. Owned by members of the Abdelmalek family, this establishment lies in one of Tangier's best neighborhoods, across the street from the Hotel El Minzah. Open Monday through Saturday from 9am to 9pm.

---

7. EVENING ENTERTAINMENT

THE ENTERTAINMENT SCENE

From belly dancers to discos, Tangier tries to please all tastes. But forget all those old movies about espionage: the nightlife of Tangier has long outlived its 1950s heyday. Bars and nightclubs today often attract the criminal element, and going to the wrong place can be life-threatening. At best, you risk your wallet or your purse. It is therefore very important to choose carefully among the offerings.

Most of the famous old places, such as the Parade Bar, have faded into history. The exterior of 1001 Nights is boarded up. This is where Brion Gysin fed his offbeat writer friends and showcased the hypnotic Master Musicians of the Joujouka. Dean's Bar, once the haunt of the likes of Tennessee Williams, Errol Flynn, Ian Fleming, and Francis Bacon, should be confined to the pages of dusty memoirs. Anything that might call itself Dean's these days simply isn't.

THE PERFORMING ARTS

Tangier isn't London or Paris. Concerts here tend to be infrequent. If any Western classical cultural entertainment is being presented, the Tangier Tourist Office will have details. Other than French-language newspapers, there is no entertainment guide published in the city from which you can glean information.

LOCAL CULTURAL ENTERTAINMENT

Moroccan music and dancing are presented nearly every evening at the major hotels. Here is your best chance to appreciate the complexity and rhythms of these unusual art forms. If your hotel doesn't have such entertainment, you can go for a drink or a meal at one of the hotels that feature such diversions.

THE CLUB & MUSIC SCENE

BELLY DANCING

MOROCCO PALACE, rue Prince Moulay Abdallah, 11. Tel. 386-14.

This is Tangier's time-tested and slightly frayed venue for belly dancing and other folkloric entertainment. After 1am, the crowd consists mainly of Moroccans, and disco music rules the night. Before that, a band plays for belly dancers. A beer costs 30

DH ($3.75). The Morocco Palace is open nightly from 10pm to 4am, with the show beginning at 10:15pm and lasting 2 hours. Bus: 12.
Admission: 50 DH ($6.25).

DANCE CLUBS

There are some suitable discos in the big hotels—safer than some of the places at night in the New Town, and certainly safer than anything in the Medina at night. However, as you move beneath the strobes and laser beams of these discos, you are far away from the culture and the locals.

ALI BABA, Cheelah Hotel, rue Allal Ben Abdallah, 47-49. Tel. 420-03.
    Housed in a four-star hotel, this is considered one of the best discos in the city, drawing for the most part a foreign crowd. The music is recorded. Beer costs 12 DH ($1.50). Nightly hours are 10pm to 2am. Bus: 12.
    Admission: Hotel guests, free; nonresidents, 50 DH ($6.25) including your first drink.

UP 2000, Hotel Les Almohades, av. F.A.R. (without number). Tel. 404-31.
    To reach this popular nightclub, take the hotel's elevator to the seventh floor and continue walking another flight up a circular staircase. You enter a dark, intimate circular room. The disco is contained within a pod shaped like a flying saucer atop one of the most stylish hotels in Tangier. Inside, the focal point, other than the big windows overlooking the sea, is a circular dance floor. Traditionally, this has been a favorite nightclub venue for oil billionaires from Saudi Arabia and their entourages, along with a number of stylish European women. Nonalcoholic drinks are 40 DH ($5); those with alcohol, 50 to 70 DH ($6.25 to $8.75). The place is open daily from 10pm to 5am. Bus: 7 or 12.

SUPPER CLUBS

EL KHAYAM, Hotel Les Almohades, av. F.A.R (without number). Tel. 404-31.
    A modern and sophisticated supper club and bar on the seventh floor of this previously recommended hotel. A Moroccan orchestra plays against a backdrop of sweeping windows overlooking the Strait of Gibraltar, the beach, the port, and the dockyards. After dinner, you can climb a flight of stairs to the Up 2000 disco (see above). Menu items at El Khayam include brochettes, couscous, harira soup, entrecôte, and fresh fish. Meals start at 150 DH ($18.75). The restaurant is open nightly from 8pm to 2am, the bar from 8pm to 5am. Bus: 7 or 12.

THE BAR SCENE

PUBS/WINE BARS

PATIO WINE BAR, Hotel El Minzah, rue de la Liberté, 85. Tel. 358-85.
    Its fame far exceeds the cramped and intimate premises it occupies near the central Andalusian-inspired courtyard of the most famous and historic hotel in Tangier. It is perhaps the only wine bar in Morocco, selling the finest vintages of the country by the glass or bottle—to which the sophisticated bartender will happily introduce you. The establishment doubles as a restaurant (see "Dining," above). If you don't plan to dine here, the perfect accompaniment for any of the wines would be a portion of the savory, herb-enhanced goat's cheese that is the house specialty. Drinks start at 40 DH ($5), and hours are Monday through Saturday from 8 to 11pm. Bus: 15.

THE PUB, rue Sorolla, 4. Tel. 347-89.
    Once past the speakeasy doors (if you make it past the guard), you confront one of the most popular and animated late-night watering holes in Tangier. Opened in 1987,

it combines pub grub with beer and some of the most urbanized clients in Tangier. Patrons of all ages and nationalities babble away in a variety of languages, especially English. Amid lithographs of English hunting scenes and portraits of both the pope and the Moroccan king, you can enjoy sandwiches, pastas, omelets, smoked palomette fish from the coast along Agadir, escalopes of veal Cordon Bleu, shepherd's pie, and pepper steak. Meals cost from 120 DH ($15). Drinks are 30 to 50 DH ($3.75 to $6.25); beer costs 14 to 28 DH ($1.75 to $3.50). Food service is available daily from noon to 3pm and 6:30pm to 1am; bar service, daily from noon to 1am. Bus: 15.

SPECIALTY BARS
Nostalgic & Expatriate Bars

CAID'S BAR, Hotel El Minzah, rue de la Liberté, 85. Tel. 358-85.

⭐ This is the most famous bar in Tangier. Through its windows or from the tables of its outdoor patios, you can enjoy views of the Andalusian garden of Tangier's best-known hotel. Inside, you sip drinks beneath a labyrinth of Moorish arches and filigreed plaster. The waiters in fezes evoke a nostalgic Morocco of long ago. Time was, there was always someone famous sitting in the bar, perhaps Tallulah Bankhead at a table across from Jean Genet, neither one knowing who the other was. Drinks cost 35 to 48 DH ($4.40 to $6); beer is 18 to 24 DH ($2.25 to $3). Caid's Bar is open daily from 10am to midnight. Bus: 15.

CAFE CENTRAL, Petit Socco. No phone.

Sheathed from floor to ceiling with the kind of ceramic tiles you might find in a cheap Hong Kong restaurant, this celebrated café in the Medina has a high ceiling supported by Corinthian-capped iron columns. Its decor is best described as "indestructible." The former nesting place of the America's Beat Generation icons, the café (as well as its staff) has seen better days, yet it retains a certain seedy charm. Few leave Tangier without having the mandatory cup of coffee at the Central, if only to say that they've been here.

Ted Morgan, the Pulitzer Prize–winning journalist and biographer of FDR, Winston Churchill, and Somerset Maugham, called the café the "meeting place and switchboard of Tangier . . . Arab guides smoking kef pipes, pimps and smugglers and money-changers, a parade of boys being appraised by expatriate queers, and above all, a parade of losers stuck in Tangier." Coffee goes for 3 DH (40¢). Transportation: On foot from the Grand Socco.

CAFE DE PARIS, place de France, 1. Tel. 384-44.

At the crossroads of five of the principal streets of Tangier, the Café de Paris is a kind of town gossip center, a meeting ground for Europeans and Arabs. Few visitors are in Tangier for more than 24 hours without paying at least one call on this centrally located café. Every imaginable transaction and assignation takes place here. And you can keep your table for as long as you like. Time was when you could pick up a lot of literary gossip here if you were seated at the right table; the ghosts of Francis Bacon, Gertrude Stein, William S. Burroughs, Cecil Beaton, Tennessee Williams, and Truman Capote still linger here. Coffee is 3 DH (40¢), available daily from 7am to 11pm. Bus: 12.

LE BAR, Grand Hotel Villa de France, rue de Hollande, 143. Tel. 314-75.

Small, snug, and cozy, this bar has attracted some of Tangier's best-known celebrity foreigners over the years. Often the staff didn't know who they were and didn't much care; ever since Henri Matisse stayed here, the Grand got used to big names. Easily reached on foot from the Grand Socco, and surrounded by a mature garden, the hotel is entered through a courtyard. The bar is at the end of a long corridor beyond the reception desk. You can also have drinks on a garden terrace. Drinks start at 15 DH ($1.90), and beer is 12 DH ($1.50). Open daily from 10am to midnight. Bus: 7.

RIF BAR, Rif Hotel, av. d'Espagne, 152. Tel. 359-10.
   Set a floor above lobby level of the hotel, this was once considered a mandatory stopover, at least for every visiting Britisher. Here in 1958 you might have spotted Winston Churchill in the bar, along with his wife, Clementine. Perhaps the most notorious patron (in a long line of rogues) was Kurt Reith, the Nazi diplomat and link to the Gestapo who engineered the assassination of Austrian chancellor Engelbert Dollfuss. You can drink at the bar or else enjoy the view of the waterfall around the grotto-inspired swimming pool. Beer costs 20 DH ($2.50). Daily hours are 8am to 1am. Bus: 7.

THE TANGERINN, rue Magellan, 1. Tel. 353-37.
   The small corner bar is generally crowded with a regular clientele of British and U.S. expatriates, so you may have to sit in one of the two rather bare rooms, one of which contains a grand piano for anyone who wants to play it. Run by John C. Sutcliffe, author of *Unknown Pilgrim,* and Peter Tuckwell for more than 20 years, there is no better place for tourists in need of information on the country or the city. No food is served here. Beer costs 9 to 16 DH ($1.15 to $2), depending on the brand. The Tangerinn is open daily from 9pm to 1am. Bus: 7.

Beach Bars

EMMA'S B.B.C., av. d'Espagne (without number). No phone.
   No one compiling a guide to the bars of Morocco could leave out the famous Emma's, established in the 1970s by an expatriate Dutchwoman who became Morocco's first female taxi driver (see "Dining," above). Gossip usually travels faster here than on the airwaves of the BBC. The "B.B.C." in the name here refers to "Beach Bar Carrousel." You can always come here for a piece of "Emma's cake" or her fish and chips, prepared British style. In the evening, however, most people arrive to drink. Beer is 16 DH ($2). Daily hours are 8am to 2am. Bus: 7 or 20.

SUN BEACH BAR, av. F.A.R (without number). Tel. 434-01.
   Sun Beach is suitable both for lunch (see "Dining," above) and for drinking. During the day, you can rent a tiny *cabine* to lock up your clothing (not necessarily safe for valuables, however), costing 5 DH (65¢) for an individual and 20 DH ($2.50) for a family. If you want a snack in the afternoon, you can drop in and order a salad and beer. It's all very casual. Tennessee Williams penned the first notes for his Pulitzer Prize–winning play *Cat on a Hot Tin Roof* as he sunbathed on the patio here. At night, the family business fades and the bar fills up mainly with men. Salads cost 8 to 12 DH ($1 to $1.50), and beer runs 9 to 16 DH ($1.15 to $2). Open daily from 9am to 1am. Bus: 7 or 20.

A Gay Bar

NUMBER ONE, bd. Mohammed V, 1. Tel. 318-17.
   This bar is attached to one of the best French restaurants in Tangier. Late at night, it is especially, though not exclusively, popular with gay people. It has a helpful and friendly staff. Drinks are 30 DH ($3.75), with beer costing 16 DH ($2). It's open daily from 11:30am to 1am. Bus: 7.

8. EASY EXCURSIONS

Even those with limited time should try to visit two attractions in the environs of Tangier: Cape Spartel and the Caves of Hercules. The distance is about 20 miles, and one should allow at least 3 hours for the tour, not counting interior visits to the caves and any stopovers along the way. Your best bet for an organized tour is to go to the

American Express representative in Tangier, **Voyages Schwartz,** bd. Pasteur, 54 (tel. 334-59).

CAPE SPARTEL

Cape Spartel, 9 miles northwest of Tangier, is a mountainous promontory looking out at the Atlantic. Planted with umbrella pines, it forms the most northwesterly point of Africa, jutting closer to Europe than any other place on the continent. Foreign diplomats erected the lighthouse in the 1870s. Cape Spartel was called "the cape of the vines" by ancient Greeks and Romans. From its precincts, there's a magnificent panorama.

There is no public transportation to the cape. However, you can take a grand taxi, which can be shared; start the round-trip negotiations at 200 DH ($25). Often visitors spend the day here, having a taxi driver take them out in the morning and return in the afternoon to pick them up. You can find these grands taxis waiting at a rank opposite the English Church on rue d'Angleterre, near the Grand Socco.

THE CAVES OF HERCULES

⭐ Going another 2½ miles west along the coast leads to these world-famous caves, once used as a limestone quarry for millstones. For many centuries, the caves were also centers of prostitution, but the most notorious excesses have been cleaned up by the Moroccan government. In the "golden era" of Tangier's status as a free port, rich expatriates such as Barbara Hutton threw fabulous parties here, sometimes even notorious parties, which were attended by many luminaries.

Inside the caves, a "sea window" is shaped like a map of Africa; the tourist department uses this unusual opening as the official cover photograph for its brochures. At high tide, the sea pours in. These natural rock chambers are open daily from 10am to sunset, with an admission charge of 2 DH (25¢). Guides will come at you from all corners, offering to show you around.

The beach below looks lovely, and the water even more inviting, but swimmers should beware. The current is dangerous, and drownings are reported every year.

CHAPTER 4

THE NORTHERN COAST

- **WHAT'S SPECIAL ABOUT THE NORTHERN COAST**
- **SUGGESTED ITINERARY**
1. **CEUTA/SEBTA (SPAIN)**
2. **TETUÁN**
3. **CHAOUEN (CHEFCHAOUEN)**
4. **ASILAH**
5. **LARACHE (EL ARAÏCH)**

Ever since the northwest corner of Africa saw the first appearances of Phoenician traders, its control has been bitterly contested among warring cultures. Spain still retains its enclaves in Ceuta and Melilla, refusing to budge even while calling for the departure of the British from Ceuta's counterpart in Gibraltar. The original Berber occupants have been uncompromisingly independent since the first military incursions by the ancient Romans. Spain and Portugal both vied for influence and trading privileges in the area. Spain was at least able to retain two coastal colonies. One of Portugal's abortive crusades into the region in 1578 was such a spectacular failure that it contributed to the eventual bankruptcy and collapse of the Portugese government, and the annexation of all of Portugal by Spain for a 60-year period.

The Moors used this territory as a base of operations for the historic conquest of Andalusia, where they established the great cities of Granada and Córdoba. Swollen in number, and embittered by defeat, they returned to this territory by the thousands after Granada fell to the attacks of the Catholic monarchs Ferdinand and Isabella.

Likewise, when the Jews were evicted from Spain, many of them fled to northern Morocco. There, as merchants operating from segregated districts known as *mellahs,* they were usually tolerated by the Muslims and often prospered. The establishment of the modern state of Israel tended to polarize the Jewish and Islamic communities of Morocco, and after Moroccan independence in 1956, many of the Jews emigrated once again, either to France or to Israel.

The towns that I've recommended in this chapter, for the most part, lie between the Mediterranean coastline and the towering barriers of the Rif mountains. Since Neolithic times, these mountains have been inhabited by the Berbers, who maintain their own dialect and culture. To get a flavor, it's best to explore Chaouen. For a glimpse of the cultural holdovers of the Spanish colonial regime, visit the former Spanish capital at Tetuán. Ceuta, Spain's present colony, prides itself on being more Andalusian than even the Spanish cities within Andalusia. Finally, if you thrill to the almost-forgotten trumpets of former glory, head west from Tangier to Larache and Asilah.

SEEING THE NORTHERN COAST
GETTING THERE

Tangier (see Chapter 3) is the gateway to the region, both for its rail and plane connections. You can fly to Tangier from Paris, London, or Madrid, then journey by rail or bus to other cities or towns along the northern coast. To visit the Spanish enclave of Ceuta, the most popular route for most visitors is via ferryboat from Algeciras on Spain's Costa del Sol.

It's relatively easy to drive up from Rabat and Casablanca to Tangier and its satellite towns. The trip takes about 3 to 3½ hours. The road has been recently widened.

WHAT'S SPECIAL ABOUT THE NORTHERN COAST

Beaches
☐ Martil, one of the best beaches along the coast, 8 miles from Tetuán toward Ceuta, stretching 6½ miles and dotted with cafés and restaurants.

Great Towns/Villages
☐ Larache, site of the ancient city of Lixus, a legend wrapped in myths.
☐ Asilah, enclosed by its old Portuguese defenses, with a famous medina.
☐ Chaouen, completely forbidden to outsiders until the 1920s, is considered one of the most beautiful towns of Morocco.

Monuments
☐ Cromlech de Msoura (meaning "holy place"), the major megalithic monument in North Africa, lies 19 miles southwest of Asilah.
☐ The ancient Roman ruins of Lixus, 3 miles from Larache.

Ace Attractions
☐ The Medina at Tetuán is a quarter filled with mosques, monuments, and souks where craftspeople ply their ancient trades.
☐ The Medina at Chaouen is filled with souks and craftspeople famous throughout Morocco for woodcarving, embroidery, metalwork, pottery, and carpets.

Amazingly, you can visit many of the cities or towns recommended in this chapter by renting a *grand taxi* in Tangier or Tetuán. The cost is surprisingly reasonable (if you can bargain), because the fare is shared between up to five or six passengers. It's a far better and more comfortable way to go than on one of the impossibly overcrowded buses.

SUGGESTED ITINERARY

Day 1: Leave Tangier and head for an overnight stay in Ceuta, the Spanish enclave at the northwest of Africa. Allow plenty of time for clearing Customs.

Day 2: Explore Tetuán, its medina and souks, and stay overnight there unless you want to explore it on a day trip from Tangier. With few scattered exceptions, its hotels are inadequate and likely to be full with beach buffs throughout the summer.

Day 3: From Tetuán, head for Chaouen, where you can explore its medina and go on a shopping expedition in its souks.

Day 4: Return to Tangier for the night.

Day 5: With Tangier as your base, explore the towns to the west, Asilah and Larache, with their medinas and ancient ruins.

1. CEUTA/SEBTA (SPAIN)

63 miles N of Tangier; 26 miles N of Tetuán

GETTING THERE   By Ferry   Car ferries take 1½ hours from Algeciras, a port on Spain's Costa del Sol. From late June to early September, 12 ferries a day operate

Monday through Friday from 8:30am to 10:30pm. Sunday service is curtailed to 6 a day. At other times of the year, there are 6 ferries a day Monday through Saturday from 8am to 9pm, and 3 on Sunday. The one-way cost is 1,150 pesetas ($10.80). In August, when many Moroccan workers are returning from their temporary homes in Europe, long delays are reported.

If you're transporting a car, expect to pay from 5,300 to 6,800 pesetas ($49.80 to $63.90). Reservations and arrangements should be made as far in advance as possible, at least a day and a half before crossing. This can be done through a travel agent if you're in some other Spanish city and plan to drive to Algeciras at the time of your crossing. Some readers who have not done this, planning to take their cars to Morocco, have had to wait in Algeciras for a day and a half until space became available. It's much easier if you don't have a car, because there always seems to be room for walk-on passengers. Ferries are operated by the **Compañía Trasmediterránea** at the Algeciras port, Recinto del Puerto (tel. 956/66-38-62 for information about departures).

By Bus Going back and forth between Morocco and Ceuta is a big hassle. Arriving in Ceuta, you do not clear Customs, as you are technically still in Spain. From the Plaza de la Constitución, take bus no. 7 for 45 pesetas (40¢) to the frontier town of Fnideq. You must wait here at least an hour—sometimes there are longer delays—to clear Moroccan Customs. There is also a baggage check by Customs, and your luggage is likely to get a thorough review. Once you clear Moroccan Customs, you can take a grand taxi to Tetuán, 70 DH ($8.75), but the price can increase if there is a strong demand on any particular day. From Tetuán, you can make bus connections to Tangier or other parts of Morocco. From Tangier, take the bus to Tetuán, the grand taxi to the border town of Fnideq, and, after clearing Customs, bus no. 7 into the heart of Ceuta.

By Car Take route S704 east from Tangier to Ceuta, but expect long delays at the border. Your car-rental firm should have given you a green insurance card and a vehicle-registration document, both of which are needed to enter this Spanish enclave. You must present your passport and fill out an immigration form. You must also swear that you have no dirhams in your possession.

Tip: If you're low on gasoline in Morocco, you can fill up at one of several stations in Ceuta more cheaply than you can in Morocco.

Jutting seaward from a peninsula attached to the Moroccan mainland, Ceuta lies north of Tetuán, following the P28, and east of Tangier, following the coastal road.

Ceuta is defined as a "territory of Spanish sovereignty on Moroccan soil." Long a bitterly disputed thorn in the side of the Moroccan government, Ceuta is most surprising in its almost total lack of anything Moroccan. There are no souks, no medinas, no mosques—nor very much of the Moorish architecture that was described in such minute detail by medieval Islamic historians.

The allure, enforced by almost a half millennium of Spanish occupation, is Iberian, with a look very similar to what you'd have expected on the opposite side of the Strait of Gibraltar. Even more galling to the Moroccans is the almost constant references (in street names, for example) to Christian, rather than Islamic, historical events.

The highest point of Ceuta was known as Abyla to the ancient Greeks, as Jebel Musa to the Arabs, and as Mount Acho to the western Europeans. In Greek mythology, it was considered as the southernmost of the two Pillars of Hercules. (Gibraltar was considered the northern bastion.) Hercules is said to have stood with a foot on each "pillar," pushed them apart, and formed the waterway that is today viewed as one of the world's most strategic.

One of the ironies of history regarding control of this strategic waterway has placed the British firmly within territory geographically connected to Spain, and the Spanish within territory geographically connected to Morocco.

The tensions generated by the Spanish presence on Moroccan soil, however, have not helped the economic prosperity of Ceuta. Most of Ceuta's economic sustenance comes via daily ferryboats from the Spanish mainland, not from the Moroccan heartland. Although Ceuta's harbor is a good one, most of Morocco's export traffic has been rerouted to the ports of Tangier and Casablanca. Ceuta is almost devoid of any viable industry other than tourism, the result of which is an increasingly expensive dependence upon Spain to keep it fiscally solvent.

Known during the Roman occupation as Septum Fratres (Seven Brothers, from which was derived its present Arabic name of Sebta), it was conquered in A.D. 429 by the Vandals and politically reattached to the Visigothic regime of Spain. In the 6th century, it was conquered by the Byzantine kingdom of Justinian, and used as a trading post for ships coming from Constantinople at the opposite end of the Mediterranean.

Around 670, the local Byzantine governor, Count Julian, declared the city independent from Byzantium's supervision, and successfully negotiated a degree of relief for the Christian city from the increasingly powerful Islamic tribes that surrounded it. However, the population of Ceuta was Islamized anyway, a victim of the massive power blocks that had developed in Islamic Andalusia and Islamic North Africa. From around 800 to 950, it passed many times between various Islamic dynasties controlling Andalusia and Morocco, and was increasingly viewed as a potent symbol of possession of the strategically important straits. During the rare moments of peace, Ceuta thrived because of its location at the meeting points of the two Islamic kingdoms.

During that period, one of the Muslim world's most famous medieval geographers, El Idrissi, was born in Sebta in 1099. In the 1100s, merchant ships from throughout the Christian world (especially Pisa, Barcelona, and Venice) dropped anchor to trade. In 1236, a consortium of merchants from Marseille arranged a special trading relation with the caliphs of Sebta. To facilitate trading profits, members of the Merenid dynasty established shipyards and a military garrison, and built luxurious houses, bathhouses, one of the best-attended Koranic universities in the Islamic world, and (according to the poets kept in the employ of the sultans) "more than a thousand mosques." The city also housed an active community of Jews, who usually lived peacefully within their own communities amid their Islamic neighbors. Sebta, as a cosmopolitan melting pot of cultures, began to rival the allure of such cities as Granada and Fez.

In 1415, as part of a disastrous crusade launched by the Portuguese monarchs, Sebta came under Portuguese rule. Although a massive Portuguese army was later lost in the Moroccan hinterlands, and fearsome ransoms were collected from the Portuguese treasury for the return of their captured aristocracy, Sebta (now Ceuta) remained in Portuguese hands. Through a complicated series of inter-Iberian alliances, Ceuta became Spanish in 1580.

Since then, the Spanish have resolutely held on to their province, despite a 17th-century Moroccan seige, which lasted for 27 years, and an 18th-century seige (1790) that cost hundreds of lives and huge amounts of money for both sides.

During the Spanish Civil War, in 1936, Ceuta was a stronghold of the nationalists.

ORIENTATION
CUSTOMS

Crossing this much-contested border is not easy. You will need a valid passport. You are technically crossing an international frontier, and whatever tensions exist at the moment of your crossing will be mirrored in the hassles you'll encounter during the transit.

If you are driving your own car, you'll need to show a *carte grise* (registration), an international driver's license (which must be accompanied by a driver's license from your home state or country), and confirmation that the car is insured.

Moroccan taxis and buses cannot cross the frontier into Ceuta. Neither, except in special circumstances, can the driver you might have hired to escort you through Morocco. If you have luggage in a taxi, bus, or rented car, you must physically carry it through both Spanish and Moroccan Customs, which might take hours, and then rent a Spanish taxi on the opposite side.

INFORMATION

The **Ceuta Tourist Office,** Muelle Canonero Data (without number) (tel. 956/51-13-79), is open Monday through Friday from 9am to 2pm and 4 to 6pm, on Saturday from 9am to 2pm.

FAST FACTS

Area Code 956.

Consulates The United States and Great Britain do not provide consulate services in Ceuta.

Currency Spanish pesetas—not dirhams—are the legal currency.

Post Office If you have letters to mail home, and plan to return to Morocco, mail them here for faster service. The **Ceuta Post Office,** Calle Cervantes, 3 (tel. 51-24-09), is open Monday through Friday from 8am to 2pm, on Saturday from 9am to 2pm.

Special Events At some point every February, Ceuta stages a carnival. Holy Week is marked by processions, similar in style to those observed in Andalusia. A procession of fishing boats takes place on July 16, honoring Our Lady of Mount Carmel. The Festival of Our Lady of Africa takes place annually on August 5.

WHAT TO SEE & DO

Many visitors head to Ceuta for an insight into a geographical and cultural oddity that is radically different from the Islamic culture surrounding it.

The archeological museum, **Sala Arqueológica,** Jardines Argentina (no phone), contains many different ceramics dating from the Neolithic, Carthaginian, and Roman eras. Some of the Roman ceramics are believed to have been imported from Gaul, from Arezzo (Italy), and from Spain. The museum's most important piece is the base of a white-marble sarcophagus with mythological scenes. Open Tuesday through Saturday from 9am to 1pm and from 4 to 6pm; on Sunday and holidays, from 10am to 2pm. Admission is 40 pesetas (40¢). Beneath the museum are many subterranean passageways, called Galerías Subterráneas, the total of which reach a length of more than a mile. They were dug by the Spanish between the 1500s and the 1600s, to assure a constant water supply for the military garrison defending the town.

Guarding the monumental entrance to the museum are a pair of bronze cannons incongruously marked with the heraldic shield of Henri IV, a 17th-century king of France.

The **Plaza de Africa,** set in the center of the town, was built upon the site of a marketplace within the former medina. Although most of the buildings surrounding it today are not especially noteworthy, they once included a palace, a Koranic school, a mosque, and an ornately ceremonial gateway. All of these were demolished in the early 1700s.

Their place on this square was taken by the **Church of Our Lady of Africa**

(Nuestra Señora de Africa). Erected between 1704 and 1726 on the site of a demolished mosque, it was consecrated to the patron saint of Ceuta, in thanksgiving for the end of an epidemic in the 1600s. Its interior is lushly baroque and, as such, is startlingly unexpected within the African setting. The main altar is dominated by a statue of the Virgin with supposedly miraculous powers of healing. It was originally carved in the 1500s. The church's treasury contains banners, Portuguese manuscripts (some of them illuminated), and paintings. It is open daily from 9am to 5pm, charging no admission.

The Cathedral, at the Plaza de Africa, is directly opposite. Only a direct edict from the Pope in Rome allowed the walls and foundations of a former mosque to be transformed into a Christian church. The actual shape and decoration of what you'll see today dates from the early 1700s. The central nave is dotted with funerary plaques marking the burial places of the colony's former bishops. The huge paintings within the church are predictably morbid views of the Crucifixion, and the Nativity. It keeps the same hours as the church.

The **Ayuntamiento (Town Hall),** on the Gran Va, is located immediately to the east of the cathedral. It was originally built in 1929. The murals of the hall inside are by one of the most prolific Spanish painters of the Moroccan Protectorate, Mariano Bertuchi.

Le Candelero was the old Portuguese fortress, built along lines inspired by Vauban. Part of its foundations are bordered by the waters of a defensive moat. This monument is best viewed crossing the moat of San Felipe.

WHERE TO STAY
EXPENSIVE

GRAN HOTEL LA MURALLA, Plaza Virgen de Africa, 15, 11700 Ceuta, Spain. Tel. 956/51-49-40. 108 rms (all with bath). A/C TV TEL **Transportation:** Taxi from the port costs 250 to 300 ptas. ($2.35 to $2.80).
$ **Rates:** 11,000 ptas. ($103.40) single; 13,000 ptas. ($122.20) double. Breakfast 900 ptas. ($8.45) extra. AE, DC, MC, V.
This four-star hotel with a swimming pool, a bar, a nightclub, and a parking lot is right in the heart of town on a pretty palm-lined square, with the Church of Our Lady of Africa across the street. Continental breakfast is available, but not included in the rates.

MODERATE

HOTEL ULISES, Camoens, 5, 11700 Ceuta, Spain. Tel. 956/51-45-10. 124 rms (all with bath). A/C TEL **Bus:** 7.
$ **Rates:** 9,400 ptas. ($88.35) single; 11,500 ptas. ($108.10) double. Breakfast 600 ptas. ($5.65) extra. AE, DC, MC, V.
With its swimming pool and air conditioning, the Ulises is a welcome relief from the hot weather and the monotony of the surrounding commercial district. Bedrooms are comfortably furnished. It's a safe haven for those experiencing "culture shock" as they cross from Europe to Africa or vice versa.

WHERE TO EAT
MODERATE

CASA SILVA, Almirante Lobo, 3. Tel. 51-37-15.
Cuisine: SPANISH. **Reservations:** Not required. **Bus:** 7.
$ **Prices:** Appetizers 600–800 ptas. ($5.65–$7.50); main dishes 1,000–1,500 ptas. ($9.40–$14.10). MC, V.
Open: Lunch Mon–Sat 1–4pm; dinner daily 8pm–11pm. **Closed:** Feb 15–Mar 1; Oct 1–15.
One of the best places in town, it's known far and wide. It serves fresh fish prepared Spanish style, often with herbs and garlic. Full meals might include hake in the house

sauce, an array of shellfish, paella, and deep-fried squid. Accompanying your dinner will be a full array of Spanish wines, as well as some Moroccan reds. Average price for a bottle is 80 DH ($10).

EL SOMBRERO DE COPA, Padilla, 4. Tel. 51-82-84.
   Cuisine: SEAFOOD. **Reservations:** Not required. **Bus:** 7.
$ **Prices:** Appetizers 600–1,000 ptas. ($5.65–$9.40); main dishes 900–1,500 ptas. ($8.45–$14.10). MC, V.
   Open: Lunch Tues–Sun 1–5pm; dinner Tues–Sun 9pm–midnight. **Closed:** Feb.
A good choice for those looking for an unpretentious seafood meal at bargain rates. You can get a wide array of both shellfish and fish here, depending on the catch of the day. Food is invariably fresh, and many of the dishes have a strong taste of Andalusia, unlike the Moroccan fare that you may have been eating.

RESTAURANT LA TORRE, Plaza de Virgen de Africa, 15. Tel. 51-49-40.
   Cuisine: ANDALUSIAN. **Reservations:** Recommended. **Transportation:** Taxi from the port 250–300 ptas. ($2.35–$2.80).
$ **Prices:** Appetizers 600–800 ptas. ($5.65–$7.50); main dishes 1,500–1,800 ptas. ($14.10–$16.90). AE, DC, MC, V.
   Open: Lunch daily 1–4:30pm; dinner daily 9–11:30pm.
In the Gran Hotel La Muralla, this well-rated restaurant, considered the best restaurant in town, provides Andalusian fare—fish dishes, stews, soups, and grilled meats. The fish dishes are always the most reliable, depending on the catch of the day. You dine in comfortable surroundings and can later enjoy a walk through the garden.

---

2. TETUÁN

26 miles S of Ceuta; 35 miles E of Tangier

GETTING THERE   By Train   Take the train from Tangier, which has links with all major Moroccan cities, then continue by bus (see below) the rest of the way.

By Bus   Twelve buses a day, taking 1½ hours, run back and forth between Tangier and Tetuán.

By Car   From Ceuta (see above), head south along route P28; from Tangier, go east on route P38.

Tetuán (also spelled Tétouan) is famous for its position as the capital of the 20th-century Spanish empire in Morocco, and for its present position as the administrative capital of the Rif mountains. A large city by Moroccan standards, it has a permanent population of at least 350,000 people. It's well known for industrial and handcrafted products that include cement, textiles, lumber, paper, processed food, leather, embroideries, and firearms.

Tetuán is, at least from a distance, one of the most memorable towns of northern Morocco, a link between the sea and the mountains. It is also the one that has remained the most authentically Hispano-Moorish in its look, with endless wrought-iron accents added by the Spanish during their tenure here. Residents of the town define themselves as the true heirs of the Islamic Andalusian culture, and refer to Tetuán as "the daughter of Granada." Translated from the Arabic, its name means "freshwater springs" or "the source."

The encircling walls that give it much of its character were the brainchild of one of the 18th century's most prolific builders, Moulay Ismail. At the northeastern edge of town rises the bulk of a ruined kasbah-fortress. The town's medina is one of the most labyrinthine and interesting in Morocco.

The new city, stretching toward the east of the Medina, is dotted with the grandiose buildings erected by the Spaniards during their reign over the city. Streets are laid out on a regularly spaced grid that seems incongruous in contrast to the claustrophobia of the Medina.

ORIENTATION

INFORMATION

In July and August, the **Tetuán Tourist Office,** av. Mohammed V, 30 (tel. 096/70-09), is open Monday through Friday from 8am to 3pm. From September to June, it is open Monday through Thursday from 8:30am to noon and 2:30 to 6:30pm, on Friday from 8:30 to 11:30am.

GETTING AROUND

The most reliable method of transportation is a *petit taxi* (a small car in which three passengers share the ride and the fare). They are most reasonable in price, but agree on the fare beforehand. If you're going to Tangier or Ceuta, you can rent one of the *grands taxis* on bouelvard Maarakah Annoual at reasonable rates, although you share the ride with others. The ride to Tangier is often no more than 25 DH ($3.15) per person, depending on your bargaining. The **CTM Bus Station** in Tetuán is at boulevard Oued al Makhazine (tel. 62-63). You can get buses from here to Tangier, Rabat, and Casablanca.

FAST FACTS

Area Code   096.

Currency Exchange   The window kiosk of the **Banque Marocaine,** located at place Moulay el Mehdi (no phone), keeps extended hours Monday through Friday from 8am to 9pm, on Saturday and Sunday from 9am to 1pm and 3 to 8pm.

Police   Tetuán is considered a dangerous city. The police are at boulevard Sidi Mandri (tel. 19), a block above avenue Mohammed V.

Post Office   The **Tetuán Post Office** is at place Moulay el Mehdi (tel. 67-98). In July and August, it is open Monday through Saturday from 8:30am to 3:30pm; from September to June, Monday through Saturday from 8:30am to noon and 2:30 to 6:30pm. You can also make both local and international calls from the post office.

Safety   The so-called guides and students who crowd around every foreign visitor to Tetuán are considered even more aggressive than those in Tangier. If you attempt to walk the streets of Tetuán on your own, you will have no peace from these young men, many of whom are pushing kef. The old Berber language translation for Tetuán meant "keep your eyes open," and the advice holds true even more today. Use only official guides from the tourist office, if only to keep the other guides from hassling you as you stroll about the town. Always carry a moneybelt and don't lug around expensive cameras. Leave the jewelry back home in a safe place. Beware of the huge number of pickpockets who hang out in the midst of the confusion of the bus station.

WHAT TO SEE & DO

✪   Because there are very few street signs and because the **Medina of Tetuán** is particularly labyrinthine, it would probably be a good idea to hire a local guide to reach the several monuments that might be of interest. It's best to choose one of the official guides from the Tetuán Tourist Office.

You can enter the Medina through the eastern corner of place Hassan II. Go through Bab er Rouah, called "the gate of the winds."

Foremost among the Medina's several attractions are the variety and color of its souks, said to rival the exoticism of the medinas at Marrakesh and Fez. Regionally distinctive in Tetuán, however, is the predominance of the color red, which is more liberally used on local artifacts than anywhere else in Morocco. (Especially noteworthy are the many carved and painted wooden boxes produced in local ateliers.)

The **Royal Palace,** at place Hassan II, built in the 1600s and enlarged early in the 20th century, is a good example of Hispano-Moorish design. It is not open to the public.

West of the Medina, a few steps northwest of the Mellah, is the **Archeological Museum** (no phone), about two blocks west of place Hassan II on boulevard Aljazaer. It contains the fruits of much of the archeological research done in the surrounding region. A walk through the garden, where obelisks and monuments from the Phoenician, Roman, and Muslim eras are heavily concentrated, reminds visitors of the rich historical legacy of this part of Morocco. Inside, of special interest, are the remnants (including some mosaics) and statues excavated from the Roman city of Lixus (Larache). You'll find rooms devoted to prehistorical artifacts, a collection of Roman vases in silver or in glass, ceramics that were probably made in Iberia, one of the best collections of Roman coins in Morocco, and several ceramics from the Muslim era. It's open daily (except Tuesday and holidays) from 9am to noon and from 2 to 6pm. Admission is 10 DH ($1.25).

At the eastern edge of the Medina is the **Musée d'Art marocain/Musée Ethnographique,** Bab el Okla (no phone). It contains musical instruments from the Andalusian tradition; a re-creation of a Moroccan bridal chamber and, nearby, an Arabic kitchen with all the accessories; a fantastic collection of skillfully adorned weapons and of ornamented horse and camel saddles; and a collection of the costumes worn by tribespeople in the nearby Rif mountains. It is open Monday through Friday from 8:30am to noon and 2:30 to 5:30pm, on Saturday from 8:30am to noon. Admission is 10 DH ($1.25).

Exposition Artisanale, Derb Seffar, 6 (tel. 41-71), displays the craft of coppersmiths, potters, and tile makers.

BEACHES

The closest beach is the one at **Martil** (formerly known as Río Martín), 8 miles away. By car, take the road toward Ceuta for less than a mile, then turn right to Martil, which is Tetuán's port. The beach is about 6½ miles long and has restaurants and cafés (the latter don't serve alcoholic beverages, however). There is also bus service.

WHERE TO STAY

The hotels of Tetuán, especially the cheap, often foul-smelling, unclassified *pensiones* of the Medina, leave much to be desired. They are also unsafe. Unless you can find a room at the chain-run hotel reviewed below, it is better to visit Tetuán on a day trip from either Tangier or Ceuta.

MODERATE

HOTEL SAFIR TETOUAN, av. Kennedy (without number), Tetuán. Tel. 096/701-44. 98 rms (all with bath). TEL **Transportation:** Petit taxi.
$ Rates: 302 DH ($37.75) single; 392 DH ($49) double. Breakfast 31 DH ($3.90) extra. AE, DC, MC, V.
Run by the Safir chain, this is the finest hotel available for those willing to spend the extra money for the added comfort. More than a mile from the town center, it has received a four-star rating from the government and offers a large garden, a swimming pool, tennis courts, and a parking lot. Rooms are pleasantly furnished, often with balconies, with several amenities. Built in 1978, the hotel was last renovated in 1989. The restaurant serves fixed-priced menus for 109 to 130 DH ($13.65 to $16.25). In an

outlying building is a nightclub, open nightly from 11pm to 3am, far removed from the hotel bedrooms to avoid disturbing anyone's sleep. Residents of the hotel enter free, and nonresidents are charged 60 DH ($7.50), including the first drink.

WHERE TO EAT

Plan to have your great Moroccan meals in such cities as Marrakesh or Rabat. In Tetuán, the goal is to be kind to your stomach. Perhaps the safest bet would be to eat at the Hotel Safir Tetouan, which serves the most consistently reliable food in the city. If you're seeking some local color, try one of the following recommendations. The least expensive meals are served in the Medina, but hygiene is not guaranteed.

INEXPENSIVE

CAFE RESTAURANT MODERNE, Pasaje Achaach, 1. No phone.
Cuisine: MOROCCAN. **Reservations:** Not required.
$ Prices: Appetizers 6–12 DH (75¢–$1.50); main dishes 18–25 DH ($2.25–$3.15). No credit cards.
Open: Daily 9am–9pm.

S The best of an unspectacular lot in this bustling district, the Moderne is a busy place near the Cinema Español, close to the bus station between avenue Mohammed V and avenue Mohammed Torres. You get the typical Moroccan dishes of *harira* soup, couscous, sometimes a grilled fresh fish, and *tajines*. One called *tajine de kefta* is made with herb-flavored meatballs.

ZARHOUN, av. Mohammed Torres, 7. Tel. 430-64.
Cuisine: MOROCCAN. **Reservations:** Not required.
$ Prices: Fixed-price menu 60 DH ($7.50). No credit cards.
Open: Lunch daily noon–4pm; dinner daily 6:30–10:30pm.

Your best bet for a typically Moroccan meal. Near the bus station, 1½ blocks from the Pasaje Achach, it is decorated in the traditional Moorish style, and offers a complete tourist meal in a Moroccan salon with low-slung sofas and brass tables from Fez.

3. CHAOUEN (CHEFCHAOUEN)

100 miles SE of Tangier; 50 miles S of Tetuán

GETTING THERE By Bus The highways from Tangier and Tetuán are good, and 10 buses daily make the 3-hour trip between Tetuán and Chaouen.

By Car From Tangier, take the P38 south in the direction of Tetuán, heading south at the junction with route P28.

ESSENTIALS The area code for Chaouen is 098.

Devotees of 20th-century cubism greatly appreciate a view of Chaouen, which spills like a series of rectangular building blocks from the pair of jagged limestone mountains that rise above it. The twin peaks lent the city its name, "The Horns," when it was established by Islamic ascetics eager to form a military bulwark in 1471 against Portuguese expansion in the Maghreb.

Today, the city sits atop one of the world's richest deposits of magnesium: an estimated nine million tons of ore containing an exceedingly rich percentage (almost 40%) of magnesium oxide.

Chaouen was established as a military stronghold in 1471 by Sherif Moulay Ali bin Rachid. Considered the patron saint of the fierce Djeballa tribes of the surrounding Rif mountains, he claimed a direct descent from the founder of the Idrissid dynasty. His intention was to block any further expansion inland by Spanish and Portuguese troops, whose coastal fortresses were becoming increasingly powerful.

Soon after its founding, the city was reinforced by large numbers of Muslims and Jews exiled from Spanish Andalusia, Catalonia, and Murcia by the Christians, an event that brought to the city much of the architectural beauty and planning which is still noticeable today. The neighborhood where the newcomers settled still bears a memory of its origins in its name, Rif el Andalous.

Before the 1920s, only three Christians had ever seen the inside of the town. Disguised as a rabbi, Charles de Foucault (as part of a cartographical expedition sponsored by the French government) paid a clandestine visit to Chaouen in 1883; Walter Harris, the famous Tangier-based correspondent for the London *Times*, saw it in 1889; and an American missionary, William Summers, was poisoned after abortively trying to spread the gospel in 1892.

In 1920, an occupying Spanish expeditionary force took over the town in an almost bloodless coup. The Europeans were welcomed, ironically, as liberators by the descendants of Jews who had been forcibly ejected 400 years previously from Andalusia. (Despite almost no contact with Spain in the previous 400 years, these Jews still spoke a Spanish dialect that had been popular in Andalusia in the late 1400s.)

The Spaniards, who by now considered the region around Chaouen the most difficult of any to subdue, were evicted from the city in 1924 during a major rebellion against them. They returned to Chaouen two years later, and held it firmly until their eventual withdrawal from the region in 1958.

WHAT TO SEE & DO

The **Medina of Chaouen** is considered one of the most charming in Morocco, thanks largely to the aesthetic sense of the Andalusian émigrés who left their imprint on the architecture of the city. It is more lavishly adorned than any other medina in Morocco with horseshoe arches, jutting arcades, bay windows, elaborate cornices, porches, and wrought-iron grilles.

Because of the impossibly narrow and unmarked streets of the Medina, all of Chaouen's attractions should be visited on foot. Park in place el Makhzen, on the easternmost edge of the Medina. Admire from afar the minaret of the local mosque and the many shops. Walk a brief distance due west, and reach place Uta el Hammam. Its chief monument is the **Grand Mosque,** which you cannot enter, and the stalls of the souk that ring its edges. At number 34, the wooden doors of an enormous gate are usually propped open to reveal the small stalls of an old caravanserai where merchants from other regions of the country could find shelter for the night for themselves and their beasts.

Also leading onto the place Uta el Hammam is the entrance to the **Kasbah.** You'll probably have to tip the guardian to enter the Kasbah, where a garden and a view of former prisons will await you. Prisoners, chained by the neck to iron rings embedded in the walls, would languish for months or years at the whim of the sultans who ruled here.

WHERE TO STAY & EAT
MODERATE

HOTEL ASMA, Sidi Abdelhamid (without number), Chaouen. Tel. 098/ 60-02. 94 rms (all with bath). TEL **Transportation:** Grand taxi.
$ **Rates:** 200 DH ($25) single; 400 DH ($50) double. Breakfast 31 DH ($3.90) extra. AE, DC, MC, V.

Built in the late 1970s north of the center of town, this hotel was named after one of the daughters of King Hassan II. It enjoys a sweeping view of both the mountains and the Medina. Each of the four floors contains well-furnished and comfortable bedrooms. Amenities include a swimming pool, a bar, two tearooms, and a good restaurant on the second floor. The hotel is part of the Kasbah Tours chain.

HOTEL CHAOUEN, place el Makhzen (without number), Chaouen. Tel. 098/61-36. 37 rms (all with bath). TEL

$ Rates: 260 DH ($32.50) single; 400 DH ($50) double. Breakfast 31 DH ($3.90) extra. AE, DC, MC, V.

Once part of a government parador, it is now part of the Maroc-Tourist chain. In the center, directly east of the Kasbah, it has rooms that are well kept. A Continental breakfast is served, with croissants fresh from the town's baker. The hotel also has a swimming pool. You can enjoy a Moroccan dinner for 105 DH ($13.15).

4. ASILAH

29 miles S of Tangier; 25 miles N of Larache

GETTING THERE   By Train   Asilah is the first stop on the Tangier train to Rabat. There are 7 trains daily from Tangier, taking 55 minutes. The station is a mile north of town.

By Bus   Seven buses run daily between Asilah and Tangier, taking 1 hour.

By Car   Take the main P2 highway running south from Tangier to Rabat, turning off when you see the signpost to Asilah.

ESSENTIALS   Orientation   There are buses from the train station to the center of town. If you miss the bus while trying to get your luggage, you can take one of the grands taxis into the center for 10 DH ($1.25). Buses deposit you right off the place Mohammed V, from where you can walk to all the attractions of town. In town, you can find taxis at place Mohammed V, across from the bus depot.

Information   There is no tourist office in Asilah, but the town is small enough so you can find your way around rather easily.

Fast Facts   The **area code** for Asilah is 091. For a pharmacy, try **Pharmacie Loukilli,** av. de la Liberté (without number) (tel. 72-78), which is about a block from place Mohammed V, opposite the police station—**Service de Police** (tel. 19).

SPECIAL EVENTS   The **International Festival of Music and Culture** in July or August; first organized in 1978 by Ravi Shankar and Keith Jarrett. The pop-art ornamentation painted onto the houses of the Medina then became well known (but not necessarily approved of) throughout Morocco.

Asilah, population 16,000, is midway between Larache and Tangier, with a reputation for producing large amounts of fish (especially tuna) from its position along the Atlantic coast southwest of Tangier.

The souk at Asilah is held every Thursday, and is noteworthy for attracting farmers and tribesmen from the surrounding region, who even today sell vegetables and live poultry (from wicker baskets), and dress in the distinctive loosely flowing burnooses and cassocks of the region, with oversized straw hats.

Founded by Phoenician mariners who used it as a harbor and trading post, Asilah, during the era of the Mauretanian Berber kings (i.e., pre-Roman), was one of the few city-states of North Africa to mint its own coins. The name of the city, which was at that time either Silus or Zili, depending on how you translate it, was inscribed on each coin in the Carthaginian alphabet.

During the Roman occupation, Asilah chose the wrong alliance in a confrontation between Bogud (a Mauretanian Berber) and the Roman emperor Octavian. To punish the city, the Romans deported each of the town's occupants to slavery in their colonies in Spain. In their place, the Romans transferred an entirely new set of colonials from Iberia, among them some retired centurions.

After the fall of the Roman Empire, Asilah was conquered by the Idrissid Muslims, members of Morocco's first dynasty, and its population of Romanized Berbers was Islamized. By the 1100s, its fortunes had declined so much that Islamic sources cited Asilah as a small hamlet with no commercial or military importance.

In 1306, the neighboring port of Ceuta became important as one of the administrative headquarters of the Merenid caliphs. Commerce grew and the Christian powers of Europe recognized the value of an active commerce with the Islamic world.

Jealously, Portugal and Spain jockeyed for influence. In 1471, an enormous flotilla of almost 500 Portuguese ships and 30,000 Portuguese soldiers invaded Asilah and conquered it. They immediately built the ramparts that still surround the city today.

A century later, the Portuguese used Asilah as the embarkation point for a disastrous crusade against "the infidels." Isolated at the extreme western end of Europe, and blocked from expanding their borders eastward by an increasingly powerful Spain, they saw North Africa as ripe for Portuguese expansionism. King Sebastian I, heading an army of 20,000 soldiers, was overwhelmingly defeated (and killed), his soldiers enslaved, and his royal officers held for one of the most expensive ransoms in Islamic history. The Portuguese treasury went bankrupt several years later, partly as a result of paying these ransoms, leading to an annexation of Portugal by Spain. Along with many other territories received by Spain during this complicated process was Asilah.

A century later, in the late 1600s, the Spanish abandoned Asilah to sultans of the Saadian dynasty after much bloodshed. In 1829, the city was heavily bombarded by seaborne artillery of Habsburg Austria, in an unsuccessful attempt to wipe out pirates who used Asilah as a base of operations. In 1860, the city was again bombarded, this time by the Spanish.

Asilah remained in Moroccan control until around 1920, when the last of the brigands and pirates were ejected by the Spaniards. Among its most famous occupants was the famous highwayman of 19th-century Moroccan history, Raisuli.

In the early 1920s, Asilah fell under the Spanish Protectorate until the independence of Morocco in 1956.

WHAT TO SEE & DO

You can reach the old town via avenue Hassan II, which is noteworthy for its encircling ramparts, built by the Portuguese during the 1400s.

Asilah's well-preserved **Medina,** with its narrow streets and alleyways, has wrought-iron accents, a legacy of both medieval Andalusia and the Spanish occupation. The Medina is accessible via three different gates—La Porte de la Kasbah, La Porte de la Mer (Bab el Bahar), and the most formal of all, Bab Homar. Bab Homar is capped with Portuguese coats of arms, which have been almost completely eradicated by erosion.

Many of the town's buildings are painted blue and white, in keeping with the colors often chosen in the north of Morocco. The wide sandy beaches that lie near the base of the Medina's fortifications are occasionally used by bathers, as well as by local fishermen for mooring their boats. It is possible to climb to many panoramic aeries along these ancient fortifications for sweeping views over the Medina and the coast.

The city's most famous building is not particularly noteworthy from an architectural point of view. The legends surrounding its builder are much more famous than the building itself. Constructed around 1900, it is known simply as the **Palais de Raisuli.** Used today as a small and underfinanced cultural center, with unpredictable hours and venues, it lies in the center of the densely narrow streets of the Medina.

WHERE TO STAY

INEXPENSIVE

**HOTEL OUED EL MAKHAZINE, av. de Melilla (without number), Asilah.
Tel. 091/7090.** 29 rms (all with bath). A/C **Transportation:** Petit taxi.
$ Rates: 125 DH ($15.65) single; 150 DH ($18.75) double. Breakfast 15 DH ($1.90) extra. No credit cards.

The best in town, near the beach, it has air conditioning, although rooms are a bit small (with tiny windows). Furnishings are done in functional modern, and the hotel is clean, offering reasonable comfort. Most rooms open onto a view of the sea. There is also a bar.

WHERE TO EAT
MODERATE

LA ALCAZABA, place Zallach, 2. Tel. 70-12.
 Cuisine: SEAFOOD. **Reservations:** Recommended.
 $ Prices: Appetizers 10–28 DH ($1.25–$3.50); main dishes 25–65 DH ($3.15–$8.15). MC, V.
 Open: Lunch daily 12:30–3pm; dinner daily 7:30–11pm. **Closed:** Nov–Mar.

Near the Portuguese tower, beneath the ramparts at the ocean end of the square, this is the most famous restaurant along the coast west of Tangier. For many years, it was operated by Lord Churchill, who built up a following among expatriate patrons from Tangier who would drive down to Asilah just to dine here. Although the emphasis is on seafood, the preparation is often either Italian or Spanish. Lobster is a specialty, and it's also the most expensive item on the menu. Try *gambas* (prawns) *à la plancha,* hot from the grill, or *calamares* (squid). You can begin with a freshly made soup or else a salad. Other dishes include spaghetti and veal scaloppine. There is a terrace with a view of the sea.

AN EASY EXCURSION

Nineteen miles southwest of Asilah, and reached by grand taxi, lies what is considered the most important megalithic monument in North Africa. The **Cromlech de Msoura** is a small-scale and very ruined version of England's Stonehenge, originally built around 2000 B.C. Approximately 200 roughly dressed stone columns are arranged in a circle around a circular funerary mound about 150 feet in diameter. Its exact function remains a mystery. By no means should you attempt to find this monument without the assistance of a guide.

To reach it, drive 14 miles from Asilah in the direction of Larache. After an unmarked hamlet named Souk Tnine de Sidi el Yamani, turn north off the highway onto a gravel-and-sand road, for an additional 4 miles in the direction of Douar Msoura. Entrance is free, other than a tip that might be solicited by a local guide and guardian. The site can be visited daily from 9am to 5pm.

5. LARACHE (EL ARAÏCH)

25 miles W of Asilah; 54 miles W of Tangier

GETTING THERE By Train There are 7 trains daily from Tangier to Rabat with a stop at Asilah. From Asilah, continue the rest of the way to Larache by bus (see below).

By Bus Five buses daily run between Asilah and Larache, taking 1 hour. If you're at Rabat, there are 4 daily connections to Larache, taking 3½ hours.

By Car From Tangier, take the P2 south, or from Rabat take the P2 north to Tangier, turning off at Larache.

ESSENTIALS The area code for Larache is 091.

Larache, whose Arabic name is El Araïch, with a population of 45,000, is an area of myriad fruit trees, which thrive in its rich soil and abundant sunlight. It has a factory for the processing and bottling of fruit juice, and also for packing fresh fruit to ship to Europe and elsewhere.

Until the construction of Casablanca by the French in the early 1900s, Larache was the most important (and the best) natural port along the Atlantic coast of Morocco. Although most of the international shipping of Fez and Meknes is now exported through Casablanca, Larache remains an important fishing port.

Under the ancient Roman regime, when Larache was called Lixus, it lay on the ancient Roman road that linked Tingis (Tangier) with Sala Colonia (Rabat). Its site was always associated with the heroic exploits of Hercules. It was at Lixus that Hercules accomplished the deed that earned him a permanent place on Mount Olympus—the harvesting of the golden apples of the Garden of the Hesperides.

WHAT TO SEE & DO

Larache is divided into roughly three different sections, including the Medina and the European-inspired new town (both of which were built on a hilltop overlooking the port), as well as the commercial dockyards at the edge of the sea.

The new town's principal avenue is **boulevard Mohammed V,** which is flanked on either side with lush and lovely gardens. The border between the new town and the Medina is the circular showcase, **place de la Libération.** Designed in the Spanish style, with a formal fountain in its center, it is lined at its edges with cafés and their terraces.

The medieval **Kasbah** of the town lies outside the Medina and, sadly, is almost completely in ruins.

The main gateway leading from place de la Libération to the center of the Medina is the **Bab el Khémis** (translated as "Thursday's Gate," because Thursday was the traditional market day at Larache). Another famous gate is the **Bab el Kasba,** which lies at the opposite end of the Medina.

Between the two gates lies a colorful maze of commerce and Muslim culture, whose souks specialize in clothes, fabrics, and foodstuffs. The headquarters of this area is called the **Socco de la Alcaicería** (Souk of the Cloth), nicknamed the **Socco Chico.** Large and bordered with arched arcades, it's considered one of the most beautiful souks in Morocco.

Encircling the Medina is an uninterrupted tall and thick **rampart.** Although you cannot enter the Medina's mosque, its terraces offer a good view of the surrounding valley of the Loukkos, a site believed by the ancient Greeks and Romans to have contained the mythical Garden of the Hesperides.

At the edge of the Medina stands a Hispano-Moorish building erected by the Spanish in 1915, which today serves as the Moroccan National Academy of Music. Nearby is a tiny **archeological museum,** open Wednesday through Sunday from 9am to noon and 3 to 5:30pm. Admission is free.

Also important is the imposing fortress known variously as the **Château de la Cigogne, Castillo de las Ciguenas, Castle of the Swan,** or **Al Fath,** a forbidding monument with angular crenellations that was ordered built by Moulay Ahmed al Manwour in 1578. The workmen were Christian slaves, most of them captured during the ill-advised Portuguese crusade.

Jean Genet, the great French writer, famous for such plays as *The Blacks, The Balcony,* and *Deathwatch,* and for his masterpiece, *Our Lady of the Flowers,* was a sometime resident of Larache. Sentenced to life imprisonment for theft in 1948, he was pardoned on petition by French writers. Fans of the author make a literary pilgrimage to his grave site (you'll need a guide to show you the way) in the Spanish graveyard directly to the south of Larache. Go by grand or petit taxi. Do not walk through the slums on the southern outskirts to reach it.

WHERE TO STAY & EAT

MODERATE

HOTEL RIAD, rue Mohammed ben Abdallah (without number), Larache. Tel. 091/26-26. 24 rms (all with bath). TEL
$ **Rates** (including half board, which is required): 300 DH ($37.50) single; 400 DH ($50) double. MC, V.

(S) The former vacation home that the duchess of Guise, mother of the pretender to the throne of France, built between 1920 and 1924, it lies midway between the Rond Point du Centre-Ville and the CTM bus terminal in the town center (not the Medina). The duchess eventually died here, and later her home was turned into a hotel set in a garden. The Hispano-Moorish–style house is built as a two-story square, with an open interior space set with stones and tiles. Surrounding the house are four separate bungalows set in the 5-acre garden, ringed with fruit trees (especially orange). The hotel prides itself on the fresh fish served here. Rooms are comfortably furnished, and a few have private terraces. Facilities include a restaurant, a tennis court, and a swimming pool with a ring-around terrace.

AN EASY EXCURSION

(★) The ancient Roman ruins of **Lixus** are 3 miles from Larache, to the left of the road leading northeast to Tangier. They include about a dozen ruined buildings in the lower (southern) extremities of the town, closest to the main highway to Tangier. They were devoted 2000 years ago to the production of *garum* and salted fish.

The site, known for its carefully chiseled pre-Roman foundations and defenses, today houses an inconspicuous Berber village known as Tchemmich. Among its ruins are a circular Roman amphitheater where wild animals battled one another. Other monuments include an acropolis, a bathhouse, at least five temples, and an array of unidentified buildings.

Much of what we know about the excavations at ancient Lixus was the result of the tireless efforts of German-born archeologist Heinrich Barth, an African specialist from the mid-1800s. Most of the objects unearthed at Lixus are today exhibited at the archeological museum at Tetuán. The site is open during daylight hours, and plenty of guides are always available.

CHAPTER 5

RABAT, CASABLANCA & THE ATLANTIC COAST

- **WHAT'S SPECIAL ABOUT RABAT, CASABLANCA & THE ATLANTIC COAST**
- **SUGGESTED ITINERARY**
1. **RABAT**
2. **CASABLANCA**
3. **ESSAOUIRA**

I f Dickens had written about Rabat and Casablanca, he might have called his yarn *A Tale of Two Cities*. So close together, they are yet so far apart—much like London and Paris.

Rabat, the center of government and the residence of King Hassan II, wasn't always the capital of the country. For a thousand years, that position was occupied by Fez or Marrakesh, even Meknes. Until the beginning of the 20th century, Rabat was a small, insignificant town at the mouth of the Bou Regreg River.

Casablanca, to the south of Rabat, was an old city, its lackluster history stretching back some seven centuries. Mainly it was just a trading post, visited either by the Portuguese or the Spanish.

Today, the situation has changed. Rabat is now the seat of political power, an attractive, well-ordered, and, to some, even a "manicured" city. Casablanca, on the other hand, is the country's leading commercial and industrial center. As Morocco's largest city, it is home to millions, many of whom live in shanties in their search for a better life.

After visiting Rabat and Casablanca in the north, you may want to continue your trip along the Atlantic coast south in the directions of Agadir. The best place for a stopover along the way is the small port of Essaouira, peopled with Berbers. This white-walled town with sandy beaches is a popular summer vacation town today, but its history goes back thousands of years, to an era when chemicals excreted by its shellfish produced the royal-purple dyes so favored by the imperial Roman emperors.

SEEING RABAT, CASABLANCA & THE ATLANTIC COAST

GETTING THERE

Casablanca is the gateway to this Atlantic coast region. It is the city where the only direct flights from North America (on Royal Air Maroc) land. If you're in Marrakesh,

WHAT'S SPECIAL ABOUT RABAT, CASABLANCA & THE ATLANTIC COAST

Great Towns/Cities

☐ Casablanca, the beloved "Casa" to millions of Moroccans—foreigners tend to love it or hate it.

☐ Salé, outside Rabat, former haunt of pirates, sultans, and various rogues, with memories of glory in the Middle Ages.

☐ Rabat, the capital of Morocco since independence, with much of historical and architectural interest.

Ace Attractions

☐ The Kasbah des Oudaïa at Rabat, a "Spanish village" created long ago by Andalusian refugees, containing Moulay Ismail's former palace.

Monuments

☐ The Necropolis of Chellah outside Rabat, the most beautiful of Morocco's ruins.

☐ The Bab Oudaïa at Rabat, built by the Almohad dynasty around 1195—the most beautiful gate in the Moorish world.

Beaches

☐ The beach of Essaouira stretching for miles toward Cape Sim—fine sands and safe swimming (if sometimes too windy).

☐ The long beach at El Jadida, most popular of the central Atlantic resorts of Morocco.

Tangier, Fez, or some other Moroccan city, you can also reach Casablanca and Rabat by train or the more uncomfortable bus (not recommended for long hauls). When you head south from Casablanca, you'll find no rail links. The only public transportation to such Atlantic resorts as El Jadida and Essaouira is by bus.

SUGGESTED ITINERARY

Day 1: Spend the day visiting the attractions of Rabat, its Kasbah, Medina, and Chellah ruins.

Day 2: Take the early-morning walking tour (see below) of Salé, a suburb of Rabat, and drive or take rail or bus to Casablanca in the afternoon. Spend the night.

Day 3: While still based in Casablanca, take a morning's excursion to El Jadida. Return along the coast for a look at the Mosque of Hassan II (from the outside only) and have dinner at one of the seafood restaurants of Aïn Diab. Stay overnight in Casablanca.

Day 4: Journey south to Essaouira for the night and explore its attractions. Spend whatever time remains on the beach.

1. RABAT

124 miles W of Fez; 171 miles S of Tangier;
200 miles W of Marrakesh

GETTING THERE   By Plane   The **airport at Rabat-Salé** (tel. 322-96) is connected to most major Moroccan cities on Royal Air Maroc or Air Inter flights. There are daily flights from Casablanca (½ hour), but the distance is so short that many visitors prefer to go overland. There are also daily planes from Marrakesh (2½ hours). For most international connections, the airport at Casablanca is used. Six

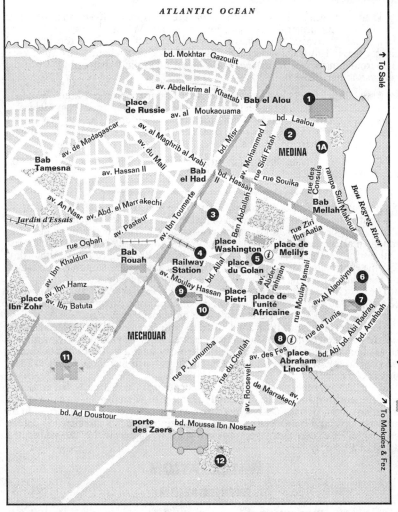

ATLANTIC OCEAN

RABAT

→ To Salé

bd. Mokhtar Gazoulit

av. Abdelkrim al Khattab **Bab el Alou** ❶

place de Russie

av. al Moukaouama

bd. Laalou

av. al Maghrib al Arabi

av. de Madagascar

av. du Mali

❷

MEDINA ❶A

rampa Sidi Makhlouf

bd. Misr

av. Mohammed V

rue Sidi Fatah

rue Souika

rue des Consuls

Bou Regreg River

→ To Salé

Bab Tamesna

av. Hassan II

Bab el Had

bd. Hassan II

Bab Mellah

av. An Nasr av. Abd. el Marrakechi

av. Pasteur

av. Ibn Toumerte

❸

rue Ziri Ibn Aatia

Jardin d'Essais

rue Oqbah

Bab Rouah

❹

place Washington ⓘ ❺

place de Melilys

av. Ibn Khaldun

av. Ibn Hamz

Railway Station

bd. Allal

place du Golan

av. Abder-rahman

rue Moulay Ismail

av. Al Alaouiyne ❻

av. Moulay Hassan ❾

❼

place Ibn Zohr av. Ibn Batuta

❿

place Pietri

place de l'unité Africaine

rue de Tunis

bd. Arrahbah

MECHOUAR

rue P. Lumumba

rue du Chellah

❽ ⓘ

place Abraham Lincoln

bd. Abi bd. Abi Radraq

av. des Fes

⓫

av. Roosevelt

av. de Marrakech

→ To Meknes & Fez

bd. Ad Doustour

porte des Zaers

bd. Moussa Ibn Nossair

City Walls

Information ⓘ

⓬

MOROCCO

Rabat

Marrakesh

Grand Mosque ❾
Kasbah des Oudaïa ❶
Mausoleum of Mohammed V ❼
Medina ❷
Moroccan National Tourist Office ❽
Musée Archéologique ❿ (Museum of Antiquities)

Museum of Oudaïa ❶A
Necropolis of Chellah ⓬
Post Office ❸
Royal Palace ⓫
Syndicat d'Initiative ❺
Tower of Hassan ❻
Train Station ❹

buses a day depart from Rabat Airport heading for Casablanca's Mohammed V International Airport, where connections abroad are made.

By Train   Reaching Rabat by train is the preferred method. The train station is right in the city center, at the junction of avenue Moulay Youssef and avenue Mohammed V. Arrivals are almost hourly from Casablanca, the trip taking 50 minutes. Seven daily trains service Rabat from Marrakesh (5½ hours). Five trains a day arrive from Tangier (4½ hours). For **train information** in Rabat, call ONCF at the train station (tel. 723-85).

By Bus   Buses from Casablanca arrive every 2 hours; trip time: 1 hour. Two daily buses connect Rabat with Tangier (5 hours). Three buses a day arrive from Meknes (4 hours), and there are 6 buses a day from Fez (5½ hours). The bus station (for **information,** tel. 751-24) is at route de Casablanca, place Mohammed Zerktouni. You can take an intercity bus or a *petit taxi* to the city center.

By Car   From Tangier, head south on route P2; from Casablanca, head north on express highway S-222.

─────────────

As the current capital of Morocco, Rabat is the primary home of King Hassan II, who maintains elaborate palaces in the other Imperial Cities as well. Once known as the Camp of Victory, Rabat today is essentially a modern city of gardens and monumental gateways. The third-largest city in Morocco, it lies on the Atlantic coast northeast of Casablanca, separated from Salé by the Bou Regreg River. Although it lacks the exotic allure of Fez or Marrakesh, I find it a rewarding stopover, especially if you take time to visit its much more colorful twin city of Salé.

The most interesting parts of Rabat are the Kasbah and the Medina, both of which are bounded on two sides by the sea and the brackish river. Along the other sides run high walls, pierced at strategic intervals with monumental gateways.

The streets of these districts are devoted to both commercial and residential uses, and are peppered with many Andalusian-inspired gardens. Outside the Kasbah and the Medina, most of the streets of the modern city form a gridwork of boulevards, and contain sidewalk cafés and modern buildings much like those found in some corners of France.

More than any other city in Morocco except perhaps Casablanca, Rabat exudes an air of efficiently organized scheduling and adherence to Western administrative values. Its citizens wear Western clothes more than in any other city in Morocco, and its businesspeople and bureaucrats seem much more hurried. Its monumental core is verdant, and its government buildings are suitably impressive for the undisputed capital of a country.

ORIENTATION

INFORMATION

Go to the **Syndicat d'Initiative,** rue Patrice Lumumba (without number) (tel. 07/232-72), open Monday through Friday from 8am to 7pm. For information about Morocco, go to the **Moroccan National Tourist Office,** rue el-Jazair, 22 (tel. 07/212-52), open in summer Monday through Friday from 8am to 2:30pm, the rest of the year Monday through Friday from 8:30am to noon and 2:30 to 6:30pm.

FAST FACTS

Area Code   07.

Bookstore   The **American Bookstore,** rue Tanja, 4 (tel. 610-16), is open Monday through Friday from 9:30am to 12:30pm and 2:30 to 6:30pm, on Saturday from 10am to 1pm.

Car Rental   These are arranged at **Hertz,** av. Mohammed V, 467 (tel. 692-27), or **Avis,** Zankat, 7 (tel. 697-59).

Currency Exchange   In the lobby of the **Hotel de la Tour Hassan,** rue de Chellah, 22 (tel. 214-01), there is a small branch of the BMCE, a national bank, open Monday through Friday from 8am to noon and 3 to 7pm, on Saturday and Sunday from 9am to 3pm.

Drugstore   The best is **Pharmacie du Chellah,** place de Melilia (without number) (tel. 247-23), open Monday through Friday from 9am to 12:30pm and 3 to 7:30pm, on Saturday from 3 to 7:30pm. When this pharmacy is closed and you need an emergency prescription, call 261-50 to find out which pharmacy in town is open. Pharmacies stay open at night on a rotational system.

Embassies and Consulates   In Rabat, the **U.S. Embassy** is at av. de Marrakesh, 2 (tel. 622-65). The consular section is open Monday through Friday from 8:30am to 5:30pm. The **United Kingdom Embassy** is at bd. de la Tour Hassan, 17 (tel. 209-05). Citizens of **Australia** and **New Zealand** go to the British Embassy, open Monday through Friday from 8am to 2pm. The **Canadian Embassy** is at Joafar Essadik Agday, 13 (tel. 713-76), open Monday through Friday from 8am to 2pm.

Emergencies   Your hotel staff will probably run to your aid in a genuine emergency. Otherwise, for an **ambulance** call 15; for the **police,** 19; and to report a **fire,** 15.

Hospital   The **Hôpital Avicenne,** av. Ibn Sina (without number) (tel. 744-11), lies in the Souissi section. Emergency treatment is rendered here. U.S. or British citizens seeking an English-speaking doctor can call their respective embassies (see above).

Laundry   Try **Rabat Pressing,** av. Hassan II, 67 (tel. 263-610), at Allal ben Abdallah, open Monday through Saturday from 8am to 12:30pm and 2:30 to 7:30pm. Most hotels will do laundry at a reasonable price.

Library   The **George Washington Library** av. el Fahs, 35 (tel. 507-88), near the Hopital Avicenne, has a collection of English-language newspapers and magazines, and is open daily from 10am to noon and 4 to 6pm.

Luggage Storage   Go to the train station (see above). Make sure your luggage is securely locked. The charge is 3 DH (40¢) per piece.

Police   The **Rabat Police Station** is located on rue Soekarno (tel. 19), about two blocks from the Rabat Post Office, lying off the main artery, avenue Mohammed V.

Post Office   The **Rabat Post Office** is found on avenue Mohammed V (tel. 207-31) near its junction with rue Soekarno. It is open Monday through Friday from 8am to 3:30pm in summer, Monday through Friday from 8:30am to noon and 2 to 6:30pm the rest of the year.

Taxis   Dial 205-18 or 303-11.

WHAT TO SEE & DO

THE MEDINA

Located adjacent to the southern edge of the Kasbah (see below), and bordered by boulevard Hassan II and avenue Misr, the Medina is the commercial and residential nerve center of Rabat. It has been likened to a medieval Andalusian town with its labyrinth of narrow streets, numerous mosques, and endless array of markets selling anything and everything. At its eastern edge, near the river, is the Mellah, which until recently was the almost exclusive domain of the city's Jews.

The Medina was originally settled by Muslims and Jews driven out of Spain by the Catholic monarchs. In memory of their homeland, in the 17th century they erected the Muraille des Andalous (Wall of the Andalusians). In those days, Rabat stretched from this wall north and west to the edges of the ancient Almohad wall.

Running along the eastern edge of the Medina is rue des Consuls (or rue Ouqqasa), at one time the required address for all foreigners and diplomats. This street overlooks the brackish, shallow river, and separates the Medina's Grand Mosque from the Mellah.

Also in the Medina is the Mechouar, the rigidly impenetrable grounds of the Royal

Palace, where King Hassan II lives. Nearby are the barracks of his soldier guards, including the all-black battalions made up of descendants of African slaves.

THE KASBAH DES OUDAÏA

✪ North of the commercial center of Rabat and across the river from Salé, above the western bank of the Bou Regreg River on the highest plateau of Rabat, sits the Kasbah des Oudaïa, former home of sultans, slaves, and pirates. Its 28-foot-high, 10-foot-thick walls were built in the 12th century by the Almohad dynasty, and later heavily fortified.

The Kasbah's most prominent entrance is the famous **Bab Oudaïa,** on the western edge. Carefully chiseled out of ocher-colored stone, this gate is considered the crowning achievement of the Almohad dynasty. Young men wait here to offer their services as guides to visitors.

The gate leads to an inner garden, designed in 1915 and richly planted with orange trees. Bougainvillea drapes the walls, and storks nest on top of the crenellated and crumbling battlements. After strolling through the gardens, stop off at the Le Café Maure, with its view over the river and the battlements of Salé.

In addition to wandering the Kasbah's alleyways, you can also visit the Muslim cemetery near its main entrance and a number of shops set within its confines. There are also a number of famous museums in the Kasbah (see below).

THE MUSEUM OF OUDAÏA, rue Bazzo (without number), Kasbah des Oudaïa. Tel. 315-37.

Reached from the Kasbah's main entrance, the Bab Oudaïa (turn right along rue Bazzo and head south within the confines of the ramparts), is one of Morocco's legendary museums. Housed within a small-scale palace that was originally built between 1672 and 1694 for the personal use of Moulay Ismail, it is flanked on its southern side with gardens, and capped with the minaret.

The building contains arcades, an elegantly symmetrical central courtyard, and a small mosque. Inside, you'll find exhibits that feature antique embroideries, Moroccan ceramics, masses of jewelry, antique and very valuable Rabat carpets, sculpted cedar chests, antique musical instruments, and a section devoted entirely to folkloric dress of the nearby region. One tableau depicts a Berber wedding ceremony, another shows the dress of the tribal inhabitants of the High Atlas. Although they are usually not on display, the museum also contains some of the oldest and rarest Koranic texts in Morocco.

Admission: 10 DH ($1.25).

Open: Wed–Mon 9–11:30am and 3–6pm. **Bus:** 2, 3, 14, or 34, then walk along the Rampe de La Douane.

TOWER OF HASSAN/MAUSOLEUM OF MOHAMMED V, av. Abi Regreg (without number).

The Tower of Hassan (Tour Hassan) is the minaret of a mosque that was built on the orders of the Almohad sultan in 1184. At the time, it was meant as a preface to what would have been the largest mosque in the Islamic world—large enough, according to legend, to have housed the entire Almohad army. Intended to rival the splendor of the Giralda in Seville, it was completely abandoned on the day of the sultan's death in 1199. Only the tower (which long ago became the symbol of the city) had been completed. The complex was raided over the remaining centuries for building materials. Finally, the 1755 earthquake that devastated Lisbon did further damage. A nearby platform, reached by ascending a ramp, offers a panoramic view over the rooftops of neighboring Salé.

At the eastern edge of the mausoleum is the carefully guarded Mausoleum of Mohammed V, father of Moroccan independence. (See "History" in Chapter 1.) Completed 10 years after his death, in 1971, it is one of the country's most impressive 20th-century buildings and is considered a masterpiece of grandly imposing Moroccan classicism. Its architect was a Vietnamese, Vo Toan. Within its interior are a mosque, a series of arcades, acres of white Italian marble, and the actual sarcophagus of the monarch, crafted from a single enormous block of white Pakistani onyx. Set at right angles to the sarcophagus is the burial place of one of the monarch's sons, Moulay Abdallah, who died in 1983. An arcade of white Carrara marble leads to a small museum chronicling the history of the Alaouite dynasty and the monarch who led his country to independence.

Admission: Free.

Open: Interior of tower not open to the public; mausoleum, open daily in summer 8am–10pm, daily in winter 8am–8pm. **Directions:** By petit taxi, go along avenue Abi Regreg, near Pont Moulay Hassan, toward Salé.

MUSÉE ARCHÉOLOGIQUE (THE MUSEUM OF ANTIQUITIES), Zankat al Brihi (without number). Tel. 622-31.

This museum houses one of the richest troves of archeological treasures in Morocco. Located two blocks east of one of the modern city's most prominent squares, place Jamaa Assouma, it contains a reproduction of a geometrical mosaic floor extracted from the ruins of Volubilis, as well as a statue of Ptolemy, son of Juba II and grandson of Cleopatra of Egypt, who was assassinated in Rome by Caligula. The museum is rich in prehistoric relics and art remnants from the Roman, Christian, and Islamic eras of Moroccan history.

Admission: 10 DH ($1.25).

Open: Wed–Mon 9am–noon and 2–6pm. **Bus:** 3.

NECROPOLIS OF CHELLAH

Located a quarter mile southeast of the city ramparts, beside the estuary of the Bou Regreg River, Chellah was the last Roman city (Sala Colonia) created along the Atlantic coast of Morocco. It sits alone on the opposite side of the valley from the 12th-century ramparts that surround King Hassan's palace. A single access road leads from one of Rabat's busiest traffic arteries, boulevard Moussa Ibn Nossair, to its only entrance, which is set into its western rampart.

The area inside its massive walls was used from the 1300s on as a cemetery for the unpretentious graves and mausoleums of many of the Moroccan aristocracy. The cemetery also contains a small mosque whose minaret was at one time capped with a stork's nest, plus the remains of an ancient Roman bath and two ancient villas. Vegetation is lush, partly because of the streams that bubble their way to a number of fountains. The place is one of the strangest, and most hauntingly memorable, in Morocco.

Once, non-Muslims were not allowed through the ornate gateway, but today that has changed. Richly decorated, it was completed by Abou el Hassan in 1339.

Admission: Free; tip appreciated.

Open: Wed–Mon 8am–8pm. **Bus:** 4.

WHERE TO STAY

Always arrive in Rabat with a confirmed reservation. Since it is the administrative center of Morocco, and a frequent venue for various conferences, its hotels fill up suddenly. In summer, when much of this business fades, package-tour-group parties often arrive en masse, so space is tight.

Prestigious visitors always stay at the Rabat Hyatt Regency and the Safir Rabat, which are the best hotels in town. After that, the hotels are unremarkable, but are generally clean and comfortable. Most of them remain very reasonable in price.

Hotels rated "Very Expensive" charge from 1,550 to 1,950 DH ($193.75 to $243.75) for a double room; those ranked "Expensive" charge from 620 to 940 DH ($77.50 to $117.50). Hotels considered "Moderate" average around 370 to 450 DH ($46.25 to $56.25) for a double room. "Inexpensive" suggests doubles in the 185 to 280 DH ($23.15 to $35) price range. All these prices are for rooms with private bath.

VERY EXPENSIVE

RABAT HYATT REGENCY, Souissi, Rabat. Tel. 07/712-34 (toll free 800/228-9000 in the U.S. and Canada). Fax 07/724-34. 220 rms (all with bath), 28 suites. A/C MINIBAR TV TEL **Transportation:** Grand taxi.

$ Rates: 1,550–1,950 DH ($193.75–$243.75) single or double; suites from 3,000 DH ($375). Breakfast 85 DH ($10.65) extra. AE, DC, MC, V.

When the Rabat Hyatt Regency opened in 1988, it was instantly recognized as one of the finest and most stylish hotels in Africa. Set in a 10-acre park whose forests border the edges of the Royal Palace, it boasts the second-largest capacity of any hotel in Morocco. Its postmodern façade of jet black with hot-pink accents contrasts with its lushly poetic Andalusian-inspired gardens in the rear. Public rooms, with much polished marble, include restaurants, bars, and other facilities.

Half of the comfortably upholstered bedrooms contain balconies overlooking the distant sea; the others open onto balconies overlooking the rear gardens. Each accommodation has a marble-sheathed private bath and a color scheme of either turquoise and blue or yellow and beige. The rooms on the seventh floor, the Regency Club, have upgraded accessories.

Dining/Entertainment: Justine's is the finest restaurant in Rabat, and the Oasis is a reasonably priced café and restaurant. See recommendations below for Justine's, El Andalous, and the Piccadilly Piano Bar.

Services: Room service, valet, laundry, massage, concierge, and business center with fax, teletype, secretarial, and multilingual translation services.

Facilities: A second-floor art gallery, with frequent expositions of new Moroccan artists; video movies and 16 in-house TV channels; a six-sided garden swimming pool and a children's swimming pool next to it; four tennis courts with instructors, rental equipment, and courtside bar and snack bar; a volleyball court; a three-hole pitch-and-putt golf minicourse, with a 175-yard driving range; discounted greens fees at the internationally famous 45-hole Dar es Salam golf course; jogging trails and paths through 10 miles of surrounding parklands; one of the most authentic Turkish-style *hammams* in Rabat, with attendants to scrub and massage clients; limousine service; and 10 different boutiques, with an adjacent tearoom.

EXPENSIVE

SAFIR RABAT, place Sidi Makhlouf (without number), Rabat. Tel. 07/72-64-31. Fax 07/31-64-14. 198 rms (all with bath); 8 suites. A/C MINIBAR TV TEL **Bus:** 16, 27, or 34.

$ Rates: 620 DH ($77.50) single; 700 DH ($87.50) double; suites from 2,000 DH ($250). Breakfast 50 DH ($6.25). AE, DC, MC, V.

This deluxe hotel is set high above the banks of the river that separates Rabat from Salé, a short walk north of the Tower of Hassan, which is visible at the end of a barren field. The Safir is designed a bit like a medieval fortress, and its monumental green-and-white-tiled entranceway evokes a majesty only rarely associated with a resort hotel. Inside are several cool rooms in white marble that radiate off courtyards, with painted ceilings and elaborately geometric mosaics. Since the place is a favorite with visiting tour groups, its facilities are frequently very crowded, a fact that detracts a bit from its architectural allure.

Originally built in 1982 as a French-owned Sofitel, and acquired in 1987 by the Moroccan-based Safir chain, it offers clean and functionally comfortable bedrooms, each decorated in a simplified Moroccan motif with a marble-trimmed bathroom.

Dining/Entertainment: Drinking and dining choices include El Mansour Restaurant, the Hanna coffee shop, and El Anbra (El Boustane) Restaurant.

Services: Concierge, currency exchange, hairdresser, travel agency, excursion arrangements.

Facilities: Car-rental office, gift shops, rooftop swimming pool with a sweeping view and nearby bar.

HOTEL DE LA TOUR HASSAN, bd. de Chellah, 22, Rabat. Tel. 07/214-

02. Fax 07/254-08. 165 rms (all with bath); 10 suites. MINIBAR TEL **Bus:** 5, 7, 9, or 17.

$ Rates: 520–760 DH ($65–$95) single; 620–940 DH ($77.50–$117.50) double; suites from 1,400 DH ($175). Breakfast 50 DH ($6.25) extra. AE, DC, MC, V.

Considered the most traditional and historic of the grand hotels of Rabat, it's set behind an Almohad-inspired façade whose intricate carvings and grand proportions might remind you of a private palace. You'll enter a lobby sheathed in white and blue tiles, with marble floors. Originally built in 1914 and enlarged in 1964, the hotel lies within a residential neighborhood near the Tower of Hassan. Despite the initial allure of this elegant and time-honored place, its bedrooms, while eminently respectable and proper, are sometimes awkwardly proportioned and not as luxurious as you might expect. Some contain air conditioning and TV. There is no swimming pool, but a garden within a courtyard provides its own appeal.

Dining/Entertainment: Two fine restaurants, La Couronne and El Mansour (see below), and an atmospheric bar (see below).

Services: Hairdresser, massage.

Facilities: Sauna, hammam (bath), access to nearby private tennis club, and Queen's Club disco/nightclub.

MODERATE

HOTEL OUDAYAS, rue de Tobrouk, 4, Rabat. Tel. 07/678-20. 35 rms (all with bath). **Bus:** 7 or 18.

$ Rates (including breakfast): 285 DH ($35.50) single; 383 DH ($47.90) double. MC, V.

Named after the elegant district of the city where it is located, this modern hotel with comfortable but Spartan bedrooms is one of the most dramatic establishments in the neighborhood. Some of the rooms open onto balconies. Its lobby, sheathed in a combination of black marble and beige stone, has a restrained French theme. The restaurant offers fixed-price meals for 105 DH ($13.15).

RABAT CHELLAH HOTEL, rue d'Ifni, 2, Rabat. Tel. 07/640-52. Fax 07/76-23-65. 120 rms (all with bath). A/C TV TEL **Bus:** 15 or 23.

$ Rates: 300 DH ($37.50) single; 368 DH ($46) double. Breakfast 31 DH ($3.90) extra. AE, DC, MC, V.

Because this hotel's entrance lies kitty-corner from the Royal Palace, you'll be able to gaze upon the green-tiled roofs of the king's residence. Well run, clean, and comfortable, the Rabat Chellah opened in 1972, but its copper-trimmed façade still looks fairly new. You register in a brick-floored lobby sheathed in elegantly crafted tilework. On the ground floor is an attractive bar, plus one of my favorite restaurants in town, the Kanoun Grill (see below).

INEXPENSIVE

HOTEL BALIMA, av. Mohammed V, 173, Rabat. Tel. 07/677-55. 71 rms (all with bath). TEL

$ Rates: 161 DH ($20.15) single; 217 DH ($27.15) double. Breakfast 23 DH ($2.90) extra. AE, DC, MC, V.

Built in 1932, across from the Moroccan Parliament, this hotel has an inviting tree-shaded courtyard filled with café and restaurant tables on its quieter side. Its official entrance lies along Rabat's major avenue in the commercial heart of the city. You register in a marble high-ceilinged lobby filled with lattices, battered furniture, art deco touches, and an allure that you might have found in colonial Cairo. The high-ceilinged bedrooms are clean and sunny, with old-fashioned baths. A fixed-priced meal is served in the restaurant (see below).

HOTEL D'ORSAY, av. Moulay Youssef, 11, Rabat. Tel. 07/613-19. 30 rms (all with bath). TEL **Bus:** 3 or 7.

$ Rates: 167 DH ($20.90) single; 209 DH ($26.10) double. Breakfast 23 DH ($2.90) extra. No credit cards.

S Close to the rail station of Rabat-Ville, this is a modern white-walled establishment with an art nouveau wrought-iron gate. The hotel has a TV lounge and clean, simply furnished accommodations, each with a shower. It was last renovated in 1984. The hotel serves breakfast, but has no restaurant.

HOTEL SHEHERAZADE, rue de Tunis, 21, Rabat. Tel. 07/222-26. 36 rms (all with bath). TEL **Bus:** 13, 14, 15, or 16.
$ Rates: 214 DH ($26.75) single; 280 DH ($35) double. Breakfast 23 DH ($2.90) extra. No credit cards.

The zigzagging façade of this modern hotel evokes the geometric designs of certain handmade Moroccan artifacts. Each bedroom has an angular bay window and comfortably upholstered furniture. For such a good hotel, the accommodations are moderately priced. Lunch and dinner are available for 83 DH ($10.40) each.

WHERE TO EAT

Restaurants rated "Very Expensive" charge from 150 to 310 DH ($18.75 to $38.75) for a meal, plus wine. Those listed as "Expensive" charge from 120 to 180 DH ($15 to $22.50) for a dinner; those listed as "Moderate," from 90 to 160 DH ($11.25 to $20); and those listed as "Inexpensive," from 40 to 80 DH ($5 to $10). Drinks are always extra.

VERY EXPENSIVE

EL ANDALOUS, Rabat Hyatt Regency, Souissi. Tel. 712-34.
Cuisine: MOROCCAN. **Reservations:** Required. **Transportation:** Grand taxi.
$ Prices: Appetizers 40–90 DH ($5–$11.25); main dishes 75–150 DH ($9.40–$18.75). AE, DC, MC, V.
Open: Dinner daily 7:30–11pm.

★ Located on the lobby level of one of the most desirable hotels in the country, this is the best Moroccan restaurant in the capital. You can select from one of the most authentic and complete Moroccan menus anywhere. In addition to the predictable array of *tajine* and couscous dishes that you find almost everywhere, you can sample an assortment of *briouates* (puff pastries stuffed with such fillings as spicy sausage and shrimp), a very unusual seafood *pastilla*, fish kebabs marinated in coriander and lemon, steamed shoulder of lamb with fresh mint, tajine of lamb with artichokes, tajine of sea perch or sea bream, and a dessert specialty of Moroccan crêpes with honey. Live regional music will accompany your meal.

JUSTINE'S, Rabat Hyatt Regency, Souissi. Tel. 712-34.
Cuisine: FRENCH. **Reservations:** Required. **Transportation:** Grand taxi.
$ Prices: Appetizers 55–185 DH ($6.90–$23.15); main dishes 110–155 DH ($13.75–$19.40). AE, DC, MC, V.
Open: Lunch daily noon–3pm; dinner daily 7–11pm. **Closed:** Lunch in summer.

★ This is Rabat's finest European restaurant, a favorite with dozens of government ministers who make it the preferred venue for social and diplomatic dinners. Located on the lobby level of the previously recommended Rabat Hyatt Regency, it features a vaguely Palladian decor that includes artfully illuminated and very large Moroccan vases set into symmetrical wall niches. Specialties include chilled fresh tomato soup with vermouth, fish soup with strips of sole, roast rack of lamb with tarragon, filet of veal with a garlic purée, pan-fried filet of beef with red-wine sauce, roasted sea bass, a lukewarm salad of red mullet in walnut oil, and a casserole of veal sweetbreads with truffles. Service is excellent.

EXPENSIVE

LA COURONNE AND EL MANSOUR, Hotel de la Tour Hassan, bd. de Chellah, 22. Tel. 214-02.
Cuisine: MOROCCAN/INTERNATIONAL. **Reservations:** Recommended.

Bus: 5, 7, 9, or 17.
$ Prices: Appetizers 30–75 DH ($3.75–$9.40); main dishes 65–90 DH ($8.15–$11.25). AE, DC, MC, V.
Open: Lunch daily 12:30–3:30pm; dinner daily 7:30–10:30pm.

Both of these restaurants are contained within the Hotel de la Tour Hassan, and offer a lavish decor that was originally installed in 1914 during the French colonial administration of Rabat. Both have impeccable service, are open the same hours, and charge the same prices.

At La Couronne, you can listen to supper-club music in the European style (at dinner only) and enjoy such international specialties as paper-thin slices of smoked fish with capers, rack of lamb, chicken with garlic, filet of sea perch grilled with fennel, and European desserts. At El Mansour, within the oldest part of the hotel, the Moroccan decor might strike some visitors as just a bit garish. You can order three kinds of pastilla (pigeon, seafood, veal), many different tajines, lamb kebabs, and the delicious specialty of the sub-Sahara, a slowly baked aromatic *mechoui* of baby lamb.

MODERATE

KANOUN GRILL, Rabat Chellah Hotel, rue d'Ifni, 2. Tel. 640-52.
Cuisine: MOROCCAN. **Reservations:** Recommended. **Bus:** 15 or 23.
$ Prices: Appetizers 23–45 DH ($2.90–$5.65); main dishes 52–85 DH ($6.50–$10.65). AE, DC, MC, V.
Open: Lunch Mon–Sat noon–2:30pm; dinner Mon–Sat 7:30–11pm.

The Kanoun Grill is the better of the two restaurants in the Rabat Chellah Hotel. Its decor is attractive and rustic, its grilled food so delicious that many employees of nearby foreign embassies swear by it. The restaurant is named after a terra-cotta brazier used by Bedouins to cook food. The ample menu includes many of Morocco's most famous dishes, including *harira* (the soup consumed at Ramadan), along with filet of sea bass flambé, grilled or poached turbot, an array of juicy tajines, roast lamb, and kebabs. You'll find a good selection of Moroccan wines. Visible from all parts of this restaurant is the dramatic grill.

KOUTOUBIA, Zankat Pierre Parent, 10. Tel. 201-25.
Cuisine: MOROCCAN. **Reservations:** Recommended. **Transportation:** Petit taxi.
$ Prices: Appetizers 20–45 DH ($2.50–$5.65); main dishes 45–85 DH ($5.65–$10.65). AE, DC, MC, V.
Open: Lunch daily noon–3pm; dinner daily 7:30–11pm.

Sitting behind a crimson façade in the bureaucratic heart of Rabat, this two-in-one establishment combines a very active and very ethnic neighborhood bar with a more upscale and formal restaurant. The dining room is brightly accented with colored glass and comfortable booths. Considered an unusual dining enclave with a distinct personality all its own, as well as a luncheon spot popular with government employees, it has attracted some famous personalities, including the king of Morocco. Three types of couscous and seven tajines are among the specialties, as well as chicken with almonds, pigeon with olives, and a flavorful brochette of lamb. A good opening would be the harira soup.

INEXPENSIVE

RESTAURANT BALIMA, Hotel Balima, ave. Mohammed V, 173 (rue Jakarta, 37). Tel. 677-55.
Cuisine: CONTINENTAL. **Reservations:** Not required.
$ Prices: Appetizers 11–24 DH ($1.40–$3); main dishes 18–30 DH ($2.25–$3.75). AE, DC, MC, V.
Open: Lunch daily noon–3pm; dinner daily 7–10pm.

Its address is officially on the major artery of town, but you'll find its entrance along a parallel street in back. A spacious outdoor terrace is almost completely covered with a screen of well-trimmed trees, creating an oasis in the middle of a busy neighborhood two blocks from the train station near the Moroccan Parliament. You can dine on the terrace or inside a semimodern room. Meals include house-style ravioli, seasonal lobster, grilled sea bass with a béarnaise sauce, pepper steak, veal kidneys with Madeira, and an array of tajines and kebabs.

CAFE RESTAURANT SAADI, av. Allal Ben Abdallah, 81 bis. Tel. 699-03.
　　Cuisine: MOROCCAN. **Reservations:** Not required. **Bus:** 13 or 16.
$ Prices: Appetizers 8–30 DH ($1–$3.75); main dishes 25–70 DH ($3.15–$8.75); 3-course menu 55 DH ($6.90). AE, DC, MC, V.
　　Open: Daily 10am–11:30pm.

Many of the neighborhood's budget-conscious diners head for this small restaurant, which lies at the end of an arcade. Very Moroccan, and very family-conscious, the establishment specializes in tajines (my favorite is the chicken with citrus). You can also order more elaborate fare, including two famous Moroccan specialties: mechoui (long-cooked lamb, a dish often reserved for festivals) and pastilla, a pastry filled with pigeon meat and flavored with ground almonds. Mint tea is the traditional finish to the meal. Under the same management is a busy café, serving only drinks and snacks beneath the arcades of a major venue running into place Mohammed V.

SHOPPING

Other than for its carpets, which have helped make it famous as a textile center, Rabat is not known for handcrafts. For the foreign shopper, greener pastures and better-stocked stores are found in Marrakesh, Fez, and the cities of the Deep South. There are, however, several exceptions to this rule that could fill some time while you're in Rabat.

HANDCRAFTS

COOPARTIM, Ensemble Artisanale, rue des Consuls, 20. Tel. 208-13.
　　Coopartim (Coopératif Artisanale) occupies a formal complex of shops and studios whose courtyards, ornamental plantings, and covered arcades might remind you of a mosque or a palace. You'll find both a bank and a currency-exchange booth on the premises, and all sales within this complex are rigidly monitored by the Moroccan government; prices are fixed and fair.
　　The 17 merchants and craftspeople here open and close, with a few exceptions, at roughly the same hours—Monday through Saturday from 8am to 1pm and 2 to 7pm. Included in their ranks are specialists in leather, copper, embroideries, and ceramics. The complex lies close to the river, near the southeastern foundation of the Medina's ramparts. Take bus no. 26 or 30 from Rabat; no. 12 or 16 from Salé.

POTTERY

QUARTIER DES POTIERS, Oulja, Salé.
　　Deposits of clay have always existed in abundance near Rabat, and for centuries local potters have fashioned it into some of the most enviable pottery in Morocco. Clustered into one well-monitored complex on low-lying flatlands about a mile upriver from both Salé and Rabat are the kilns, workshops, and showrooms of 22 different manufacturers. Each specializes in a particular form and firing technique, and their products range from run-of-the-mill commercial knickknacks to elegant reproductions of timeless designs perfected after centuries of experimentation.
　　Many manufacturers make up to 1,500 pieces daily (hours are 8am to 7:30pm), and then fire them in kilns heated either by firewood or by gas. Firings traditionally take place every afternoon, at which time a pall of smoke from wood fires hangs densely over the complex. Two of the largest manufacturers are **Oulja Poterie Salé,** Shop 10 bis, Oulja, Sale (tel. 818-56), and **Poterie Demnate,** Shop 12, Oulja, Salé (tel. 807-25).
　　In addition to pottery, you'll find baskets, chairs, benches, and settees made of wicker. Take bus no. 26 or 30 from Rabat; no. 12 or 16 from Salé.

EVENING ENTERTAINMENT

DISCO QUEEN'S CLUB, Hotel de la Tour Hassan, bd. de Chellah, 22. Tel. 214-02.
Connected to the Hotel de la Tour Hassan, with a separate entrance onto boulevard de Chellah, this is the most popular disco club in town. It's open nightly from 10:30pm to 3 or 4am. Bus: 5, 7, 9, or 17.
Admission: 50 DH ($6.25), including first drink.

BAR DE L'HOTEL DE LA TOUR HASSAN, bd. de Chellah, 22. Tel. 214-02.
The allure here is one of an almost-forgotten, politely restrained, and slightly dowdy charm. Your waiter will wear a fez and a dark jacket, and the decor hasn't been altered since 1914. In other words, come here for the ambience as much as for the drink, and perhaps stay for dinner at one of the hotel's restaurants (see above). Beer costs 20 DH ($2.50), and daily hours are 10am to midnight. Bus: 5, 7, 9, or 17.

PICCADILLY PIANO BAR, Rabat Hyatt Regency, Souissi. Tel. 712-34.
Set adjacent to the marble lobby of the finest hotel in Rabat, the Piccadilly opens its doors to the fragrances of the hotel's spectacular Andalusian gardens. Decorated in sophisticated teal blue and pink, it features a jazz band nightly from 10pm to 1am (it opens at 5pm). Considered the best watering hole in Rabat, the Piccadilly is one of the capital's very few piano bars. It draws a well-traveled and international clientele. Beer is 15 DH ($1.90), and drinks cost 45 DH ($5.65). Transportation: Grand taxi.

AN EXCURSION TO SALÉ

Salé—reached by bus no. 12, 15, or 16, as well as by ferry from the Kasbah des Oudaïa—lies across the Bou Regreg River from Rabat. Famous in the 17th century as a pirates' haunt, this was the port whence the corsairs launched frequent attacks on the French and English fleets. Robinson Crusoe, you may recall, was captured by the Salé rovers.

In the Middle Ages it flourished as a merchant port and entrepôt for the west coast of Africa. The town is believed to date from the 11th century; the encircling ramparts were built by the Merenids in the centuries to follow. The Merenids were also responsible for the **Bab Mrisa,** the former entrance to the harbor. The 13th-century gateway leads to the Mellah, or Jewish quarter. The Merenids are further credited with the **Medersa of Abou Al Hassan,** a college built in 1341 by the so-called Black Sultan. It is across from the **Grand Mosque,** which dates from the 12th century (you can observe it only from the outside). If you're traveling with a guide (highly recommended), ask to be shown both the **Fondouk Askour,** a 14th-century hospice noted for its gateway, and the most prized monument of Salé, the **Tomb of Sidi Abdallah ben Hassoun,** the city's patron saint. The latter is characterized by its curious dome and its galleries in many colors. Also worth visiting is the **Mausoleum of Marabout Sidi ben Achir,** only two stories tall, but by far the tallest monument in the area. It contains the remains of a 14th-century Islamic saint known for his miracles, particularly relating to healing nervous and emotional disorders. These are but some of the monuments that have earned Salé the reputation as a city of sanctuaries.

Of course, most of your time will be spent walking through the narrow streets and looking at the shops. Salé is known for its matting work, a specialty of the local craftspeople. On rue Kechachine, you'll see carpenters and stone carvers, and on rue Haddadine, blacksmiths and brass workers. Many Andalusian Moors, fleeing Spain after the Reconquest, settled in Salé, and perhaps for that reason the appearance of the town is often compared to that of a Muslim town in Andalusia before the fall of Granada.

Allow at least half a day for exploring Salé.

2. CASABLANCA

63 miles S of Rabat; 147 miles W of Marrakesh

GETTING THERE By Plane   See "Planning a Trip to Morocco" in Chapter 2. Most international flights arrive at Mohammed V International Airport, about 12 miles south of Casablanca. From there, an ACTM bus will take you into the city terminal for 20 DH ($2.50). Taxis should cost about 165 DH ($20.65). Some drivers will try to charge more. For **airport information,** call 36-41-84.

By Train   Casablanca has two train stations, the **Casa Port,** at port de Casablanca (tel. 22-30-11), in the vicinity of the CTM Station, and **Casa Voyageurs,** located on boulevard Ba Hammed (tel. 24-58-01). The Casa Port is for most northbound services to such places as Rabat and Tangier, and the Casa Voyageurs is for southbound service to such places as Marrakesh. Trains arrive more or less hourly from Rabat, the trip taking 50 minutes to 1½ hours. Four trains a day pull in from Tangier via Rabat (6 hours), and 4 trains a day arrive from Marrakesh (5 hours).

By Bus   The bus station in Casablanca is **CTM,** rue Léon L'Africain, 23 (tel. 26-80-61), off rue Colbert. Eighteen buses a day run from Rabat to Casablanca (1 hour, 40 minutes), and two buses a day come down from Tangier (6½ hours). Three buses a day link Marrakesh and Casablanca (4 hours).

By Car   From Rabat and the north, take the S222 express highway south; and from Agadir in the south, take the P8 north. From Marrakesh in the east, follow route P7 north.

Casablanca is the largest city in Morocco and the fourth-largest city in Africa after Cairo, Alexandria, and Lagos, with a population conservatively estimated at 3.5 million. It is the undisputed commercial center of Morocco, a brash, bold city where family ties and aristocratic heritage matter less than perhaps anywhere else in Morocco. It contains five different schools of higher learning, some of the worst slums and some of the best modern architecture in Morocco, and the country's only airport capable of receiving transatlantic flights.

The size (750 square miles) and influence of modern Casablanca are especially noteworthy because as recently as 1830 its population was a mere 600. It required the mercantilistic fervor of the 19th century and early 20th century, a surge in Moroccan exports, and the advent of the steam engine to radically transform the small ruin of a town, which had previously based its income and survival exclusively upon piracy, into a thriving metropolis.

Winter is mild and dry, with a temperature of around 60° to 65°F. Summer is hot, but not scorching.

ORIENTATION

INFORMATION

The **Moroccan National Tourist Office** is at rue Omar Slaoui, 55 (tel. 0/27-11-77). Hours are Monday through Thursday from 8:30am to noon and 2:30 to 6:30pm, on Friday from 8:30 to 11am and 3 to 6:30pm. For information strictly about Casablanca, go to the **Syndicat d'Initiative,** bd. Mohammed V, 98 (tel. 0/22-15-24), across from the CTM Station, open Monday through Saturday from 9am to noon and 3 to 6:30pm, on Sunday from 9am to noon.

GETTING AROUND

Buses in Casablanca are designed mainly to transport workers to their homes or jobs in the suburbs. They are hot, uncomfortable, and often impossibly overcrowded. For

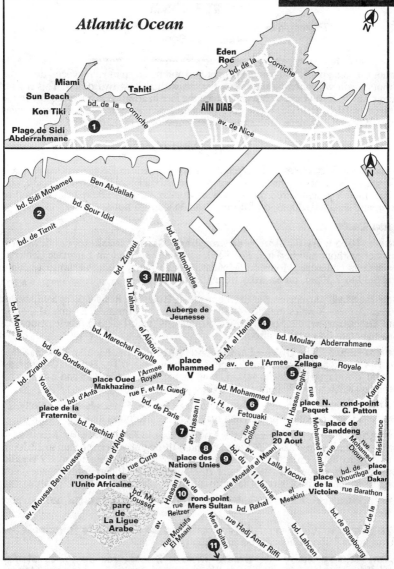

CASABLANCA

Atlantic Ocean

Eden Roc

bd. de la Corniche

Miami

Tahiti

Sun Beach

Kon Tiki

bd. de la Corniche

AÏN DIAB

av. de Nice

Plage de Sidi Abderrahmane ❶

bd. Sidi Mohamed

Ben Abdallah

bd. Sour Idid

❷

bd. de Tiznit

bd. des Almohades

bd. Ziraoui

bd. Tahar

❸ MEDINA

Auberge de Jeunesse

bd. Moulay

bd. de Bordeaux

bd. Marechal Fayolle

el Alaoui

bd. M. el Hansali

❹

bd. Moulay Abderrahmane

place Mohammed V

place Zellaga

av. de l'Armee

Royale

l'Armee Royale

av. de l'Armee

❺

place Oued Makhazine

rue F. et M. Guedj

bd. Mohammed V

rue Hassan Seghir

rond-point G. Patton

bd. Ziraoui

Youssef

bd. d'Anfa

bd. de Paris

av. H. el Fetouaki

place N. Paquet

❻

Karachi

place de la Fraternite

bd. Rachidi

av. Hassan II

rue Colbert

bd. du 20 Aout

place de Banddeng

rue Mohamed Diouri

rue Resistance

rue d'Alger

❼

rue Mohamed Smiha

place de Dakar

av. Moussa Ben Noussair

rue Curie

❽ place des Nations Unies ❾

bd. du Mostafa el Maani

av.

rue Mostafa el Maani

Lalla Yacout

place de la Victoire

bd. de Khouribga

rue Barathon

rond-point de l'Unite Africaine

bd. My Youssef

Hassan II av. de

❿ rond-point Mers Sultan

el Meskini

rue 11 Janvier

rue Reitzer

bd. Rahal

bd. de Strasbourg

parc de La Ligue Arabe

av.

rue Mostafa El Maani

Mers Sultan

rue Hadj Amar Riffi

bd. Lahcen

bd. de la

⓫

MOROCCO

☆ Rabat

Casablanca

Aquarium ❷	Notre Dame de Lourdes ⓫
Casa Port Train Station ❹	Old Medina ❸
Court of Justice ❾	Place des Nations Unies
CTM (Bus Station) ❺	(United Nations Square) ❽
Hassan II Mosque ❶	Post Office ❼
Moroccan National	Syndicat d'Initiative ❻
Tourist Office ❿	

IMPRESSIONS

This could be the beginning of a beautiful friendship.
—HUMPHREY BOGART

---

about the same price, you can hail a petit taxi and be taken in your general direction, although you will often have to share the cab with at least two others. This is a far better way to travel than by bus. Negotiate the fare in advance. An average fare in the city costs 10 DH ($1.25). Petit taxis can be caught at avenue des Forces Armées Royales (F.A.R.) or place Mohammed V, but most often they are hailed on the street.

FAST FACTS

American Express The representative for American Express in Casablanca is **Voyages Schwartz,** rue du Prince Moulay Abdallah, 112 (tel. 27-31-33). This office doesn't accept wired money. Open Monday through Friday from 8:30am to noon and 2:30 to 6:30pm, on Saturday from 8:30am to noon.

Area Code 0.

Bookstore Try the **American Language Center Bookstore,** bd. Moulay Youssef (without number) (tel. 27-95-59), beneath the American Language Center at place de la Fraternité. Hours are Monday through Friday from 9:30am to 12:30pm and 3:30 to 7:30pm, on Saturday from 10am to 1pm.

Car Rental Arrangements can be made at **Budget,** Résidence es Safir, av.des Forces Armées Royales (tel. 30-14-80); **Hertz,** rue de Foucauld, 25 (tel. 31-22-23); and **Europcar,** av. des Forces Armées Royales, 44 (tel. 31-37-37). These companies also maintain desks at the airport.

Consulates The **United States Consulate** is at bd. Moulay Youssef, 8 (tel. 22-41-49), and hours are 8am to 4:30pm Monday to Friday. The **British Consulate** is at bd. d'Anfa, 60 (tel. 26-14-41), and hours are 8:30am to 12:30pm and 2 to 6pm on Monday, 8:30am to 12:30pm and 2 to 5:30pm Tuesday to Friday.

Doctor For an English-speaking doctor, call **Dr. A. El Kouhen,** rue Nolly, 24 (tel. 27-53-43), Monday through Saturday from 9am to noon and 3 to 7pm.

Drugstores A good pharmacy is **La Pharmacie Principale,** av. Mers Sultan (without number) (tel. 22-01-74); open Monday through Friday from 9am to 12:30pm and 3:30 to 8pm, on Saturday from 9am to 12:30pm. You might also try **Kyalid Bennani Pharmacie 2000,** Centre 2000, boulevard Moulay Abderrahane (Gare Casa Port; tel. 27-54-53); open daily from 9am to 12:30pm and 3 to 7pm.

Emergencies For an **ambulance,** call 30-30-30; for the **police,** 19; to report a **fire,** 15.

Eyeglasses Optician services are available at **La Pharmacie Principale** (see "Drugstores," above). Ask for Georges Loufrani.

Film/Photography At **Studio Riviera Photo,** rue du Prince Moulay Abdallah, 77 (tel. 27-55-68), film can be developed in one day. It's open Monday through Saturday from 9am to 12:30pm and 3:15 to 8:30pm.

Hairdresser **Coiffure Rouika,** in the Sheraton Casablanca, av. des Forces Armées Royales, 100 (tel. 31-78-78), is reached via a number of labyrinthine passages on the third floor of this deluxe hotel. It caters to both women and men, charging around 100 DH ($12.50) for shampoo and styling. Hours are daily from 9am to 9pm.

Laundry/Dry Cleaning For both services, try **Pressing Mers Sultan,** av. Mers Sultan, 116 (tel. 26-41-94), open Monday through Saturday from 8:30am to 12:30pm and 2:30 to 8:30pm.

Medical Emergency medical services are available at **Croissant Rouge Marocain,** bd. El Massira El Khadia (without number) (tel. 25-25-21).

Post Office The main branch of the **Casablanca Post Office** is at place des Nations Unies. Do not attempt to call; go there to conduct business in person. It is open Monday through Thursday from 8:30am to 12:15pm, on Friday from 8:30 to 11:30am. Mail sent c/o General Delivery should be marked "Poste Restante"; bring your passport to pick it up. Collect phone calls can be made from here.

Religious Services Jewish worshipers in Casablanca can attend the synagogue, **Ein Habanim,** rue Lusitania, 14 (tel. 26-69); Protestants gather at **Eglise Protestante de Casablanca,** rue Azilal, 33 (tel. 30-19-22), which has Sunday services at 10:30am; **Eglise Anglicane,** rue F & M Guedj (without number) (tel. 25-10-22), offers Anglican services Sunday at 10:30am; and **Notre-Dame de Lourdes,** Rond-Point d'Europe (without number) (tel. 22-08-52), holds Catholic masses on Sunday at 11am and 7pm.

WHAT TO SEE & DO

Considered the folkloric heart of Casablanca, the **Old Medina,** bounded by boulevard Sidi Mohammed ben Abdallah, place Mohammed V, and avenue des Forces Armées Royales, is a maze of narrow streets and whitewashed buildings. I personally find this particular medina less interesting than some in Morocco, but I always enjoy visiting its souks. It also contains a Grand Mosque erected under Sidi Mohammed ben Abdallah (1757–90), open to Muslims only, and three gateways— Bab Kedim, Bab El-Assa, and Bab El-Marsa—that connect it to the port.

South of boulevard Victor Hugo and north of the rail lines is the **New Medina,** built by the French in 1921 and more intriguing than the old. Resembling a filmmaker's version of a medina, it sprang up around a high-walled garden encompassing the Royal Palace (built after World War I), where King Hassan II stays. Another important monument is the Mahkama, or Court of Justice. More interesting is the *joutiya* (handcrafts market), where you can bargain for copperware and Mediouna carpets.

The most monumental square in Casablanca, and the administrative center of Morocco, is **United Nations Square,** conceived in 1920 under the French regime and executed by an architect named Marrast. Impressive buildings surround the square, whose center is ornamented with lush gardens, fountains, and the booming traffic of avenue Hassan II. On the east side of the square is the Palais de Justice, flanked by the French Consulate. To the south stands the Préfecture, with a clock tower. On the north side is the Banque de Maroc and nearby is the rectangular Parc de la Ligue Arabe, with promenades and ornamental lakes.

On boulevard Rachidi (rue d'Alger) is the **Cathédrale du Sacré-Coeur,** a gleaming white building named after, and inspired by, its counterpart in Paris. Note, in particular, its lovely stained-glass windows. It was designed by French architect Paul Tornon.

Another European church, noted for its remarkable stained glass, is **Notre-Dame de Lourdes,** on boulevard Mohammed Zerktouni. Completed in 1956, it is decorated with tapestries that depict the story of the Immaculate Conception and apparitions that were reported to have been seen at Lourdes. Admission to the church is free. It's open daily from 8:30am to noon and 3 to 7pm.

Considered one of the wonders of the Islamic world, the **Hassan II Mosque,** begun in 1980, is the most imposing monument on the Casablanca skyline, visible from many miles around. It is located on the coastal flatlands of a residential area called Aïn Diab, along the northwestern edge of the city. As yet uncompleted, this is the second-largest mosque in the world, second only to the Grand Mosque at Mecca. When completed, it will include within its precincts a Koranic university, an Islamic library, ornamental gardens, and miles of decorative adornments. Its minaret will be the tallest in the world, 562 feet high. Like all mosques in Morocco, it will be open to Muslims only.

WHERE TO STAY

With few exceptions, the third-class hotels of Casablanca are definitely third-rate, and some of the best bargains don't appear to be safe for the average visitor. Therefore, I suggest that if you're going to stay in Casablanca, you spend more than our usual budget allows if you want clean, respectable, and more secure accommodations.

For those who can afford it, Casablanca has some of the best hotels in Morocco, particularly those affiliated with American chains, such as Hyatt. Prices reflect Casablanca's status as a business center. It caters far more to the commercial community than to the tourist market.

The rating "Very Expensive" (all the big chain hotels) means 1,500 to 2,100 DH ($187.50 to $262.50) for a double; "Expensive," about 800 DH ($100) for a double; and "moderate," 380 to 530 DH ($47.50 to $66.25) for a double. Anything in the neighborhood of 200 DH ($25) is considered "Inexpensive."

VERY EXPENSIVE

CASABLANCA HYATT REGENCY, place Mohammed V (without number), **Casablanca. Tel. 0/26-12-34,** or toll free 800/228-9000. Fax 0/220-180. 171 rms (all with bath); 58 suites. A/C MINIBAR TV TEL **Transportation:** Petit taxi. **$ Rates:** 1,550–1,950 DH ($193.75–$243.75) single or double; suites from 3,000 DH ($375). Breakfast 85 DH ($10.65) extra. AE, DC, MC, V.

One of the most stylish and innovative hotels in North Africa, the Hyatt Regency is a rose-colored glass structure rising above the best-known square in Casablanca. The marble lobby has black surfaces, highlighted with Rabat carpets and intricate tilework. Throughout the public room, dozens of high-tech accessories are softened by splashing fountains, comfortable seating niches, and a gorgeously majestic sandstone replica of a dome-covered Andalusian courtyard. Throughout the sprawling complex, Regency-style armchairs are mixed with carved masks from Central Africa and a life-size menagerie of carved horses and camels from 19th-century Venice.

The plush bedrooms are spacious and decorated much like a cosmopolitan apartment. Each has mirrored surfaces, a walk-around bar, luxurious carpeting, curtains, upholstery in shades of blue-gray or persimmon, air conditioning, stylish bathrooms, and a TV with U.S.-based news broadcasts and in-house movies. The most elegant accommodations are in the Regency Club, for which you pay more for such services as your own concierge and butler service, complimentary breakfast, and evening drinks.

Dining/Entertainment: Three meals a day are served at the café-restaurant Golden Gates, on the lobby level of the hotel, and there's a summer-only restaurant, Bougainvillea, around the pool. Others include Dar Beida, Restaurant Wong Kung, and Restaurant Valentino as well as the late-night spots Bar Casablanca and the Black House disco (for all five, see below).

Services: 24-hour room service, outside laundry and dry cleaning, limousine service, airport representative to meet you, valet parking, baby-sitting, doctor on call, express checkout, 24-hour concierge service, hairdresser, beauty parlor.

Facilities: Resort-style outdoor swimming pool, health club, squash courts, steam bath, sauna, business center, shopping arcade, and art gallery.

EL MANSOUR, av. des F.A.R., 27, Casablanca. Tel. 0/31-30-11. Fax 0/31-25-83. 148 rms (all with bath), 22 suites. A/C MINIBAR TV TEL **Transportation:** Petit taxi. **$ Rates:** 1,700 DH ($212.50) single or double; suites from 2,500 DH ($312.50). Breakfast 80 DH ($10) extra. AE, DC, MC, V.

Built in 1952 and extensively renovated in 1988, this was for many years the grand-scale hotel of Casablanca. Set behind a soaring Moorish arched entry from a position three blocks from place Mohammed V, it's managed today by the London-based chain of Trusthouse Forte. The core of the hotel is a greenhouse-covered winter garden, where cascades of water decorate one wall within earshot of one of the most pleasant watering holes and tearooms in Casablanca, the Diplomat Bar (see below).

Dining/Entertainment: Drinking and dining establishments include International Restaurant Volubilis, Restaurant Douira (see below), a coffeeshop, and the aforementioned Diplomat Bar.

Services: Room service, hairdresser, concierge with lists of available baby-sitters, massage.

Facilities: Health club with sauna.

HOLIDAY INN CROWN PLAZA HOTEL, Rond Point Hassan II, Casablanca. Tel. 0/29-49-49. Fax 0/29-30-29. 183 rms (all with bath), 24 suites. **Bus:** 6 or 28.

$ Rates: 1,400 DH ($175) single; 1,500 DH ($187.50) double; suites from 2,600 DH ($325). Breakfast 80 DH ($10) extra. AE, DC, MC, V.

Built in 1989 on a location five blocks south of place Mohammed V, the hotel boasts a stylish design reminiscent of a white-painted concrete version of a monarch's crown. You'll register within an all-white lobby covered in marble and staffed by a well-trained bevy of porters and receptionists. Bedrooms contain tastefully modernized Moroccan touches of ornate plasterwork, comfortably upholstered furniture, and satellite reception on the TV.

Dining/Entertainment: Two restaurants, Les Ambassadeurs (French) and El Bahia (Moroccan); poolside snack bar; and the Ascot Bar.

Services: Hairdresser, 24-hour room service, concierge.

Facilities: Business center, rooftop swimming pool.

SHERATON CASABLANCA, av. des F.A.R., 100, Casablanca. Tel. 0/31-78-36. Fax 0/31-51-36. 306 rms (all with bath), 16 suites. A/C MINIBAR TV TEL **Transportation:** Petit taxi.

$ Rates: 1,800 DH ($225) single; 2,100 DH ($262.50) double; suites from 3,300 DH ($412.50). Breakfast 95 DH ($11.90) extra. AE, DC, MC, V.

The newest five-star hotel of Casablanca sits behind a dramatically angular façade whose mirrored windows reflect a location several blocks west of place Mohammed V. Its stone lobby rises many stories in a ziggurat-inspired series of angles to a ceiling covered in Moorish geometrics. The third-floor swimming pool is ringed with parasol-shaded tables, with a bar nearby. Each of the bedrooms contains satellite TV reception, a tile-and-marble bath, block prints by Moroccan artists, and a stylish international decor.

Dining/Entertainment: Five restaurants—Trianono (French), Andaluz (Lebanese/Moroccan), Sakura (Japanese), Dafra (coffee shop/buffet), Oasis (poolside lunch restaurant); a nightclub; and three bars.

Services: Hairdresser, massage, laundry, concierge.

Facilities: Courtyard swimming pool, special rooms for nonsmokers and handicapped guests, fitness club, sauna, hammam (bath), and business center.

EXPENSIVE

HOTEL SAFIR, av. des F.A.R., 160, Casablanca. Tel. 0/31-12-12. 310 rms (all with bath). A/C MINIBAR TV TEL **Transportation:** Petit taxi.

$ Rates: 700 DH ($87.50) single; 800 DH ($100) double. Breakfast 75 DH ($9.90) extra. AE, DC, MC, V.

Hotel Safir, near the air terminal in the center of the city, was designed as one of the most prominent skyscrapers in Casablanca. Built in 1983, it has 16 floors of well-furnished and attractive bedrooms, each with a private bathroom, radio, alarm clock, and soundproofing. Cascading water cools the stone-trimmed lobby with its Moroccan-tile arches. Facilities include a third-floor swimming pool, massage facilities, four restaurants serving meals costing from 110 DH ($13.75), two bars, and Le Palace nightclub.

MODERATE

HOTEL LES ALMOHADES, av. Moulay Hassan 1er (without number), Casablanca. Tel. 0/22-05-05. Fax 0/22-05-05. 138 rms (all with bath). MINIBAR TV TEL Transportation: Petit taxi.

$ Rates: 334 DH ($41.75) single; 424 DH ($53) double. Breakfast 32 DH ($4) extra. AE, DC, MC, V.

⑤ The Hotel Les Almohades, directly south of place Mohammad V, stands on one of the busiest streets in town, but its stippled façade is softened by a small cascade of water pouring into a fountain. A modern entrance leads into a lobby where a circle of low couches frames a view of a tiled courtyard and a green-and-white reflecting pool. This attractive hotel has well-furnished and comfortable bedrooms decorated in a modern style. It also offers an international restaurant and an elegant Moroccan dining room.

HOTEL BASMA, bd. Moulay Hassan ler, 135, Casablanca. Tel. 0/22-33-23. 117 rms (all with bath), 18 suites. MINIBAR TV TEL **Transportation:** Petit taxi.

$ Rates: 300 DH ($37.50) single; 380 DH ($47.50) double; 460 DH ($57.50) triple; suites from 850 DH ($106.25). Breakfast 31 DH ($3.90) extra. AE, DC, MC, V.

⑤ This comfortable modern hotel sits only about a block from the southwestern edge of place Mohammed V. Considering its facilities and the comfort of its rooms, it offers good value for the money. *Basma* means "smile," and fittingly enough, the attentive staff will greet you warmly. The lobby-level bar Baramica is an all-black and very cozy enclave of Moroccan decor and hospitality. Bedrooms are outfitted with Moroccan detailing, Sahara-inspired tones, and doors that open onto breeze-filled balconies. A fixed-price meal in the second-floor restaurant, Balaba, costs 109 DH ($13.60) at lunch and 150 DH ($18.75) at dinner. The hotel offers 24-hour room service.

KANDARA HOTEL, bd. d'Anfa, 44, Casablanca. Tel. 0/26-29-37. Fax 0/22-06-17. 213 rms (all with bath), 11 suites. A/C MINIBAR TV TEL **Transportation:** Petit taxi.

$ Rates: 420 DH ($52.50) single; 530 DH ($66.25) double; suites from 2,000 DH ($250). Breakfast 40 DH ($5) extra. AE, DC, MC, V.

⑤ Rising above one of the city's most sought-after locations, a 10-minute walk northwest of place Mohammed V, is the angular façade of this comfortable hotel, built in 1986. Rated four stars by the Moroccan government, it contains a swimming pool on its ground floor; two restaurants, plus a coffee shop; a business center; and a comfortable bar with a strongly defined Moroccan decor. The earth-toned bedrooms are simply but comfortably outfitted with Moroccan accessories; some rooms have private balconies overlooking the cityscape, and many of them contain minibars.

HOTEL TOUBKAL, rue Sidi Belyout, 9, Casablanca. Tel. 0/31-04-50. Fax 0/31-22-87. 66 rms (all with bath). A/C MINIBAR TV TEL **Transportation:** Petit taxi.

$ Rates (including breakfast): 317 DH ($39.65) single; 428 DH ($53.50) double. AE, DC, MC, V.

⑤ The Toubkal's central location northwest of place Mohammed V makes it a convenient choice, and its "Moroccanized" art deco style makes it almost irresistible. This hotel was built in 1971, and a renovation in the early 1980s transformed its public areas with the addition of black-marble and ziggurat-shaped arches. The bedrooms are comfortable, the quietest rooms overlooking a rear garden filled with palms. There's a disco on the premises, Nightclub Toubkal.

INEXPENSIVE

HOTEL GEORGES V, rue Sidi Belyout, 1, Casablanca. Tel. 0/31-24-48. 34 rms (17 with bath). **Transportation:** Petit taxi.

$ Rates: 109 DH ($13.60) single without bath, 134 DH ($16.75) single with bath; 130 DH ($16.25) double without bath, 188 DH ($23.50) double with bath. Breakfast 15 DH ($1.90) extra. No credit cards.

Situated across from the Royal Mansour, one of the most glamorous hotels in Casablanca, the Georges V, built in the 1930s, charges only moderate prices. The small hotel is quite plain inside, with a simple lobby, a two-passenger elevator, and painted furniture in the bedrooms. All rooms are clean and comfortable. You'll find it two blocks northeast of place Mohammed V.

WHERE TO EAT

Casablanca has some of the best restaurants in Morocco, rivaling those of Marrakesh and Rabat. Both Moroccan specialties and international food, especially French, are offered. In fact, some of the old French restaurants look like holdovers from colonial days. Only problem is, prices here are the highest in Morocco.

If it's summer, consider driving or taking a taxi to the boulevard de la Corniche, which not only hugs the beachfront but contains many delightful seafood and international restaurants. It's also a good way to beat the heat. See "An Excursion to Anfa and Aïn Diab," below.

Casablanca has dozens of independent restaurants, the majority of which are of poor quality, but there are also gems to be found here. Many of its finest specialty restaurants are located in hotels such as the Hyatt Regency and El Mansour.

Every Moroccan city has a slightly different price scale in its restaurants. Actually, Casablanca doesn't have any terribly expensive restaurants. Here, "Expensive" suggests meals ranging upward from 180 to 220 DH ($22.50 to $27.50); "Moderate" offers dining tabs from 130 to 200 DH ($16.25 to $25); and "Inexpensive" suggests meals below 100 DH ($12.50).

EXPENSIVE

DAR BEIDA, Casablanca Hyatt Regency, place Mohammed V (without number). Tel. 26-12-34.
    Cuisine: MOROCCAN. **Reservations:** Required. **Transportation:** Petit taxi.
$ Prices: Complete menu for 220 DH ($27.50). AE, DC, MC, V.
    Open: Daily 7pm–1:30am.

On the lobby level of this hotel in the center of the city, Dar Beida is both a sumptuous choice for dining and also a major venue for typically Moroccan entertainment. Every night a band, complete with singers and a belly dancer, entertains guests. Decorated like an Arabian tent, it is considered both the most colorful and the best Moroccan restaurant in Casablanca. The food is famous, and many affluent Moroccans take their foreign guests here for an evening on the town. All the major Moroccan classic dishes, including lamb tajines, couscous, and fresh fish, are served here, along with several versions of chicken, plus various salads and pastries. Later you can have mint tea in this atmosphere of the Thousand and One Nights.

RESTAURANT DOUIRA, Hotel El Mansour, av. des F.A.R., 27. Tel. 31-30-11.
    Cuisine: MOROCCAN. **Reservations:** Recommended. **Transportation:** Petit taxi.
$ Prices: Appetizers 45–85 DH ($5.65–$10.65); main dishes 90–180 DH ($11.25–$22.50). AE, DC, MC, V.
    Open: Dinner daily 4–11:30pm.

A charming and attentive staff serves exotic Moroccan meals here amid a gloriously ornate decor. It is neither the most prestigious nor the most expensive dining spot within this prestigious hotel, but it is the favorite of many of its regular customers. The name of the restaurant is translated as "small house," probably because of an intimate layout that permits the seating of only 30 guests at a time. Menu specialties include harira soup, pigeon with lentils, lamb couscous, and marinated orange slices with ground cinnamon.

MODERATE

AL MOUNIA, rue du Prince Moulay Abdallah, 95. Tel. 22-26-69.
  Cuisine: MOROCCAN. **Reservations:** Recommended. **Transportation:** Petit taxi.
  $ Prices: Appetizers 28–48 DH ($3.50–$6); main dishes 58–75 DH ($7.25–$9.40). DC, MC, V.
  Open: Lunch Mon–Sat noon–2pm; dinner Mon–Sat 8–11pm.

⭐ The palatial Al Mounia, located behind the Palais de Justice and the Fire Station, is one of the finest Moroccan dining establishments in Casablanca, and it's reasonably priced. Two French-born sisters operate this restaurant, located in a century-old villa that you enter through a filigreed stone gate opening into a verdant courtyard. You dine in one of two ornate Moroccan-style dining rooms. Regular clients who call in advance—at least before 3:30pm—can enjoy Morocco's special slow-roasted lamb dish, mechoui, that night. The traditional first course is the local soup, harira, while main-dish specialties include tajine with almonds, couscous, and pastilla. Moroccan pastries and mint tea round out your dining adventure.

LA CORRIDA, rue Gay-Lussac, 59. Tel. 27-81-55.
  Cuisine: SPANISH. **Reservations:** Recommended. **Transportation:** Petit taxi.
  $ Prices: Appetizers 24–50 DH ($3–$6.25); main dishes 65–85 DH ($8.15–$10.65); fixed-priced lunch 60 DH ($7.50). AE, DC, MC, V.
  Open: Mon–Sat 11am–2pm and 7–11pm.

Located off boulevard du II Janvier, this restaurant, whose entrance is marked with depictions of a pair of Iberian bulls, is Casablanca's most vivid reminder of its former Spanish heritage. If you come here on a summer's night, you can dine by candlelight under the palm trees of an enclosed courtyard. House specialties include paella and *zarzuela de pescados,* a savory fish stew.

RESTAURANT VALENTINO, Casablanca Hyatt Regency, place Mohammed V (without number). Tel. 26-12-34.
  Cuisine: ITALIAN. **Reservations:** Recommended. **Transportation:** Petit taxi.
  $ Prices: Appetizers 30–50 DH ($3.75–$6.25); main dishes 65–130 DH ($8.15–$16.25). AE, DC, MC, V.
  Open: Mon–Sat noon–3pm, and 7pm–midnight.

This winning combination of high-tech architecture and flavorful Italian food draws an animated crowd from throughout Casablanca, many of whom consider an evening amid the dramatic architecture of the Hyatt Regency to be entertainment of its own. You'll have to cross the hotel's shopping arcade and climb a flight of stairs to the restaurant, where a uniformed maître d' will seat you. A buffet of desserts and another of antipasti offer visual temptations as soon as you enter. You can order such specialties as tomato-and-mozzarella salad; eggplant parmigiana; pasta, including tagliatelle, spaghetti, and fettuccine prepared according to your taste; saffron-flavored risotto; sea bass with fennel; saltimbocca; and T-bone steaks.

RESTAURANT WONG KUNG, Casablanca Hyatt Regency, place Mohammed V (without number). Tel. 26-12-34.
  Cuisine: CHINESE. **Reservations:** Required. **Transportation:** Petit taxi.
  $ Prices: Appetizers 35–150 DH ($4.40–$18.75); main dishes 60–190 DH ($7.50–$23.75). AE, DC, MC, V.
  Open: Tues–Sun 7pm–midnight.

Restaurant Wong Kung, the most elegant Chinese restaurant in town, is set behind pagoda-style columns near the Moorish dome in the lobby of the Hyatt Regency. You sit at lacquered tables in a quadrangle marked by four huge enameled vases on teakwood pedestals, near a lacquered screen. Wonton soup, corn-and-crabmeat chowder, Hunan-style beef, sweet-and-sour veal, cold soya-stuffed duckling, fried Cantonese ravioli, and many excellent seafood dishes are served. The last include Szechuan shrimp, fresh lobster sautéed with black beans and chili, and fresh fish platters with Chinese vegetables.

INEXPENSIVE

RESTAURANT DES FLEURS, av. des F.A.R., 42. Tel. 31-27-51.
Cuisine: FRENCH/MOROCCAN. **Reservations:** Not required. **Transportation:** Petit taxi.
$ Prices: Complete menu downstairs 55 DH ($6.90); complete menu upstairs 80 DH ($10). AE, DC, MC, V.
Open: Lunch daily noon–3pm; dinner daily 7pm–midnight.

S   The exterior looks like any of the other commercial buildings that surround it, but the interior is an elegantly decorated multilevel dining emporium. It stands at the congested intersection of two major avenues in the center of the city, near the El Mansour hotel. The ground-floor restaurant, with its cost-conscious menu, remains open from 7am to midnight daily for drinks and snacks, which include salads and plats du jour.

The allure of the place, however, isn't visible until you reach the second floor. There, you'll find two radically different, very elegant dining rooms. You can dine on low banquettes in one of the most elaborately tiled Moroccan settings in town. If you prefer a European ambience, there's a darkly paneled, spacious French-style dining room with all the accoutrements of a Parisian restaurant. In either section, you can enjoy sole with almonds, swordfish in a white-wine sauce, red mullet *en papillote,* and an array of shellfish (including lobster). The list of classic Moroccan dishes includes a pastilla of pigeon, couscous, chicken with almonds, and kebabs.

PETIT POUCET, bd. Mohammed V, 86. Tel. 27-54-20.
Cuisine: FRENCH. **Reservations:** Not required. **Transportation:** Petit taxi.
$ Prices: Appetizers 10–55 DH ($1.25–$6.90); main dishes 30–65 DH ($3.75–$8.15). AE, MC, V.
Open: Lunch daily noon–2:30pm; dinner daily 6:30–10:30pm.

S   The floral murals were stained with water years ago, and the pseudo-baroque curlicues on the ceiling haven't seen paint in several decades. Founded in 1920, in time to feed and entertain French philosopher Antoine de Saint-Exupéry before his expeditions into the Sahara, the Petit Poucet is reminiscent of Morocco's French colonial era. You'll find such dishes as grilled sea bass, head of veal with a ravigote sauce, filet mignon, terrine of the chef, and a dessert soufflé flavored with Grand Marnier. Don't confuse this establishment with the less recommendable brasserie that lies next door.

SHOPPING

Save your serious shopping for Fez or Marrakesh if you are planning to visit either of those cities. While in Casablanca, you might also want to take a look at **Centre 2000,** located at boulevard Enphrette Boignet (formerly boulevard Mohammed el Hanssali) and Moulay Abderrahane. This complex is the closest thing in Casablanca to a North American shopping mall, and it contains about 30 different shops and at least five restaurants and cafés. It's open daily from 9am to 12:30pm and 3 to 7:30pm.

For leather, try **LaGriffe Skalli,** av. des Forces Armées Royales, 6 (tel. 22-39-46), which sells *haute cuir* worthy of the boutiques of Paris, but for much less money. LaGriffe is open daily from 8am to 8:30pm. Take a petit taxi or bus no. 7.

For a variety of gift items, visit **Bel Bacha,** av. des Forces Armées Royales, 8. Here you'll find luxurious European-style accessories on the street level and more typical souvenir merchandise in the basement, including jewelry and crafts. The place is open daily from 8am to 8:30pm. Take a petit taxi or bus no. 7.

EVENING ENTERTAINMENT

BAR CASABLANCA [RICK'S BAR], Casablanca Hyatt Regency, place Mohammed V (without number). Tel. 26-12-34.
Its 1930s-style ceiling fans and Foreign Legion decor re-create the kind of setting

where Humphrey Bogart might once again captivate Ingrid Bergman. Its speakeasy-style entrance, inspired by Rick's Café Américain, is near the reception desk of one of the most dramatic hotels in the center of town, but much of its business comes from affluent residents of the city. It's a bit like an elegant version of a French-Moroccan desert outpost, with lots of exposed hardwood, a dark-oak floor, movie posters, and a beat-up piano. The video eternally plays *Casablanca,* and music is heard from 6:30pm until midnight. Beer costs 27 DH ($3.40), and daily hours are 11am to 1am. Transportation: Petit taxi.

BLACK HOUSE, Casablanca Hyatt Regency, place Mohammed V (without number). Tel. 26-12-34.

Although it lies within the most exclusive and interesting hotel in Casablanca, its patrons are by no means limited to hotel guests. This is the safest, most international, and most sought-after disco in this part of Morocco, with a conscientious battalion of bouncers and a hip clientele. There's a long stand-up bar, plus giant video screens and special lighting effects synchronized with the music. As its name implies, the color scheme is based on the dramatic use of black. There is no strictly defined dress code, but smart and casual is preferred. Entry is restricted to those over 18, and hours are 10pm to 2am Thursday through Saturday. Transportation: Petit taxi.

Admission: 120 DH ($15), including first drink (second drink 30–45 DH [$3.75–$5.65]).

DIPLOMAT BAR, Hotel El Mansour, 27. av. des F.A.R. Tel. 31-30-11.

This is one of the most elegant and charming bars in the city, ensconced within a verdant glass-covered courtyard. The tables and chairs are wicker, the bar is richly polished mahogany in the English style, and a cascade of water spills down the side of one of the encircling walls. At teatime, a pianist fills the atrium with polished renditions of classical and popular music. Tea costs 30 DH ($3.75), alcohol-free drinks are 30 DH ($3.75), and alcoholic drinks go for 80 DH ($10). The place is open daily from 10pm to midnight or 1am, with tea served from 3 to 6pm. Transportation: Petit taxi.

AN EXCURSION TO ANFA & AÏN DIAB

Anfa is a Europeanized suburb with some of the most beautiful homes in Morocco. This quarter, reached from place Mohammed V, along boulevard Hassan I, was the site of the world-famous Anfa Hotel (torn down in 1973), the meeting place of Churchill, Roosevelt, and de Gaulle for the Casablanca Conference of World War II. The conference, in January of 1943, planned the invasion of Sicily, and here Roosevelt announced that "unconditional surrender" was being demanded of the Axis powers.

In addition to being one of the wealthiest suburbs of Casablanca, Anfa is also the oldest and most historic. It was the site of the original Phoenician trading post whose boundaries eventually grew into the modern city of today.

Although the upper reaches of Anfa include some of Casablanca's most upscale residential buildings, they are all dwarfed by a sparkling white complex whose encircling ramparts are impossible to miss from the coastal boulevard de la Corniche. The massive complex, completed in 1985 and containing several different palaces, a mosque, and a large library, is one of the many homes of the royal family of Saudi Arabia.

Aïn Diab, situated on the rocky peninsula of El Fank, is a pleasantly unhurried residential suburb. It is also one of the fastest-growing sea resorts in Morocco, receiving hordes of city residents on summer weekends and adding new hotels every year.

Aïn Diab is famous as the site of the impressive Hassan II Mosque, whose construction began in 1980 (see "What to See and Do," above). The principal boulevards are the coastal boulevard de la Corniche and boulevard de Biarritz.

WHERE TO STAY
Expensive

RIAD SALAM LE MERIDIEN, bd. de la Corniche (without number), Aïn Diab. Tel. 0/39-13-13. Fax 0/39-13-45. 218 rms (all with bath), 10 suites. **Bus:** 9 from boulevard de Paris.

$ **Rates:** 680 DH ($85) single; 790 DH ($98.75) double; extra bed 100 DH ($12.50); suites from 1,300 DH ($162.50). Breakfast 60 DH ($7.50) extra. AE, DC, MC, V.

This stylish French-owned hotel sits behind a façade of white stucco and flowing fountains, each of which acts as a prelude to the interior's extravaganza of Moorish carved filigree. The accommodations encircle a series of simulated lagoons, each traversed by footbridges, and a huge circular fountain whose waters drip into a swimming pool. Each room has its own terrace or balcony and is furnished in the "kasbah-boudoir" style.

Dining/Entertainment: Dining facilities include Restaurant Dar Andalous, Restaurant l'Océan, Restaurant La Pizzeria, and Restaurant La Brasserie. Bar Churchill and the hotel's disco are popular at night.

Services: Room service, concierge.

Facilities: Seawater Therapy Center (sea-mud skin treatments, saunas, gymnastics, Turkish baths), outdoor swimming pool.

Inexpensive

HOTEL BELLERIVE, bd. de la Corniche (without number), Aïn Diab. Tel. 0/39-14-09. 35 rms (all with bath). TEL **Bus:** 9.

$ **Rates:** 188 DH ($23.50) single; 228 DH ($28.50) double. Breakfast 23 DH ($2.90) extra. V.

This informal waterfront hotel provides nondescript accommodations containing all the necessities, including armchairs, desks, reading lamps, and complete baths. Most rooms have private balconies with ocean views. The hotel is often heavily booked by Europeans on beach holidays. Fixed-priced lunches and dinners are available for 83 DH ($10.40).

WHERE TO EAT
Moderate

LA CAMBUSE, bd. de la Corniche (without number). Tel. 36-71-05.
Cuisine: SEAFOOD. **Reservations:** Recommended. **Bus:** 9.

$ **Prices:** Appetizers 35–80 DH ($4.40–$10); main dishes 55–150 DH ($6.90–$18.75); fixed-priced menu 75 DH ($9.40). AE, DC, MC, V.
Open: Lunch daily noon–3pm; dinner daily 7:30–11:30pm.

La Cambuse rates as one of the best seafood restaurants along the coast. Its most popular dining area is the lively ground-floor brasserie, where big windows illuminate the knotty paneling. There's a more sedate upstairs dining room, with fewer tables, marine-inspired frescoes, and panoramic windows. A particularly good house specialty is a filet of John Dory meunière. Other dishes include brochette of swordfish, fondue bourguignonne, *couscous royal*, house-style stuffed mussels, scallops Provençale, lobster thermidor, and, for dessert, bananas flambé.

RESTAURANT LA MER, boulevard de la Corniche (without number), Phare d'el Hank. Tel. 36-33-15.
Cuisine: FRENCH. **Reservations:** Recommended. **Bus:** 9.

$ **Prices:** Appetizers 38–46 DH ($4.75–$5.75); main dishes 48–75 DH ($6–$9.40). AE, DC, MC, V.
Open: Lunch daily noon–2:30pm; dinner daily 8–10:30pm.

⭐ At this chic French-inspired seafood restaurant, you'll rub elbows with some of the most discerning diners in town. Set a few feet from the rocks and tidal flats of the Atlantic, it might remind you of eateries along the Côte d'Azur. During his tenure as president of France, Valéry Giscard d'Estaing visited this place.

You'll pass through a grottolike rock garden and, once inside, you'll be seated in one of a pair of lattice-decorated dining rooms filled with exposed cedar and large windows overlooking the coastline. Menu specialties focus on fresh fish and shellfish, such as oysters marinara, a classic fish soup, grilled filet of sole, red mullet en papillote, John Dory au gratin, grilled sea bass flambéed with fennel, and a changing array of daily specials. A limited number of meat dishes include filet mignon with shallots, succulent lamb chops, and veal.

MA BRETAGNE, bd. Sidi Abderrahane (without number). Tel. 36-21-12.
Cuisine: FRENCH. **Reservations:** Required. **Transporation:** Bus 9 or petit taxi.
$ Prices: Appetizers 45–125 DH ($5.65–$15.65); main dishes 55–125 DH ($6.90–$15.65). AE, DC, MC, V.
Open: Lunch daily noon–2:30pm; dinner daily 8–10:30pm.

⭐ The low-lying and unpretentious concrete villa that houses Ma Bretagne lies within its own gardens 2 miles from the other hotels and touristic facilities of the Aïn Diab/Anfa beachfront. You'll drive along a lonely and sun-flooded stretch of coastal highway, park under the oleanders of a partially covered parking lot, and head through glass doors into this restaurant, which has a lovely view of the sea and its coastline. Some critics say that this is the best restaurant in Casablanca, if not in all of Morocco. In any case, it offers a French-inspired *cuisine du marché*—daily menus based on the freshest and the finest ingredients of the day. The focus is usually on fresh fish. The wine list is excellent, especially the vintage Moroccan reds.

AN EXCURSION TO EL JADIDA

El Jadida, 62 miles south of Casablanca, is easily reached by buses that leave Casablanca every half hour, or by daily bus service from Marrakesh.

El Jadida Tourist Office is located on rue Ibn Khaldoun (tel. 27-24). In summer, hours are 8:30am to 3pm Monday through Friday; from mid-September to June, 8am to noon and 2 to 6pm Monday through Friday. The area code for El Jadida is 034.

During the days of the sailing ships, El Jadida's port was considered the best along the entire Atlantic coast of Morocco. Today, the city is a beach resort with a solid industrial base and a recently improved deepwater-port facility about a mile to the south, at Jorf Lasfar, where many of El Jadida's 150,000 inhabitants work. It is one of the few modern Moroccan cities whose architecture was not established by the Berbers or the Arabs, but rather by the Portuguese.

WHAT TO SEE & DO

El Jadida is a beach resort made popular by the annual influx of wealthy families from Marrakesh that began in the 1930s.

Today, the 16th-century **Portuguese citadel,** set to the south of an artificial seawall and to the north of the Ville Nouvelle, is the city's most interesting historical district. Many visitors walk along the top of the ramparts, admiring the view of the sea, the sky, and the four bastions of the old town.

Later, you can inspect the most famous enclosure in El Jadida, the **Portuguese cistern.** Originally designed as a storage place for munitions, it was built in the early 1500s. Its vaulted masonry ceiling, supported by five elegantly symmetrical rows of hand-hewn and brick-edged columns, is pierced with a single oculus window. The effect of sunlight interplaying with a layer of water below the stone vaulting has been described by many visitors as mystical. The entrance to the cistern is from a square in the center of the old town still known by the Portuguese name of Praça do Terreiro. Admission is 10 DH ($1.25). It's open Monday through Friday from 9am to noon and 2 to 6pm.

In 1921, the French restored the old Portuguese **Church of Our Lady of the Assumption,** on place Moussa. It has an arcaded front, and its former bell tower is now the pentagonal minaret of a mosque.

WHERE TO STAY & EAT

HOTEL CLUB SALAM DOUKKALA, av. de la Ligue Arabe (without number). Tel. 034/3737. 80 rms (all with bath) MINIBAR TV TEL **Transportation:** Bus from Casablanca's Safir Hotel; 15 DH ($1.90) one way.

$ Rates: 290 DH ($36.25) single; 368 DH ($46) double; breakfast 31 DH ($3.90) extra. MC, V.

Built in 1977, the Hotel Club Salam Doukkala looks like a high-tech version of a Moroccan kasbah complete with swimming pool and a view of one of the country's most famous beaches. Each bedroom has a small salon separated from the main room; furnishings are functionally modern in style. There is no air conditioning, but the ocean breezes usually make life tolerable around here. Meals cost 120 DH ($15). The in-house nightclub is open Tuesday through Sunday.

3. ESSAOUIRA

106 miles W of Marrakesh; 218 miles SW of Casablanca

GETTING THERE   By Bus   Buses run daily from Casablanca to Essaouira, the trip taking 5 hours. For information about departures, call 31-17-46 in Casablanca. Departures are from the City Terminal behind the Sheraton Casablanca, av. des Forces Armées Royales, 100. There are also SATAS bus arrivals from Marrakesh at the rate of 1 per day (5 hours). There is 1 bus per day arriving from Agadir in the south (3½ hours).

BY CAR   From Casablanca, take Route P8 south.

ESSENTIALS   The staff of the **Essaouira Tourist Office,** located at place Moulay el Hassan (tel. 234), across from the Porte Portugaise at the harbor, speak French and Arabic. The **area code** for Essaouira is 047.

Located at the end of a peninsula jutting into the Atlantic, Essaouira is the favorite beach resort of many Moroccan families, and it would be more popular year round were it not for strong winter tidal currents. Most of the year, however, its weather is considered almost perfect for swimming, and its beach is one of the loveliest anywhere. This, plus the nearby exoticism of medieval ramparts that ring the Medina, two kasbahs, and the abandoned Mellah (Jewish quarter), makes the city memorable.

Beginning in classical times, merchants and traders courted Essaouira for the purple dyes that were made there. Reduced from smelly messes of shellfish dug from the harbor sands, the dye became the symbolic color of imperial Rome, and an essential element in the robes of both the Roman and Byzantine aristocracy.

Between 1506 and 1628, the city was annexed by the Portuguese, who constructed a fort there (little of it remains). Most of the city was built after 1760, when a local sultan, envious of the splendor of nearby Agadir, began construction of the ramparts that still give Essaouira its distinctively fortified look.

By the early 1800s, its port, funneling 40% of all maritime traffic into Morocco, was the single most important destination for the many caravan routes originating in the Sudanese fortress of Timbuktu. Today, most maritime traffic has abandoned Essaouira in favor of the bigger and more commercially viable ports at Casablanca, El Jadida, and Tangier. Hampered by its small size, Essaouira handles only 3% of the country's merchandise, most of it fish. As a beach resort, however, it does a thriving business, mostly with Europeans.

The allure of Essaouira became well known during the hippie era, when Jimi Hendrix dropped in to turn on, and the rest of the flower generation followed his lead. Regarded as anathema to traditional Moroccan values, this behavior was not tolerated by the local police, and those hash-filled evenings are now only a memory.

WHAT TO SEE & DO

The **Great Mosque** is the major sight in Essaouira, although the **walled town** itself, founded in 1760 and once known as Mogador, is also worth the trip.

Essaouira's industrious people are fascinating. Many are employed in fishing and woodworking, and they're known for making furniture out of thuya wood.

From the **Skala,** an 18th-century fort lined with cannons at the harbor, you'll have a panoramic view of the sea and the "Purple Islands." Stroll along the waterfront, with its lovely gardens and mimosas and palm trees, and shop in the Medina, one of the most colorful along the Atlantic coast.

WHERE TO STAY

MODERATE

HOTEL DES ILES, bd. Mohammed V (without number), Essaouira. Tel. 034/23-29. 70 rms (all with bath). TV TEL

$ Rates: 295 DH ($36.90) single; 378 DH ($47.25) double. Breakfast 31 DH ($3.90) extra. AE, DC, MC, V.

The glamour of the Hotel des Iles, with its 1940s façade, outdistances everything else in town. One of its outlying poolside buildings housed soldiers during the French occupation of Morocco, but after their departure in 1956 the barracks were transformed into some of the hotel's most alluring accommodations. Other units, fronted with vines and flowers, encircle a large courtyard, and at the center are a swimming pool and a modernized version of a Bedouin tent. There's a cedar-paneled bar with large windows overlooking the pool. Each of the traditional, rather formal bedrooms in the main building sports dark paneling, big windows, and a renovated bathroom. Fixed-priced meals in the dining room cost 125 DH ($15.65).

HOTEL TAFOUKT, bd. Mohammed V, 58, Essaouira. Tel. 034/25-05. 40 rms (all with bath). A/C TEL

$ Rates: 193 DH ($24.15) single; 228 DH ($28.50) double; 312 DH ($39) triple. Breakfast 23 DH ($2.90) extra. MC, V.

The name of this little hotel means "sun" in Berber dialect. In many ways, its clean bedrooms offer the best value in town, and the management welcomes foreign visitors. Built in 1977, the Tafoukt sits in a garden-filled residential section of town, across the street from a promenade flanking the beach. Its three-story green-and-white façade has concrete flowerboxes and wooden balustrades. Each of the sunny rooms has a private bath and simple modern furnishings, and 10 of them come with a private balcony. Don't overlook the two Moroccan tearooms on the ground floor, where geometric tilework contrasts with the thuya and lemonwood paneling of the other public rooms.

WHERE TO EAT

The most adventurous readers will stroll along the quayside and purchase freshly grilled sardines straight from the sea from the many vendors.

MODERATE

CHALET DE LA PLAGE, bd. Mohammed V, 1. Tel. 21-58.
  Cuisine: FRENCH. **Reservations:** Not required.
$ Prices: Appetizers 20–40 DH ($2.50–$5); main dishes 45–60 DH ($5.65–$7.50); set menu 70 DH ($8.75). AE, DC, MC, V.
  Open: Lunch daily 12:30–3pm; dinner daily 7:30–10:30pm.

The best restaurant at the resort is a beachfront club-bistro located opposite the Hotel des Iles. The ambience is both stylish and fun, and the house specialties are good. Few dishes are finer than its shellfish and well-seasoned whitefish dishes—the pride of chef Khaled ben Ghadda. He also turns out a tasty fish soup, pigeon with almonds, grilled lamb cutlets, and a wide choice of omelets.

CHAPTER 6

MEKNES, FEZ &
THE MIDDLE
ATLAS

- **WHAT'S SPECIAL ABOUT MEKNES, FEZ & THE MIDDLE ATLAS**
- **SUGGESTED ITINERARY**
1. **MEKNES**
2. **FEZ**
3. **TAZA**

Although lying within an hour's drive of each other, Meknes and Fez (Fès in French) have radically different histories.

Meknes was created and built within a single generation by perhaps the most tyrannical monarch in the history of Morocco, Moulay Ismail. It slumbers today in the past glory of an era when its power controlled most of northwestern Africa and most of the Sudan, and emissaries from the capitals of Europe considered its splendor the Islamic answer to the court of Louis XVI at Versailles.

Today, Meknes is a market town filled with bustling souks that, although exotic, do not equal the vast labyrinth of the Medina at Fez. Meknes makes an excellent base for exploring Volubilis, the best-preserved Roman site in the country. It is also well suited for visits to the hilltop fortress of Moulay Idriss, where, until 1916, any European setting foot was likely to be imprisoned and killed.

Fez enjoyed a privileged status as a religious and academic stronghold from the beginning of the Islamic conversion of Morocco. It was the capital of the Merenid, Wattasid, and Alaouite dynasties. The cultural heart of Morocco, it has a thousand-year-old history and a medina that is a three-star attraction of the Arabic world. Some historians consider it the best-preserved medieval city in the Middle East.

From Fez you can take excursions into the Middle Atlas, the mountain range before Marrakesh and the High Atlas, which eventually leads to the sub-Sahara.

Fez and Meknes, the "birthplace" of Morocco, lie only 40 miles apart and getting to one or the other is relatively easy, but it is foolhardy and just too exhausting to try to explore both cities in one day, as many visitors attempt to do. The two cities are rivals, each vying for the tourist market. Fez has far better and more comfortable hotels, however, as those in Meknes tend to be limited.

SEEING MEKNES, FEZ & THE MIDDLE ATLAS

GETTING THERE

The best international arrival point is the airport at Casablanca. From there, it's an easy transfer by train to Meknes, with continuing service to Fez in the east. It's also possible to fly to Fez from Casablanca. CTM buses also link the cities of Meknes and Fez with Rabat and Casablanca.

WHAT'S SPECIAL ABOUT MEKNES, FEZ & THE MIDDLE ATLAS

Great Towns/Villages

☐ Fez, the most complete Islamic medieval city in the world, with a thousand-year-old history.

☐ Meknes, the imperial city of Moulay Ismail, lying in the heart of Morocco.

☐ Taza, the ancient fortress city in the east, once the capital of Morocco.

Monuments

☐ Volubilis, the Roman city outside Meknes, which enjoyed its heyday from A.D. 45 to 285.

☐ The Bou Inania Medersa, at Fez, the most exuberant example of a Merenid monument.

Ace Attractions

☐ The Medina of Fez, dating from 925—a labyrinthine and nostalgic time warp.

☐ The Medina of Meknes, with its memories of the infamous Moulay Ismail.

☐ Dar Jamaï, a 19th-century vizier's palace in Meknes, now a museum of Moroccan arts and crafts.

Special Events/Festivals

☐ Moussem of Moulay Idriss, Fez, in September—a fantastic festival of dance, music, and parades.

SUGGESTED ITINERARIES

Day 1: Explore the ancient Medina of Meknes and the city's other attractions.

Day 2: Based in Meknes, spend a day in its environs, seeing Volubilis and Moulay Idriss.

Days 3–4: Continue on to Fez and spend all your time (and you'll need every bit of it) getting to know this fascinating but often confusing city.

1. MEKNES

70 miles E of Rabat; 37 miles W of Fez

GETTING THERE **By Train** The **train station** (tel. 52-00-17 and 52-06-89), located on avenue de la Basse, lies half a mile east of the center of the New Town (Ville Nouvelle). Eight trains a day arrive from Rabat (2½ hours), and 7 trains from Fez (45 minutes).

By Bus The **CTM bus station** is at bd. Mohammed V, 47 (tel. 225-83). Hourly buses arrive from Fez (1 hour) and 3 buses a day arrive from Rabat (4 hours).

By Car From Rabat take route P1 east. From Fez, take Route P1 west.

Technically, Meknes is composed of a pair of cities, one richly medieval and historic, and the other a function of the French colonial regime of the 1920s. They lie on twin plateaus, facing each other across the valley of the Oued Boufekrane River. When combined, the twin cities compose the fifth-largest metropolis in Morocco, with a population of around 650,000. The triplicate ramparts and bastions of the old city measure more than 28 miles in length, and rank as one of the country's architectural wonders. There are nine gates with four-sided towers, and minarets of many different mosques pierce the skyline.

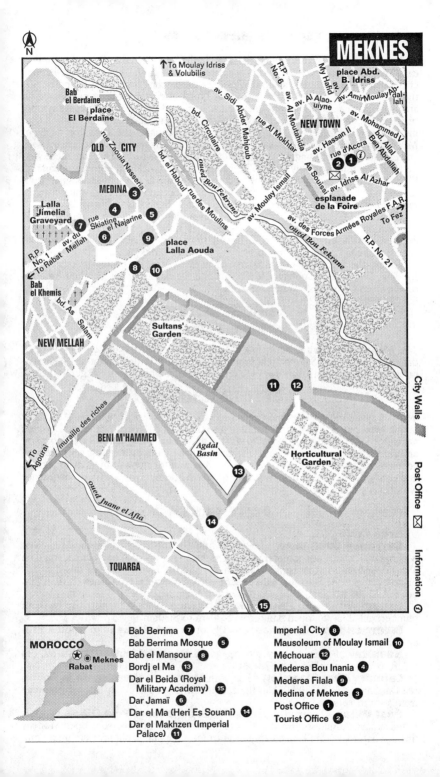

MEKNES

To Moulay Idriss & Volubilis

place Abd. B. Idriss

NEW TOWN

Bab el Berdaïne

place El Berdaïne

OLD CITY

rue Zaouia Nasseria

MEDINA 3

Lalla Jimelia Graveyard

rue Skiatine

el Najarine

7

4 5

6 9

8 10

place Lalla Aouda

R.P. No. 1 To Rabat

av. du Mellah

Bab el Khemis

bd. As Selam

NEW MELLAH

BENI M'HAMMED

Sultans' Garden

11 12

To Agourai / muraille des riches

Agdàl Basin

13

Horticultural Garden

oued Jnane el Afia

14

TOUARGA

15

av. Sidi Abder Mahjoub

R.P. No. 6

My Hard

av. Al Alaouiyne

av. Amir Moulay Abdallah

av. Al Moutahida

rue Al Mokhtar

av. Mohammed V

av. Hassan II

rue d'Accra

2 1 i

As Souissi

av. Idriss Al Azhar

Ben Abdallah

esplanade de la Foire

av. des Forces Armées Royales F.A.R.

To Fez

R.P. No. 21

oued Bou Fekrane

av. Moulay Ismaïl

bd. el Haboul

rue des Moulins

oued Bou Fekrane

bd. Circulaire

City Walls ■

Post Office ⊠

Information ⊙

MOROCCO

Rabat ● Meknes

Bab Berrima 7
Bab Berrima Mosque 5
Bab el Mansour 8
Bordj el Ma 13
Dar el Beida (Royal Military Academy) 15
Dar Jamaï 6
Dar el Ma (Heri Es Souani) 14
Dar el Makhzen (Imperial Palace) 11

Imperial City 8
Mausoleum of Moulay Ismail 10
Méchouar 12
Medersa Bou Inania 4
Medersa Filala 9
Medina of Meknes 3
Post Office 1
Tourist Office 2

Having survived in dusty obscurity as a dimly remembered trading post from as early as the 10th century, Meknes was the brainchild and almost single-handed creation of Sultan Moulay Ismail (1672–1727). After the Pharaohs of Egypt, he was the greatest single builder in the history of North Africa. Meknes is considered an architectural manifestation of his megalomania, and an awesomely impressive symbol of the enforced slavery of his enemies and the almost unchallenged domination over his citizens. His supervision of the city's construction is the basis for many of Morocco's legends. Setting an example to his workers by wielding a pickaxe himself, and constantly supervising the construction, Moulay Ismail would execute those who performed slipshod or slow work. The army of laborers included both European and Black African slaves captured in battle, convicts, as well as rebellious tribesmen from the surrounding region. The city was enlarged to contain vast stables, water cisterns, mosques, palaces, and a harem reported to contain hundreds of his wives.

Contrary to the wishes of Moulay Ismail, his heirs did not approach the glorification of Meknes with the same zeal as their father. After his death, the expansion of the city slowed and eventually stopped as the new sultans moved their capital and chief residence first to Fez and then to Marrakesh.

Today, the ocher-colored ramparts of Meknes, the bargaining masses of the Medina, the militarily impregnable Kasbah, and the exotic gardens combine into one of Morocco's fabulously grandiose cities.

ORIENTATION

INFORMATION

The **Meknes Tourist Office,** place Administrative, 27 (tel. 05/212-86), is open daily in summer from 8am to 3pm. From mid-September to June, hours are 8:30am to noon and 2:30 to 6pm. You can pick up information and hire official guides here.

GETTING AROUND

You can reach most addresses within both the Ville Nouvelle and the Medina by taking local bus no. 5, 7, or 9. You will also, as in all Moroccan cities, find *grands taxis* (for longer hauls) and *petits taxis* (for shorter hauls), which will transport you around the city and its environs. Obviously, since taxi rates for most runs are very economical, it is preferable to take a taxi than to wait for an overcrowded, hot, stuffy, and erratically scheduled bus. Even in most taxis, however, you'll have to share space with other passengers.

FAST FACTS

Area Code   05.

Currency Exchange   The limited number of banks within the Medina of Meknes will usually not accept traveler's checks, so for any such transaction, you'd be well advised to do your banking within the Ville Nouvelle. One of this district's biggest banks is the **Banque Marocaine du Commerce Extérieur** (BMCE), av. des F.A.R., 98 (tel. 203-52), open daily from 10am to 2pm and 4 to 8pm.

Drugstore   Go to **Pharmacie d'Urgence,** place Administrative (without number) (tel. 233-75), open daily from 8:30am to 8:30pm.

Emergencies   For **police,** call 19; for an **ambulance** or to report a **fire,** call 15.

Hospital   For emergency service, go to **Hôpital Moulay Ismail,** av. des F.A.R. (without number) (tel. 228-06).

Laundry/Dry Cleaning   For both services, try **Pressing de la Poste,** rue Dar Smen, 14 (tel. 309-03), in the Medina. It is open Monday through Saturday from 9am to 1pm and 3 to 8pm.

Post Office   For mail and stamps, go to the **Meknes Post Office,** which is found at place Administrative (don't try to phone—show up in person); open Monday through Saturday from 8am to 2pm. You can use the public phones here until 9pm.

WHAT TO SEE & DO

BAB MANSOUR, place El Hedim.

The city's most interesting gate was begun during the reign of Moulay Ismail and completed by his son and successor, Moulay Abdullah, in 1752. Its Ionic and Corinthian columns came from the ruins of Volubilis (see below). Opposite the gate, characterized by an ogival horseshoe-shaped archway, sprawls the vast (about 650 feet by 330 feet) rectangular place El Hedim, the main square of the Medina. On the other side is a smaller gateway, Bab Djama En Nouar, dating from the 18th century. If you're driving, incidentally, you can leave your car here (tip the attendant).

THE MEDINA OF MEKNES

The Medina of Meknes is not as big, as rich, or as well supplied with merchandise as that of its nearby counterpart at Fez. There are, however, many worthwhile diversions here, most of which involve the work of Moulay Ismail. Almost everything in the old part of Meknes dates from the late 1600s and early 1700s.

The Medina's mazelike alleyways, few of which are marked, almost compel visitors to engage an official guide from the tourist office or an unofficial one from among the masses of young men who will present themselves during your visit.

While in the Medina you may want to visit the **Medersa Bou Inania,** Souk Sebbat, a college founded during the reign of the Merenid sultan Abou El Hassan (1331–50); and an outstanding example of Merenid architecture. Note especially the bronze door and intricate carving. Stand in the courtyard, with its large ablution basin, and look up to see where the students lodged. From its rooftop terrace you'll have a view of the Grand Mosque of the Medina, Mosquée Kebira, which is not open to the public. The college is open daily in summer from 9am to noon and 4 to 7pm; in winter, daily hours are 8am to noon and 2:30 to 6pm. Admission is 10 DH ($1.25).

Also worth seeing is the **Medersa Filala,** located on rue Sebab, which was built during the reign of Moulay Ismail near the Grand Mosque. It is not open to the public.

DAR JAMAÏ, place El Hedim (without number). Tel. 308-63.

At the far end of the "Square of Destruction" stands Dar Jamaï, a palace constructed by the vizier Djamaï during the reign of Moulay Hassan (1873–94). Now a museum of Moroccan arts and crafts, it has served many functions in its day—from a military hospital to a harem. Pass through the handsome courtyard and proceed through one ornamental salon after another, observing the antique Meknes embroideries and old Berber silver jewelry. The reception room is furnished in classic Moroccan style. Copies of the Koran on display date from the 17th century.

Admission: 10 DH ($1.25).
Open: Wed–Mon 9am–noon and 3–6pm. **Bus:** 5, 7, or 9.

MOSQUE OF BAB BERRIMA, rue Sekkakine (without number).

The Mosque of Bab Berrima, built during the reign of Sidi Mohammed Ben Abdullah (1757–90), forms a corner of the Berrima quarter, which used to be the Kasbah. The Berrima quarter is surrounded by a high four-cornered wall that separates it from the walled Mellah, the former Jewish quarter. The Mellah is now inhabited mainly by Muslims, since most Jews left either for France or Israel after Morocco was granted independence in 1956.

Bus: 5, 7, or 9.

IMPERIAL CITY

This quarter, entered through the gate called Bab Mansour, was almost completely the work of Moulay Ismail. Much of what remains is in ruins, including the palace of the former sultan, **Dar Kebira,** found on place Lalla Aouda. Now hardly more than a shell, the palace, dating from 1677, at one time comprised nearly two dozen buildings. Today, the section is mainly residential.

Since streets often have no names and major monuments are often unmarked, it is necessary to explore this district with an official guide from the tourist office (see above). That way, you'll know what you're looking at. By passing through the Bab

Filala, you reach the **Koubbet El Khiyatine,** a pavilion where Moulay Ismail used to receive foreign ambassadors.

At the opposite side of place Lalla Aouda stands the **Mausoleum of Moulay Ismail,** the only mosque in Morocco open to non-Muslims. You can't go in to see the actual tomb, but you may enter a main courtyard and, once you have removed your shoes, a smaller courtyard after that. The mausoleum is usually open daily from 9am to noon and 3 to 6pm. Sometimes admission is refused, particularly if men and women, especially women, are too skimpily attired. Wear clothes that cover most of your arms and legs. The custodian guide expects a tip for letting you in; otherwise, no admission is charged.

Standing beside the Koubbet El Khiyatine (see above), on place Lalla Aouda, is the so-called **Christian Prison,** which is touted as the place where Christian slaves were imprisoned, although scholars dispute such a claim. A guard is usually here to unlock the door and show you through these damp, macabre underground cellars, which are open Saturday through Thursday from 8:30am to noon and 2:30 to 6pm, on Friday from 8am to noon and 3 to 6pm. No admission is charged, but you should tip the guard.

Directly south of the Mausoleum of Moulay Ismail stands a gateway called **Bab Er Rih** (Gateway of the Wind). Here you come upon the **Dar el Makhzen,** the imperial palace where King Hassan II stays whenever he is in town; naturally, entrance to the public is forbidden. In 1697, this was the chief palace of the sultan.

If you follow the long wall protecting the king's palace, you will come to the **Bordj el Ma** (Bastion of Water), where the precious water of the town was stored. You will have entered the colonnaded **Méchouar,** where former sultans received adulations and gifts from their subjects.

To the east of this stands the **Kasbah of Hedrache** (also called Kasbah Hadrach), which used to be the barracks of the Bukharis—the elite guard of the sultan's army, with warriors carefully chosen from the Sudan.

From this point, ask your guide to direct you to **Heri Es Souani,** a short walk from the Kasbah. Sometimes referred to as Dar el Ma, this is a large granary warehouse with vaulted underground silos.

From here, a lane leads to **Dar el Beida,** directly to the southeast, an 18th-century fortress whose pavilions and gardens were originally constructed by Sidi Mohammed ben Abdallah, an 18th-century sultan. Ever since the father of the present king turned it into a military academy in the late 1950s, admission to its courtyard and gardens has been forbidden.

Below the military academy stands the **Mosque of Er Rouah** (Mosque of the Stables), which Sidi Mohammed, the sultan, ordered constructed in 1790. These stables are said to have once sheltered 12,000 horses and mules. In ruins and exposed to the sky, the vast chambers are impressive for their size alone; they are enclosed by walls and divided by arches. A former palace built over the stables contained nearly two dozen pavilions, and the barracks of the king's Black Guard were here as well. The descendants of these former slaves are reputed to form King Hassan II's bodyguard today. The reservoir nearby, comprising approximately 10 acres, was completed with the help of 50,000 slaves.

WHERE TO STAY

Meknes has very few really good hotels and many of the hotels in the Medina are not even adequate. The following recommendations are clean and reasonably comfortable. By the price standards of Meknes, the Hotel Transatlantique is considered "Very Expensive," with double rooms at 474 DH ($59.25), whereas the Hotel Rif or Hotel Zaki is judged "Expensive," with doubles renting for 340 to 400 DH ($42.50 to $50). "Moderate" suggests doubles costing 235 DH ($29.40) a night, and "Inexpensive" means doubles at 210 DH ($26.25). Anything under that is "Budget."

VERY EXPENSIVE

HOTEL TRANSATLANTIQUE, rue El Meriniyine (without number), Meknes. Tel. 05/200-02. Fax 05/200-57. 30 rms (all with bath). A/C MINIBAR TV

TEL **Transportation:** Grand taxi.
$ Rates: 437 DH ($54.65) single; 474 DH ($59.25) double. Breakfast 45 DH ($5.65) extra. AE, DC, MC, V.

The best hotel in town, the five-star Transatlantique (just north of the Medina) dates from the 1930s and the French colonial heyday. Greatly enlarged and improved in 1967, it is an elegant building offering views of the Medina. Bedrooms are all well equipped and within earshot of the muezzin when he calls the faithful to prayer (this may seem less than a joy at daybreak, around 3:30am in summer). You can take a taxi to the center of town, or walk through the pleasant suburban area.

Dining/Entertainment: Restaurant Bellevue serves international cuisine and Restaurant Ismailia concentrates on Moroccan dishes (see below). There is a good bar that serves tasty hors d'oeuvres, plus a snack bar.

Services: Laundry, dry cleaning.

Facilities: Two swimming pools, parking.

EXPENSIVE

HOTEL RIF, Zankat Accra (without number), Meknes. Tel. 05/225-91.
120 rms (all with bath). A/C MINIBAR TEL **Bus:** 2 or 3.
$ Rates: 260–310 DH ($32.50–$38.75) single; 340–398 DH ($42.50–$49.75) double. Breakfast 31 DH ($3.90) extra. MC, V.

The accommodations here are adequate, with most units opening onto the inner courtyard and swimming pool. Some rooms contain a TV. The entire hotel has a pleasing decor, the use of chalk white offset by a different color on each floor. Overlooking the courtyard is the dining room, where a fixed-priced meal costs 109 DH ($13.65). An afternoon sit-down mint tea is recommended in the Moroccan salon. In the evening, both belly dancing and dancing to records take place in the lower-level nightclub, where the first drink costs 30 DH ($3.75) and each additional drink goes for 20 DH ($2.50). The nightclub is open nightly from 10:30pm to 2:30am, with an occasional presentation of a folkloric show.

HOTEL ZAKI, route de l'Ifrane, 40, Meknes. Tel. 05/200-63. 163 rms (all with bath). TV TEL **Transportation:** Petit taxi.
$ Rates: 300 DH ($37.50) single; 398 DH ($49.90) double. Breakfast 30 DH ($3.75) extra. AE, DC, MC, V.

On the outskirts of the Ville Nouvelle, 2 miles from the Medina, is this owner-managed Moroccan-style hotel (named, in fact, for the owner). The walls of its lobby are covered with red brick set into geometric patterns. Both of the hotel's two restaurants (one Moroccan, one European) serve lunch and dinner daily. The bedrooms are modern, clean, unpretentious, and comfortable.

MODERATE

HOTEL BAB MANSOUR, rue Amin Abdelkadar (without number), Meknes. Tel. 05/252-39. 65 rms (all with bath). TEL **Bus:** 2 or 3.
$ Rates: 191 DH ($21.90) single; 234 DH ($29.25) double. Breakfast 25 DH ($3.15) extra. AE, MC, V.

The newest three-star hotel in Meknes was built in 1988 close to the railway and bus (CTM) stations of the Ville Nouvelle. You'll find a bar, a restaurant, and a nightclub on the premises. All rooms are comfortably but simply furnished in an international style; some, but not all, of them are air-conditioned.

GRAND HOTEL VOLUBILIS, av. des F.A.R., 45, Meknes. Tel. 05/201-02. 36 rms (all with bath). TEL **Bus:** CTM.
$ Rates: 191 DH ($23.90) single; 234 DH ($29.25) double. Breakfast 23 DH ($2.90) extra. No credit cards.

Close to the CTM bus station and a short walk from the railway station, this simple but clean and pleasant place has good-size bedrooms, most with shower and toilet, phone, and central heating. The hotel's restaurant offers a tourist menu for 70 DH ($8.75), and the Oriental Cabaret is open nightly until 3am. Although it has seen better days, this is one of the more nostalgic hotels of Meknes.

INEXPENSIVE

HOTEL DE NICE, Zankat Accra, 10, Meknes. Tel. 05/203-18. 30 rms (all with bath). TEL **Bus:** 2 or 3.
$ Rates: 167 DH ($20.90) single; 208 DH ($26) double. Breakfast 23 DH ($2.90) extra. No credit cards.

⑤ This establishment lies in the Ville Nouvelle, near the post office and the Hotel Rif. Built in the 1950s and refurbished in 1974, the small, semimodern Hotel de Nice offers functionally furnished, clean bedrooms, a restaurant, and a "New York" bar. A fixed-priced menu in its Moroccan restaurant costs 83 DH ($10.40).

HOTEL PALACE, rue du Ghana, 11, Meknes. Tel. 05/257-77. 40 rms (all with bath). TEL **Bus:** 2 or 3.
$ Rates: 167 DH ($20.90) single; 208 DH ($26) double. Breakfast 23 DH ($2.90) extra. No credit cards.

Built in the 1950s, the three-floor Hotel Palace is still fairly modern, though without an elevator. It stands in the Ville Nouvelle, opposite the post office. You'll find neon lighting and plastic furnishings; however, the bedrooms are compact and scoured daily—and the rates are not bad.

WHERE TO EAT

MODERATE

RESTAURANT BELLEVUE, Hotel Transatlantique, rue El Meriniyine (without number). Tel. 200-02.
   Cuisine: INTERNATIONAL/MOROCCAN. **Reservations:** Not required. **Transportation:** Grand taxi.
$ Prices: Appetizers 35–45 DH ($4.40–$5.65); main dishes 45–100 DH ($5.65–$12.50). AE, DC, MC, V.
   Open: Lunch daily 12:30–2:30pm; dinner daily 8–10:30pm.
Located one floor above street level in the best hotel in Meknes, within the oldest and most historical core, Restaurant Bellevue enjoys a sweeping view of the northern edge of the old town's majestic ramparts. Service is formal, eminently correct, and evocative of the last days of the French colonial regime in Morocco. You can get the usual array of beef, chicken, and lamb dishes, prepared in a rather bland style, but a better bet might be one of the Meknassi dishes such as *djaja taret* (chicken with chick peas and raisins) or *couscous au lait.* The aromatic mint tea served here is considered among the best in the country.

RESTAURANT ISMAILIA, Hotel Transatlantique, rue El Meriniyine (without number). Tel. 200-02.
   Cuisine: MOROCCAN. **Reservations:** Recommended. **Transportation:** Grand taxi.
$ Prices: Appetizers 30–42 DH ($3.75–$5.25); main dishes 48–105 DH ($6–$13.15). AE, DC, MC, V.
   Open: Daily dinner 8–10:30pm.
This restaurant is located on the lobby level of the newest wing of the historic Hotel Transatlantique (see above). Specialties include a wide array of *tajines,* couscous dishes, and kebabs—plus a delectable version of lamb *mechoui,* so tender from its long cooking process that the meat literally falls off the bone. A team of Moroccan musicians, playing from a dais at one end of the elegantly ornate dining room, adds their contribution to your meal.

INEXPENSIVE

BAR RESTAURANT LA COUPOLE, av. Hassan II (without number). Tel. 224-83.
   Cuisine: FRENCH. **Reservations:** Not required. **Bus:** 2 or 3.

$ Prices: Appetizers 15–35 DH ($1.90–$4.40); main dishes 18–45 DH ($2.25–$5.65); fixed-priced menu 60 DH ($7.50). No credit cards.
Open: Daily 7am–3am.

Situated in the Ville Nouvelle near the Rif Hotel, La Coupole is not particularly chic, but it does serve good food in a pleasant atmosphere. The tourist menu includes hors d'oeuvres, salade niçoise or tomato salad, then entrecôte with vegetables. The à la carte selection is made up of many appetizers (salads, fish, and vegetables), tajine of lamb with prunes or lemon and olives, kebab El Maghour, chateaubriand, and rabbit with mushrooms. *Pastilla* and mechoui are available on request.

LA HACIENDA, route de Fez–Meknes. Tel. 210-92.
　Cuisine: FRENCH. **Reservations:** Not required. **Transportation:** Grand taxi.
$ Prices: Appetizers 18–30 DH ($2.25–$3.75); main dishes 35–65 DH ($4.40–$8.15). MC, V.
　Open: Lunch daily 12–3:30pm; dinner daily 7–11pm.

La Hacienda is a country inn about 2 miles outside of Meknes on the road to Fez (signs point the way through a woodland). It's ideal for leisurely luncheons or dinners in a holiday atmosphere. As its name suggests, it is built hacienda-style around a swimming pool, with a rustic, farm-motif interior. The menu offers many French dishes, such as escargots. Main dishes include entrecôte with anchovies and hamburger. Try a basket of fruit for dessert. If you order the house specialty, a small charcoal stove will be placed on your table so that you can cook the meats to your satisfaction—you'll be given a kebab or two, sausages, a lamb chop, and a small beefsteak. In the evening, there is entertainment in the basement nightclub (open from 10:30pm to 1am), often featuring folk dances from the Middle Atlas. Admission is 30 DH ($3.75), including one drink.

ROTISSERIE KARAM, rue du Ghana, 2. Tel. 224-75.
　Cuisine: MOROCCAN/INTERNATIONAL. **Reservations:** Not required. **Bus:** 2 or 3.
$ Prices: Appetizers 4–7 DH (50¢–90¢); main dishes 20–55 DH ($2.50–$6.90); fixed-priced menus 26 and 31 DH ($3.25 and $3.90). No credit cards.
　Open: Lunch daily 12:30–3pm; dinner daily 7:30–10:30pm.

The Rôtisserie Karam, in the Ville Nouvelle a block from the Hotel Palace, offers a good low-cost dinner. The dining room is clean, the service courteous and speedy. You can order a salad, followed by meat or chicken, along with french fries, bread, dessert, and a beverage. Try the grilled brains, filet of entrecôte, or a Wiener Schnitzel. I suggest you skip the hamburger made with horse meat, a favorite of the locals.

ONE-DAY EXCURSIONS
VOLUBILIS & MOULAY IDRISS

Only 19 miles north of Meknes lie the finest Roman ruins in Morocco—at **Volubilis,** one of the country's oldest cities. Situated on a windswept plain surrounded by rugged scenery, Volubilis became a royal residence and the capital of Mauretania Tingitana during the reign of Juba II (25 B.C.–A.D. 23). Eventually, it was annexed to the Roman Empire. Rome abandoned the colony in 285, and the city drifted along until the appearance of Islam in 684. Again Volubilis fell into decay and serious excavations were begun only in 1915. Although you may have seen more dramatic ruins, you'll find the scope of these impressive. Volubilis sprawls over 100 acres encircled by a 2nd-century rampart approximately 1½ miles long.

The most notable structures include the House of Orpheus (named for a large mosaic in the reception room depicting Orpheus at play with a group of animals); the Baths of Galius (the most important in Morocco, although badly decayed); the Triumphal Arch, commissioned by Silvius Aurelius Sebastianus; the Basilica, with two large apses; the 3rd-century Forum; the House of the Youth, with its central patio typical of the private villas of that time; the House of the Labors of Hercules with its mosaics; the House of the Beasts, noted for its wild-animal mosaics; and the colonnade of the Palace of Gordius, ranging upward to the Tangier Gate, from which there is a superb panorama of the archeological garden.

Guides at the entrance will direct you through the ruins for a fee. Admission costs 15 DH ($1.90), and the ruins are open daily from 8am to 6:30pm, closing at 5:30pm in winter.

Volubilis lies 2 miles from Moulay Idriss. It's often possible for several people to rent a collective grand taxi from Meknes to both Volubilis and Moulay Idriss for 75 DH ($9.40) round trip for the whole taxi. You can also just occupy a seat in a taxi going there.

✪ About 2 miles from Volubilis (21 miles north of Meknes), **Moulay Idriss** is one of Morocco's most venerated sites. Sitting on two rocky spurs split by a deep gorge, this ancient city is considered sacred because it contains the *zawiya* (sanctuary) of Moulay Idriss, the founder of the Idrissid dynasty, the first Arab dynasty to rule over Morocco. His mausoleum, whose green-tiled roof dominates the city, is the site of an annual pilgrimage—called a moussem—in August and September. Non-Muslims may not enter. In fact, at one time foreigners were not welcome under any circumstances in Moulay Idriss, but happily that ruling has been changed.

Even if the city were not holy, you might still want to visit it just for its scenery. Pull your car or taxi into the market square, where it's easy to secure a guide. He may speak little or no English, but you should consider his services nevertheless. Although a walk through the town is interesting, the most moving sights are in the town's periphery. You'll need help getting up and down the narrow streets and over the encircling roads (many of which lead to blind alleys). Outside the town, incidentally, are hot springs once used by the Romans.

You may want to conclude your tour by walking through the teeming souks of the Medina. The town hasn't quite arrived in the 20th century, but electricity has been installed in some places. As of yet, there is no recommendable hotel or restaurant. If you're hungry, and not fastidious, you can get lamb kebabs grilled over an open charcoal brazier in the marketplace.

Because there are no tours from Meknes, many tourists take a collective taxi for about 7 DH (90¢) per seat. Buses to Moulay Idriss leave the Bab Mansour station in Meknes about every hour, costing 4 DH (50¢). Motorists should take route P6 northwest of Meknes, turning right at the signposted secondary road to Moulay Idriss.

EN ROUTE TO AZROU

The route from Meknes to Azrou, a town known for its handcrafts, is quite beautiful. You go through some 15½ miles of rolling farmland interspersed by equally fertile, postage-stamp-size plots of local owners, who cultivate and harvest them in the old-fashioned way.

Along this road, you come to **El Hajeb,** perhaps Morocco's cleanest village, where there are bright, primitive pictures carefully painted on the walls of buildings, an old fort, and steps carved into the hillside. This is the wine-growing region, and the fields are spiky with vines. The road starts to climb, and fir trees clothe the slopes and heavy cows graze in green fields.

You'll see a sign on the right, **Auberge Amros,** just 3 miles before you reach Azrou and 38½ miles from Meknes. Turn into the yard and wander into the tiny, dark, highly polished bar, where more than six people make a crowd. The spotless dining room, with its red-checked tablecloths, is always open at lunchtime (from 12:30 to 3pm), but you may decide to return here for the night—to sleep in the silence of the countryside, a silence broken only by the creaking of storks nesting on the roof and in every available fir tree. Bedrooms off the garden are simple, as is the plumbing; 50 DH ($6.25) for a double. Dinner (from 7:30 to 11pm) will consist of whatever is available, the charge being based on what and how much you eat. Even this paradise of quiet can become busy when locals drive out from Azrou to eat. The telephone

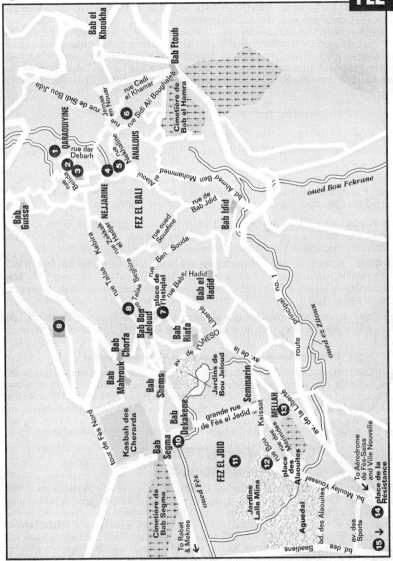

FEZ

Bab el Khoukha

Bab Ftouh

rue Cadi el Khamar

QARAOUIYINE

rue de Sidi Bou Jida

Jenaa en Nouar

rue Sidi Ali Ai Boughaleb

Cimetière de Bab el Hamra

rue dar Debarh

rue Nejjaine

ANALOUS

Alaoui

bd Ahmed Ben Mohammed

oued Bou Fekrane

rue Bellida

NEJJARINE

FEZ EL BALI

rue de Bab Jdid

Bab Guissa

rue el Hababe

rue Talaa Kebira

rue oued Souafine

Ben Souda

Bab Idid

rue Talaa Seghira

rue de Bab el Hadid

rue Babl el Hadid

Bab el Hadid

Place d'Istiqlal

Bab Bou Jeloud

Liberté

FUNESO

tour de Fès Nord

Bab Chorfa

Bab Mahrouk

av. de la

route

principal nou 1

oued ez Zitoun

Kasbah des Cherarda

Bab Shems

Bab Riafa

Jardins de Bou Jeloud

Semmarin

Ksissat

MELLAH

av. de la Liberté

Cimetière de Bab Segna

Bab Segna

Bab Dekakene

grande rue de Fès el Jedid

rue des Merinides

rue Bou

place des Alaouites

To Aérodrome de Fès-Saiss and Ville Nouvelle

oued Fès

To Rabat & Meknes

FEZ EL JDID

Jardins Lalla Mina

Aguedal

bd. Moulay Youssef

place de la Résistance

bd. des Alaouites

Saadiens

bd. des

av des Sports

MOROCCO
Fez
Rabat

Andalusian Quarter ❻
Armory Museum ❾
Attarine Medersa ❸
Bou Inania ❽
Dyers' Street & Souk ❺
Great Mosque ❷
The Medina ⓫
The Mellah ⓭
Moroccan National Tourist Office ⓮
Museum of Moroccan Art and Handcrafts ❼
Old Mechouar Courtyard ❿
Royal Palace (Palais Royal) ⓬
Seffarin Medersa ❹
Syndicat d' Initiative ⓯
Tanners Quarter ❶

number is 5 "par la poste," which means you must ask for the post office at Azrou and ask to be connected with the establishment.

Drive on into the commercial part of **Azrou,** the first real town of the Middle Atlas, where gasoline is refined, passing on into the old town. After lunch at the Hotel du Panorama, you'll have time to drive down to Fez and back to Meknes. If you have the time to spare, turn off the Fez road before Immouzer for the **Tour Touristique des Lacs,** a drive of about 34 miles around five tranquil lakes and through beautiful country.

---

2. FEZ

124 miles E of Rabat; 182 miles E of Casablanca;
37 miles E of Meknes; and 203 miles S of Tangier

GETTING THERE   By Plane   Royal Air Maroc has 3 flights a week from Paris. From Casablanca, Royal Air Inter has daily connections to Fez via Rabat. The **Aérodome de Fès-Saiss** (tel. 237-12) is 7½ miles from town.

By Train   From Tangier, there are 3 trains a day, taking 6 hours. From Rabat, 8 trains arrive daily (4 hours). The **train station** is at rue Chenguit and avenue des Almohades (tel. 250-01) at the northern edge of the Ville Nouvelle.

By Bus   Buses arrive hourly from Meknes (1 hour). Six buses a day run from Rabat to Fez (5½ hours), and 3 buses a day arrive from Marrakesh (8½ to 11 hours). The **bus station,** Gare Routière CTM (tel. 220-41), lies next to place Baghdadi, at the western edge of Fès el Bali.

By Car   From Rabat, continue east along route Pl. From Tangier in the north, take route P38 toward Tetuán, then go south along the P28 until the junction with the P3 into Fez.

The third-largest city of Morocco, Fez is the oldest of the four Imperial Cities and perhaps the best preserved. Its role as the capital of the first Moroccan dynasty and as the center for the intellectual elite (who seem always to have lived there), as well as its reputation as a fervently committed religious stronghold, has made it one of the most prestigious cities in the Muslim world. It is the cultural capital of Morocco, and the city most committed to preserving the glory that was Islamic Andalusia.

ORIENTATION

INFORMATION

The **Moroccan National Tourist Office** is at place de la Résistance (tel. 06/234-60), at avenue Hassan II. It is open in summer Monday through Friday from 7am to 2pm; from mid-September to June, Monday through Friday from 8:30am to noon and 2:30 to 6:30pm. The local tourist office for Fez, **Syndicat d'Initiative,** on boulevard Mohammed V (tel. 06/247-69), is found in the BMCE building. Here you can rent official guides for about 30 DH ($3.75) per half day. It is open in summer Monday through Friday from 8am to 3pm; and from mid-September to June, Monday through Friday from 8:30am to 12:30pm and 2:30 to 6:30pm.

GETTING AROUND

Instead of buses, which are awkward because of their unreliable schedules and complicated routes, I recommend that you hail one of the petit taxis on the street.

IMPRESSIONS

Fez where all is Eden, or a wilderness.
—Anonymous

These are surprisingly inexpensive, usually 6 DH (75¢); of course, you must share your ride with at least two other persons, which keeps the costs low. Grands taxis are preferred for trips into the environs. Taxis can usually be found at the post office or the tourist office. Remember that both bus fares and taxi rates in the city double after 8pm.

FAST FACTS

Area Code 06.

Bookstore The **English Bookstore of Fès,** Hassan II, 68 (tel. 208-420), is in the vicinity of place de la Résistance. It is open Monday through Friday from 8:30am to 12:30pm and 3 to 7pm.

Currency Exchange A branch of **BMCE** operates at place Mohammed V (no phone), near the tourist office. It is open Monday through Friday from 8:30am to noon and 3 to 5pm.

Drugstore Pharmacie, Municipalité de Fez, bd. Moulay Youssef (without number) (tel. 233-80), is the late-night pharmacy for Fez, open daily from 8pm to 8am.

Police Call 19 in an emergency. The station is located on avenue Mohammed V.

Post Office Have your mail sent to the **Fez Post Office,** avenue Hassan II and boulevard Mohammed V (don't try to phone—just show up), in Ville Nouvelle. Telephone calls can also be placed here. It is open in summer Monday through Friday from 7am to 2:30pm; from mid-September through June, Monday through Friday from 8:30am to 6:30pm.

WHAT TO SEE & DO
FÈS EL BALI

THE MEDINA

The ancient city offers a decaying array of palaces, mosques, souks, national monuments, and medersas (former schools or colleges, now relatively abandoned). Once home to the wealthy as well as the poor, it is now home to the poor alone. A guide is essential, even for those who pride themselves on getting around Moroccan cities without local help—the Medina has been called the most complicated square mile on earth.

The streets, a labyrinth of alleyways, are extremely narrow, and cars or taxis may not enter. The houses rise high, blocking the sun. Inside, the buildings are often dark and musty, especially in winter, when windows and doors are closed. Yet many of the buildings, in spite of their unprepossessing façades, conceal private courtyards and extravagantly decorated salons.

Aside from the historical monuments outlined below, take time to observe the everyday life—by far the most enduring attraction of the Medina. Notice, for example, the women making dough for their bread at home, and then taking it to the baker to be popped into his ancient oven. You can wander past almost any door (except for the mosques and private homes) and watch the artisans practice their age-old crafts.

The soul of the Medina is its series of souks, or marketplaces, sometimes called bazaars. The most interesting is the **Souk el Henna,** the spice bazaar, which is reached by taking a right turn just before the Attarine Arch at the Souk el Attarin. Hundreds of years ago it was the site of a madhouse, but later got its name from the henna leaves and henna paste sold here. Although more and more potters are moving

IMPRESSIONS

There is scarcely a view of Fez that is not beautiful,
scarcely a glimpse that is not sad.
—Walter Harris

in, you can still fill your other shopping needs here, especially if you're interested in some dried skins of lizards or snakes. You can purchase mascara in its original rock form, aphrodisiacs, health potions (with exaggerated claims), extracts of perfumes, ambergris, cooking spices, and, yes, even poisons.

Some may find it a memorable, if somewhat offensive, diversion to visit the **Tanners' Quarter,** along rue el Mechattine. I strongly suggest that you buy a sprig of mint from one of the many vendors in the alleyways before venturing in. First you'll be taken through the section of vats where the animal hides are treated by scantily clothed men, the stench of freshly killed animals permeating the air. You'll proceed to a terrace where you can look down at the dye-filled vats in which the treated hides are submerged.

You can also visit the **Dyers' Street,** called Souk Sabbighin, lying directly below the Séffarin Medersa (see below). Brilliantly colored yarn and cloth can be seen drying in the desert heat. You can see workers toiling over centuries-old cauldrons, making multicolored dyes based on "recipes" handed down from the Middle Ages.

ANDALUSIAN QUARTER, crossed by Mohammed El Alaoui.

The Quartier des Potiers (Potters' Square) is in the Andalusian Quarter. As you approach, you'll receive countless offers from prospective guides to show you through for a fee. The potters practice their craft with consummate skill, most of them trained by their fathers to carry on an ancient family tradition.

The quarter takes its name from the Mosque of the Andalusians, built for refugees from Córdoba and dating from the 9th century. The present structure, however, is mainly from the 13th century. It is closed to non-Muslims, but you can get a glimpse of the restored porch roof over the north doorway.

Directions: To enter the quarter, take the bridge Bein El Moudoun over the Oued Fès.

MUSEUM OF MOROCCAN ART AND HANDCRAFTS, place l'Istiqlal. No phone.

The Medina is traditionally entered through the Bab Boujeloud, actually two gates, the newer one built in 1913. You come first to the Dar Batha, a 19th-century palace turned into the Museum of Moroccan Art and Handcrafts. Sultan Hassan I and his son, Moulay Abd el Aziz, described as the "playboy of Fez," lived here in the declining years of Moroccan decadence under the French colonial powers. The Hispano-Moorish interior is filled with embroideries, tapestries, pottery, ceramics, manuscripts, wool carpets, funereal art, jewelry, and leatherwork. The Moorish garden is especially attractive.

Admission: 10 DH ($1.25).

Open: Wed–Sat 9am–noon and 3–6pm. **Transportation:** Petit taxi or bus no. 9 to Bab Boujeloud.

BOU INANIA MEDERSA, just inside Bab Boujeloud.

From the palace of Dar Batha, you can make your way to the Bou Inania Medersa, a former college complex for studying the Koran that dates from the 14th century, and a fine example of Merenid architecture. It was constructed by Sultan Abou Inan in the 1350s. Note the mosaic-covered walls, the carved plaster, and the elaborate cedarwood friezes. Its roof is superbly decorated as well, and its courtyard is paved with onyx and pink-and-white marble. The rooms upstairs housed the former students. The so-called clock, perhaps a former carillon, is a curiosity. Only men are admitted to the Hall of Ablutions. Finally, staircases lead to the Mosque of the Dead.

Admission: 10 DH ($1.25).

Open: Daily 8:30am–1pm and 4–7pm. **Transportation:** Petit taxi or bus no. 9 to Bab Boujeloud.

ATTARINE MEDERSA, rue de Souq el Attarine.

Another college is the Attarine Medersa, even older than the Bou Inania—it dates from 1325. Built by Sultan Abou Said, it is a smaller complex, and in some ways more graceful. If you climb to the terrace, you'll enjoy a view of the monumental Karaouyine Mosque, founded in the 9th century; with its 270 columns

and 16 naves, it is the second-largest in North Africa. It literally dominates the Medina. Of course, non-Muslims are forbidden to enter; but nobody will stop you if you walk around it, glancing into its many doorways.
Admission: 10 DH ($1.25).
Open: Sat–Thurs 8am–noon and 4–7pm. **Transportation:** Petit taxi or bus no. 9 to Bab Boujeloud.

PLACE NEJJARINE

A short walk from the Karaouyine Mosque is Place Nejjarine (Carpenters' Square), one of the most delightful spots in the city. The plaza is known for its mosaic fountain. The much-photographed Nejjarine Fondouk has an entrance surmounted by a handsome portico. A *fondouk* functioned as an inn and stable; this one dates from the 18th century. From this point, you can venture into the Nejjarine souk, with its compelling odors of thuya and cedarwood, worked by cabinetmakers. The ancient Kissaria, or fabric market, has unfortunately been destroyed by fire, although the flamboyantly colored fabrics—many with gold embroidery—are still there in rebuilt premises. Perhaps you'll get to see an auction.
Transportation: Petit taxi or bus no. 9 to Bab Boujeloud.

ZAWIYA OF MOULAY IDRISS II, rue Mjadiyn.

Near the Nejjarine Fondouk is the Zawiya of Moulay Idriss, a sanctuary dedicated to the founder of Fez. It is sacred to Moroccans, and visitors should act accordingly. Wooden beams bar the streets leading to it, marking the limit of the so-called *horm,* or holy asylum. You definitely cannot go inside the sanctuary; in fact, you're advised not to get too close to the horm limit.
Transportation: Petit taxi or bus no. 9 to Bab Boujeloud.

SEFFARIN MEDERSA, place Séffarin.

Make sure your guide takes you to the Séffarin Medersa, the oldest in Fez, dating from 1280. It is near the sector where the coppersmiths ply their trade, on place Séffarin.
Admission: Free, but the guide will expect a tip.
Open: Sat–Thurs 8am–noon and daily 4–7pm. **Transportation:** Petit taxi or bus no. 9 to Bab Boujeloud.

TETUANI FONDOUK

The Tetuani Fondouk, reached along Bou Touil, was originally a caravanserai for the merchants and their camels who came down from Tetuán. The goods and camels were kept downstairs, the beds placed in cramped quarters above. Notice especially its delicately carved 14th-century ceiling.

FÈS EL JEDID

Crossing through the Boujeloud Gardens, you leave Fès el Bali and enter Fès el Jedid, or New Fez, reached by petit taxi or bus no. 4 or 9. Less colorful, but interesting nevertheless, New Fez contains the **Dar el Makhzen,** place des Alaouites, the imperial palace complex, where King Hassan II stays when he is in town. The palace, its grounds, and adjoining buildings occupy nearly 200 acres, or exactly one half of Fès el Jedid. As the king's private residence, it is closed to the public.
The **Mellah,** the old Jewish quarter, is enclosed behind walls. Dating from the early 14th century, today this former ghetto has few Jews and lots of Muslims. Some of the most fascinating shops are run by Jewish goldsmiths. You'll find these at the top of the grande rue des Merinides. In addition to a Jewish cemetery, there are a few synagogues in the Mellah as well. Unlike the mosques, these can be visited; see especially the Serfati and the Fassiin (also spelled Fasyne or Fasiyin).
Perhaps what will interest you most about Fès el Jedid is the **Old Méchouar courtyard,** Petit Méchouar, surrounded by high walls. In the afternoon, jugglers, fortune tellers, soothsayers, acrobats, and dancers entertain.
Also in this district are the **Great Mosque,** founded in 1276, and the Mosque of

Moulay Abdullah, surrounded by an interesting quarter of the same name. The quarter is entered through an arch on Petit Méchouar. Entrance to the mosques is forbidden to non-Muslims.

VILLE NOUVELLE

Sometimes called Fez Debibagh, the New Town, dating mainly from the 1920s, overlooks Fès el Jedid. Built on a grid system, this section doesn't have the charm that you're likely to find in modern sections of such cities as Rabat. It is viewed more as a service area for tourists, with its restaurants, cafés, and banks. Most of Fez's hotels are here. Many buses and taxis run between the New Town and the ancient sectors.

NEARBY ATTRACTIONS

Before the sun sets, strike out by grand taxi for the **route du Tour de Fès,** a corniche highway above the town, that encircles Fez for about 10 miles. If you stop for drinks on the terrace of the Hotel Les Mérinides, you can enjoy a view of the old town, the Sebou River, Mount Senhadia, and the Atlas mountain range.

You might also want to stop over at the badly deteriorated **Merenid necropolis** on the hill of El Kolla, reached via a footpath leading down from the Hotel Les Mérinides. This was the last major gravesite built for the rulers of the Merenid dynasty. Built for the most part during the 1300s, the necropolis affords a sweeping view of the oldest section of the Medina of Fez, whose ramparts begin on the opposite side of a ravine.

Two hundred years after its completion, it was described as lavishly ornamented with sculpted marble, Koranic kufic texts, and tilework. Today, none of the ornamentation remains, only a weirdly earth-toned assemblage of arches, columns, and ruined masonry walls. With its breathtaking view, echo of fallen dynasties, and convenient proximity to the bars and restaurants of one of the best hotels in Morocco (Hotel Les Mérinides), the necropolis makes for a very pleasant excursion.

Housed in a small fort beyond the hotel at Bordj Nord is the **Armory Museum,** containing weapons from around the world—Spain, Iran, Tunisia, Japan, France, Turkey, and Senegal, for example. Even prehistoric weapons and American-made Colts and automatic pistols are displayed. Note especially the 16th-century Milanese armor and the 15th-century Moroccan cannons. Admission is 10 DH ($1.25), plus tip for the guide. The museum is open Wednesday through Monday from 8:30am to noon and 2:30 to 6pm.

WALKING TOUR —— New Fez (Fès el Jedid)

Start: Royal Palace

Finish: Bab Boujeloud

Time: 3 hours

Best Time: Any day from 9am to 5pm

Fès el Jedid is the rampart-ringed section of the old town whose traffic flows and overall plan were more or less defined during the 1200s. It is 500 years "younger" than the oldest section of Fez, which gradually evolved from many different migrations that began around A.D. 800. Fès el Jedid contains the power center, the vast sprawl of the (strictly private) Royal Palace. In earlier days, it contained the mint and fiscal headquarters of the Moroccan empire. Fès el Jedid is relatively easy for a newly arrived pedestrian to navigate, less complicated in its layout than the vastly more complex and labyrinthine Fès el Bali, a short distance to the northeast, which can be toured only with a guide.

Begin your tour in front of the seven massive and ornate doors at the western facade of the:

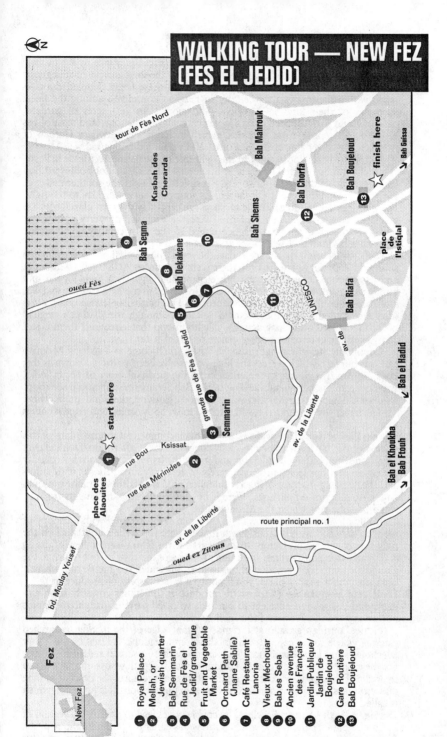

WALKING TOUR — NEW FEZ (FES EL JEDID)

N

tour de Fès Nord

Bab Mahrouk

Bab Boujeloud

☆ finish here

⟶ Bab Guissa

Kasbah des Cherarda

Bab Chorfa

⑫

⑬

Bab Shems

place de l'Istiqlal

Bab Segma

⑨

Bab Dekakene

⑩

⑧

l'UNESCO

oued Fès

⑤ ⑥ ⑦

⑪

Bab Riafa

av. de

grande rue de Fès el Jedid

④

Bab el Hadid ↙

☆ start here

rue Bou

Ksissat

Semmarin

③

av. de la Liberté

① ②

rue des Mérinides

Bab el Khoukha
Bab Ftouh ↙

place des Alaouites

av. de la Liberté

route principal no. 1

bd. Moulay Yousef

oued ez Zitoun

Fez

New Fez

① Royal Palace
② Mellah, or Jewish quarter
③ Bab Semmarin
④ Rue de Fès el Jedid/grande rue
⑤ Fruit and Vegetable Market
⑥ Orchard Path (Jnane Sabile)
⑦ Café Restaurant Lanoria
⑧ Vieux Méchouar
⑨ Bab es Seba
⑩ Ancien avenue des Français
⑪ Jardin Publique/Jardin de Boujeloud
⑫ Gare Routière
⑬ Bab Boujeloud

1. **Royal Palace.** Tradition dictates that this, the official entrance to the historic residence of King Hassan II, can be used only by the king and his invited guests on the most ceremonious of occasions. Behind these finely chiseled doors—made within the last quarter century in Fez and considered among the finest examples of their kind in Morocco—lie more than 160 acres of gardens, pavilions, and palaces, occupying a large percentage of the total land mass of Fès el Jedid. The entire royal complex, which includes the legendary Garden of Adgal, is ringed by almost 2 miles of carefully guarded ramparts.

   Facing the brass doors, walk to the right side of the palace, to rue de la Poste. (This will also be referred to as either boulevard Boulakhsissat or boulevard Bou Khessissat, depending on your source.) Turn left, and skirt the southern edge of the wall surrounding the Royal Palace. As your path curves slightly to the right, note the arcaded buildings whose rooftops are capped with green-glazed tiles. (In medieval days, green-glazed roof tiles were the exclusive property of royal or religious buildings, but that practice ended in the 19th century.) The arcade marks the beginning of what used to be the:

2. **Mellah, or Jewish quarter.** Today, the Jewish population of Fez is estimated at around 260, but as late as 1966 there were as many as 70,000 Jews within Fez and its environs. These decaying but elegant buildings, with their loggias and jutting balconies, were built in a style that originated in the 13th century and was always associated with the Jews of Morocco. This particular Jewish quarter was originally settled under the Merenid sultans. Although the district's original occupants moved away long ago, the neighborhood that surrounds them is still considered the commercial nerve center of Fès el Jedid.

   Continuing straight along rue de la Poste, you'll come to a soaring Moorish gate on your left, which pierces the high wall you've been skirting. Known as the:

3. **Bab Semmarin,** it marks the entrance to the medieval heart of Fès el Jedid. Even beneath the peripheral vaulting of the Bab Semmarin itself you'll see shops selling such uninspiring everyday wares as shoes, clothing, glass, and kitchenware.

   The street you've entered is still referred to by both Arabic and French names of:

4. **rue de Fès el Jedid/grande rue.** The main commercial thoroughfare of this section of Fez, it's likely to be especially congested in the afternoon. Don't expect lavish presentations of handcrafts and artwork. Its edges contain a workaday collection of shops frequented only rarely by foreign visitors. Kiosks with tailors and their sewing machines, lingerie salesmen, and a handful of minor mosques will surround you on all sides. Were it not for the plastic implements for sale, you'd imagine yourself in the Middle Ages.

   Eventually the street narrows and the open sky is covered with a canopy of wooden slats and woven canes. From time to time you'll see a courtyard off the right side of this street. Detour from the grande rue if you want a view of the fig and quince trees, dusty vines, and calmer recesses of this district, but return to the grande rue for the continuation of this tour. At the end of the grande rue, where it broadens into a sort of plaza, you'll notice a lavish display of produce at the:

5. **Fruit and Vegetable Market.** Its produce is sometimes enviably fresh and juicy, and is displayed adjacent to butchers who sell parts of slaughtered lambs not usually seen in Western food markets.

   Notice, on high ground at the most distant edge of the market, an arched gateway whose top is capped with medieval crenellations. It leads to the Vieux Méchouar, and you should note its location because you will return to it later. For the moment, however, descend the unmarked footpath whose entrance lies to the right of that gateway. The beginning of this path requires the descent of nine masonry steps. You will probably not see a sign posted along this footpath, which is called the:

6. **Orchard Path (Jnane Sabile).** Its cobblestones lead to an isolated section of the largest public park in Fez, which is known as either the Jardin Publique or the Jardin de Boujeloud. Formerly reserved for the use of the sultan and his entourage, this park is one of the only breathing spaces in the otherwise

jam-packed Medina; with its century-old trees and crumbling masonry, it is a legendary site of romantic trysts and family outings. At the bottom of the path, a sign will point to your:

REFUELING STOP   One of the most charming and verdant corners of Old Fez is the **7. Café Restaurant Lanoria,** Jardin de Boujeloud (tel. 254-22). This is a European-inspired café with a large stand-up bar, a vine-covered arbor, and an outdoor terrace that abuts the iron grillwork of a decaying water wheel. The menu includes coffee, pastries, tajines, and couscous dishes, and you receive a warm welcome from the owner, Belbhar Gillali. Tajines and couscous each cost 25 DH ($3.15), the coffee goes for 3 DH (40¢), and the mineral water is pure and plentiful. The café is open daily from 6am to 10pm.

After your refreshment and rest, retrace your steps up the slope of the Orchard Path to the nine steps you descended at the entrance to the park. As you ascend, note the foundation of a building constructed high above the path on your right. This building formerly housed the slaves and servants of the Merenid sultans.

Enter the square containing the vegetable market, and pass beneath the arches of the crenellated gateway. Pass beneath it and enter the:

8. Vieux Méchouar, the square marking the southernmost, and most frequently used, entrance to the Royal Palace. The elaborately tiled green, yellow, and white gateway to your right (at the highest elevation of the square) is the Bab Dekakine (or Bab Dekaken), where a battalion of guards forbid entrance to unauthorized persons. Opposite the brilliantly colorful Bab Dekakine is an monochromatic, somewhat eroded three-arched gateway, the:

9. Bab es Seba, which was originally intended to guard the entrance to the courtyard that precedes the entrance to the palace. It was from the crenellations of this gateway that the body of Ferdinand, Infante (heir to the throne) of Portugal, was hung upside down for four days in 1443. His execution followed six years of imprisonment that resulted from his capture near Tangier during an ill-advised crusade to establish Portuguese territories within the interior of Morocco. His rotting corpse was publicly displayed within a coffin whose lid remained open for an additional 29 years.

Now, with your back to the Royal Palace, pass beneath yet another ornamental gateway (this one with two arches) to your right, and enter the straight and rather dusty promenade known as the:

10. ancien avenue des Français. Keeping an iron fence and a concrete irrigation ditch on your right, negotiate the uncurving edge of this busy walkway, which rambles beside quarters formerly occupied by the sultans. Walk in a straight line toward the twin arches of a distant ornamental gateway. Just before you reach it, notice the wide steps leading down into the main and most-visited entrance to gardens you visited briefly during your refueling stop, the:

11. Jardin Publique/Jardin de Boujeloud. Formal, rambling, and verdant, the garden was transformed early in the 20th century into a public park on orders of the French colonial government. Entrance is free and hours are daily from 6am to 8pm. Exit through your original path of entry. Continue toward the ornamental gateway, pass beneath it, then descend the slope that turns steeply downhill. Traffic and congestion will become ever busier as you pass near the undistinguished and traffic-clogged place Baghdadi and approach the distant Medina of the oldest section of Fez. The wall on your right at this point marks the border of the Lycée Moulay Idriss, a school established by the French in 1917, where many of the leaders of modern Morocco were trained and educated. Always keep ahead of you the soaring minaret of the Mosque of Boujeloud. Your goal will be the southwestern entrance of the oldest section of Fez, Fès el Bali. Pass the perimeter of the:

12. Gare Routière (long-distance bus station) of Fez, easy to recognize because of the roar of large vehicles pulling into parking spaces after long treks through the countryside. Continue a steep descent toward the ornamental blue-and-white-tiled gateway named the:

13. Bab Boujeloud. Built in 1913, it is considered one of the most photogenic gateways in Fez. The tilework facing the exterior of the ramparts is blue, the symbolic color of Fez, that facing the interior is green, the symbolic color of Islam. This gateway marks the southwestern entrance to Fès el Bali, and one of the two neighborhoods within Fès el Bali where dye pits and tanneries emit some of the most exotic sights and scents of Morocco. It also marks the end of your walking tour.

WHERE TO STAY

Reservations should be made well in advance, as hotels tend to be heavily booked by tour groups during peak summer months. If you plan to be in Fez during the summer, try for a hotel with air conditioning if you can afford it.

Fez has one or two of the best hotels in Morocco, but most of the accommodations, while clean, comfortable, and safe havens, are merely adequate. But what you lose in style, you get when it comes time to pay the bill, as most hotels are either moderate or inexpensive in price.

"Very Expensive" suggests hotels charging from 800 DH ($100) and up for a double room with bath. "Expensive" means doubles in the 620 DH ($77.50) price range, and "Moderate" gives you doubles at 370 DH ($46.25). Nearly all the recommendable "Inexpensive" hotels charge about the same price: 240 DH ($30) for a double with bath.

VERY EXPENSIVE

HOTEL LES MERINIDES, Borj Nord, Fez. Tel. 06/22-12-54. Fax 06/26-01-61. 90 rms (all with bath), 11 suites. A/C MINIBAR TEL **Bus:** 21.

$ Rates: 650 DH ($81.25) single; 800 DH ($100) double; 860 DH ($107.50) triple; suites from 900 DH ($112.50). Breakfast 75 DH ($9.40) extra. AE, DC, MC, V.

Named after the Moroccan dynasty that contributed more than any other to the architecture of Fez, this is the modern and extremely stylish five-star answer to the antique ambience of the Hotel Palais Jamaï. Built in the 1960s and renovated in the 1980s, it sits in isolated grandeur on an arid and sun-blasted hilltop north of the Medina, separated from it by a ravine. A few paces from its entrance are the dramatically ethereal ruins of the Merenid tomb, whose crumbling walls seem oddly to complement the modern life and glamour of their stylish neighbor.

The hotel's marble and plant-ringed lobby has panoramic windows and comfortable settees, and an international kind of spaciousness. The upper hallways, accented with tiles in geometric patterns, lead to modern, stylish bedrooms, each of which has a balcony and a radio.

Dining/Entertainment: Restaurants include La Tour Mérinide (French; see below); La Kouba du Ciel (Moroccan; see below), whose painted rooftop rolls away for a view of the evening sky; an international coffee shop; and a main dining room frequented by groups. The hotel also has a pool-terrace restaurant (open in summer only); two different bars, one with a panoramic view; and Nightclub Les Mérinides (see below).

Services: Hairdresser, valet and laundry service, in-house medical facility, and a "solve-everything" concierge.

Facilities: Garden, outdoor swimming pool with a spectacular view of the Medina and the Merenid ruins, and a handful of boutiques.

HOTEL PALAIS JAMAÏ, Bab el Ghuissa, Fez. Tel. 06/343-31, or toll free in the U.S. 800/223-6800. 140 rms (all with bath), 20 suites. A/C MINIBAR TV TEL **Bus:** 10.

$ Rates: 700–950 DH ($87.50–$118.75) single; 850–1,100 DH ($106.25–

$137.50) double; suites from 2,500 DH ($312.50). Breakfast 75 DH ($9.40) extra. AE, DC, MC, V.

✪ Located on the northern edge of the Medina of Fès el Bali, this is considered one of the finest hotels in Morocco. An opulent 19th-century palace of Grand Vizier Jama, with additional bedrooms set within an Almohad-inspired wing added in the 1930s, this structure was originally created for "rest and evasion, the pleasure of the eyes and the peace of the soul."

Many of the bedrooms have sweeping views over the rooftops of the most famous medina in Morocco, as well as every conceivable comfort and an international decor with specific Moroccan accessories. The hotel is built around a garden inhabited by raucous peacocks. As you swim in the large sapphire-colored pool, the ziggurat-shaped decorative crenellations of the hotel evoke some of the mystery of Fez. In high season, a room booked here is a much-sought-after prize in such cities as Paris.

Under a different name, this hotel was immortalized in the Paul Bowles's novel *The Spider's House* as the ancestral pleasure palace of the Jama family.

Dining/Entertainment: The Djenina Restaurant serves international cuisine in an elegant dining room or on the spacious courtyard terrace beside the swimming pool. The Al Fassia Moroccan restaurant (see below) is richly exotic with live music. The high-tech "Nightclub" draws a chic crowd (see below).

Services: Hairdresser, valet and laundry service, currency exchange, translation and secretarial services.

Facilities: A very large swimming pool set as the centerpiece of the enclosed and verdant courtyard, a tennis court, transportation to a golf course in Meknes, horseback riding, *hammam* (Turkish steam bath), car rentals, shops and boutiques, parking.

EXPENSIVE

HOTEL DE FES, av. des F.A.R. (without number). Tel. 06/230-06. Fax 06/204-86. 300 rms (all with bath), 5 suites. A/C MINIBAR TV TEL **Transportation:** Petit taxi.
$ **Rates:** 535 DH ($66.90) single; 620 DH ($77.50) double; suites from 1,300 DH ($162.50). Breakfast 50 DH ($6.25) extra. AE, DC, MC, V.

This sprawling, spacious, elegant hotel, built in 1971 and renovated several times since, lies within a well-established garden in a residential section of the Ville Nouvelle. Its appealingly airy lobby is artfully decorated with Moroccan-inspired geometric patterns in fine hardwoods and tiles. There's a feeling of a resort hotel here: serpentine paths wind to outlying wings of the hotel, and signs point the way to its facilities. Each of the bedrooms is comfortably upholstered, with sliding glass windows overlooking either the street or the garden.

Dining/Entertainment: Restaurant El Minzah (French) and Restaurant Nejjarine (Moroccan) are both recommended below. Le Riyahd Coffeeshop serves food to guests on the run.

Services: Massage, helpful concierge.

Facilities: Sauna and hammam (Turkish steam bath), swimming pool, boutiques.

MODERATE

HOTEL ZALAGH, rue Mohammed Diouri, 6, Fez. Tel. 06/255-31. 74 rms (all with bath). TEL **Transportation:** Petit taxi.
$ **Rates:** 300 DH ($37.50) single; 370 DH ($46.25) double. Breakfast 31 DH ($3.90) extra. AE, DC, MC, V.

Though the Zalagh, built in 1952, is listed as a four-star hotel by the government, its bedrooms frankly need restoration. They are large and airy, with French doors opening onto private balconies; each contains a private bathroom. Only the public rooms are adequately air-conditioned, however. On the premises you'll find a swimming pool surrounded by a flagstone border, as well as a wide concrete terrace jutting out from the bar, which on hot nights is a popular watering hole (open daily from 10am to 3am). The modern blue-and-white dining room, with its helpful staff, is one of the hotel's most endearing areas. Meals cost from 110 DH ($13.75) each.

INEXPENSIVE

HOTEL DE LA PAIX, av. des Palmiers, 44 (av. Hassan II, 44), Fez. Tel. 06/26-880. 42 rms (all with bath). TEL **Transportation:** Petit taxi.
$ Rates: 193 DH ($24.15) single; 238 DH ($29.75) double. Breakfast 23 DH ($2.90) extra. MC, V.

Built in 1935 in the Ville Nouvelle, this three-star "A"-category hotel was renovated in 1986. It sits upon a wide boulevard, behind a modern stucco-sheathed façade. Its clean, tile-covered lobby is placed near a staircase leading down into the establishment's cellar restaurant, the Nautilus, where a fixed-priced meal goes for 130 DH ($16.25). There's a bar on the premises. Each room is clean, modern, and comfortably simple, with Moroccan-motif headboards and flowered bedspreads.

LE GRAND, bd. Chefchaouini (without number), Fez. Tel. 06/255-11. 83 rms (all with bath). TEL **Bus:** 9.
$ Rates: 193 DH ($24.15) single; 238 DH ($29.75) double. Breakfast 23 DH ($2.90) extra. No credit cards.

Le Grand, built in the 1930s and standing in the center of the Ville Nouvelle, is probably the best architectural expression of art deco in Fez. Each of the high-ceilinged public rooms is air-conditioned, and each has a deliberately simple Moorish-inspired decor of airy spaciousness. Most of the bedrooms—only some are air-conditioned—are relatively large. Renovated several times since the hotel's construction, they have a comfortable but relatively simple decor. A three-course tourist menu costs 86 DH ($10.75); a gastronomic menu, 110 DH ($13.75). Both are served in the hotel's La Normandie Restaurant, which is open daily from noon to 3pm and 7 to 9pm.

HOTEL MOUNIA FES, rue Asilah, 60, Fez. Tel. 06/248-38. 95 rooms (all with bath). A/C TEL **Bus:** 9.
$ Rates: 193 DH ($24.15) single; 238 DH ($29.75) double; 312 DH ($39) triple. Breakfast 23 DH ($2.90). AE, MC, V.

Set upon a busy street corner of the Ville Nouvelle, opposite the CTM bus depot, this comfortable and unpretentious hotel boasts an unexpectedly ornate series of public rooms. Built in 1989, it also has an earth-tone façade designed to look like a modernized version of a kasbah; an elevator; and five floors of clean and simple bedrooms decorated in a blandly international style. On the premises are a sauna, a hammam, and a "honeymoon salon" off the lobby with a gloriously filigreed plasterwork ceiling. A fixed-price menu in the dining room costs between 86 DH ($10.75) and 100 DH ($12.50).

WHERE TO EAT

Some visitors dine in their hotels, requesting the half-board plan (a room with breakfast and one main meal, usually dinner). However, there are several good independent restaurants.

Fez doesn't have any really expensive restaurants. Those rated "Moderate" charge from 180 to 220 DH ($22.50 to $27.50) for dinner, and restaurants rated "Inexpensive" charge less than 90 DH ($11.25) for dinner. In all listings, wine or drinks are extra.

MODERATE

AL FASSIA, Hotel Palais Jamaï, Bab el Ghuissa. Tel. 343-31.
Cuisine: MOROCCAN. **Reservations:** Recommended. **Bus:** 10.
$ Prices: Appetizers: 50–100 DH ($6.25–$12.50); main dishes 95–160 DH ($11.90–$20); fixed-priced menu 230 DH ($28.75). AE, DC, MC, V.
Open: Dinner daily 7:30–11:30pm.

★ Al Fassia is housed within the original 19th-century core of a hotel that was built as the private palace of the most powerful vizier in the region. The decor is as headily opulent as you'd expect from a Moroccan salon that once welcomed many of the grandest names in the Muslim and European worlds; the restaurant, in fact, is considered the architectural gem of the hotel. You sit on low cushioned sofas in private alcoves lit by lanterns. Moroccan violin, drum, and lute music is played. A specialty is *panaché de briouates* (puff pastry filled with minced meat and rice). Couscous is made with chicken, fish, pigeon, or lamb, and is accompanied by *harissa*, a fiery red-pepper sauce. One of the tajine specials, arriving in a cone-headed vessel, is lamb cooked with prunes, tomatoes, and almonds. Quail is also prepared in a tajine with dried apricots, and duck with figs is another special dish.

RESTAURANT AL FIRDAOUS, rue Jenjfour, 10, Bab Ghuissa Fès. Tel. 343-43.
  Cuisine: MOROCCAN. **Reservations:** Recommended. **Transportation:** Petit taxi.
  $ Prices: Fixed-priced menu 130–160 DH ($16.25–$20). DC, MC, V.
  Open: Lunch daily noon–3pm; dinner daily 8:30–11:30pm.

★ Located a short walk downhill from the entrance to the landmark Hotel Palais Jamaï, at the northern edge of the Medina, this restaurant was built in 1926 as the private home of a Fez merchant. Its courtyard is covered with folds of fabric, creating the effect of a massive and well-furnished tent. Tables are grouped within the courtyard, as well as within a series of small rooms clustered around its perimeter. The dinner menu includes such Moroccan specialties as *harira* soup, tajines, couscous with seven vegetables, and a succulent version of slow-baked mechoui of lamb. Every evening at 9pm there's a spectacular show that includes dancers and entertainers for 40 DH ($5) extra.

RESTAURANT DAR SAADA, Souk Attarine, 21. Tel. 333-43.
  Cuisine: MOROCCAN. **Reservations:** Not required. **Bus:** 9 to Bab Boujeloud.
  $ Prices: Fixed-priced menu 90–200 DH ($11.25–$25). AE, DC, MC, V.
  Open: Daily 6am–7:30pm.

This restaurant, which serves morning tea, lunch throughout the day, and afternoon tea, lies deep within the section of the Medina devoted to the sale of carpets and occasionally dubious antiques. The building is a century-old palace whose interior is far larger than you might suspect at first. Eat either within a patio courtyard or on the balcony that overlooks it, or penetrate even deeper into the recesses to discover an additional, cedar-sheathed dining room beyond the most distant point of the upper balcony. The four fixed-priced menus include one featuring fish and another offering chicken and red meat.

DAR TAJINE, Ross Rhi, 15. Tel. 341-67.
  Cuisine: MOROCCAN. **Reservations:** Recommended. **Bus:** 9 to Bab Boujeloud.
  $ Prices: Fixed-priced lunch 145 DH ($18.15); fixed-priced dinner 170 DH ($21.25). MC, V.
  Open: Lunch daily 12–3:30pm; dinner daily 7:30–10pm.

★ Located just inside the Medina, Dar Tajine is a delightful restaurant, though difficult to find. The unobtrusive doorway, marked only with a small sign, leads to a sort of pasha's palace—130 years old and the home of the Lebbar family during most of that time. The beautiful dining rooms have tall decorative columns, tile floors, and small fountains; far above, birds flit between the rafters of transparent roofs. In the Moroccan tradition, there are no windows, as it is not considered polite to demonstrate one's wealth to a neighbor who might not be so fortunate. Around the walls are small chambers with low sofas and tables, some downstairs and some high in the galleries above.

For lunch, choose from the salads displayed on a buffet. They might include combinations of both mild and fiery tomatoes with onions, spinach, beetroot, and potatoes. Your main dish might be brochettes of local sausages or beef, a tajine, or couscous. The evening menu is more elaborate, with items such as soup, kefta or brochettes, salads, lemon chicken, pastilla (for which a supplement is usually charged), and *mrouria* (a joint of lamb simmered with raisins).

DJENINA RESTAURANT, Hotel Palais Jamaï, Bab el Ghuissa. Tel. 343-31.
   Cuisine: INTERNATIONAL. **Reservations:** Recommended. **Bus:** 10.
$ **Prices:** Appetizers 70–200 DH ($8.75–$25); main dishes 110–200 DH ($13.75–$25); fixed-priced menu 230 DH ($28.75). AE, DC, MC, V.
   Open: Lunch daily 12:30–3pm; dinner daily 7:30–10:30pm.

⭐ In winter, the restaurant is housed within a beautifully proportioned dining room where a beamed ceiling contrasts with the intricate Moroccan tilework adorning the walls. In summer, all of the tables are moved to the tile-covered terrace beneath the courtyard's arcade, near the edge of the swimming pool. Choices from the menu, beautifully served, might include barely cooked marinated rockfish with coriander; a mousseline of pink shrimp with *beurre blanc,* stuffed into ravioli and served with a confit of onions; saffron-flavored seafood stew with a mosaic of vegetables; lamb with eggplant; grilled filet steak with béarnaise sauce; and, for dessert, a palette of ice creams.

RESTAURANT EL MINZAH, Hotel de Fès, av. des F.A.R. (without number). Tel. 23-06.
   Cuisine: FRENCH. **Reservations:** Recommended. **Transportation:** Petit taxi.
$ **Prices:** Appetizers 50–95 DH ($6.25–$11.90); main dishes 80–155 DH ($10–$19.40); fixed-priced 4–course menu 155 DH ($19.40). AE, DC, MC, V.
   Open: Daily for lunch noon–3pm; dinner 6–10pm.

The walls that separate the El Minzah from its neighboring restaurants within the Hotel de Fès can be collapsed at will for more flexible seating arrangements, so you never know which of the two dining rooms you might occupy. My favorite has wraparound murals showing scenes of café life during the French Protectorate, with many of the men wearing the tassel-topped hat named after the city you're in. Menu specialties include an escalope of seawolf with black pepper and ginger, a soufflé of turbot, pâté of fish, and an escalope of rabbit with a *chiffonade* of endives. If you go for lunch, it's best to arrive either early or late to avoid the organized tour groups that usually fill the courtyard. If you plan on an evening meal here, it's a good idea to arrange your menu during your morning or afternoon tour of the Medina.

LA KOUBA DU CIEL, Hotel Les Mérinides, Borj Nord. Tel. 22-12-54.
   Cuisine: MOROCCAN. **Reservations:** Recommended. **Bus:** 21.
$ **Prices:** Appetizers 30–60 DH ($3.75–$7.50); main dishes 70–175 DH ($8.75–$21.90). AE, DC, MC, V.
   Open: Lunch daily noon–3pm; dinner daily 7:30pm–midnight.

⭐ At one of the most extraordinary restaurants in North Africa, Moroccan culinary traditions are accented with a show-biz flair that many visitors find almost irresistible. La Kouba du Ciel is located on the third floor of the Hotel Les Mérinides, in a room ringed with 36 ornately tiled columns, a decorative arcade, and wraparound windows that offer an illuminated nighttime view of the Medina and the nearby tombs of the Merenids. Best of all, the ornately painted ceiling retracts into carefully engineered slots for an unparalleled view of the heavens. As you dine, troupes of musicians and dancers will entertain you in the style of the Arabian Nights. Menu specialties include pastilla with almonds; tajines of fish, sausage, chicken, or lamb; couscous; and brochettes.

RESTAURANT NEJJARINE, Hotel de Fès, av. des F.A.R. (without number). Tel. 230-06.
   Cuisine: MOROCCAN. **Reservations:** Recommended. **Transportation:** Petit taxi.
$ **Prices:** Appetizers 30–86 DH ($3.75–$10.75); main dishes 65–175 DH ($8.15–$21.90). AE, DC, MC, V.

Open: Dinner daily 7:30pm–midnight.

An army of decorators draped the interior of a windowless room with acres of fabric, gathered the folds into decorative bunches, and—assisted by a scattering of carpets, artful lighting, and the sounds of a Moroccan orchestra—created the illusion of a Bedouin's tent. Together with the kindly staff, it all contributes to a warm and welcoming experience of the Moroccan cuisine. Menu specialties include harira soup, pastilla (with pigeon), stuffed fish, couscous with seven vegetables, and a wide array of brochettes and tajines. Dessert might be a honeyed pastry or a succulent salad of sliced oranges with cinnamon. The restaurant is named after one of Fez's most famous fountains, a 14th-century waterspout.

PALAIS DE FES, Boutouil Karaouyine, 16. Tel. 347-07.

Cuisine: MOROCCAN. **Reservations:** Not required. **Bus:** 9 to Bab Boujeloud.
$ Prices: Appetizers 20–80 DH ($2.50–$10); main dishes 60–200 DH ($7.50–$25). AE, DC, MC, V.
Open: Lunch daily noon–3pm.

A meal here in a historic and very old setting might be accompanied by a display and sales presentation of Moroccan carpets. Come here to explore the building and to gain insight into merchandising as much as for the food. Regardless of what you eat, the experience will be remembered. Enter the palace's courtyard from a quiet street in the Medina near the Karaouyine Mosque. The courtyard's soaring arcades are hung with dozens of carpets, with thousands more stacked in the corners. A staff member will direct you to a labyrinth of impossibly steep and narrow stairs that wind upward to a carefully decorated trio of dining rooms outfitted in the Moroccan style with low banquettes and carpets. After the climb, you'll appreciate the breezes that blow constantly through the casement windows.

The all-Moroccan menu includes pastilla, three kinds of brochettes, tajine with plums, mechoui of lamb (when available), and three different kinds of couscous. For a well-deserved tip, one of the waiters will serve your after-lunch tea within a green-and-white-tiled gazebo on the roof of the palace, where you'll enjoy an unparalleled view of the rooftops of the Medina and the minaret of the Karaouyine Mosque.

PAVILLON LAMBRA, Laraichi, route d'Immouzer, 47 bis. Tel. 416-87.

Cuisine: MOROCCAN. **Reservations:** Recommended. **Transportation:** Petit taxi.
$ Prices: Fixed-priced menu 180 DH ($22.50). MC, V.
Open: Lunch daily 12pm–3pm; dinner daily 7:30–10:30pm; snacks daily 9am–10pm.

Run by a prestigious old Fassi family, this restaurant is in a private house at the entrance to the Ville Nouvelle. It draws upon the styles of the 14th century, and is richly decorated with many antiques and handcrafts. In spacious surroundings, seated on low sofas, you dine on such specialties as pastilla; chicken with olives, lemons, and almonds; oven-baked lamb; keftas (skewered meat); and tajines (meat and vegetables simmered in earthenware dishes). The price includes mineral water, fresh fruit, ice cream and mint tea, as well as service. There is an à la carte menu, but my recommendation is not to ask for it, as the items are likely to be unavailable; order from the menu that was prepared that day, as it's sure to be fresh. The restaurant has a patio overlooking the garden where guests can order snacks, and a back room is loaded with Moroccan jewelry and antiques, one of the best selections in Fez. Dining here is a totally Moroccan experience that's worth the price.

LA TOUR MÉRINIDES, Hotel Les Mérinides, Borj Nord. Tel. 452-25.

Cuisine: FRENCH. **Reservations:** Recommended. **Bus:** 21.
$ Prices: Appetizers 35–70 DH ($4.40–$8.75); main dishes 60–105 DH ($7.50–$13.15). AE, DC, MC, V.
Open: Lunch daily noon–3pm; dinner daily 7:30pm–midnight.

Tasteful, subtle, and charming, this European restaurant is attached to one of the best hotels in town—and is accessible through the ornate Moroccan premises of the previously recommended Kouba du Ciel. No other dining spot has quite as spectacular a view of the imperial glories of Fez as this one. It contains a charming corner bar, and tables set upon a series of platforms offer a sweeping view of the Medina and the nearby Merenid tombs. The menu includes shrimp bisque soup, suprême of John Dory with almonds, seawolf grilled with fennel, grilled or poached turbot with hollandaise, grilled chicken *à la dijonnaise,* and a filet mignon of Charolais beef with green peppercorns.

INEXPENSIVE

L'ADOUR RESTAURANT, rue Abdelkrim El Khattabi, 9. Tel. 221-48.
   Cuisine: FRENCH/MOROCCAN. **Reservations:** Not required. **Bus:** 9.
$ Prices: Fixed-priced menu 90 DH ($11.25). AE, DC, MC, V.
   Open: Lunch daily 12:30–3pm; dinner daily 7:30–10:30pm.
L'Adour, which is part of the Splendid Hotel, is one of your best bets for French cooking in the Ville Nouvelle, offering a tourist menu as well as sandwiches and salads. I recently enjoyed some tempting hors d'oeuvres, followed by a Moroccan tajine and a selection of fruit. At lunch, try the spaghetti bolognese or an omelet. The sole meunière is also fine. Many Moroccan dishes, such as couscous, are available.

PALAIS MNEBHI, Souk Ben Safi Talaa Sghira, 15. Tel. 338-93.
   Cuisine: MOROCCAN. **Reservations:** Required. **Bus:** 9 to Bab Boujeloud.
$ Prices: Fixed-priced menus 80–250 DH ($10–$31.25). DC, MC, V.
   Open: Sat–Thurs 12:30–3:30pm.
Centered around a symmetrical and fully enclosed courtyard in the Medina, the building that contains the Palais Mnebhi was constructed in the 1840s as a private residence. There isn't even a sign to indicate its presence on a narrow street, although its existence is a matter of public record for almost everyone in the Medina. Phone in advance for alcohol-free meals, which, in the case of the least expensive possibility, include such Moroccan dishes as a tajine, followed by couscous and mixed salad, tea, and pastry.

SHOPPING

Do not make purchases while accompanied by an "official" guide. One reporter, after an investigation, estimated that the guide sometimes receives as much as a 50% commission on any particular sale. If you see some merchandise you really want while accompanied by a guide, note the shop and return on your own to purchase it. You'll get a better price. One local told the press, "The rug merchants are employed by the guides, not vice versa."
   The Medina of Fez is one giant souk. Here one shop cannot be recommended over another, as wares are constantly changing. So wander at will, looking to see whatever catches your eye, while at the same trying to fend off overly aggressive merchants. The eagerness to sell here sometimes borders on the hysterical.

COOPARTIM CENTRE ARTISANALE, Ensemble Artisanale, bd. Allal Ben Abdullah (without number). Tel. 256-54.
   Owned and operated by the Moroccan government, this complex contains a staggering amount of handcrafted merchandise linked to studio space for 10 local artists. It's housed within a cool white-tiled pavilion dotted with greenery in the Ville Nouvelle, and is open Monday through Saturday from 9am to 2pm and 4 to 7pm. Visitors can watch the creative process as it unfolds in a kind of living museum of Moroccan crafts. Know in advance that prices are fixed (that is, not negotiable). Although the thrill of the negotiating process is gone, a visit to the sales area gives a good idea of the going rates for similar merchandise sold with much more energy and passion in the souks. Bus: 9, 19, or 29.

EVENING ENTERTAINMENT

NIGHTCLUB LES MERINIDES, Hotel Les Mérinides, Borj Nord. Tel. 452-25.

This is one of the most fashionable nightclubs and discos in Fez, owned and operated by the Hotel Les Mérinides. Located in the basement, it has a separate entrance, so its music doesn't disturb sleeping guests. Completely European in flavor, it has an all-black decor accented with mirrors, and a gridwork of metal pipes above the dance floor. Drinks cost 50 DH ($6.25), and nightly hours are 9:30pm to 3am. Bus: 21.

Admission: 50 DH ($6.25), including first drink.

"NIGHTCLUB," Hotel Palais Jamaï, Bab el Ghuissa. Tel. 343-31.

The walk through the lobbies and corridors of the most legendary hotel in Fez is part of the fun of coming here. Located within the Palais Jamaï's basement, this is one of the most fashionable and unusual nightclubs in town. The hotel's parabolic antenna helps to project large-screen video onto the screen beyond the dance floor. The entire effect is like an electronic and high-tech version of an Islamic kasbah, the combinations of which are absolutely fascinating. Some kind of live performance, usually by a *danseuse orientale*, interrupts the otherwise electronic sound and light every night at around 1:15am. Drinks are 60 to 80 DH ($7.50 to $10), and nightly hours are 10pm to 3am. Bus: 10.

Admission: Free "to suitably attired and behaved guests."

---

3. TAZA

47 miles E of Fez; 374 miles NE of Marrakesh

GETTING THERE By Train Four daily trains arrive from Fez (2 hours).

By Bus There are 3 buses a day from Fez (2½ hours).

By Car Continue east from Fez along route P1, toward the Algerian border.

Located midway between the Rif and the Anti-Atlas mountains, Taza occupied a historically strategic position, dominating the mountain gap through which passed most of the traffic leading from the eastern steppes and plateaus into the fertile plains of western Morocco. Each of the country's many invaders over the centuries, including the Arab armies spreading the message of Islam, coveted it as an artery of transit and communication. During portions of three different dynasties (the Almohad, the Merenid, and the Alaouite), Taza was designated the capital of Morocco, but its importance is now limited to its role as the headquarters of a relatively populous province.

ORIENTATION

INFORMATION

The **Taza Tourist Office,** located on avenue Hassan II (no phone), will arrange guides for you. Hours in summer are 8am to 3:30pm Monday through Friday; from September to mid-June, 8:30am to noon and 2:30 to 6:30pm Monday through Friday.

GETTING AROUND

The best way to get around is by a petit taxi, which you can hail in the streets. You must share the ride—and the expense—with at least two others. Fares are reasonable. For example, the trip from the Ville Nouvelle (New Town) to the Medina costs only 3 DH (40¢). Trains arrive on the northern periphery of the Ville Nouvelle, about a 45-minute walk from place de l'Indépendance. You can also take a petit taxi for about 6 DH (75¢). Buses arrive right off place de l'Independance at the CTM depot.

FAST FACTS

Area Code 067.

Police The **Taza Police Station,** Hôtel de Police (tel. 19), lies on place de l'Indépendance.

Post Office The **Taza Post Office,** rue Moussa Ibn Noussair at rue Allal ben Abdallah (don't call—show up in person), is in the vicinity of place de l'Indépendance. It is open in summer Monday through Friday from 8am to 3:30pm; from September to mid-June, Monday through Thursday from 8am to noon and 4 to 7pm, on Friday from 9am to noon, and on Saturday from 4 to 6pm. On Saturday you can pick up mail sent poste restante, but no other services are offered. In the same building is a phone office where you can make calls.

WHAT TO SEE & DO

Taza's most striking sight is the more than 2 miles of **peripheral walls**—probably the most hotly contested ramparts in Moroccan history. Skillfully incorporated into the region's natural cliffs, they were originally laid out in the 1100s by the Almohad sultan Abd el Moumen, and later embellished and strengthened many times. The rectangular bastion along the rampart's southeast corner was erected relatively late during the history of the town, by the Saadians during the 1500s. The rampart's northwestern entrance, the **Bab er Rih (Gate of the Wind),** offers the most sweeping views over the valleys and mountains that surround the legendary city.

Contained within these ramparts are a pair of 11th-century mosques (the **Grand Mosque** and the **Mosque of the Andalusians**), located along the northern and southern perimeters of the town, respectively. Entrance to both is forbidden to non-Muslims, although the ornate portals and mosaics of their exteriors are endlessly interesting. Between them sprawls the labyrinth of the town's **souk,** which, because of its occupation by the Beni Ouarain tribe, has a distinctly Berber flavor.

WHERE TO STAY & EAT

HOTEL FRIOUATO, bd. Bel Hassan Al Wazzani (without number), Taza. Tel. 067/25-98. 60 rms (all with bath). A/C TEL **Transportation:** Petit taxi.

$ **Rates:** 193 DH ($24.15) single; 238 DH ($29.75) double. Breakfast 60 DH ($7.50) extra. AE, DC, MC, V.

Built in 1975, this three-star hotel is owned by the Salam hotel chain. Named after a famous nearby grotto, it lies midway between the Ville Nouvelle and the medieval Medina, a 12-minute walk from either. It is considered the best hotel in Taza. Each bedroom, theoretically air-conditioned, is modern, somewhat Spartan, and clean. None has a balcony. On the premises are a swimming pool, a bar, and a restaurant where fixed-priced meals cost from 83 DH ($10.40) to 100 DH ($12.50).

GRAND HOTEL DU DAUPHINE, place de l'Indépendance (without number), Taza. Tel. 067/35-67. 26 rms (16 with bathroom). TEL **Transportation:** Petit taxi.

$ **Rates:** 69.50 DH ($8.70) single without bath, 132.50 DH ($36.55) single with bath; 86 DH ($10.75) double without bath, 155 DH ($19.40) double with bath. Breakfast 15 DH ($1.90) extra. No credit cards.

Although Taza provides several hotels even less expensive than this one, none of them are recommendable. This, our budget choice, was built in the Ville Nouvelle more than 50 years ago, during the heyday of the French Protectorate. Some visitors like its nostalgic creakiness and sense of a long-departed foreign legion: the pinewood bar and old-fashioned staircase are easily evocative of a slightly tatty *Beau Geste* film. Each of the rooms has a balcony and a high ceiling. There's a garage on the premises, as well as an in-house restaurant serving fixed-price meals for 61 DH ($7.65).

CHAPTER 7

AGADIR, THE SOUSS & THE ANTI-ATLAS

- • **SUGGESTED ITINERARY**
- • **WHAT'S SPECIAL ABOUT AGADIR, THE SOUSS & THE ANTI-ATLAS**
- **1. AGADIR**
- **2. TAROUDANNT**
- **3. TIZNIT**
- **4. TAFRAOUTE**

U nlike the High Atlas mountains farther north, the Anti-Atlas region of Morocco is neither high enough nor moist enough for significant snows ever to accumulate. This region marking the north-western edge of the rarely charted expanses of the Sahara is dry, with little vegetation—a mass of pinkish-beige rocks. Wherever a rare stream or artesian well surfaces, goats and sheep are raised along with figs, olives, and a drought-resistant strain of barley. Although there are some tiny pockets of fertile soil created by ancient volcanic eruptions, much of the area lacks both the water and the organic soil needed to sustain widespread agriculture.

Despite the austerity of the countryside, many visitors find the region beautiful, and it has many attractions to make a visit worthwhile. It contains one of the most desirable resorts in Africa—Agadir.

A warning: If you venture out in the sun, you must protect yourself. Do as the locals do and shield your head and body from prolonged exposure to the sun. Carry bottled water in your car, to avoid dehydration and in the event of an overheated car radiator.

GETTING THERE

Agadir is the "gateway" to the region. It's most easily reached by plane from either Europe or one of the major cities of Morocco, such as Casablanca. From Agadir, the major attractions of the Anti-Atlas are best explored by privately rented car. They can also be reached by bus (not by rail).

SUGGESTED ITINERARY

Days 1–2. Spend enjoying the beaches and attractions of Agadir.
Day 3. Drive south to Tiznit for an overnight stopover.
Day 4. Overnight in Tafraoute in the east, using it as a base for exploring the Valley of the Ameln.
Day 5. Head north ot Taroudannt for the night and take a ride around its ancient walls at sunset. Bargain for some of the region's legendary Berber jewelry and crafts.

WHAT'S SPECIAL ABOUT AGADIR, THE SOUSS & THE ANTI-ATLAS

Beaches
☐ Agadir Beach, most desirable and safest beach for swimming on the west coast of Africa.

Great Towns/Villages
☐ Agadir, called the "Miami Beach of Africa" for sun-and-fun seekers from Europe.
☐ Taroudannt, chief market town of the fertile Souss valley, and the original capital of the Saadian dynasty in the 16th century.

☐ Tiznit, legendary stronghold of the 19th-century Blue Sultan, with a medina encircled by 3 uninterrupted miles of ramparts.
☐ Tafraoute, also in the Anti-Atlas, lying in a fertile valley, the almond tree center of North Africa.

Ace Attractions
☐ The walls of Taroudannt, some of the best preserved in Morocco.
☐ The Valley of the Ameln, outside Tafraoute, one of the greatest scenic drives in Africa.

1. AGADIR

323 miles S of Casablanca, 190 miles W of Marrakesh

GETTING THERE By Plane   Inezgane, the Agadir airport, is the only one in the region, and many charter flights filled with beach lovers from Europe land here. Scheduled flights on Royal Air Maroc touch down at either Casablanca or Tangier before continuing on their way south to Agadir. The airport is 5 miles east of the resort and easily accessible by taxi, the trip costing about 12 DH ($1.50). In Agadir, you can reconfirm your tickets at **Royal Air Maroc,** located on avenue General Ketani (tel. 220-06).

By Train   There are no rail links this far south in Morocco.

By Bus   There are three buses daily from Casablanca, taking 5 hours, and 6 buses daily from Essaouira, taking 3½ hours. From Marrakesh, there's a daily bus (4 hours).

By Car   From Casablanca, continue south along the coastal route P8.

It's the Miami Beach of Morocco, unashamedly commercial and sybaritic, eager to show sun-worshipping Europeans the many attractions of its glittering beachfront. It is the closest point to Europe that offers the possibility of sea bathing in both summer and winter, and as such, does a thriving year-round business. It is estimated that at least 350 days of the year are suitable beach weather. With 300,000 visitors annually, it is the undisputed capital of Moroccan tourism.

The city's modern appearance is the result of the rebuilding that followed one of the worst earthquakes in recent memory, on February 29, 1960.

"If destiny has decided upon the destruction of Agadir, its reconstruction will be a result of our faith and of our force of will," are the words of Mohammed V engraved on a memorial plaque. The new city, remarkably larger, better equipped, and more glamorous than the old, lies a short distance to the south of the original site.

Today, Agadir is divided into three main sections. The industrial quarter of Anza is the home of fish-processing plants—after the more southerly port of Tan-Tan, Agadir produces the second-richest haul of sardines and mackerel in Morocco—cement factories, and oil depots. To the south lies the tourist and residential district, with many of Morocco's most plushly upholstered hotels. Separating these two areas, with a sweeping view over the port, is a hill capped with a ruined kasbah (never repaired after the 1960 earthquake). If Agadir continues its present rate of enormous growth, urban planners predict that the city boundaries will, within several generations, extend all the way to the delta of the Souss River, 6 miles to the south.

ORIENTATION

INFORMATION

The **Moroccan National Tourist Office,** located at place du Prince Héritier Sidi Mohammed (tel. 08/228-94), is open in summer Monday through Friday from 8am to 3pm; from mid-September through June, Monday through Friday from 8am to noon and 2:30 to 6:30pm. The local tourist office, the **Syndicat d'Initiative,** found at avenue Mohammed V and avenue du Général Ketani (tel. 08/226-95), keeps the same hours as the tourist office listed above.

GETTING AROUND

Agadir is spread out and the best way to get around is one of the *petits taxis.* A petit taxi is small, carrying about three passengers, and in Agadir it is always painted orange. The meter begins at 1.40 DH (20¢). If you have a lot of luggage, and are arriving at the airport, always take a *grand taxi* and negotiate the price in advance with the driver. Grands taxis are painted blue. To call a grand taxi, dial 82-20-17.

FAST FACTS

American Express   Voyages Schwartz, avenue Hassan II, near the town market (tel. 228-94), represents American Express. Open Monday through Friday from 9:30am to 12:30pm and 3 to 6pm.

Area Code   08.

Currency Exchange   Banks are open Monday through Friday from 8:30 to 11:30am and 2:30 to 4:30, and will make currency exchanges. Off-hours, you can try the hotels (the bigger the better), which will often exchange your checks (with proper identification such as a passport). Hotels, of course, don't give the same favorable rates offered by most banks, but sometimes the lower rate is worth the extra convenience.

Emergencies   For an **ambulance** or to report a **fire,** dial 15; for the **police,** at the **Hôtel de Police,** rue XVIII Novembre, call 19. For **medical attention,** the **Hôpital Hassan II,** route de Marrakech (tel. 414-77), is reliable.

Pharmacy   Pharmacie, Municipalité d'Agadir (tel. 82-03-49), is open 24 hours.

Post Office   It's located on place du Marché and is open Monday through Friday from 8:30am to noon and 3 to 6:30pm, on Saturday in the morning only. In July and August, it is open Monday through Friday from 8am to 2pm, on Saturday in the morning only. Don't try to call—show up in person.

WHAT TO SEE & DO

One of the sites ruined by the 1960 earthquake was the **Kasbah,** whose position atop the region's tallest hill gives it a sweeping view of the town and the harbor. It was built in 1540 by the Saadian sultan Mohammed ech Cheikh as a departure point for the raids he planned (and completed) the following year against the Portuguese-controlled harbor fortifications. After the Portuguese were ousted, the sultans continued to maintain it briefly as protection against raids from insurrectional Berber tribes and a return of the Iberians.

Other than the rebuilt original ramparts and the head-spinning view, there's very little to see here. Be careful amid the ruins—rusted edges of sheet-metal roofs are still wedged around.

To reach the Kasbah, take a winding hilltop road that turns off from the coastal road at the northern perimeter of Agadir. A small sign pointing to it is simply marked KASBAH. Park your car at the wide terrace near the top and explore the rest on foot. Be prepared to be accosted by local peddlers.

Since Agadir was carefully rebuilt after the earthquake, its urban plan is unlike anything else in Morocco. Wide boulevards, verdant parks, and modern plazas make it unique. Among the several noteworthy buildings are the Mosquée Principale, on avenue des Forces Armées Royales (open only to Muslims), and the strikingly modern Central Post Office on avenue du Prince Moulay Abdallah.

Visit the municipal market on avenue Hassan II, a two-story mall filled with the scent of spices and with modern shops selling everything from kaftans to silver jewelry.

By all means, walk or take a petit taxi to the heart of town, and promenade in the early evening along either avenue du Prince Moulay Abdallah or avenue du Président Kennedy, where the bustling cafés make it one of the most convivial urban scenes in the region.

WHERE TO STAY

Agadir has one of the highest concentrations of hotels in all price ranges of any place in North Africa. Hotels rated "Very Expensive" charge 730 to 800 DH ($91.25 to $100) for a double room; those considered "Expensive," 640 to 720 DH ($80 to $90) for a double. "Moderate" rooms are 400 to 550 DH ($50 to $68.75), and "Inexpensive" ranges from 255 to 400 DH ($31.90 to $50).

Hotels usually do not include house numbers as part of their addresses, but most of them are easy to find once you reach the boulevard on which they are situated. Don't look for house numbers, but big signs with the name of the hotel.

VERY EXPENSIVE

CLUB PLM DUNES D'OR, Secteur Balnéaire, Agadir. Tel. 08/201-50. 440 rms (all with bath), 10 suites. **Transportation:** Petit taxi.
$ Rates (with half board included): 730 DH ($91.25) single; 1,200 DH ($150) double; suites from 2,000 DH ($250). AE, DC, MC, V.
This is the largest hotel in Agadir, built in 1978, and it abuts the beach. Famous for its tennis courts (far more than any other hotel in Morocco) and its position as annual host for several important tennis tournaments, it is careful to define itself as a club, rather than a hotel, in an attempt to emphasize group activities and entertainment for its guests. Included in the room price are breakfast and dinner, an hour of daily tennis instruction, and free use of the sauna and *hammam* (bath). Rooms are simple and modern, with either balconies or terraces but without telephones.
Dining/Entertainment: Five restaurants, including ones specializing in Moroccan food, Italian food, and fish; four bars; and Nightclub Byblos (see below).
Services: Tennis lessons, an "animateur" to keep the party rolling during meals, massage.
Facilities: 21 tennis courts, volleyball, handball, basketball, weight room and gym, availability of water sports, deep-sea fishing, and horseback riding.

EUROPA HOTEL SAFIR, bd. du 20 Août, Agadir. Tel. 08/212-12. Fax 08/234-35. 221 rms (all with bath); 16 suites. A/C MINIBAR TV TEL **Transportation:** Petit taxi.
$ Rates: 600 DH ($75) single; 730 DH ($91.25) double; suites from 1,300 DH ($162.50). Breakfast 50 DH ($6.25) extra. AE, DC, MC, V.
One of the most interestingly designed hotels in town, this soaring skyscraper was originally built as a series of interlocking hexagons in 1975. In 1990, its original core was completely renovated and a brown sandstone Almohad-inspired entranceway was added. Bedrooms have private balconies, wall-to-wall carpeting, Moroccan decor, and wall safes.
Dining/Entertainment: The Restaurant President, serving dinner only, is a

stylish re-creation of something you'd expect to find in France; the Restaurant Marocain Al Ambra serves Moroccan food; Le Cockpit, near the pool, serves drinks and snacks; and Le Coq d'Or Ryad is the international restaurant for breakfasts.

Services: Concierge, 24-hour room service, laundry and dry-cleaning service, hairdresser for men and women, currency exchange, translation and typing, travel and recreational services (including shark fishing and deep-sea fishing).

Facilities: Boutiques, art gallery/gift shop, piano bar, tennis courts, swimming pool.

SAHARA AGADIR, bd. Mohammed V, Agadir. Tel. 08/206-60. 234 rms (all with bath), 27 bungalows, 12 suites. A/C MINIBAR TV TEL **Transportation:** Petit taxi.

$ Rates: 520–580 DH ($65–$72.50) single; 600–780 DH ($75–$97.50) double; bungalows and suites from 1,500 DH ($187.50). Breakfast 54 DH ($6.75) extra. AE, DC, MC, V.

The least flashy of the five-star hotels of Agadir, it's located at the southern edge of the Secteur Balnéaire, about a quarter-mile from the beach. Bedrooms have earth-tone decor with geometric accents and private balconies. Bungalows are scattered throughout the surrounding gardens.

Dining/Entertainment: Choices include Moroccan and international restaurants; and the Abou Nouasse piano bar, with a view of the tropical garden; the Al Kaytoune tent erected beside the swimming pool, with a cocktail bar and snack bar; and the Nightclub Schéhérazade (see below).

Services: Translator, hairdresser, massage, group activities, including supervised stretching classes beside pool.

Facilities: Sauna, hammam (bath), drugstore and boutiques, sports and recreational facilities (volleyball, children's wading pool), five tennis courts, a large swimming pool for adults, conference facilities.

EXPENSIVE

HOTEL ATLAS-AMADIL, route de l'Oued Souss, Agadir. Tel. 08/84-06-20. Fax 08/82-36-68. 312 rms (all with bath); 12 suites. A/C TEL **Transportation:** Petit taxi.

$ Rates: 600 DH ($75) single; 720 DH ($90) double; suites from 1,250 DH ($156.25). Breakfast 50 DH ($6.25) extra. AE, DC, MC, V.

Within a 15-minute walk of the commercial center of town, in a district somewhat removed from the tourist zone, the Atlas-Amadil is virtually on Agadir's beach. There's a landscaped atrium with glass-sided elevators on the side. Rooms have radios, terraces or balconies, and safes. Part of the nationwide Atlas hotel chain.

Dining/Entertainment: Choices include Restaurant Belle Epoque (French, see below), an international main dining room, the wine bar Le Tonneau, two bars, a coffee shop, and the Alcazar cabaret and nightclub.

Services: Massage, hairdresser, laundry and dry cleaning, translation, and secretarial services.

Facilities: A minilibrary, TV and video room, large swimming pool, tennis courts, easy availability of water sports, boutiques, and gift kiosks.

HOTEL TAMLELT/HOTEL AGADOR, Quartier des Dunes d'Or, Secteur Balnéaire, Agadir. Tel. 08/84-15-25. 659 rms (all with bath). A/C TV TEL **Transportation:** Petit taxi.

$ Rates (including breakfast): 430 DH ($53.75) single; 640 DH ($80) double. AE, MC, V.

The Tamlelt/Agador complex is the largest and one of the most elaborate tourist facilities in Agadir. The Hotel Tamlelt is the older and smaller of the two, although many guests prefer it for its medina-inspired design and comfort. Many rooms are arranged around symmetrical courtyards with Andalusian fountains.

The Hotel Agador, with 409 rooms, is the most unusual and dramatic interpretation of a kasbah in Agadir. Built in 1986, it is futuristically angular in design and appeals to lovers of unusual architecture, who marvel at its soaring interior spaces and coldly postmodern pizzazz.

In the sprawling gardens between the hotels are swimming pools, endless cascades of water, scattered fountains, restaurants, Moorish pavilions, banks of seasonal flowers, and bars capped with palm fronds.

Dining/Entertainment: Four restaurants, including Restaurant Chez Salah (Moroccan), and the Blackjack Disco (see below). Various "theme" nights with Moroccan dance and music are presented throughout the week.

Services: Hairdresser, concierge, water-sports arranger, tour desk.

Facilities: Four swimming pools, several bars.

MODERATE

AGADIR BEACH CLUB, Centre Balnéaire, Agadir. Tel. 08/84-07-91. Fax 08/257-63. 350 rms (all with bath); 24 suites. TEL **Transportation:** Petit taxi.

$ Rates: 450 DH ($56.25) single; 550 DH ($68.75) double; suites from 800 DH ($100). Breakfast 40 DH ($5) extra. AE, DC, MC, V.

⭐ Agadir's newest and most architecturally impressive hotel. Designed as a series of concentric circles that radiate outward from a circular swimming pool (connected directly to the beach by a covered passageway), it is a Moorish fantasy combining avant-garde building techniques embellished with the ancient Moroccan construction technique of *tadlakt* (lime, sand, egg yolks, and pigments applied like stucco and polished to resemble marble). The result: soaring public rooms accented with cerulean blues, desert reds, and imperial gilt. The effect is majestic. Each accommodation is comfortably plush, with an elegant bathroom and a terrace or balcony.

Dining/Entertainment: At press time, there were three working restaurants, although ambitious plans existed for the creation of seven more, a nightclub, and at least two additional bars scattered throughout the hotel. The in-house disco is the Flamingo Club.

Services: 24-hour room service, laundry and dry cleaning, massage, and a concierge who books car rentals and solves travel problems.

Facilities: Three tennis courts, fitness center with sauna, Jacuzzi, and massage; hairdressers; handcraft boutiques; parasols and chaises longues for use on the beach; circular swimming pool and adjacent bar-and-grill restaurant.

HOTEL ATLAS, bd. Mohammed V, Agadir. Tel. 08/84-32-32. Fax 08/443-79. 156 rms (all with bath), 40 bungalows (all with bath); 2 suites. TEL **Transportation:** Petit taxi.

$ Rates (including breakfast): 341 DH ($42.65) single; 460 DH ($57.50) double; suites from 950 DH ($118.75). AE, DC, MC, V.

Located on the edge of town close to the beach, the Atlas is perhaps a bit better managed and more imaginatively furnished than many of its competitors. Bedrooms have contemporary earth-tone decor and balconies. There are also bungalows on terraced gardens along the hillside below for the same price. Fixed-price meals in one of the hotel's two restaurants are 98 DH ($12.25) each. Tennis courts, a swimming pool, and a nightclub are also available at this pleasant establishment.

INEXPENSIVE

HOTEL ARGANA, bd. Mohammed V, Agadir. Tel. 08/84-00-70. 174 rms (all with bath). TEL **Transportation:** Petit taxi.

$ Rates (including breakfast): 240 DH ($30) single; 295 DH ($36.90) double. AE, DC, MC, V.

Ⓢ Constructed in 1976, the Argana has some of its rooms arranged around a plant-filled atrium. Some balconies overlook either the sea or the hotel's circular swimming pool. Facilities include a plush bar, a restaurant offering meals for 83 DH ($10.40), and a helpful, English-speaking staff.

HOTEL MABROUK, av. du 20 Août, Agadir. Tel. 08/406-06. 41 rms (all with bath). **Transportation:** Petit taxi.

$ **Rates** (including breakfast): 193 DH ($24.15) single; 254 DH ($31.75) double. No credit cards.

Ⓢ Built in 1966 on one of the city's major avenues near more expensive hotels, the Mabrouk sits behind a brick-and-iron fence and a stretch of lawn. The swimming pool is an almost perfect square set within a courtyard. The modern, simply furnished, and clean rooms overlook the pool, the garden, or the sea.

HOTEL ROYAL, bd. Mohammed V, Agadir. Tel. 08/406-75. 73 units (all with bath). TEL **Transportation:** Petit taxi.

$ **Rates** (including breakfast): 200 DH ($25) single; 264 DH ($33) double. No credit cards.

Ⓢ My favorite accommodations are the roughly textured bungalows with vine-covered entrances amid the bougainvillea-filled gardens, though others may prefer the modern rooms in the main building, each with either a terrace or a balcony. There's an intimate bar with a Moorish fountain, plus a rooftop terrace with panoramic view and a sunny restaurant. Fixed-price meals go for 90 DH ($11.25). Facilities include a swimming pool.

WHERE TO EAT

Agadir has one of the widest range of restaurants—both international and Moroccan—in the country. All of the major ones, and a lot of the minor ones, were established for tourists, most of whom fly in from Europe.

Restaurants classified as "Expensive" charge 110 to 460 DH ($13.75 to $57.50) for dinner. The higher price applies only if you order something very expensive, such as lobster. Restaurants considered "Moderate" charge 100 to 160 DH ($12.50 to $20) for dinner, and those ranked "Inexpensive" charge 65 to 120 DH ($8.15 to $15). In all the prices cited, drinks are extra.

Look for the signs advertising the restaurant, not a building number, as most of them are unnumbered.

VERY EXPENSIVE

GOLDEN GATE, Complexe Tafoukt, bd. du 20 Août. Tel. 408-20.
Cuisine: INTERNATIONAL. **Reservations:** Not required. **Transportation:** Petit taxi.
$ **Prices:** Appetizers 25–64 DH ($3.15–$8); main dishes 70–193 DH ($8.75–$24.15); children's menu 47 DH ($5.90). AE, DC, MC, V.
Open: Daily 11am–midnight.

One of the most popular wining and dining facilities in Agadir. With three distinct dining and drinking areas on two levels, the heart and soul of the place is a floor above street level—a Moroccan dining room with a richly filigreed ceiling and a parquet dance floor that serves as a platform for folkloric spectacles presented every evening at 8pm.

Just as popular is the street-level dining room. Also at street level is a very large, vaguely Teutonic bar (see "Evening Entertainment"). Prices on the street level are probably 10% less expensive than upstairs, although the menus are easily interchangeable. Menu specialties in both sections include fresh fish according to the day's deliveries, freshly smoked eel, filet of fresh mullet meunière, escalope Cordon Bleu, *mechouis,* and an array of *tajines.*

LA TOUR DE PARIS, av. Hassan II. Tel. 84-09-06.
Cuisine: FRENCH. **Reservations:** Recommended. **Transportation:** Petit taxi.
$ **Prices:** Appetizers 55–145 DH ($6.90–$18.15); main dishes 55–230 DH ($6.90–$28.75). DC, MC, V.
Open: Lunch 11:30am–2:45pm; dinner 7–11pm. **Closed:** Sat.

Its art nouveau decor was redone in 1990, creating one of the most elegant and unapologetically Parisian interiors in Agadir. Surrounded by white marble and etched glass, you can enjoy a sophisticated cuisine that is described by its owner as a combination of nouvelle cuisine with traditional sauces based on the use of wine, cognac, and Cointreau. Representative specialties include fresh pasta with seafood, lobster salad, terrine of seawolf with tarragon, pot au feu de la mer, a gigot of monkfish in the Parisian style, and a house specialty, *trois petits feuilletes*, composed of three different puff pastries containing three different types of fish, served with three different versions of dill sauce.

MODERATE

RESTAURANT BELLE EPOQUE, Hotel Atlas-Amadil, route de l'Oued Souss. Tel. 84-06-20.
Cuisine: INTERNATIONAL. **Reservations:** Recommended. **Transportation:** Petit taxi.
$ Prices: Appetizers 45–60 DH ($5.65–$7.50); main dishes 75–90 DH ($9.40–$11.25). AE, DC, MC, V.
Open: Dinner daily 8:30pm–midnight.
Located off the lobby of the hotel, the Belle Epoque makes a refreshing change from ethnic Moroccan cuisine. As its name implies, its decor is reproduction art nouveau with lots of etched glass. Specialties include fish dishes (whose exact ingredients and preparation vary according to what's available in the markets), rack of lamb with herbs, and breast of chicken with honey-vinegar, grapefruit, and orange sauce.

DARKHOUM RESTAURANT MAROCAIN, av. du Général Kettani. Tel. 84-06-22.
Cuisine: MOROCCAN. **Reservations:** Recommended. **Transportation:** Petit taxi.
$ Prices: Appetizers 25–35 DH ($3.15–$4.40); main dishes 50–90 DH ($6.25–$11.25); 4-course fixed-priced menu 120 DH ($15). AE, MC, V.
Open: Dinner only, nightly 7:30pm–midnight.
Located in the commercial heart of town, it is a beautifully decorated Moroccan restaurant in the cellar of the Hotel Sud Bahia. Moroccan musicians play in the early evening and a Moroccan dancer performs at 9pm. Specialties include stuffed patties known as *briouates, harira* soup, brochettes of fish and meat, and an array of tajines, some of them flavored with almonds.

LE DOME, bd. Hassan II. Tel. 414-35.
Cuisine: INTERNATIONAL. **Reservations:** Not required. **Transportation:** Petit taxi.
$ Prices: Appetizers 15–30 DH ($1.90–$3.75); sandwiches 25–45 DH ($3.15–$5.65); main dishes 45–60 DH ($5.65–$7.50); beer 10–15 DH ($1.25–$1.90); whisky 25–40 DH ($3.15–$5). AE, DC, MC, V.
Open: Daily 7am–midnight.
Located in the heart of the town's busiest section, it's the most famous and popular café in Agadir. Although there's a modern two-level dining room, most patrons prefer to sit on the sprawling terrace. No one will mind if you order just a beer, coffee, ice cream, or soda. For meals, dishes include shrimp in a spicy *pil-pil* sauce, brochettes of beef, grilled filet steak, fish soup, shrimp salad, assorted sandwiches, and bananas flambé. The menu for this place is translated into an astonishing number of languages.

JARDIN D'EAU, bd. du 20 Août. Tel. 84-01-95.
Cuisine: FRENCH. **Reservations:** Recommended. **Transportation:** Petit taxi.
$ Prices: Appetizers 20–40 DH ($2.50–$5); main dishes 45–90 DH ($5.65–$11.25). AE, DC, MC, V.
Open: Daily 11am–11:30pm.
In a courtyard with a half-dozen fountains in the tourist area, it is the single most charming restaurant in Agadir. Your meal might include fish soup, pigeon in puff pastry, calamari, roasted monkfish with spinach, filet of sole (prepared many different ways), or a Moroccan mechoui of lamb.

RESTAURANT MARINE HEIM, bd. Mohammed V. Tel. 221-31.
Cuisine: GERMAN. **Reservations:** Recommended. **Transportation:** Petit taxi.
$ **Prices:** Appetizers 11–98 DH ($1.40–$12.25); main dishes 48–80 DH ($6–$10); children's platters 34 DH ($4.25). MC, V.
Open: Daily noon–11pm.
Established by Mohammed Fadil and his German-born wife, Hilde, this is without doubt the best German restaurant in Agadir, with a helpful Moroccan staff fluent in English and German. There are a bar and a dining room on the street level, but the most refreshing spot is on the second floor, with tables on a balcony overlooking the avenue below. The restaurant's decor adopts much of the paraphernalia of the German navy, where Hilde's father spent most of his career. Specialties include filet of John Dory with a sauce of white wine, onions, and shrimp; sauerkraut with sausages and ham hock; sole au gratin accented with ham strips or shrimp; ragoût of fish with rice; and one of the best versions of fish soup in Agadir. The dessert specialty is a high-caloric version of German cheesecake with German coffee. Lobster, priced by the kilo, is one of the house specialties.

VIA VENETO, av. Hassan II, 89. Tel. 414-67.
Cuisine: INTERNATIONAL. **Reservations:** Recommended. **Transportation:** Petit taxi.
$ **Prices:** Appetizers 20–30 DH ($2.50–$3.75); main dishes 45–70 DH ($5.65–$8.75). AE, DC, MC, V.
Open: Daily 11:30am–midnight.
This cozy bistro lists specialties in six different languages, probably the result of the international clientele attracted by one of its owners, Charles Blasa, who arrived from Switzerland 50 years ago and never left. Dishes include osso buco, four different preparations of shrimp, three different preparations of filet steak, sole meunière, kebabs of calamari, fish soup, seafood gratin, and flavorful salads usually made without lettuce.

INEXPENSIVE

CHEZ JO RESTAURANT CACHER, Complexe l'Agador, bd. du 20 Août, 41. Tel. 82-33-05.
Cuisine: KOSHER/SEPHARDIC (BETH-DINN). **Reservations:** Recommended. **Transportation:** Petit taxi.
$ **Prices:** Appetizers 15–30 DH ($1.90–$3.75); main dishes 30–55 DH ($3.75–$6.90). MC, V.
Open: Lunch daily noon–3pm; dinner daily 7pm–midnight.
At the edge of the broad commercial esplanade that flanks the entrance to the Agador section of the Hotel Tamlelt/Hotel Agador, this is the only kosher restaurant in Agadir and one of the very few kosher restaurants in Morocco. Specialties include lamb cutlets, brochettes of lamb heart, grilled sole, grilled steaks, a mixed fry of tiny fish, and several variations of reddish spicy sausages called *merguez* that probably originated in Tunisia.

CHEZ REDY, av. du Prince Héritier Sidi Mohammed. Tel. 84-25-27.
Cuisine: INTERNATIONAL. **Reservations:** Recommended. **Transportation:** Petit taxi.
$ **Prices:** Hamburgers 14–20 DH ($1.75–$2.50); pizzas and salads 28–40 DH ($3.50–$5); main dishes 38–55 DH ($4.75–$6.90); fixed-priced 3-course daily special 90 DH ($11.25). MC, V.
Open: Daily 8am–1am.
It's the closest thing in Agadir to a revival of the freewheeling conviviality of the 1960s—an all-day food-and-drink emporium, with a long rectangular bar, a scattering of wooden tables cooled by breezes blowing through lattices, and courtyards both front and back. In the evening, a giant-screen video displays an oft-repeated series of rock-and-roll concerts. If you want to dine, there are grilled

dishes, sandwiches, and pizzas (nine different kinds), but many people come only for what owner Redy Renal calls "a pitcher of happiness." This, for 40 DH ($5), mixes red or rose wine with 7-Up into a bubbly concoction something like sangría.

RESTAURANT DU PORT, Yacht-Club, Port d'Agadir. Tel. 84-37-08.
   Cuisine: SEAFOOD. **Reservations:** Recommended. **Transportation:** Petit taxi.
$ Prices: Appetizers 22–42 DH ($2.75–$5.25); main dishes 34–56 DH ($4.25–$7). AE, V.
   Open: Lunch daily noon–3pm; dinner daily 7–10pm.

⭐ To reach Agadir's most famous seafood restaurant, you'll have to drive into a slightly sinister-looking industrial zone beside the port of Agadir. The bistro-style confines are more French than you might have imagined. The specialties will depend on the catch of the day, but several highly recommended dishes include brochette of *lotte* or monkfish; fried filets of red mullet, hake, or sole; grilled sea bass with fennel; and a local version of *ombrine* prepared in the style of Grenoble.

LA PAMPA, Immeuble A, place du Prince Héritier Sidi Mohammed. Tel. 228-31.
   Cuisine: INTERNATIONAL. **Reservations:** Recommended. **Transportation:** Petit taxi.
$ Prices: Appetizers 15–60 DH ($1.90–$7.50); main dishes 25–60 DH ($3.15–$7.50). AE, DC, MC, V.
   Open: Daily 10am–11pm.

⭐ On the ground floor of the shopping mall that also houses the city's tourist office, it's owned by the most famous caterer in Agadir, Ahmed Boutabaa. (The famous couscous he made in February 1990 for a state dinner attended by Britain's Prince Philip measured 15 feet in diameter and included 200 chickens, 20 sheep, and 2 tons of semolina.)
You might enjoy an apéritif at the Churchill Bar (see "Evening Entertainment"), and follow it with a meal in one of two dining rooms decorated in European and Moroccan styles. Choices from the European menu include pepper steak flambéed with champagne, filet mignon with *cèpe* mushrooms, a pampa-style hamburger, fish soup, grilled seawolf flambéed with *pastis,* and local eel carefully smoked over a fire made from the aromatic *arganier* tree. The Moroccan menu includes a tajine of lamb, a regional variation of a traditional mechoui called *m'hammar, couscous royale,* and *djaj m'qualli* (a regional version of chicken with a confit of lemon and olives).

SHOPPING

Prices in the shops of Agadir are higher than those in Marrakesh. Granted, the merchandise is often exquisite and much of it is geared to European and North American tastes. If you're planning day trips, hold off on serious purchases until you visit the souks of such places as Taroudannt, where items are much more reasonably priced.

EVENING ENTERTAINMENT

NIGHTCLUB BYBLOS, Club PLM Dunes d'Or, Secteur Balnéaire. Tel. 201-50.
   This glittering club is in the largest hotel in Agadir, located near the beach. Its French clientele and its high-tech amplification system create a beachfront version of something you might find in Paris. Beer costs 15 DH ($1.90). The place is open nightly from 9:30pm to 5am. Transportation: Petit taxi.
   Admission: Hotel residents, free; nonresidents, 60 DH ($7.50).

NIGHTCLUB SCHEHERAZADE, Hotel Sahara Agadir, bd. Mohammed V. Tel. 206-60.
In this cavelike cellar full of curves, rounded corners, and bars, a sophisticated sound system—reputedly one of the best in Agadir—can blast you off the dance floor, but many of the foreign clients seem to enjoy it. Beer costs 15 DH ($1.90). Nightly hours are 10pm to 4am. Transportation: Petit taxi.
   Admission: Hotel residents, free; nonresidents, 25 DH ($3.15).

BLACKJACK DISCO, Hotel Agador, Quartier des Dunes d'Or, Secteur Balnéaire. Tel. 84-15-25.
It's probably the most fun, whimsical, and energetic disco in Agadir, filled with European tourists and hip locals. Set within the cellar of the Agador section of the Hotel Tamlelt/Hotel Agador, it has a teakwood dance floor centered amid wraparound balconies, batteries of musically synchronized lasers, an all-black decor, and two bars. Go late. Drinks cost 40 DH ($5). Nightly hours are 9:30pm to 5am. Transportation: Petit taxi.
   Admission: 60 DH ($7.50), including first drink.

GOLDEN GATE, Complexe Tafoukt, bd. du 20 Août. Tel. 408-20.
There are two floors of restaurant facilities connected to this place in the heart of the tourist zone (see "Where to Eat"), but many guests come just to drink at the circular and vaguely alpine bar. There is a wide selection of Teutonic beers, including Holstein, Heineken, and Flagg, as well as snacks to soak up the drinks. Under the same management, a sidewalk pizzeria nearby sells several different kinds of pizzas. Beer costs 13 to 20 DH ($1.65 to $2.50); pizzas are 30 to 45 DH ($3.75 to $5.65). The place is open daily from 11am to midnight. Transportation: Petit taxi.

CHURCHILL BAR, Restaurant La Pampa, Immeuble A, place du Prince Héritier Sidi Mohammed. Tel. 228-31.
You'll find it tucked away behind the two dining rooms of the previously mentioned restaurant—an unexpectedly charming leather-upholstered bar, similar to what you'd expect in Bristol or Liverpool, adorned with a portrait of Sir Winston himself. A selection of whiskies and beers is available, and the Moroccan clientele might be engrossed in a locally televised soccer match. Beer costs 10 to 15 DH ($1.25 to $1.88), and the place is open daily from 11am to 3pm and 6pm to 1am.

2. TAROUDANNT

50 miles E of Agadir; 140 miles SW of Marrakesh

GETTING THERE   By Bus   From Marrakesh's CTM station, daily buses depart at 4am, taking 8½ hours over Tizi n'Test, the mountain pass. Connections are better from Agadir to Taroudannt, with 4 daily buses making the 2½-hour trip.

By Car   From Agadir, take route P32 east until you see the signposted turnoff for Taroudannt.

ESSENTIALS   Orientation   Nearly all roads in town will lead either to place Tamoklate or to place Assarag. Petits taxis are a good way to get around; either hail one on the street or go to place Tamoklate. You can also ride in a horse-drawn calèche, usually found in the center of town. The city is best covered on foot.

Fast Fact   Area code is 085.

With a population of 30,000, Taroudannt is the capital of the agricultural district of the Souss Valley. The town is considered one of the important centers of handcrafts in Morocco, with a thousand-year history of great distinction. It is the chief city of the Chleuh tribe, whose members are particularly noted for their heavy silver jewelry.

Without the carefully husbanded irrigation systems that funnel water down from the High Atlas mountains to the north, Taroudannt and most of the life around it would cease to exist.

WHAT TO SEE & DO

✪ The **walls of Taroudannt,** over 3 miles long and pierced with five gates, are the most memorable feature of the town. Some historians consider them the best-preserved walls of their kind in Morocco. In the early 1700s, on much older foundations, they were crafted from *pise,* a form of battered sun-dried earth reinforced with chopped straw and palmwood. Maintained over the years by each new generation of city residents, they are at their most impressive in the late afternoon (a vehicular circumnavigation of the ramparts takes about 30 minutes), when the setting sun gives them a russet-colored glow. Groves of oranges and olives spread out from the base of the walls.

Within the walls, the **souks** are most impressive with more exotic merchandise on sale here than almost anywhere else in southern Morocco.

Because of the frequent pillagings of this town, there is a notable absence of specific monuments. The two major squares of the town are the **place Assarag,** and the **place Tamoklate,** where visitors can park near the arrival point of the overland buses from Marrakesh, and where a flotilla of blue-sided petits taxis await arriving visitors.

WHERE TO STAY
VERY EXPENSIVE

LA GAZELLE D'OR, route de Amezgou, Taroudannt. Tel. 085/85-20-39. 30 rms (all with bath). A/C MINIBAR TV TEL **Transportation:** Petit taxi.
$ **Rates** (including half board): 1,525 DH ($190.65) single; 2,000 DH ($250) double. AE, DC, MC, V. **Closed:** July 20–Sept. 1.

✪ A mile from the center of town, the hotel charges rates that are acceptable by European standards but stratospheric by Moroccan ones. Still, because of its beauty, some readers will consider the price well worth paying. The 9-acre site was bought in 1938 by French-born Baron von Pellenc, who dreamed of building a vacation paradise for himself and a handful of occasional visitors. There are huge tracts of orange groves, some of the most beautiful gardens in the region, and, inside, the kinds of exotic artifacts and paintings that in their day created a legend in the glamorous salons of Europe and America. Thirty one-story bungalows, with vine- and flower-covered walls and terraces, are stylishly furnished in Moroccan style and have fireplaces. There are two tennis courts, waterfalls, a swimming pool where lunchtime buffets are served, and dozens of rose-lined pathways. The main clubhouse has a dining room, a bar, and a Moroccan-inspired zodiac chart set in mosaic into the floor of one of the salons.

EXPENSIVE

HOTEL PALAIS SALAM, route de Ouarzazate, Taroudannt. Tel. 085/25-01. 174 rms (all with bath). TEL **Transportation:** Petit taxi.
$ **Rates** (including breakfast): 300 DH ($37.50) single; 450 DH ($56.25) double. MC, V.

Situated within an 18th-century Moorish palace that skirts the inner walls of the town's medieval fortifications, it became a hotel in the 1940s and offers pasha-style grandeur to its guests. The newer accommodations are in bungalows along pathways draped with vines, flowers, and trees; the older accommodations, in what was originally the palace, encircle several old courtyards containing Moorish fountains and small groves of banana trees. All but the oldest rooms have air conditioning; the high ceilings also compensate a bit for the sometimes oppressive heat. Facilities include two lavishly decorated Moroccan restaurants, a less dramatic restaurant serving international food, and a bar/salon covered with some of the most elaborate tilework in town. You'll find the staff cooperative.

INEXPENSIVE

HOTEL SAADIEN, Borj Oumansour, Taroudannt. Tel. 085/25-89. 50 rms (all with bath). **Transportation:** Petit taxi.
$ Rates (including breakfast): 149 DH ($18.65) single; 188 DH ($23.50) double; 200 DH ($25) half board per person. No credit cards.

This attractive modern hotel (1980) is inside the Medina, on a dusty street barely wide enough for two cars. The simple rooms are filled with Bedouin-inspired furniture and Moroccan carpets. No alcohol is served in the Moroccan tearoom upstairs. There's a rooftop lounge for breakfast, with plants, panoramic views, and an open terrace. Facilities include a swimming pool in the garden.

HOTEL TAROUDANNT, place Assarag, Taroudannt. Tel. 085/24-16. 20 rms (11 with bath). TEL **Transportation:** Petit taxi.
$ Rates: 54 DH ($6.75) single without bath, 93 DH ($11.65) single with bath; 73 DH ($9.15) double without bath, 105 DH ($13.15) double with bath. Breakfast 26 DH ($3.25) extra. No credit cards.

Located on one side of the main square, it's the bargain hotel in town. The accommodations are very simple and basic (no air conditioning), and the plumbing varies widely, although the more expensive rooms have full baths. Each unit is decorated with a combination of Bedouin artifacts and textiles. There's a restaurant, with fixed-priced meals costing 60 DH ($7.50), plus a bar.

WHERE TO EAT

EXPENSIVE

LA GAZELLE D'OR, route de Amezgou. Tel. 85-20-39.
Cuisine: MOROCCAN/INTERNATIONAL. **Reservations:** Required. **Transportation:** Petit taxi.
$ Prices: Complete meal 320 DH ($40). AE, DC, MC, V.
Open: Dinner daily 8–10pm.

About a mile from the center, this hotel serves the finest food in southern Morocco. An international coterie of guests dine in a huge tented dining room, where the menu changes daily. You might begin with a fish soup. Moroccan dishes are always featured, including *pastilla au pigeon* (shredded pigeon with cinnamon, eggs, and almonds, enclosed in puff pastry). Delectable desserts include thin layers of light, fluffy pastry filled with custard (made by the hotel's own pastry chef). You might also try fresh pears in wine. Waiters wear white *gundura* outfits, white stockings, and white slippers. It's customary to take tea outside the main room, where a waiter, sitting cross-legged on a carpet scattered with rose petals, makes an elaborate ritual of pouring your tea from a brass pot.

SHOPPING

MAGAZIN LICHIR, Souk Smata, 36. Tel. 21-45.
There are dozens of shops throughout the medinas of most Moroccan cities, but Magazin Lichir is so unusual that it deserves special mention. It's set within the labyrinth of the most exotic part of the souk, surrounded by spice vendors, shoe salesmen, and coffee merchants. Its two floors contain genuinely antique jewelry, carpets, furniture, and a valuable collection of 18th- and 19th-century Moroccan arms and pistols. But the Bedouin carpets attract the most attention. The owner will unfold dozens of them for you, and price negotiations are welcomed. The place is

open daily from 8am to 8pm and is reached only on foot, since it lies in the center of the souk.

3. TIZNIT

56 miles S of Agadir; 379 miles S of Casablanca

GETTING THERE   By Bus   Four buses daily, taking 3½ hours, connect Tiznit with Tafraoute (see below). Four buses daily travel between Tiznit and Agadir (2 hours).

By Car   Head south from Agadir along route P30.

ESSENTIALS   The area code is 086.

Despite the ancient appearance of the ramparts that surround it, Tiznit was founded in 1882, along a caravan route 10 miles from the Atlantic coastline. Though the surrounding region is arid, with only almond and argan trees seeming to grow with any degree of good health, there are an estimated 250,000 inhabitants occupying the surrounding steppes and plains. The richness of the town's souks, the exoticism of its landscape, and the curiously invigorating quality of its dry heat make for an interesting excursion.

WHAT TO SEE & DO

The geographical heart of town is **place Méchouar,** a combination of parking lots, bus depots, and merchants' stalls. It is at its most animated every Thursday, when dozens of Bedouin traders arrive from the outlying regions. Scattered among the fruit and vegetable stalls are stands selling unusual jewelry of varying quality. Look especially for the good-luck symbols of the hand of Fatima, crafted in honor of the favorite daughter of the Prophet Muhammad.

Despite the town's relative youth, it is nonetheless imbued with local legends. For example, the minaret of the **Grand Mosque,** less interesting than older mosques throughout the countryside, is adorned with perches similar to those you might have expected birds to roost upon. It was ordained by local imams as a resting place for the souls of the dead, presumably so they will gain wisdom from their nearness to the prayers of the Faithful.

Also interesting is an insipid-looking concrete basin that local guides will point out as the legendary source of the **blue springs of Lalla Tiznit.** It marks the site where, according to legend, an ancient city called Tiznit was founded by a repentant prostitute whose holiness so impressed Allah that he created a flowing spring at the site of her martyrdom. Today, the spring is kept filled with an electric pump.

Two eroded gates on the northern edge of the ramparts, the **Bab Targua** and the **Bab El Kehmis,** provide occasional solid footing (this is recommended *only* for the athletic) for a panoramic view over the surrounding countryside.

WHERE TO STAY & EAT
INEXPENSIVE

HOTEL TIZNIT, rue Dirinzarn (without number), Tiznit. Tel. 086/24-11.
40 rms (all with bath). **Transportation:** Petit taxi.
$ Rates: 193 DH ($24.15) single; 238 DH ($29.75) double; 312 DH ($39) triple. Breakfast 23 DH ($2.90) extra. AE, DC, MC, V.

The best in Tiznit, this three-star hotel is set at the edge of town, near the commercial crossroads and within sight of the old fortified city. Each of the comfortable rooms has big windows and its own bath. Guests can enjoy a swimming pool, banks of oleander, and a large and sunny restaurant one floor above ground level, serving meals for 83 DH ($10.40).

4. TAFRAOUTE

69 miles E of Tiznit; 53 miles S of At-Baha (the last gas
station); 79 miles SE of Agadir

GETTING THERE By Bus There are 5 buses daily from Agadir via Tiznit,
taking 4½ hours and costing 40 DH ($5) one way.

By Car From Agadir you can travel along the S509 via Blougra and At-Baha. You'll
cut through some of the most beautiful valleys of the Anti-Atlas along a highway that
is treacherous in places and recommended only to skilled drivers. Although you'll
miss the best scenery, you can follow the bus route along a better road: route P30
south from Agadir to Tiznit, then route 7074 east to Tafraoute.

ESSENTIALS The area code is 080.

SPECIAL EVENTS Market day, Wednesday of each week.

The landscape is even more arid than that of Tiznit, but the 69-mile drive eastward is
considered one of the most beautiful in Morocco. A good road cuts into the heart
of the Anti-Atlas mountains to reach this town of jumbled rocks and sun-blasted
bleakness, much like a lunar landscape.

Rectangular houses huddle against cliffs, and occasionally a motorist will spy a
goat that has managed to climb onto the lower limbs of a dust-covered tree to munch
at the fruit and leaves. Where an oasis bubbles through mud to the surface, a verdant
grove of palms, olives, almonds, and figs will glow against the otherwise monochromatic terrain. Among the most memorable times to visit is in mid-February, when
delicate clouds of almond blossoms add beauty to the area around Tafraoute. (A local
legend claims that one of them blooms at the site of the murder of a local swain,
Ibrahim, and that the petals that adorn his grave, and the roots that entwine his
corpse, are those of his lover, Malika, whose grief transformed her into an almond
tree at the moment of his death.)

Tafraoute, with a population of only 1,200, is usually deserted except on
Wednesday, when it's market day. The town has a good hotel, described below, and
provides an excellent base for exploring the other attractions of the Anti-Atlas
mountains.

WHERE TO STAY & EAT
MODERATE

**HOTEL LES AMANDIERS, route de Oumesnat, Tafraoute. Tel. 080/
0008.** 62 rms (30 with bath). TEL
$ Rates: 201 DH ($25.15) single without bath, 247 DH ($30.90) single with bath;
245 DH ($30.65) double without bath, 302 DH ($37.75) double with bath.
Breakfast 31 DH ($3.90) extra. MC, V.
Positioned atop a hill, a 5-minute walk from the town center, the Hotel Les
Amandiers is the most prominent building in town. It was electrified in 1989. Some of
the older accommodations, with the highest ceilings, are arranged around an interior
courtyard and fountain. Plumbing varies from room to room. The public salons
contain dozens of deep armchairs, filigreed ceilings, and lots of unused space.
Fixed-priced meals in the slightly faded dining room run 90 to 100 DH ($11.25 to
$12.50).

AN EASY EXCURSION

An interesting detour, 2½ miles north along the S509 highway toward Agadir
and Igherm, takes you to the rocky bluffs that ring the town of Tafraoute and
give way to a sweeping view of the verdant **valley of the Ameln.** Watered by
a series of oases that inexplicably bubble to the surface, it incorporates almost 30

different villages within a serpentine route whose precariously perched kasbahs, palm groves, and rocky abutments provide some of the most memorable sights in Morocco. Be warned that I cannot recommend hotels or restaurants along this route: only a glorious spectacle of unparalleled views.

Continuing along the gravel-covered and potholed road to Igherm is not recommended. The road to Agadir, however, is fine.

CHAPTER 8
MARRAKESH

- **WHAT'S SPECIAL ABOUT MARRAKESH**
- **1. ORIENTATION & GETTING AROUND**
- **FAST FACTS: MARRAKESH**
- **2. ACCOMMODATIONS**
- **FROMMER'S SMART TRAVELER: HOTELS**
- **FROMMER'S COOL FOR KIDS: HOTELS**
- **3. DINING**
- **FROMMER'S SMART TRAVELER: RESTAURANTS**
- **FROMMER'S COOL FOR KIDS: RESTAURANTS**
- **4. ATTRACTIONS**
- **DID YOU KNOW . . . ?**
- **SUGGESTED ITINERARIES**
- **FROMMER'S FAVORITE MARRAKESH EXPERIENCES**
- **5. SAVVY SHOPPING**
- **6. EVENING ENTERTAINMENT**
- **7. EASY EXCURSIONS**

An ancient caravan town, full of gardens and palaces, Marrakesh sits poised on the edge of the Sahara. With Rabat, Fez, and Meknes, it's classified as one of the four Imperial Cities of Morocco, yet in many ways its prestige is greater than that of any of its royal counterparts.

It so impressed early European visitors that they gave its name (Marrakesh, later Morocco) to the country that contained it. Its stones seem to bear the imprint of every monarch who ever thirsted for its allegiance or raged against its rebuttals. The lifespan of entire dynasties is defined upon Moroccan datelines by the year of their conquest or loss of Marrakesh.

Fez, the traditional rival of Marrakesh, is known for its Arabic and Islamic purity and its canonization of traditional Andalusian values. Marrakesh, a staunchly Berber rather than an Arab capital, is known better for the tidal waves of power that repeatedly swept from the Sahara into its inner sanctums.

Some have called Marrakesh the most mysterious town in Africa. Unlike Tangier and Casablanca, it is deeply rooted in the continent, far removed from the Mediterranean and its European influence. African rhythms—amplified through Marrakesh—add a complicated grace note to the soul of Morocco.

The city is at its best in winter, when snow gleams on the peaks of the nearby Atlas mountains, and temperatures are dry, invigorating, and (according to some) aphrodisiacal.

Marrakesh is probably the most chic and sophisticated city in Africa. In any season (but especially in winter) it has attracted the rich, the notorious, and the famous. Winston Churchill used to visit frequently, spending many hours on the veranda of his hotel painting the date palms and the mountains. Many sophisticated Europeans, including a scattering of titled aristocrats from France, live within villas in the Ville Nouvelle or within Muslim palaces within the Medina, keeping alive the nostalgia, the social forms, and the memories of the country's colonial era. Famous part-time residents have included lions from the haute-couture empires of Paris, including (with their entourages) Pierre Balmain, Pierre Cardin, and Yves St. Laurent. Even the Shah of Iran, fleeing from a fundamentalist Islamic revolution, escaped to find refuge at Marrakesh's most famous hotel (the Mamounia) in 1979.

WHAT'S SPECIAL ABOUT MARRAKESH

Historic Districts
- ☐ Jemaa el Fna, the most famous market square in North Africa.
- ☐ The Medina, overflowing with artifacts on sale and a labyrinth of souks.

Buildings
- ☐ Koutoubia Minaret, the towering symbol of the city and a souvenir of the once-mighty Almohad dynasty.
- ☐ Tombs of the Saadians, extravagantly decorated resting place of a great imperial family.

Parks/Gardens
- ☐ The Aguedal, a splendid imperial oasis of reflective calm laid out by the Almohads in the 12th century.
- ☐ Jardin Menara, set in an extensive olive grove, where Almohads dallied with their favorites.

- ☐ The palm groves of Marrakesh, the oldest of which are more than a thousand years old, covering nearly 30,000 acres.

Ace Attractions
- ☐ The red-toned Ramparts of Marrakesh, stretching almost 10 miles around the city.
- ☐ The souks of the Marrakesh Medina, the best place in North Africa for finely crafted leather, wood, brassware, and carpets.

Special Events
- ☐ National Folklore Festival in June, one of the largest and most fervent cultural showcases in the world.

Today, the population of Marrakesh incorporates a seam-busting half-million inhabitants. Its environs are witnessing the greatest real-estate boom in Moroccan history, a dizzying expansion that fuels itself on Marrakesh's reputation as the most frequently visited (after Agadir) city in Morocco. Dozens of exciting hotels are being erected faster than a sandstorm, but whether they will flourish is something that will depend only on time, world events, and the mysterious allure of Marrakesh,

1. ORIENTATION & GETTING AROUND

Marrakesh is the major city of southern Morocco and the gateway to the Sahara. As you begin to explore Marrakesh, particularly its Medina, you are likely to be besieged by prospective guides aggressively selling their services. In a land of some 80% male unemployment, with nearly half the population under 21, unofficial guides will attempt to corner you at every turn.

You will not be left alone, and you might as well accept this as a fact. Do not, under any circumstances, accept one of the wads of chocolate-colored hashish that are a legendary product of the Jemaa el Fna (the city's open marketplace), or any other drugs. The consequences could be more horrible than you ever dreamed, the most obvious being that your dealer is also an informant for the police.

You may legitimately want someone to show you around, especially the labyrinthine Medina of Marrakesh. It is best to go to the tourist office (see below) and arrange for one of the official guides. They are regulated by the government and have to meet certain linguistic and ethical requirements.

Even if you don't really want a guide, an official guide will keep the hustlers away from you and let you sightsee with a modicum of peace. Agree on the price before setting out. The rates, as fixed by the tourist office, are reasonable: 50 DH ($6.25) for a half day, 100 DH ($12.50) for a whole day. Of course, the guide will be most happy to accept a tip. Get used to tipping a lot in Marrakesh. It is always wise, as soon as possible, to acquire small change in dirhams. Technically, you're not supposed to dispense foreign currencies for services rendered, even though guides may specifically request that you pay them in dollars or German marks.

Even with an official guide, purchases made in shops, even meals consumed at restaurants, may carry a small hidden surcharge. Many of the guides return later to the store in which you bought something—perhaps a small Moroccan carpet—to demand their commission. They even go to restaurants and demand a commission for having taken you there. Well used to this practice, the shopkeeper or restaurant owner simply adds the "commission" to your purchases.

This information is presented not to deter a visit or even to disappoint. It's an accepted way of life in Marrakesh, and it's important to be forewarned.

ARRIVING

BY PLANE

Royal Air Maroc and **British Airways** fly from London, and Royal Air Maroc and **Air France** leave from Paris several times weekly. **Royal Air Inter** connects Marrakesh to most major Moroccan cities.

In Marrakesh itself, the ticket office for both Royal Air Maroc and Air France is the same, and it's found on avenue Mohammed V (tel. 319-38).

Domestic and international flights arrive at the **Aéroport de Marrakech Menara** (tel. 303-38), 3 miles south of the center. There is no bus service into the center, but **taxis** usually only cost 50 DH ($6.25).

BY TRAIN

The **train station** is at avenue Hassan II (tel. 311-07 for rail departure information). Seven trains a day travel west to Casablanca, taking 3 hours. There is also a direct overnight train heading north to Tangier, departing Marrakesh at 8:15pm and taking 4 hours. You can also make rail connections to Meknes, six trains daily, taking 3 hours. Six trains daily also run between Fez and Marrakesh, taking 4 hours.

BY BUS

Buses depart from a congested depot by Bab Doukkala on place Mouarabiten. Unfortunately, you can't phone but should go to one of the windows selling tickets. The **CTM** window is no. 10, and that of its major rival, **SATAS,** is no. 14. There are many competing private bus companies, but their standards are always lower than those of these two major companies.

Three buses daily run between Marrakesh and Casablanca, taking 4 hours, and two buses daily go back and forth to Fez, taking 11 hours. You can also get one of four buses leaving for Ouarzazate, taking 4½ hours, and four buses for Zagora, taking 10 hours.

BY CAR

From Casablanca, take route P7 south. From Fez, head south along route P24 toward Azrou. Continue along this route via Beni Mellal all the way to Marrakesh.

TOURIST INFORMATION

The **Moroccan National Tourist Office** is located at place Abdel Moumen ben Ali along avenue Mohammed V (tel. 04/302-58). It is open daily in summer from 8am to 2:30pm. From September through June, daily hours are 8am to noon and 2 to 6pm. It is probably the best-managed tourist office in all of Morocco, with an especially strict supervision of official guides. For information exclusively about the city of Marrakesh, go to the **Syndicat d'Initiative,** avenue Mohammed V, 176 (tel. 04/330-97). It's open in summer Monday through Friday from 9am to 1:30pm and 4 to 7pm. From mid-September through June, it's open Monday through Friday from 8am to noon and 3 to 6pm, on Saturday from 8am to noon.

CITY LAYOUT

MAIN ARTERIES & STREETS

The **Jemaa el Fna,** an open marketplace overshadowed by the Koutoubia Minaret, is the spiritual and geographical heart of Marrakesh. From the Jemaa el Fna, turn right, with your back to the old city, onto **avenue Mohammed V;** continue until you reach a crossroads with a fountain in the middle. (If you wish to walk around town, I recommend hiring a guide.) To the left is **avenue El Yarmouk,** which runs along the side of the ramparts. When the fortifications turn from the avenue at right angles, enter the Medina, choosing one of two gateways, **Bab er Rob** or **Bab Agnaou.**

Inside are the **Kasbah** and the Grand Mosque, with the Saadian Tombs in a walled garden nearby. After seeing the tombs, turn right onto **rue de la Kasbah** and take the second street on the left to reach **Bab Berrima** and El Badi Palace, now in ruins but the site of the annual folklore festival. Farther along to the right, go around the Royal Palace, or Dar el Maghzen, to the external and internal assembly places near the walled Aguedal gardens, with their ancient olive trees.

Back at the Koutoubia, go through the quarters on the right, known as **Riad Zitoun Kebir** and **Riad Zitoun Jedid,** to El Bahia Palace and its lovely gardens, and to Dar Si Said, a palace turned art museum. Take the street on the left on the far side of the Jemaa el Fna, and enter the covered alleyways lined with shops selling rugs from Chichaoua, Ouarzazate, and the High Atlas mountains. You'll come to a maze of small streets redolent of the cedar, sandal, and thuya wood used by cabinetmakers. Visit a little square with a country air, and go under a "bridge" composed of colorful skeins of wool strung across the dyers' souk.

Farther on is the Moulay Youssef Mosque, near which, on lower ground, is a *koubba* shrine dating back to the 11th century. Near the Ben Youssef Mosque, visit the *medersa* (Koranic school) of the same name, attended by students since 1565. Here you'll find the Chrob ou Couf fountain, decorated with geometrically arranged stalactites and woodcarvings inscribed with kufic and Arabic script. Farther on are the *zaouias* (sanctuaries near the mausoleums of Islamic saints) of Sidi Ben Abbes es Sebti, Sidi Ben Slimane and Jazouli, Sidi Abdelaziz, Kaid Ayad, Sidi El Ghezouani, and Sidi Es Soyhli. On the way you'll pass the Grand Mosque and several fine fountains.

The **Ville Nouvelle,** or **Guéliz,** is the new part of the city constructed mainly by the French, lying along avenue Mohammed V, past the Koutoubia Minaret. In this section you will find the train station, the bus station, the tourist offices, the travel agencies, and the luxury and first-class hotels.

FINDING AN ADDRESS

Buildings that have numbers (most do not) are even on one side and odd on the other, running in consecutive order. But don't plan on locating a building by a house number. It is far better to look for the name of the establishment—hotel, restaurant, travel agent—as these letters will be far more prominent than some usually nonexistent house number. If you're seeking a specific address, it is always better to find out the cross street, instead of wandering up and down avenue Mohammed V, for example, trying to find a place.

Guéliz, or the New Town, is the best mapped, but the Medina is a maze. Sometimes street names are used, often not. The first-time visitor can usually get around the New Town without a guide (although you'll be besieged at every turn). But looking for specific addresses in the Medina without the assistance of a guide is virtually impossible.

NEIGHBORHOODS IN BRIEF

"Neighborhoods" in Marrakesh are rather easily defined. There is the New Town, or Ville Nouvelle, most often referred to as Guéliz; and there is the Old Town, or Medina, in the geographic center.

The Medina The souk-filled Medina of Marrakesh is a giant handcrafts market, although many people also live here. Its main artery is Souk Semarine, traditionally a souk for potters, although the rigid classification of souks by craft orientation no longer holds true. The Rahba Kedima is a small square with both a spice souk and a carpet souk. The Souk Attarine contains most of the silver and carpet merchants. At the Souk aux Bijoutiers you can purchase chunky silver (at least we think it is silver, not pewter) and amber Berber jewelry (be warned, however, that much of the amber sold here is fake).

Guéliz The Ville Nouvelle, laid out by a French architect in the colonial era, is the New Town of Marrakesh, a natural outgrowth of the Medina when it could no longer contain the developing city's many businesses and interests. Some of the streets are planted with olive trees, and the city officials jealously guard their long-held right to harvest the fruit in December. The heart of the New Town is where four famous café-terraces meet on avenue Mohammed V, including the Atlas, the Café les Négociants, the Glacier Adra, and the Renaissance. Because of its wide boulevards and flat lands, Guéliz can be explored by bicycle. It's about a 15-minute ride from the Jemaa el Fna (which is spelled Djemaa el Fna just as frequently).

STREET MAPS

A really good map of Marrakesh has yet to be published. Before setting out—assuming you are walking—it is always best to ask at your hotel to have the direction traced for you on your inadequate map.

You can get a free map at the tourist office (see above), but it pinpoints only the major arteries. The best map published to date is issued by **Berlitz**. It has a fairly good plan of the New Town, with an index that will help you find the location of various streets. But even Berlitz gives up when it comes to the Medina, outlining in boldface letters only the major districts and a few of the major arteries. The map is sold at virtually every newsstand and at nearly all hotel news and magazine shops.

GETTING AROUND

The options are by bus, by bicycle (often quite practical), by *petit taxi*, and on foot. There are no discount passes on public transportation: everybody pays the same fare.

BY BUS

Local buses serve the city, but often you'll find a petit taxi preferable for not much more money (see below). From the Jemaa el Fna, you can catch bus no. 1, which will take you along avenue Mohammed V, the main street of Guéliz, the New Town. Bus no. 3 travels avenue Mohammed V and avenue Hassan II to the train station, and bus no. 4 takes you along avenue Mohammed V to El Jadida road. Bus no. 5 goes to the Beni Mellal road and is useful for reaching Souk el Khemis. Bus no. 7 travels avenue Hassan II, and no. 8 goes along both avenue Mohammed V and avenue Hassan II. Bus no. 10 goes to the gate of Bab Doukkala and the Safi highway. Most fares are 1.20 DH (18¢).

BY TAXI

The preferred method of getting around Marrakesh, and the cost, at least by most Western standards, is relatively small. Taxis aren't metered, so you'll have to bargain. One taxi driver told us in French that his fare "depends upon the charm—or lack of it, monsieur—of the passenger."

Petits taxis are small, carrying no more than three passengers (usually), and can be hailed on the streets. *Grands taxis* are much larger and more suitable for longer hauls, and even these are collective taxis where the passengers divide the fares among themselves. For example, it is customary for a group of four tourists to band together and rent a grand taxi for the day if they'd like to make an excursion into the High Atlas in the environs of Marrakesh. These taxis, along with petits taxis, are located at the Jemaa el Fna and by the gateway Bab er Rob.

If you're going out in the evening, you can have your hotel call a *taxi privé* (private taxi).

BY CAR

Cars are not a practical means for touring Marrakesh, but may be ideal for exploring the environs. For a list of some major car-rental companies, see "Fast Facts: Marrakesh," below.

Parking

Parking is free at hotels that have the space, and most of them have guards. When you go to get your car, you should, of course, tip the guardian. You can also park along streets, including any place available off the main street, avenue Mohammed V, in Guéliz. Even there, you'll also have a guard for your car, usually displaying an official badge. Parking is unmetered but, again, you should tip the guard.

There is a parking lot in the old bus depot, across from the CTM Hotel at the Jemaa el Fna. You can park your car here if you're planning to tour the Medina from this square. Never leave any possessions, especially luggage, in a car. There are also garages at **Ourika,** avenue Mohammed V, 66 (tel. 301-55), and at **Tazi,** located on rue Bab Agnaou (tel. 223-39).

BY BICYCLE

Bicycles, which might be an interesting way to tour the city's ramparts, can be rented at the **Foucauld Hotel,** Jemaa el Fna (tel. 454-99). They cost 40 DH ($5) for a half day or 65 DH ($8.15) for a full day.

ON FOOT

This is the ancient way to explore Marrakesh, and no one has improved on it yet. Guéliz (New Town), however, is too spread out for this kind of exploration. Otherwise, if you confine your touring to the main geographic heart of Marrakesh, including the souks of the Medina, you will find that your feet are not only the preferred way to see the Medina but the *only* way. Get some comfortable walking shoes before you set out.

BY HORSE AND BUGGY

In Marrakesh, these are called calèches. Once they were the way all foreign visitors, usually the French, toured Marrakesh, especially the long circuit of the ramparts, but in recent years their ranks have dwindled to less than 150. Calèches rent for about 50

DH ($6.25) per hour, although you can bargain for less, especially if business is slow. Often you'll find them waiting in front of major hotels, and you can also locate them at the edge of the Jemaa el Fna across from the Banque du Maroc. In Guéliz, they are often seen waiting at spots along avenue Mohammed V.

FAST FACTS *MARRAKESH*

American Express   The local representative is **Voyages Schwartz,** Immeuble Moutaouskil, rue Mauritania (tel. 333-21). Off avenue Mohammed V in Guéliz, it is open Monday through Friday from 8:30am to 12:30pm and 3 to 6:30pm, with banking hours from 8:30am to noon only.

Area Code   04.

Baby-Sitting   There is no local agency that specializes in baby-sitting. Arrangements can be made—as far in advance as possible—through the various hotels. Usually a staff member will shoulder this responsibility for a negotiated fee. It is often difficult to find a baby-sitter who speaks English.

Bookstores   Two good bookstores with English-language books include **Librairie Elouaa,** rue Fatima Zorah, 15 (tel. 44-52-24), and **Librairie La Maison des Livres,** rue Clemenceau, 38 (tel. 43-07-72).

Business Hours   See "Fast Facts: Morocco" in Chapter 2.

Car Rentals   Try **Avis,** av. Mohammed V, 137 (tel. 337-27); **Europcar,** rue Mansour Eddahbi, 59 (tel. 484-84); or **Hertz,** av. Mohammed V, 154 (tel. 346-80). **Budget,** av. Mohammed V, 213 (tel. 332-24), often offers some of the best deals.

Climate   The summer months, although hot, are never humid. Sometimes the sun is obscured by a violent sandstorm raging in the Sahara. In winter, the temperature averages around 68°F, but in July and August, midday temperatures of 100° are frequent.

Currency   See "Information, Entry Requirements, Customs, and Money," in Chapter 2.

Currency Exchange   For the convenience of their guests, hotels will exchange dollars, pounds, pesetas, and francs into dirhams, but they get a good commission. Sometimes travel agents will exchange money. Legally, they are supposed to convert at the official rate, although sometimes that is not the case. Know what the official rate is and ask for a receipt. Hustlers in the Medina will approach you with offers to exchange money on the black market. Such transactions are against the law in Morocco and could get you in trouble with the police. Whenever possible, exchange money at one of the major banks. Convenient central banks include **BMAO,** rue Bab Agnaou, 75 (tel. 42-56-00), and **ABM** Banque, bd. Zerktouni, 55 (tel. 44-89-12).

Dentist   For an English-speaking dentist, call **Dr. Hamid Laraqui,** av. Mohammed V, 203 (tel. 332-16).

Doctor   For an English-speaking doctor, call **Dr. Ahmed Mansouri,** whose office is on rue de Sebou (tel. 43-07-54).

Drugstores   Centrally located is **Pharmacie Guéliz,** located on avenue Moulay Rachid Marrakech (tel. 43-12-30). Another good pharmacy is **Pharmacie Atlas,** found on avenue Mohammed V (tel. 43-06-75).

Electricity   See "Fast Facts: Morocco" in Chapter 2.

Embassies/Consulates   The nearest embassies and consulates of the United States and the U.K. are in Rabat and Casablanca.

Emergencies   Dial 19 for **police;** dial 15 for **fire** or an **ambulance.**

Eyeglasses   One of the best opticians is **Wrede,** av. Mohammed V, 142 (tel. 43-16-32).

Hairdressers/Barbers   Both sexes can try **Salon Soumair,** av. Zerktouni, 34 (tel. 471-89). In addition, many of the major hotels have hairdressers on their premises.

Holidays   See "When to Go" in Chapter 2.

Hospitals   Only in the direst of emergencies should you go to such local clinics as **Avenzoar,** on avenue Sidi Mimoun (tel. 420-19), or **Ibn Tofail,** on avenue Abdelwahab Derraq (tel. 480-11). It is nearly always better to have your hotel put you in touch with a private physician.

Information   See "Tourist Information," above.

Laundry/Dry Cleaning   Both laundry and dry cleaning are arranged through your hotel. Someone at the hotel, even at the smaller ones, often washes and irons your clothes, or has them cleaned somewhere in the Medina.

Lost Property   Usually, this is a lost cause in Marrakesh, a city of extremely poor people. Call the police at 19 and report the loss, providing you can find someone at the station who speaks English. Give the name of your hotel and the date of your departure from Marrakesh. You can also leave a forwarding address. Don't spend too much time waiting for a reply.

Newspapers/Magazines   Copies of London papers and editions of the *International Herald Tribune* are sold at newsstands throughout Marrakesh and at hotel gift shops. Copies of *Newsweek* and *Time* are also sold.

Photographic Needs   An outlet for this exists at the **Hotel Mamounia,** on avenue Bab Jdid (tel. 489-81).

Police   See "Emergencies."

Post Office   The **Marrakesh Post Office** is at place XVI Novembre, off avenue Mohammed V (don't attempt to call—show up in person). Expect a long line at all the windows. In the dire case where you need to send your mail to Marrakesh general delivery, mark it "Poste Restante." But lines waiting for mail are S-L-O-W. Saturday is the worst day. Hours are 8am to 9pm Monday through Saturday. Both local and international telephone calls can be made from here.

Radio/TV   There are no broadcasts in English. Both radio and TV broadcasts are either in Arabic or French.

Religious Services   If you are a Muslim, you will have no problem, as places of worship are found virtually everywhere. Non-Muslims, however, are forbidden to enter mosques. Catholic services are conducted at **Eglise des Saints-Martyrs,** located on rue El Imam Ali (tel. 43-05-85); Protestant services at the **Protestant Church,** located at bd. Moulay Rachid, 89 (tel. 43-14-79); and Jewish worship at **Synagogue Bet-el-Guéliz,** located at Arset El Maash (tel. 44-78-32).

Rest Rooms   Hotels, cafés, terminals, restaurants, and bars all have toilets, some of them not well maintained. Public toilets, if available, are of the squat variety and recommended only in an emergency. It's best to go to a café and order mineral water and use cleaner facilities.

Safety   As guides, use only official tourist office personnel or someone recommended by the tourist office, not someone who solicits you on the street. Likewise, it is not advisable to exchange money outside a bank or hotel—and always get a receipt. Don't wander at night on the streets. After dark, it's best to use a taxi to get where you're going. It's cheap and will get you there safely.

Shoe Repair   Itinerant cobblers come into the Jemaa el Fna every day, setting up little stands on the square. It's a novel way to get your shoes repaired while you wait, or else a shine.

Taxes   Marrakesh imposes a hotel room tax of 5% to 7%, plus the 17% to 19% government tax added to hotel and restaurant bills. The exact percentage is based on the government rating of the establishment.

Taxis   See "Getting Around," above.

Telegrams/Telex/Fax   A telex can be sent from most hotels. Fax machines are available only at the bigger hotels, which will usually let you send a fax for cost plus a small surcharge.

Transit Information   For **airline** information, call 303-38, and for **rail** information, call 311-07. However, the person on the other end may not always speak English. For **bus** connections, show up in person at one of the windows that sell tickets outside the Medina walls at Bab Doukkala. There is no central booking office.

Weather   See "Climate," above.

Yellow Pages   Chances are, if you do find a phone book (highly unlikely), you won't be able to read Arabic or even know the French names for various services. Ask at the hotel reception desk or, if the hotel is big enough, get the address and phone number of a particular establishment from the concierge.

2. ACCOMMODATIONS

The best and most sumptuous hotels in all of Morocco are found in Marrakesh, including the deluxe charmer of them all, the Hotel Mamounia. The prices are often what second-class hotels charge in Western European capitals.

Many are, frankly, tour-oriented, which is a great drawback to the individual traveler. Packaged tourism has also led to a wholesale decline in the quality of service for which Marrakesh was once known.

Many of the major hotels have sports facilities, at least large swimming pools. In summer, try to find a hotel that offers air conditioning. The air conditioning may not always work at the cooling temperature to which you are accustomed, but it is better than no air conditioning at all.

Hotels ranked "Very Expensive"—and there is only one in this category, the world-famous Mamounia—charge from 1,800 to 3,200 DH ($225 to $400) for a double. "Expensive" hotels offer doubles in the average range of 800 to 900 DH ($100 to $112.50), and those considered "Moderate" charge 500 to 640 DH ($62.50 to $80). "Inexpensive" hotels cost about 320 to 400 DH ($40 to $50) for a double, and anything under 200 DH ($25) is definitely "Budget."

Most of the hotels do not have building numbers.

VERY EXPENSIVE

HOTEL MAMOUNIA, av. Bab Jdid, Marrakesh. Tel. 04/489-81. Fax 04/449-40. 179 rms (all with bath), 49 suites. A/C MINIBAR TV TEL **Transportation:** Petit or grand taxi.

$ **Rates:** 1,500–2,800 DH ($187.50–$350) single; 1,800–3,200 DH ($225–$400) double; suites from 4,000 DH ($500). Rates significantly higher during Christmas week and Easter. Continental breakfast 110 DH ($13.75) extra. AE, DC, MC, V.

Sprawled near the Koutoubia Minaret a short walk east of the Jemaa el Fna, it is the most famous hotel in Africa. Its roster of famous former residents includes Winston Churchill and the Shah of Iran.

In late 1986, King Hassan's then-favorite decorator, French-born André Paccard, was commissioned to remodel and enhance the interior decor. Emphasizing the art deco origins of a landmark hotel originally built in 1923, he retained most of the original public rooms but enhanced some of the restaurants, bars, and bedrooms with a swirl of fabrics and art deco accessories, and added a casino with slot machines. Those public rooms are a theatrical fantasy of intricate geometric carvings, tilework, Moorish arcades, and cedar beams. The hotel's 34 acres of gardens are enclosed with a carefully guarded 12th-century wall.

Dining/Entertainment: Choices include the Imperial French restaurant (open only in winter); the Restaurant Marocain du Mamounia, a Moroccan dining spot set around a fountain within a forest of Andalusian columns (see below); the Three Palms Garden Restaurant, named after the trio of palms growing from an island in the swimming pool; La Calèche, a French brasserie; and for Italian food, the Mamounia Club Restaurant. Le Grand Casino de La Mamounia, the only casino in Marrakesh, and the Piano Bar are recommended separately (see "Evening Entertainment").

Services: Massage, 24-hour room service, a salon of "haute coiffure," concierge.

MOROCCO

Rabat

Almoravides, Hotel-Club Les **8**
Atlas Asni **19**
Chems **9**
El Andalous **16**
Es Saadi **14**
Grand Imilchil **7**
Imperial Borj **13**
Koudou, Le **12**
Koutoubia **4**
Mamounia **10**
Marrakesh, Le **5**
Menara, Hotel de la **6**
Méridien Marrakesh, Le **1**
Palais el Badia **18**
PLM N'Fis **17**
Pullman Mansour Eddahbi **20**
Safir Siaha **15**
Tafilalet **2**
Tichka **3**
Toubkal **11**

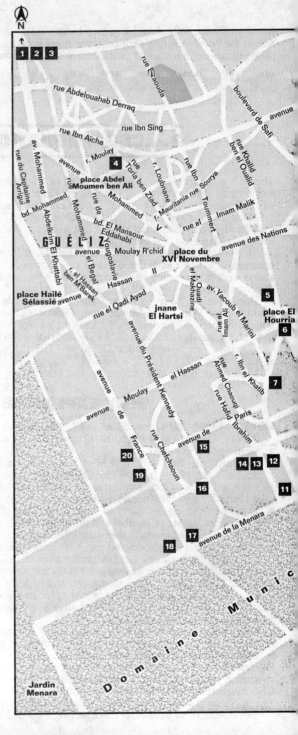

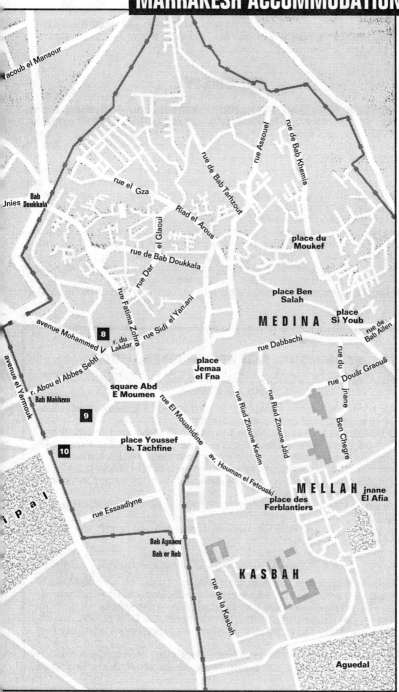

acoub el Mansour

rue Assouel

rue de Bab Khemis

rue el Gza

rue de Bab Tarhzout

Bab
Jnies Doukkala

Riad el Arous

place du
Moukef

rue d'el Glaoui

rue de Bab Doukkala

rue Dar

place Ben
Salah

place
Si Youb

rue Fatima Zohra

rue Sidi el Yamani

MEDINA

rue de
Bab Aïlen

avenue Mohammed V

8

r. du
Lakdar

rue Dabbachi

rue du
Jnane

rue Douâr Graouâ

avenue el Yarmouk

r. Abou el Abbes Sebti

place
Jemaa
el Fna

Bab Makhzen

**square Abd
E Moumen**

rue El Mouahidine

9

Ben Chegra

rue Riad Zitoune Kedim

rue Riad Zitoune Jdid

10

place Youssef
b. Tachfine

av. Houman el Fetouaki

MELLAH

jnane
El Afia

ipal

rue Essaadiyne

place des
Ferblantiers

Bab Agnaou

Bab er Rob

KASBAH

rue de la Kasbah

Ramparts

Aguedal

Facilities: Squash court, two tennis courts, beautiful garden ornamented with Andalusian fountains, outdoor swimming pool, health club with weights and exercise machines, *visagiste* specializing in skin care and scalp treatments, sauna, *hammam* (bath), *parfumerie* boutique, gift boutique.

EXPENSIVE

HOTEL CLUB PULLMAN MANSOUR EDDAHBI, av. de France, Marrakesh. Tel. 04/482-22. Fax 04/481-68. 403 rms (all with bath), 38 suites. A/C TV TEL **Transportation:** Petit taxi.

$ Rates: 950 DH ($118.75) single or double occupancy; suites from 1,800 DH ($225). Breakfast 70 DH ($8.75) extra. AE, DC, MC, V.

At the junction of two broad avenues in Guéliz, this is the largest hotel in Morocco. Built in 1989, it contains the most comprehensive conference facilities in Africa, as well as auditoriums, gardens, and rococo-edged swimming pools and fountains. Scattered over more than 16 acres of land, its accommodations are contained within six kasbah-inspired buildings, two of which are devoted solely to suites. Its lobby is an echoing stone forest of marble columns that support vaulted ceilings and illuminated domes, some visitors comparing it with the vast stone mosques of 11th-century Andalusia. Bedrooms are plushly comfortable, with balconies, eight-channel TVs, radios, and built-in furniture. All are painted differently—blue, brown, red, or beige—according to the building that contains them.

Dining/Entertainment: Seven different restaurants, scattered throughout the

---

 FROMMER'S SMART TRAVELER: HOTELS

VALUE-CONSCIOUS TRAVELERS SHOULD TAKE ADVANTAGE OF THE FOLLOWING:

1. Off-season reductions. Although they don't advertise it, many hotels reduce rates during the hot summer months—from April to October—often at least 20%. But you have to ask. Winter brings the high season and the high prices.
2. The price you pay in cheaper hotels depends on the plumbing. Rooms with showers are cheaper than rooms with private tub baths. Even cheaper is a room with hot and cold running water (with use of the corridor bath).
3. Parents should ask if their children can stay free in the same room or at a greatly reduced rate.
4. At the cheaper hotels that take credit cards, ask if payment in cash will get you a reduction.
5. If you're going to spend a week in Marrakesh, ask about any special "long-term" discounts.

QUESTIONS TO ASK IF YOU'RE ON A BUDGET

1. Is there a surcharge either for local or long-distance phone calls? Usually there is. In some cases, it is an astonishing 40%. Better to know beforehand, so you can make your calls from the post office if phone rates are too high.
2. Are service charge (10% to 15%), the government tax (17% to 19%), and the room tax (5% to 7%) included? It could mean a big difference when your final bill is tallied.
3. Is breakfast included in the rate? Sometimes it isn't and you pay extra for a Continental breakfast. You always pay extra for an American or English breakfast.

compound, including Moroccan, kosher, international, Italian, and dietetic cuisine; three bars; and Disco Paradise (see "Evening Entertainment").

Services: Massage, concierge, secretarial and translation services.

Facilities: Three swimming pools (including a semiprivate, partially enclosed pool), wading pool for children, daytime "disco" for children aged 12 to 17, health spa with *hammam* (bath), sauna.

HOTEL IMPERIAL BORJ, av. Echchouada, quartier Hivernage, Marrakesh. Tel. 04/473-22. Fax 04/462-06. 120 rms (all with bath), 20 suites. A/C MINIBAR TV TEL **Transportation:** Petit taxi.

$ Rates: 750 DH ($93.75) single; 950 DH ($118.75) double; suites from 1,800 DH ($225). Breakfast 50 DH ($6.25) extra. AE, DC, MC, V.

One of the most appealing new hotels in Marrakesh. Its majestic walls are colored both inside and out in the same reddish tones as the ramparts of Marrakesh. Designed like a balconied version of a Saharan kasbah, it has a lobby sheathed almost completely in red, blue, and white marble—coming, respectively, from Turkey, Brazil, and Morocco—with sunlight streaming down a balconied atrium. The luxurious bedrooms have balconies, a combination of Moroccan and European decor, and lacquered maple and elmwood furniture.

Dining/Entertainment: Four restaurants, a poolside cafeteria/snack bar, and the refreshingly formal Bar Acajou, which has a charming staff (see "Evening Entertainment").

Services: Room service, concierge.

Facilities: A large swimming pool with jutting palm trees and an encircling rose garden.

HOTEL LE KOUDOU, rue Echchouada, Marrakesh. Tel. 04/43-50-07. 42 rms (all with bath), 6 suites. A/C MINIBAR TV TEL **Transportation:** Petit taxi.

$ Rates: 700 DH ($87.50) single; 800 DH ($100) double; suites from 1,800 DH ($225). Breakfast 50 DH ($6.25) extra. AE, DC, MC, V.

On a lavishly landscaped acre of land in the most affluent section (Hivernage) of Guéliz, this hotel is most famous for its trio of restaurants (see below). Considered one of the small, innovative, and stylish new hotels in town, it's managed by a former director of the Hotel Mamounia, Jacques Vandeghen. El Koudou is currently rated "four-star A" by the Moroccan government, a rating that will probably be upgraded to five stars after completion of additional renovations. Bedrooms are very comfortable, decorated in the Moroccan style with lots of fabric and comfortable upholsteries. Each of the suites has a private balcony.

Dining/Entertainment: Three of the most desirable restaurants in Marrakesh are located here (see below), plus a paneled and leather-upholstered bar inspired by the private clubs of London.

Services: 24-hour room service, translation service, and concierge.

Facilities: A swimming pool, an array of boutiques, a chocolate shop selling European confections made on the premises.

LE MERIDIEN MARRAKECH, route de Casablanca, Marrakesh. Tel. 04/43-13-77 (or toll free in North America, 800/543-43-00). Fax 04/44-71-27. 174 rms (all with bath), 6 suites. A/C TV TEL **Transportation:** Petit taxi.

$ Rates: 550–720 DH ($68.75–$90) single; 600–920 DH ($75–$115) double. Breakfast 60 DH ($7.50) extra. AE, DC, MC, V.

In the same complex as the Tichka and the Tropicana hotels, this French-owned place is very popular with Gallic tour groups. Formerly the Semiramis Hotel, it has an interior of reddish-colored marble, a shady garden, and comfortable bedrooms with modern accessories.

Dining/Entertainment: A comfortable modern piano bar, the Oasis bar beside the pool, and four different restaurants, the most amusing of which is an Italian emporium called La Strada.

Services: Massage, hairdresser, room service, concierge.

Facilities: A swimming pool designed "in the Hollywood style," sometimes with surrounding buffet.

MODERATE

ATLAS ASNI, av. de France, Marrakesh. Tel. 04/470-51. Fax 04/333-08. 317 rms (all with bath). A/C TEL **Transportation:** Petit taxi.

$ Rates: 480 DH ($60) single; 580 DH ($72.50) double. Breakfast 40 DH ($5) extra. AE, DC, MC, V.

This four-star property, opened in 1986 by Royal Air Maroc, is one of the most stylish hotels in town. Located on a wide and sunny boulevard, it has a highly desirable swimming pool (with poolside food service) and a landscaped garden. The public rooms glisten with white stone and hand-glazed tiles and are serviced by a cooperative staff. Each well-furnished bedroom has a balcony and plushly comfortable summer furniture; some bedrooms contain TVs. The hotel boasts four outdoor tennis courts, of which two are lit for night play, as well as two good restaurants and a nightclub, L'Alcazar. On the premises you'll find both a bank and a ticket office for Royal Air Maroc.

HOTEL PALAIS EL BADIA, av. de la Menara, Marrakesh. Tel. 04/489-77. Fax 04/489-74. 280 rms (all with bath), 15 suites. A/C TEL **Transportation:** Petit taxi.

$ Rates: 400 DH ($50) single; 496 DH ($62) double; 620 DH ($77.50) triple; suites from 1,200 DH ($150). Breakfast 40 DH ($5) extra. AE, DC, MC, V.

Originally built as a Holiday Inn, and later purchased by a Moroccan hotel group, this modern facility is set in what used to be an open field at the edge of town. You'll enter a lobby with an elaborately carved wooden ceiling and dozens of red-wool carpets. Modern, comfortably furnished rooms sprawl around a U-shaped courtyard with a shady lawn and a swimming pool; some rooms have minibars and TVs. Sports facilities include tennis courts and access to golf and horseback riding. There are three Moroccan restaurants, an international dining room, and a bar with folkloric singing and dancing. Fixed-priced meals run 120 DH ($15).

PLM N'FIS HOTEL, av. de France, Marrakesh. Tel. 04/487-72. 282 rms (all with bath). A/C TEL **Transportation:** Petit taxi.

$ Rates: 629 DH ($78.65) single; 638 DH ($79.40) double. Breakfast 31 DH ($3.90) extra. AE, DC, MC, V.

The hard-to-pronounce name is derived from a nearby and historic Moroccan river. The focus of the lobby is a star-shaped fountain encased in emerald-green tiles. A skylight illuminates Moroccan carpets, brass tables, and the otherwise modern design. In back, you'll find a landscaped swimming pool ringed with multilevel terraces, bars, and intricate tilework. Many planned activities are available. After dark, life centers around the Byblos disco. The hotel's very French clientele appreciates the pair of restaurants, the bar, and the bedrooms contained in a trio of outlying buildings, each with a private balcony.

HOTEL TICHKA, Semlalia, Marrakesh. Tel. 04/487-10. Fax 04/486-90. 129 rms (all with bath), 8 suites. A/C TV TEL **Transportation:** Petit taxi.

$ Rates: 545 DH ($68.15) single; 600 DH ($75) double; suites from 1,300 DH ($162.50). Breakfast 45 DH ($5.65) extra. AE, DC, MC, V.

After it was built in 1986, the Tichka's California-born designer, Bill Willis, was praised for one of the most imaginative commercial interpretations of Moorish architecture in the world. Its features include a majestically proportioned octagonal lobby that soars into a series of arcades, and lavish use of an ancient Berber form of stucco (*tadlak*) that combines lime with sand, soap, egg yolks, pigments, and endless hours of polishing to create a richly colored form of artificial marble. About 30 of the attractively furnished Moroccan-style bedrooms have private balconies, and 40 of them overlook a swimming pool. The Johara restaurant serves only dinner, every night from 7:30pm to midnight, for a fixed price of 185 DH ($23.15).

FROMMER'S COOL FOR KIDS

HOTELS

Hotel Club Les Almoravides *(see p. 213)* The best bet in all of Marrakesh. Its "Mini Eldo" welcomes children 4 and up with an entertainment program. In the dining room, a guest table shared with other children awaits your kids, who are given a special menu. Baby-sitting can be arranged at night.

Hotel Palais El Badia *(see p. 212)* Set on 7 acres of beautifully landscaped gardens with palm and orange trees, this is a safe "oasis" for children. Rooms are large and comfortable, and extra beds can easily be added.

INEXPENSIVE

CHEMS, av. Homane el Fetouaki, Marrakesh. Tel. 04/348-13. 150 rms (all with bath). A/C MINIBAR TEL **Transportation:** Petit taxi.

$ Rates: 264 DH ($33) single; 330 DH ($41.25) double. Breakfast 31 DH ($3.90) extra. AE, DC, MC, V.

In a Europeanized section of town amid an orange grove, an easy walk from the Medina and the Jemaa el Fna, Chems is near the deluxe Hotel Mamounia. From the pool in the hotel garden you can see the tower of the Koutoubia. Bedrooms are clean and well maintained, furnished along simple modern lines and quite comfortable; most of them open onto private balconies. Guests can enjoy a cocktail lounge and disco, a restaurant serving international cuisine, and a poolside grill and snack bar. Facilities include outdoor tennis courts and a guarded parking lot.

HOTEL CLUB LES ALMORAVIDES, Arset D'Jnan Lakhdar, Marrakesh. Tel. 04/451-42. Fax 04/431-33. 103 rms (all with bath). A/C TEL **Transportation:** Petit taxi.

$ Rates: 264 DH ($33) single; 324 DH ($40.50) double. Breakfast 50 DH ($6.25) extra. AE, MC, V.

This four-star hotel has its own garden and a king-size swimming pool, with poolside umbrella tables where you can order refreshments or meals. More than half of the modern, streamlined bedrooms overlook the garden, and also have a view of the minarets (you'll hear the wailing prayer calls five times daily). Sliding glass doors open onto private balconies. The general atmosphere is plush, and the hotel has a comfortable bar with a stage where entertainment is presented in winter, plus an agreeable Moroccan restaurant that serves a fixed-price lunch or dinner for 120 DH ($15). Some sports activities are also available, especially on the tennis courts.

EL ANDALOUS, av. du Président Kennedy, Marrakesh. Tel. 04/482-26. Fax 04/47-195. 200 rms (all with bath). A/C TEL **Transportation:** Petit taxi.

$ Rates: 320 DH ($40) single; 394 DH ($49.25) double. Breakfast 31 DH ($3.90) extra. AE, DC, MC, V.

The decor of this pleasant establishment celebrates the era when all of southern Spain was a Moorish dominion. It's set at the edge of a wide boulevard within walking distance of the medieval ramparts. The sun-flooded lobby has a filigreed plasterwork ceiling, a floor covered in glistening white marble, and walls softened with leather, tilework, and carefully oiled paneling. Comfortable bedrooms contain their own loggias and radios. There's a large swimming pool surrounded with latticed arbors entwined with flowering vines, plus a solarium, tennis courts, and a fitness center. Fixed-price meals in one of the three restaurants cost between 110 DH ($13.75) and 130 DH ($16.25).

HOTEL GRAND IMILCHIL, av. Echchouada, Marrakesh. Tel. 04/476-33.
97 rms (all with bath). A/C TEL **Transportation:** Petit taxi.
$ Rates (including breakfast): 198 DH ($24.75) single; 244 DH ($30.50) double; 310 DH ($39.50) triple. No credit cards

This modern hotel is in Hivernage, a district midway between the European community of Guéliz and the Medina. Rooms are simply furnished and have balconies, and the hotel restaurant serves fixed-price meals for 95 DH ($11.90). There's a swimming pool.

HOTEL LE MARRAKECH, place de la Liberté, Marrakesh. Tel. 04/343-51. 350 rms (all with bath), 15 suites. A/C TV TEL **Transportation:** Petit taxi.
$ Rates: 263 DH ($32.90) single; 330 DH ($41.25) double; suites from 650–1,200 DH ($81.25–$150). Breakfast 31 DH ($3.90) extra. AE, DC, MC, V.
The design of this modern hotel was heavily influenced by traditional Moroccan themes. Its busy interior contains a pair of covered oval atriums, exposed paneling, and dozens of carpets. The many French and German tour groups welcomed here transform the poolside terrace into one of the busiest social centers in town. Bedrooms are furnished in a streamlined functional style, relieved by occasional Moroccan artifacts. Services include dozens of organized activities.

HOTEL TAFILALET, av. de Casablanca, Marrakesh. Tel. 04/345-18. 90 rms (all with bath). A/C TEL **Transportation:** Petit taxi.
$ Rates: 300 DH ($37.50) single; 334 DH ($41.75) double. Breakfast 31 DH ($3.90) extra. No credit cards.
One of the best small hotels in town, this family-owned place sits behind a barricade of semitropical plants along an outlying road filled with bigger, and sometimes less desirable, hotels. The spacious lobby has honey-colored slabs of marble; courtyards enhance a sense of airy comfort. The gardens surrounding the swimming pool are laid out in brilliant banks of roses, pansies, petunias, geraniums, and phlox that line palm-fringed walkways. The rooms are clustered into a handful of Navajo-style buildings with log detailing and thick walls—a study in artful rusticity. Each room has its own spacious tile bath, a balcony or terrace, and a radio. A la carte meals cost 130 DH ($16.25) in Le Rissania Restaurant, with dinner accompanied by folkloric song and dance. There's also a piano bar.

HOTEL TOUBKAL, rue Haroun Er Rachid, Marrakesh. Tel. 04/488-72.
120 rms (all with bath). A/C TEL **Transportation:** Petit taxi.
$ Rates: 264 DH ($33) single; 332 DH ($41.50) double. Breakfast 40 DH ($5) extra. AE, DC, MC, V.

Part of the PLM chain, the Toubkal stands in a quiet residential neighborhood filled with manicured gardens and flower-dotted lawns. The salmon-colored stucco exterior sports evergreens and rubber trees that almost conceal it from view. Inside, low-slung couches provide comfortable seating in a high-ceilinged bar overlooking the garden, the pool, the tennis courts, and the dozens of sunbathers. The breezy, comfortable accommodations are in five-story wings flanking two edges of the garden. A restaurant serves Moroccan and international dishes, and there's a disco with live music.

3. DINING

After dark, the adventurous will head for the Jemaa el Fna for dinner. If you're interested in local food, you'll find it here . . . and how! You'll discover open-air stands where each chef is noted for a different specialty. At one, tiny fish will be deep-frying; at another, a young boy will be cooking chunks of lamb on a charcoal brazier; then there are the large bowls of food, both salads and spicy dishes. You sit at benches and place your order with the main cook. Everything is accompanied by round loaves of barley bread. Frankly, many people are horrified at the unsanitary conditions here; but the Jemaa el Fna remains a dining tradition for many travelers. At least go for a look, but sample the fare at one of the restaurants recommended below, some of which are considered among the finest in North Africa.

In Marrakesh, restaurants considered "Very Expensive" charge 350 to 600 DH ($43.75 to $75) for a dinner; restaurants ranked "Expensive," generally 200 to 380 DH ($25 to $41.50); those considered "moderate," 70 to 150 DH ($8.75 to $18.75). Any dinner under 80 DH ($10) is considered "Inexpensive." Wines are extra.

IN GUÉLIZ (VILLE NOUVELLE)

EXPENSIVE

AL FASSIA, av. Mohammed V, 232. Tel. 340-60.

Cuisine: MOROCCAN. **Reservations:** Recommended. **Transportation:** Petit taxi; bus no. 1.

$ **Prices:** Appetizers 39–95 DH ($4.85–$11.85); main dishes 75–125 DH ($9.35–$15.60). AE, DC, MC, V.

Open: Lunch Tues–Sun noon–2:30pm; dinner Tues–Sun 7:30–11pm.

One of the best New Town choices for refined Moroccan cuisine, it occupies the ground floor of an apartment building in the suburb of Guéliz. You can dine beneath the bougainvillea of the walled forecourt or inside the cool, white dining room. The couscous is superb, even for people who say they don't like the dish. You'll find one of the best desserts of the Moroccan kitchen, *pastilla au lait*, served with flair here. Almost unrealistically large when presented, it is reduced to a very thin crepe, which is covered with sesame seeds and almonds. Recooked in hot milk right at your table, it's then folded into a light pastry. Copious amounts of mint tea follow your dinner.

LE JACARANDA, bd. Mohammed Zerktouni, 32. Tel. 472-15.

Cuisine: FRENCH. **Reservations:** Recommended. **Transportation:** Petit taxi; bus no. 1 or 20.

$ **Prices:** Appetizers 30–135 DH ($3.75–$16.85); main dishes 70–130 DH ($8.75–$16.25). AE, DC, MC, V.

Open: Lunch Thurs–Mon noon–3pm; dinner Wed–Mon 8–11pm.

Near the junction of several of Guéliz's broadest boulevards (place Abdel Moumen), and named after the violet-flowered jacaranda trees that bloom along the avenue outside, this has been viewed as one of the city's most charming and consistently good restaurants since it was originally established in the day of the French Protectorate. Managed today by Lille-born Alain Demars, it has the kind of tall fireplace you might find in a country *auberge* in Normandy, plus a small bar and an upstairs balcony for additional seating. Although the menu contains a token scattering of Moroccan fare, the emphasis is on imaginative French dishes. From the fresh fish that arrives twice weekly from Casablanca, you might choose the escalope of John Dory served with strips of smoked Atlantic salmon and an almond sauce. Other flavorful main dishes include tournedos with *cèpe* mushrooms, fricassee of chicken, and shrimp with curry sauce. A dessert specialty is almond crêpes.

RESTAURANTS LE KOUDOU, rue Echchouada (without number). Tel. 350-07.

Cuisine: FRENCH/MOROCCAN. **Reservations:** Recommended. **Transportation:** Grand or petit taxi.

$ **Prices:** Lunch appetizers 18–60 DH ($2.25–$7.50), lunch main dishes 60–80 DH ($9.50–$10); dinner appetizers 80–170 DH ($10–$21.25), dinner main dishes 80–300 DH ($10–$37.50); fixed-price menus 260–350 DH ($32.50–$43.75). AE, DC, MC, V.

Open: Lunch Tues–Sat in Le Jardin noon–3pm; dinner Tues–Sat in La Cascade and El Nejma, 8–11pm.

 Located in the Hivernage district of Guéliz, this newest, most interesting, and most exciting restaurant complex in Marrakesh lies behind a sprawling formal garden containing ornamental ponds with shimmering goldfish, a menagerie of

MOROCCO

Rabat

Al Fassia **5**
Bagatelle **8**
Brasserie des Négociants **3**
Café de France **20**
Calèche, La **13**
Chez Jack'Line **2**
Dar Fez **23**
El Bahia **17**
Eucalyptus **11**
Foucauld, de **15**
Haj Iddir **22**
Hotel Mamounia **13**
Iceberg **16**
Jacaranda, Le **4**
Koudou, Le **12**
Palais Gharnatta **18**
Petit Poucet **1**
Relais al Baraka **21**
Restaurant Marocain
   du Mamounia **13**
Rôtisserie du Café
   de la Paix **9**
Stylia **14**
Taverne, La **6**
Trattoria de Gian Carlo, La **7**
Villa Rosa **10**
Yacout **19**

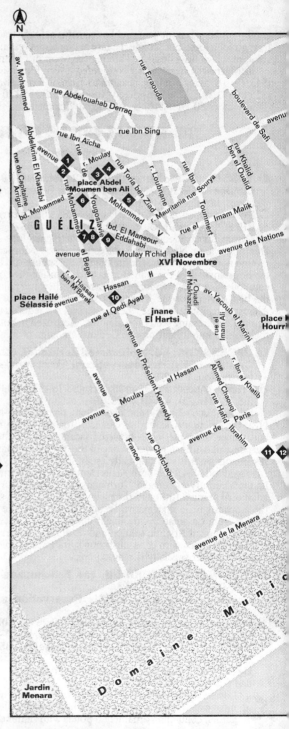

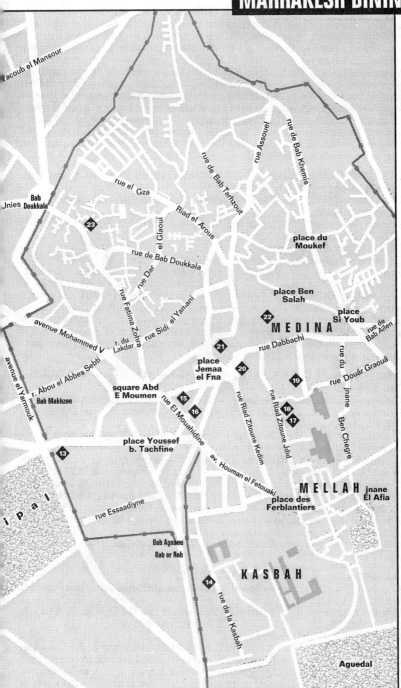

acoub el Mansour

rue Assouel

rue de Bab Khemis

rue de Bab Tarhzout

rue el Gza

Bab
Jnies Doukkala

Riad el Arous

23

rue el Glaoui

place du
Moukef

rue de Bab Doukkala

rue Dar

rue Fatima Zohra

place Ben
Salah

place
Si Youb

avenue Mohammed V

r. du
Lakdar

rue Sidi el Yamani

22 **MEDINA**

rue de
Bab Allen

rue Dabbachi

rue du Douâr Graouâ

21

place
Jemaa
el Fna

20

rue du jnane Ben Chegre

avenue el Yarmouk

r. Abou el Abbes Sebti

Bab Makhzen

square Abd
E Moumen

rue El Mouahidine

15

16

rue Riad Zitoune Kedim

rue Riad Zitoune Jdid

19

18

17

place Youssef
b. Tachfine

13

av. Houman el Fetouaki

MELLAH jnane
El Afia

ipal

rue Essaadiyne

place des
Ferblantiers

Bab Agnaou

Bab er Rob

KASBAH

14

rue de la Kasbah

Aguedal

pink flamingos, and bridges arching over ornamental waterfalls. With its emerald-glazed roof, double cupolas, and ornamental stone porches, it could easily pass as a private royal residence. The three restaurants are carefully tailored for different ambiences and menus. La Cascade is a French dinner restaurant; Le Jardin, a slightly less formal lunchtime restaurant; and El Nemja, an elegant Moroccan restaurant.

Menu specialties at La Cascade and Le Jardin are prepared by an expert in nouvelle cuisine imported from Paris, and include a succulent variation of a traditional Provençale *bourride,* a filet of sole prepared with three different herbs, *magret* of duckling with wild-honey sauce, and filet of red snapper with a sesame-flavored cream sauce. Upstairs at El Nemja (The Star), where floral carvings and painted arabesques mingle with the succulent odors of Maghrebi cuisine, dishes include chicken pickled with a confit of lemons and olives, two different versions of couscous, an array of *tajines,* and a selection of fine salads.

RESTAURANT MAROCAIN DU MAMOUNIA, Hotel Mamounia, av. Bab Jdid (without number). Tel. 489-81.

Cuisine: MOROCCAN. **Reservations:** Recommended. **Transportation:** Grand or petit taxi.

$ Prices: Appetizers 65–130 DH ($8.15–$16.25); main dishes 120–200 DH ($15–$25). AE, DC, MC, V.

Open: Dinner daily 8–11pm.

★ Climb the theatrically ornamental marble staircase and enter one of the most richly decorated rooms anywhere, amid a forest of marble columns centered around a massive chandelier of Venetian glass. Traditional specialties are listed on the menu in both French and a rarely used Moroccan dialect. They include *chorba* or *harira* soup, couscous, a suger-dusted pastilla with pigeon meat, brochettes of lamb, and an array of meat and fish tajines. One of the dishes that appear only rarely on menus throughout the country is this restaurant's version of *kedra touimiya* (pigeon stuffed with almonds and onions). A tastefully restrained Moroccan spectacle begins every night around 9:15pm.

LA TRATTORIA DE GIAN CARLO, rue Mohammed El Begal, 179, Guéliz. Tel. 326-41.

Cuisine: ITALIAN. **Reservations:** Recommended. **Transportation:** Petit taxi.

$ Prices: Appetizers 39–95 DH ($4.35–$11.85); main dishes 75–130 DH ($9.40–$16.25). AE, DC, MC, V.

Open: Lunch Tues–Sun 10am–3pm; dinner Tues–Sun 8:30pm–midnight.

Closed: One week in Jan; lunch in Aug.

★ This trattoria was established by a likable and enterprising Italian whom everyone in Marrakesh calls simply Gian Carlo. Housed in a 1927 art deco villa, it boasts a plush decor that includes elaborate plaster ceilings, ornamental brasswork, pasha-style upholstery, working fireplaces, and period chandeliers. The restaurant stands behind a lovely courtyard filled with palms and flowers. Selections include pastas such as spaghetti with clams and tagliatelle with salmon, while the many veal dishes include saltimbocca, osso buco, and veal marsala. The dessert extravaganza is a temptingly caloric zabaglione. There's a good selection of wines, and service is impeccable.

VILLA ROSA, av. Hassan II, 64. Tel. 308-32.

Cuisine: ITALIAN. **Reservations:** Recommended. **Transportation:** Petit taxi; bus no. 3.

$ Prices: Appetizers 40–120 DH ($5–$15); pastas 50–110 DH ($6.25–$13.75); main dishes 95–110 DH ($11.85–$13.75). AE, DC, MC, V.

Open: Dinner daily 7–midnight.

This intimate Italian restaurant is shielded from a busy boulevard in the European section of Guéliz by a high wall. You can dine on a sheltered outdoor terrace beneath orange trees or in a candlelit dining room; pink napery and a tiny apéritif bar in one corner add to the allure. Fish and pasta are the house specialties. The ten kinds of pasta include carbonara, *matriciano,* double-cream tagliatelle, and tagliatelle with mushrooms. You'll also find three kinds of soup, spicy shrimp, four kinds of veal, seasonal asparagus, filet Stroganoff, three kinds of sole, monkfish with pink peppercorns, and poached filet of John Dory.

MODERATE

RESTAURANT BAGATELLE, rue Yougoslavie, 101. Tel. 302-74.

Cuisine: FRENCH. **Reservations:** Recommended. **Transportation:** Petit taxi.

$ **Prices:** Appetizers 18–40 DH ($2.25–$5); main dishes 35–60 DH ($4.40–$7.50). AE, MC, V.

Open: Lunch Thurs–Tues noon–2:30pm; dinner Thurs–Tues 7:30–10:30pm in winter, and 8–11pm in summer. **Closed:** Sept.

Located in Guéliz, two blocks west of place du 16 Novembre, behind a pink bistro-style façade, this is an excellent bet for unpretentious French meals served with Gallic flair. There is an airy dining room with a high ceiling, plus additional tables set up in an ivy-draped enclosed courtyard. The house canapé served with your apéritif is a deliciously cheesy concoction made with freshly cured cheese, cream, thyme, and herbs of Provence. This might be followed with one of the plats du jour, veal kidneys *marchand de vin*, escalope of veal, pepper steak in cream sauce, or an array of fresh fish.

ROTISSERIE DU CAFE DE LA PAIX, rue Yougoslavie, 68. Tel. 331-18.

Cuisine: MOROCCAN. **Reservations:** Recommended. **Transportation:** Petit taxi.

$ **Prices:** Appetizers 8–45 DH ($1–$5.65); main dishes 30–55 DH ($3.75–$6.90). AE, DC, MC, V.

Open: Lunch Mon–Sat noon–3pm; dinner Mon–Sat 7–11pm.

A virtual landmark since 1949, the place does not reveal its true beauty until you reach the circular garden courtyard, where tables are set up next to splashing fountains. There's also a trio of Moroccan-style rooms, but except in uncomfortably chilly weather, I prefer the rose garden. A dinner might include well-flavored brochettes, grilled chicken, various tajines, paella (every Saturday), and couscous (every Friday). However, the chef's specialty is charcoal-grilled meats.

FROMMER'S SMART TRAVELER: RESTAURANTS

VALUE-CONSCIOUS TRAVELERS SHOULD CONSIDER THE FOLLOWING:

1. Look for the daily special, which is often cheaper in price than the regular fare on the à la carte menu.
2. Watch the booze. Liquor and wine are very expensive in Marrakesh, and your tab will mount rapidly.
3. To keep costs low, patronize the Moroccan restaurants, as they are invariably cheaper than the international ones—especially the French places in Guéliz—which tend to be pricey.
4. Have a light lunch of sandwiches or hamburgers at one of the many cafés during the day and save your big meal for the evening.
5. Go to places that feature a set menu for one price. These are almost always more economical than ordering from an à la carte menu.
6. Make sure that tax is included in the prices quoted. It's another 19% and could make a big difference when it comes time to pay your bill.

INEXPENSIVE

PETIT POUCET, av. Mohammed V at the corner of rue Mohammed le Bequat. Tel. 482-38.
Cuisine: FRENCH. **Reservations:** Recommended. **Transportation:** Petit taxi.
$ Prices: Appetizers 10–25 DH ($1.25–$3.15); main dishes 25–40 DH ($3.15–$5); fixed-price menus 60 DH ($7.50). MC, V.
Open: Lunch daily noon–3pm; dinner daily 7:30–11pm.

⑤ Located in the heart of Guéliz, Petit Poncet was established at the turn of the century as a bistro. Today, it evokes a faded nostalgia for the working-class Gallic presence in Marrakesh. Servings include huge portions of such grandmotherly dishes as cream of vegetable soup, grilled kidneys, sautéed rabbit, sole meunière, steak tartare, and tomatoes Provençale.

IN THE MEDINA

VERY EXPENSIVE

RESTAURANT PALAIS GHARNATTA, Derb el Arsa, 56 (Riad Zitoun Djedid). Tel. 452-16.
Cuisine: MOROCCAN. **Reservations:** Recommended. **Transportation:** Petit taxi.
$ Prices: Fixed-price menus 350–600 DH ($43.75–$75). AE, DC, MC, V.
Open: Lunch daily noon–3pm; dinner daily 7:30pm–midnight.

Considered one of the most beautiful of the restaurant-palaces of the Medina, it's located several buildings north of El Bahia Palace. Patrons have included film crews from Hollywood (part of *The Return of the Pink Panther* was shot within its courtyard) and luminaries such as the Aga Khan and Jacqueline Onassis. It was originally built of stone, cedarwood, plaster, and tiles in the 1500s, and there's an alabaster fountain reputedly carved by Italians even earlier, in the 13th century. Menu choices include salads, pastilla, sausage kebabs, several different kinds of tajine, and couscous.

EXPENSIVE

EL BAHIA, Riad Zitoun Jedid, 1. Tel. 413-50.
Cuisine: MOROCCAN. **Reservations:** Recommended. **Transportation:** Petit taxi.
$ Prices: Fixed-price menus 250–300 DH ($31.25–$37.50). AE, MC, V.
Open: Lunch daily noon–3pm; dinner daily 8:30–11:30pm.

When it was originally built in the 19th century, it served as one of the courtyards for the harem connected to El Bahia Palace. Today, its central fountain is filled with flowers, and its ornate double-tiered arcade has been embellished with painted panels. The effect is very beautiful, and an appropriate setting for the nightly Moroccan entertainment beginning at 9:30pm. Dishes include pastilla with pigeon, couscous, varied brochettes, and chicken with a confit of lemons.

DAR FEZ, rue El Gza (without number) (Riad Laarous). Tel. 417-93.
Cuisine: MOROCCAN. **Reservations:** Recommended. **Transportation:** Petit taxi.
$ Prices: Fixed-price menus 250–380 DH ($31.25–$47.50). AE, DC, MC, V.
Open: Dinner daily 8pm–2am.

★ The most upscale of the many Moroccan restaurants within the Medina, with a star-studded international clientele, it lies in a century-old palace. The beautiful blue-and-white decor, the sybaritically comfortable sofas, and the theatricality of a troupe of Saharan entertainers help provide one of the most vivid memories of a visit to Marrakesh.

The cuisine of Fez (considered the best in Morocco) is enhanced by the sophisticated adaptations of the restaurant's owner, Brittany-born Michel le Goff. He will describe each night's fixed-price menus. Dishes include the best *keftas* (sausages) in the Medina, imaginative salads, succulent tajines, brochettes, and couscous—each fresh, flavorful, and beautifully presented.

RESTAURANT STYLIA, rue Ksour, 34. Tel. 435-87.
    Cuisine: MOROCCAN. **Reservations:** Recommended. **Transportation:** Petit taxi.
$ Prices: Fixed-price menu 320 DH ($40). AE, MC, V.
    Open: Dinner daily 8–11:30pm.

The thick-walled palace in the heart of the Medina was built in 1436 for one of the Saadian pashas, and it now serves as the memorable setting for some of the best Moroccan food in Marrakesh. Your taxi will deposit you in a teeming cul-de-sac about three labyrinthine blocks from the restaurant. An employee will then lead you down the narrow, dusty streets of the Medina to a brass doorway that opens onto the carpeted and perfumed interior of this most charming restaurant. The staff is eager to describe the nouvelle-cuisine twists given to traditional Moroccan dishes such as a salad of oranges with cinnamon, harira soup, fish, meat, and fowl tajines.

RESTAURANT YACOUT, Sidi Ahmed Soussi, 79. Tel. 419-03.
    Cuisine: MOROCCAN. **Reservations:** Recommended. **Transportation:** Petit taxi.
$ Prices: Fixed-price meals including wine, 400 DH ($50). AE, DC, MC, V.
    Open: Dinner, Tues–Sun 8pm–midnight. **Closed:** Aug.

East of the Jemaa el Fna, within a corner of the Medina usually ignored by foreign visitors, the Yacout offers one of the most dramatic entrances of any restaurant in Morocco, and an ambience that has already been appreciated by all manner of celebrities—royalty, jet-setters, and politicians. Your taxi will deposit you at the mouth of a network of Medina streets, where djellabah-clad employees of the restaurant will guide to its door. Don't expect a street sign announcing this 17th-century palace: only a collection of flickering candles, a litter of freshly picked rose petals, and an eerily expectant silence mark the entrance.

The owners, the Zkhiri family, deliberately avoided installing electricity for all but the most essential uses. In summer, you'll ascend a dizzying set of circular stairs to the palace's flat rooftop, where there are more candles and views of the sprawling Medina. In winter, meals are served within a series of small, majestically restored salons. All meals here have a fixed price, and include wine, cooked salads, an array of tajines, brochettes, and couscous.

INEXPENSIVE

RESTAURANT DE FOUCAULD, av. El Mouahidine (without number). Tel. 454-99.
    Cuisine: MOROCCAN. **Reservations:** Recommended. **Bus:** 1.
$ Prices: Appetizers 10–30 DH ($1.25–$3.75); main dishes 25–80 DH ($3.15–$10); fixed-price menus 65–75 DH ($8.15–$9.40). AE, DC, MC, V.
    Open: Lunch daily noon–4pm; dinner daily 6pm–1am.

This friendly and unpretentious restaurant, near the Koutoubia Minaret and the Jemaa el Fna, offers at least 14 typically Moroccan dishes at lunch and dinner, including pigeons stuffed with almonds and poulet with prunes. Naturally, you get couscous prepared either with mutton or chicken, and the tajines are prepared in a number of ways (one method is with fish). The chef will also prepare an entrecôte or a steak, perhaps tournedos, even some spaghetti or an American hamburger. A good French dish in season is the roast rabbit (*lapin*) with mustard sauce.

ICEBERG, av. El Mouahidine (without number). Tel. 429-51.
    Cuisine: MOROCCAN. **Reservations:** Not required. **Bus:** 1.
$ Prices: Appetizers 10–22 DH ($1.25–$2.75); main dishes 42–60 DH ($5.25–$7.50); fixed-price menu 50 DH ($6.25). No credit cards.

Open: Lunch daily noon–3pm; dinner daily 6–11:30pm.

For budget dining, try this curiously named cafe-restaurant near the Koutoubia Minaret. It specializes in Moroccan dishes, and considering its quality and scope, I find it the best dining value in Marrakesh. A meal might include a selection of hors d'oeuvres, an omelet, leg of lamb, potatoes, and dessert (cheese, flan, or strawberries in season). Among the specialties is lemon chicken. English is spoken by affable owner Moulay Driss Alaoui, who, if you're planning to return to his restaurant, will often suggest a special dinner for you, which he'll insist you eat Moroccan style—with your fingers.

SPECIALTY DINING
DINING WITH A VIEW

RESTAURANT LA CALECHE, Hotel Mamounia, av. Bab Jdid (without number). Tel. 489-81.
Cuisine: FRENCH. **Reservations:** Required in wintertime only. **Transportation:** Petit or grand taxi.
$ Prices: Appetizers 60–250 DH ($7.50–$31.25); main dishes 130–280 DH ($16.25–$35). AE, DC, MC, V.
Open: Lunch daily 12:30–2:34pm; dinner daily 8–11pm.

Located beneath a wide porch attached to the main reception rooms of the most famous hotel in town, the restaurant owes its main allure to the perfect weather of Marrakesh and to the ancient garden that begins a few feet from your table. Specialties here include carpaccio of duckling with basil, terrine of duckling with muscadet sauce, risotto with shrimp, *crevettes royales en brochettes,* filet of beef with pepper sauce, and a dessert specialty of crêpes Suzette flambéed at your table.

LOCAL FAVORITES

RESTAURANT RELAIS AL BARAKA, Jemaa el Fna. Tel. 44-23-41.
Cuisine: MOROCCAN. **Reservations:** Recommended. **Transportation:** Petit taxi.

FROMMER'S COOL FOR KIDS
RESTAURANTS

Restaurant Relais Al Baraka (see p. 222) Kids delight in the 19th-century building, once a private home of a grand local family, but now one of the few restaurants in town with a menu specifically for them.

Rôtisserie du Café de la Paix (see p. 219) In a garden courtyard setting, with splashing fountains, a reasonably priced place to introduce kids to some Moroccan specialties. Should they balk at the idea, the chef will quickly put a piece of chicken on the grill or else a small cut of beef.

Restaurant de Foucauld (see p. 221) Escaping from the teeming life of the Jemaa el Fna, kids can enjoy this oasis and such concoctions as pigeon stuffed with almonds. But should that fail to entice, spaghetti or an American hamburger might attract instead.

Chez Jack'Line (see p. 223) This is not truly a fast-food joint, but it is the next best thing in Marrakesh. When you're on the run and want to get to the Medina, try one of the grilled steaks and order your kid a brochette.

$ Prices: Fixed-price menus 200–300 DH ($25–$37.50); student and children's menus 100–150 DH ($12.50–$18.75). No credit cards.
Open: Lunch daily noon–3pm; dinner daily 8pm–midnight.

In a less hectic section of the Jemaa el Fna, a few paces to the left of the police station, you'll find a rectangular courtyard with semitropical shrubbery and seasonal flowers, ringed with three different dining rooms and a scattering of fountains and small pavilions. Each of the high-ceilinged dining rooms has a view of the garden and is forested with columns, ornate arches, and Berber artifacts. Meals include traditional Moroccan dishes such as tajines, couscous, brochettes, keftas, and salads.

FAST FOOD

CHEZ JACK'LINE, av. Mohammed V, 63. Tel. 475-47.

Cuisine: INTERNATIONAL. **Reservations:** Not required. **Transportation:** Petit taxi.
$ Prices: Appetizers 13–45 DH ($1.65–$5.65); main dishes 45–62 DH ($5.65–$7.75). AE, DC, MC, V.
Open: Lunch daily noon–3pm; dinner daily 6–11pm.

The ambience—thanks partly to its owner, Jack'line Pinguet—is French, vivacious, and somewhat reminiscent of a bustling pizzeria, and the cuisine is flavorful and refreshingly uncomplicated. You can order tajines, osso buco, diet-conscious brochettes, sangría, grilled steaks, and escalopes of veal.

AFTERNOON TEA

HOTEL MAMOUNIA, av. Bab Jdid (without number). Tel. 489-81.

Cuisine: MINT TEA. **Reservations:** Not required. **Transportation:** Petit or grand taxi.
$ Prices: Tea 25 DH ($3.15). AE, DC, MC, V.
Open: Daily 2–5pm.

Sitting on the terrace of this hotel indulging in a mint tea, with perhaps a Moroccan pastry to accompany it, is considered one of the grandest tea breaks in all of North Africa. Even more exciting than the tea is the walk through the walled-in gardens, once the royal stamping grounds of the Saadians, who built a series of pavilions here. Don't jump into the swimming pool, however, as it's reserved strictly for hotel guests. You can request (permission not always granted) a tour of the older wing of the hotel, where the suite of a former guest, Sir Winston Churchill, is preserved more or less as he left it. Even editions of his books are still on the shelves, and the bed in which he slept also survives.

SIDEWALK CAFES

One of the popular pastimes in Marrakesh is sitting at a sidewalk café. A most interesting panorama unfolds at the **Café de France,** Jemaa el Fna (tel. 417-29). The café is simple, but not the action taking place in front of it. An inside staircase leads up to a terrace with an unobstructed view of the marketplace. For the price of a coffee, only 3 DH (40¢), probably the cheapest entertainment in the city can be yours. A fixed-price French menu costs 65 DH ($8.15). Open daily from 8am to midnight.

In the center of Guéliz is the **Brasserie des Négociants,** av. Mohammed V, 110 (tel. 310-94). If you want to spread a rumor around Marrakesh quickly, launch it here. As you sit sipping coffee at 3 DH (40¢) or drinking Moroccan beer at 11 DH ($1.40), at least 10 boys will offer to shine your shoes. Often the same ones will approach you two or three times, just in case you should change your mind. Hours are 5am to 1am daily.

? **DID YOU KNOW . . . ?**

- The Koubba El Mouravide is all that is left from the golden age of the 12th-century Almoravid dynasty.

- Jemaa el Fna—the liveliest, most exhausting, and teeming "carnival" square in all of Morocco—translates as "rendezvous of the dead."

- At the turn of the century, a black slave, Si Ahmed ben Moussa, rose to become the grand vizier of Marrakesh. He built El Bahia Palace.

- The Saadian Tombs, sealed for centuries, were only rediscovered in 1917 because of the overview provided by a French aerial map.

- The Hotel Mamounia and its gardens were Sir Winston Churchill's favorite stopping place.

4. ATTRACTIONS

The peculiar charm of Marrakesh certainly isn't reflected in the New Town, or Guéliz, which was founded in 1913 about 1½ miles west of the Old Town, or the Medina. Unlike the Medina, Guéliz is characterized by wide boulevards, palaces, gardens, and modern structures. You'll spend much time in this quarter, as the majority of the hotels and restaurants are here. However, life in Marrakesh really centers on its main square, the Jemaa el Fna, and the Medina.

Warning: The opening hours given below for attractions are not written in stone. Even though hours are posted, places will often be closed for no apparent reason. Sometimes visitors facing closed doors are told that the palace or museum guards inside "are praying." Count yourself fortunate if you can get into all the places advertised as "open to public."

SUGGESTED ITINERARIES

IF YOU HAVE 1 DAY

Day 1: With an official guide from the tourist office, head for the Jemaa el Fna (also called Djemaa el Fna, or "the big square") to begin your tour of the souks of the Medina. After a day spent wandering these webs of alleyways, retire to the Café de France on the Jemaa el Fna for the ritual cup of coffee. Dine in one of the Moroccan restaurants in the Medina or at one of the big hotels where folk music and entertainment are presented.

IF YOU HAVE 2 DAYS

Day 1: As indicated above.
Day 2: Concentrate on specific sights, such as the Saadian Tombs, the Medersa Ben Youssef, and El Bahia Palace and its gardens.

IF YOU HAVE 3 DAYS

Days 1–2: As indicated above.
Day 3: In the early morning, take a horse-drawn carriage ride around the ramparts of Marrakesh. After lunch in a Moroccan restaurant, have a guide return you to the Medina, and this time explore the Mellah, the old Jewish quarter.

IF YOU HAVE 5 DAYS

Days 1–3: As indicated above.
Day 4: Take a one-day excursion from Marrakesh to the beautiful Ourika Valley (see

Chapter 9), the most popular one-day excursion from "the red city," as Marrakesh is called.

Day 5: Return to the Medina, where you virtually will never see the same sights twice, as it holds endless fascination. Visit Dar Si Said, a 19th-century palace that is now a museum of art. After lunch, explore the famous gardens of Marrakesh, including Aguedal and Menara. Have afternoon tea at the Mamounia, a deluxe hotel whose gardens date from the Saadian era.

FROMMER'S FAVORITE
MARRAKESH EXPERIENCES

Mint Tea and the Mamounia Gardens   The royal grounds laid out by the Saadian dynasty are now the property of the Mamounia, the most deluxe of Marrakesh hotels. Winston Churchill painted here for 20 years. After your stroll, have a mint tea on the terrace and let the world go by.

Overlooking the Jemaa el Fna from the Café de France   Far removed from the crowded square, you can oversee the action from this café's rooftop. On the square below, a carnival of one-eyed beggars, fake water sellers (waiting for a tourist with a camera), pickpockets, dancing boys, snake charmers, acrobats, medicine men, and carpet merchants compete for center stage, where a goat-head soup bubbles vigorously over a charcoal brazier.

Shopping the Souks of the Medina   Wander through North Africa's grandest marketplace, a labyrinth of alleyways and congested streets with a bewildering array of merchandise. Souk by souk, discover a world of handcrafts, carpets, and aggressive merchants. It is bewildering, confusing, and never in your whole life will so many people try to sell you so many things—everything from a live duck to a "diamond" ring.

A Horse-and-Buggy Ride Along the Ramparts   Colonial tourists had the best idea. They rented a horse-drawn calèche and toured the ramparts of Marrakesh, built in the Almoravid reign. The walls, depending on the time of day, take on various hues—ocher, gold, nut brown, dusty pink. It's an easy, safe way to see a panorama of desert life.

THE TOP ATTRACTIONS

JEMAA EL FNA

The largest souk in Morocco—and the most famous address in Marrakesh—is a world unto itself. Camera-carrying tourists and kef-smoking young people rub shoulders with Berber men from the Atlas mountains or wandering tribesmen from the Sahara in indigo-blue robes. If you go at 2 o'clock on a winter afternoon (4 or 5 o'clock in summer), you'll meet a cast of characters that might include occasional acrobats of Amizmiz, monkey trainers, soothsayers, palm readers, trick cyclists, pate-polishing barbers, magicians, jugglers, *fellahs* (small farmers), flame eaters, lottery sellers, snake charmers, acupuncturists, and scribes. You can even see "dentists" pulling teeth. To be frank, this square isn't the three-star attraction it used to be. One Moroccan explained it this way: "Many of us have TV now. We stay home and watch a show in our living room and don't have to go to the square to see one."

The most characteristic star in this drama is the red-clad water seller—a goatskin

MOROCCO

★ Moknos

● Rabat

Aguedal Gardens **14**

Bab Agnaou **9**

Bab er Rob **10**

Dar Si Said (Museum
of Moroccan Art) **6**

El Bahia Palace **7**

Jemaa el Fna **4**

The Kasbah **12**

Koutoubia Minaret **5**

Medersa Ben Youssef **1**

The Medina **2**

The Mellah
(Jewish Quarter) **8**

Royal Palace
(Dar el Makhzen) **13**

Saadian Tombs **11**

The Souks of the Medina **3**

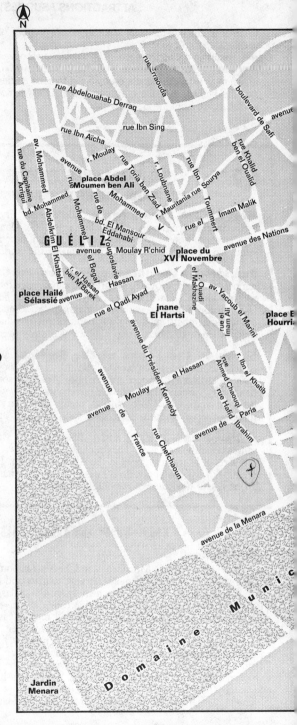

acoub el Mansour

Bab
nies   Doukkala

rue el Gza

Riad el Arous

rue de Bab Tarhzout

rue Assouel

rue de Bab Khemis

rue de el Glaoui

rue de Bab Doukkala

place du
Moukef

①

rue Dar

rue Fatima Zohra

r. du
Lakdar

rue Sidi el Yamani

②

③

place Ben
Salah

place
Si Youb

MEDINA

rue de
Bab Ailen

avenue Mohammed V

rue Dabbachi

④
place
Jemaa
el Fna

r. Abou el Abbes Sebti

Bab Makhzen

square Abd
E Moumen

⑤

rue El Mouahidine

rue du jnane

rue Douâr Graouâ

⑥

⑦

Ben Chegre

enue el Yarmouk

place Youssef
b. Tachfine

av. Houman el Fetouaki

rue Riad Zitoune Kedim

rue Riad Zitoune Jdid

⑧

MELLAH   jnane
El Afia

place des
Ferblantiers

p a l

rue Essaadiyne

⑨

Bab Agnâou

Bab er Rob

⑩

⑪

⑫   **⑬**

K A S B A H

rue de la Kasbah

⑭
Aguedal

Ramparts

sack draped across his back, a necklace of brass cups dangling from his neck—who tinkles his bell as he makes his way through the crowd. Today he earns more money posing for tourists who give him tips than he does selling water from the gold faucet of his goatskin sack.

Everybody in the Jemaa el Fna has something to sell, and you are the prime target.

If Allah is smiling on you during your visit, you'll have a chance to see a performance by the black Muslims of Mauritania, who are known for their acrobatic feats and barefoot dancing. Scarlet-colored sashes are slung around their ivory-toned garb, a dramatic sight as they move rhythmically to the tam-tam.

Although the drama peaks in the late afternoon, the square is an experience at any time. At night, you can see the Chleuh boy dancers, accompanied by jarring cymbals, sending out their age-old sexual invitations; or musicians playing their skin-covered *ginbris*, or guitars (usually three strings). The black Gnaouas are trance-healers beating out hypnotic rhythms. Storytellers are dying out (again, TV is to blame) but there are still a few who weave intricate plots for a dirham. In an atmosphere that Brueghel would love to have painted, the nightly dinner ritual begins. Salads are spread before you, and there are stands dispensing exotic juices. In some of the vats, goat-head soup is brewing, as it seems to be a favorite. Fish and mutton are frying on the braziers, as are vegetables and chickens.

As the most adventurous of tourists (those with cast-iron stomachs) sample the wares, children—seemingly under 12 years of age—peddle hashish or veiled women appear out of the night to offer handmade Berber trinkets.

You can also purchase some fried chameleons, a fake Rolex watch, or a djellabah. Perhaps when it all becomes too much, you can retire to the roof terrace of the Café de France on the square and take in the rest of the action from there.

Incidentally, the name of this square is translated roughly as "Rendezvous of the Dead." It must be the worst-named square in Morocco.

Bus: 1 from Gueliz.

KOUTOUBIA MINARET, Jemaa el Fna.

Dominating the city is this 222-foot-high minaret of a 12th-century pink sandstone mosque. The tower is crowned with three decorative gilt balls which, according to legend, were presented by the wife of Sultan Yaacoub el Mansour, "The Victorious One," and which are carefully guarded by *djin*. The Koutoubia, or the Mosque of the Scribes, is the equivalent of the Giralda Tower at Seville and the Tower of Hassan at Rabat—both of which are imitations of this, the oldest of the three.

Regrettably for sightseers, non-Muslims are forbidden to enter this most enduring and characteristic monument of Marrakesh.

Bus: 1.

THE SOUKS OF THE MEDINA, directly south of Jemaa el Fna.

After you've learned the ground rules of the Jemaa el Fna, you'll be ready to venture into the nearby maze of souks, beginning at the northern edge at either Bab er Rob or Bab Agnaou gateway. Some of the finest craftspeople in Morocco are found on these narrow streets.

Everybody heads for the dyers' souk, as it is, naturally, the most colorful (but not on Friday). Hanging on lines strung across the streets are silk and woolen skeins in every hue of the rainbow. Leather workers, bookbinders, shoemakers, brass and copper artisans ply their crafts. The aromas alone will lure you to the exotic spice section. Fabric is sold in the *kissarias*, and the bright sunlight only enhances the brilliance of the gold embroidery.

IMPRESSIONS

You can't come as far as Casablanca without visiting my beloved Marrakesh, the Paris of the Sahara.
—WINSTON CHURCHILL TO FDR

Some of the alleyways are covered with latticework, casting slanting shadows. Merchants tempt you with all sorts of kettles and braziers, wrought-iron lanterns, silver daggers, camel-hair blankets. Perhaps the rugs will catch your eye—especially those from Chichaoua, with their red backgrounds and geometric designs.

For specific suggestions for browsing, see "Savvy Shopping," below.

Bus: 1.

THE SAADIAN TOMBS, Bab er Rob.

Built during the reign of the Saadian monarch Ahmed El Dehbi in the 16th century, this is the most lavish, most visited, and most memorable mausoleum in Morocco. Entrance is through a small passage south of the Kasbah Mosque. You enter an enclosed rectangular garden planted with shrubbery and flowers; the prayer hall can be seen on your left. This is an ancient cemetery used by the Shorfa, descendants of the Prophet, long before the Saadians began their rule in Marrakesh. The tombs contain the remains of all but five of the Saadian rulers. The royal burial ground wasn't discovered until 1917. Wanting to "erase" the memory of his predecessors, Sultan Moulay Ismail had them walled off, and they were simply forgotten until their rediscovery on a French aerial map. All in all, the necropolis forms the most dramatic architecture in the city, and of the three halls, the most elegant is the Chamber of the 12 Columns. Many of the tombs contain the remains of children or royal concubines.

Admission: 10 DH ($1.25).

Open: Daily 8am–noon and 2:30–5:30pm. **Directions:** Follow the signs from the gateway, Bab er Rob.

MEDERSA BEN YOUSSEF, rue Ben Youssef.

This monument was built during the reign of Abou Hassan, a 14th-century Merenid sultan. The Saadian monarch Moulay Abou Abdallah (Abdullah el Ghalib) rebuilt it in 1565. The style is traditional, with a quartet of ornately decorative inner façades surrounding a central courtyard. Look for the 11th-century marble basin with its heraldic birds. Until 1956 the medersa was used as a university, filled with medical students who lived in the cell-like rooms upstairs.

Admission: 10 DH ($1.25).

Open: Daily 9am–noon and 3–7pm. **Transportation/Directions:** Bus no. 1. Lies north of the Jemaa el Fna. Take a right turn at the fork of Souk Semarine onto Souk el Kbir.

EL BAHIA PALACE, rue Zitoun el Said, opposite Bab Berrima.

If King Hassan II isn't putting up a VIP guest or one of his relatives isn't in town, you might gain entrance to this splendidly decorated palace, whose name means "brilliance." It was built between 1894 and 1900, and is noted not only for its decor but for its Moorish gardens.

Formerly the residence of the Si Ahmed ben Moussa (also known as Bou Ahmed), grand vizier in the twilight years before the colonial takeover of Morocco, the palace was stripped of its finery and trappings after his death, as vividly recounted in *Morocco That Was* by Walter Harris. In the reporter's words, "His women fought and stole to get possession of the jewels. Safes were broken open, documents and deeds to titles extracted, precious gems were torn from their settings, and even murder took place." Later the building was occupied by French resident governors. The Moorish gardens, with their smell of sweet jasmine, are irrigated by water from an artificial lake.

It is the only "royal palace" in Morocco that can be visited by the public.

Admission: 10 DH ($1.25).

Open: Wed–Mon 9:30am–noon and 2:30–5:30pm. **Transportation/Directions:** Bus no. 1 to Jemaa el Fna. From the main square, fronting the closed CTM station, go left through a gateway onto rue Zitoun el Said and follow it to place des Ferblantiers.

DAR SI SAID, rue Zitoun el Jdid.

Now the Museum of Moroccan Art, this palace was erected at the end of the 19th century by the brother of Bou Ahmed, grand vizier of Sultan Moulay Hassan. You enter via a sweet-smelling patio garden filled with birds. The two-story collection is interesting, especially the handcrafts from the High Atlas mountains, including wood carving from the Glaoui kasbahs. The rugs and capes are exceptional, as is the Berber jewelry. There's a room of engraved daggers, muskets, and powderhorns. Note also the waterbags of camel skin, the copper and brass work, the Safi and Zagora pottery, even the decorated doors to Berber houses.

Admission: 10 DH ($1.25).

Open: Wed–Mon 9am–noon and 4–7pm. **Bus:** 1 to Jemaa el Fna.

THE MELLAH

Reached by heading south from place Jemaa el Fna, along rue Zitoune Keddim, past intersections of about 14 different alleyways, the old Jewish quarter (the Mellah) isn't what it used to be, as most of the Jews emigrated either when the state of Israel was formed in 1948 or when Moroccan independence was granted in 1956. Some went to live in the more tolerant city of Casablanca, and many moved to Paris. A few still live here, and most of them are old. As one local put it, "They were too poor to move."

The quarter was created in 1558. Jews were ordered into this area by Abdullah el Ghalib, a sultan of the Saadian dynasty. His motives are not entirely clear, as he had moved them into the safety of his kasbah. Some have suggested it was to keep an eye on them so he could tax them more heavily—they were a prosperous community of merchants, bankers, traders, and metalsmiths, among other professions. Many were jewelers working in precious metals. The Jews built their own gardens with fountains, their own synagogues, and their own merchandise-loaded souks.

Buildings in the Mellah tended to be taller than in other parts of the Medina, but the streets and little stores appear smaller. Until the French took over, Jews could not own real estate. They weren't even allowed to ride outside the Mellah. They could walk, but only if they went barefoot. If a Jew accidentally wandered into a mosque, he was given two choices: he could either convert to Islam immediately or else be set afire.

The center of the old Mellah is called **place des Ferblantiers,** although it used to be known as place du Mellah. There are many souks here, including a jewelry souk, as Moroccan craftsmen gradually replaced the former Jewish artisans. Spice and textile souks are also found here.

One of the most interesting and characteristic squares is place Souweka. Lying about 200 yards from the square is the old Jewish cemetery, **Mihaara.** A number of synagogues still exist in the Mellah, but you'll have to locate them with a guide if you're interested. Getting inside one of them depends in large part on how good your guide is, as people now live in them. Your best chance is to visit one that is operated more or less like a Jewish-American hostel, and you'll definitely need help finding it.

MORE ATTRACTIONS

The **Royal Palace (Dar el Makhzen),** where King Hassan II lives when he is in Marrakesh, is not open to visitors, but you can ride around it in a horse-drawn carriage. The trip around the high walls is about 2 miles.

GARDENS

Marrakesh is famous for its gardens. The best known is the 2-mile-long **Aguedal,** splendid imperial gardens laid out by the Almohads in the 12th century. Studded with olive trees, they are irrigated by pools. Sultan Moulay Abd Er Rahman is credited with giving the Aguedal its present form in the 19th century.

One of the pavilions, Dar el Beida, was constructed at the time for the harem of

Moulay Hassan. In 1873, Sultan Sidi Mohammed ben Abd Er Rahman drowned while boating in a large tank of water, Sahraj el Hana, in the gardens. A previous sultan, Moulay Rachid, was killed in these same gardens in 1672 while galloping through citrus groves on a horse. He broke his skull on a tree branch. To reach the Aguedal, follow the road outside the ramparts below either Bab er Rob or Bab Agnaou. Make a left as you are about to leave the Old Town at Bab Irhli. Go across a parade ground alongside King Hassan II's Royal Palace, which will eventually lead to the corner *bab* (gateway) of the Aguedal.

Surrounded by an adobe enclosure full of olive trees, the **Jardin Menara** was originally laid out by the Almohads. In the 19th century, Sultan Sidi Mohammed ben Abd Er Rahman erected a pavilion surrounded by a 12-foot-wide parapet. Apparently, the sultan met his "favorites" here in this tranquil setting around a massive water tank. On the site of a ruined Saadian *minzah* (pavilion), the sultan constructed another, in green tiles, in 1869. A stopover here is considered mandatory during all coach tours of the city. To reach the gardens on foot, follow avenue de la Menara from Bab Jdid.

The **Jardin Majorelle,** found on rue Majorelle, was originally planted by the 19th-century artist and designer Jacques Majorelle. In 1978, 2 acres of exotic greenery were purchased by Yves St. Laurent, the French couturier, as part of the grounds surrounding his nearby villa. Visitors can stroll beneath soaring promenades of bamboo and past tile-ringed pools of lotus blossoms. The villa is strictly private. The gardens, however, are open daily from 8am to noon and 2 to 6pm. Admission is 10 DH ($1.25); children are not admitted. From the Jemaa el Fna, take bus no. 1 to Guéliz. The location is north of avenue Yaacoub el Mansour, lying between avenue El Jadida and boulevard de Safi.

SCENIC ROUTES

No trip to Marrakesh is complete without a tour of the celebrated **route de la Palmeraie,** the choicest part of the palm grove northeast of the city, and a horse-drawn carriage ride around the Ramparts of Marrakesh (see below). The cost depends on your negotiations with the driver, but expect to pay from 50 DH ($6.25) per hour. After 8pm, it goes up 50%. Stretching on for nearly 12 miles, the palm oasis covers an area of about 30,000 acres; there are reputed to be 150,000 trees. (At some point, you may want to get down from your carriage and mount a camel.) Before your visit to the grove, you can circle the ramparts. Trips usually begin at place de la Liberté and last for nearly 5 miles. This way, you'll get to see the interesting gates of Marrakesh—Bab Doukkala, of Almoravid origin, and the especially delightful Bab Agnaou, from the 12th century. The palm oasis was planted by the Almoravids, but the trees are here only for scenic purposes, as they are too far north in Africa to bear fruit.

The **Ramparts of Marrakesh** are 10 miles of walls circling the "red city." They are traditionally toured by horse and buggy, although many prefer to bicycle around them (not recommended on a hot day in summer). A few intrepid visitors even walk the entire circuit. The walls were the idea of a sultan in 1126, Ali ben Youssef of the Almoravid dynasty. Twenty-nine feet high, they were studded with some 200 towers and pierced by some 20 gateways, including Bab Khemis, which leads to the souks, and Bab ed Debbagh, which leads to the tanneries. Visitors often comment on the changing light or color displays of the walls, the exact shade depending on the time of day the ramparts are viewed. You may want to begin your tour of the ramparts at the Jemaa el Fna, where carriages can be rented.

COOL FOR KIDS
TOP CITY ATTRACTIONS

The Jemaa el Fna *(see p. 225).* People eat fire, drink boiling water, or charm cobras in this square. The acrobats of Amizmiz entertain, as do monkeys and their trainers. Your kid may never watch TV again.

The Souks of the Medina *(see p. 228).* The great souks of Marrakesh are filled with wonder at every turn. For adults, it's always a question of whether to shop or look. Your kid will definitely want to look . . . and look.

The Ramparts *(see p. 231).* Few adventures delight kids more than to hop aboard a calèche (horse and buggy) at the Jemaa el Fna and tour the Ramparts of Marrakesh. They can stop and have their pictures taken on one of the camels just waiting for that purpose outside the walls.

ORGANIZED TOURS

What is available changes from season to season and year to year, with a curtailed schedule in summer. Your best bet is to go to the American Express representative in Marrakesh, **Voyages Schwartz,** Immeuble Moutaouskil, rue Mauritania (tel. 333-21). Off avenue Mohammed V in Guéliz, it offers not only tours in Marrakesh but also excursions into the High Atlas. It is open Monday through Friday from 8:30am to 12:30pm and 3 to 6:30pm.

WALKING TOUR — Marrakesh

Start: Bab Agnaou

Finish: Jemaa el Fna

Time: About 2½ hours

Best Time: Daily from 8am to 5pm, but only with the assistance of a guide, as street names are often unmarked and maps are inadequate.

Worst Time: After dark.

Begin at the Medina's eastern edge, at one of its most famous gates:

1. **Bab Agnaou.** The name translates as Gate of the Hornless Ram, and since two towers that originally flanked either side have been demolished, its name is appropriate. Along with its defensive counterpart a short walk to the southeast (Bab er Rob), it forms a defensive unit frequently cited as early as the 1100s. The gates formerly guarded a kasbah that no longer exists. They and the narrow space between them were famous for centuries as a place where the severed heads and mangled bodies of the enemies of the sultans were displayed. The space between these two gates is place de la Kasbah, although there is little within it other than some trees and the nostalgia of a once-mighty fortress.

   If you haven't already passed beneath the archway of Bab Agnaou, do so now so that you are standing within the encircling ramparts of the ancient city. From Bab Agnaou, continue straight along:

2. **rue de la Kasbah.** After one block, turn right onto rue Botweil. The first large white building with the Almohad-inspired crenellations is the:

3. **Mosque of the Kasbah,** which non-Muslims cannot enter. Originally built by the Almohads between 1185 and 1190, it was embellished by the Saadians during the late 1500s. When it reaches the mosque, the street will turn to conform to its edges, but continue walking. A short walk later, on the left, you'll see signs pointing to TOMBEAUX SAADIENS, which are the:

4. **Saadian Tombs.** One of the most famous monuments of Marrakesh, they are also one of the few holy places in Morocco open to non-Muslims. Within their splendid and somber setting, the actual tombstones, in the Islamic style, are noticeably simple. Most of the tombs date from the mid-1500s, although a few of the more eroded ones were placed here around 1350. Wishing to conceal forever the burial places of his predecessors, a later sultan (Moulay Ismail) walled them off from public view, where they lay forgotten until a French aerial photograph revealed their presence during the Protectorate.

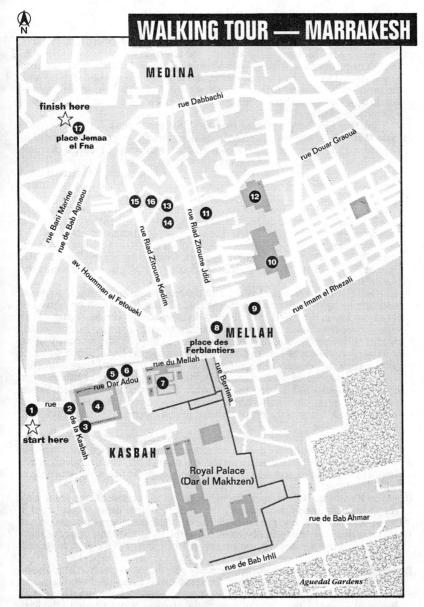

WALKING TOUR — MARRAKESH

N

MEDINA

rue Dabbachi

finish here
☆ 17
place Jemaa el Fna

rue Douar Graoua

rue Bani Marine
rue de Bab Agnaou

15 16 13
14

12

rue Riad Zitoune Kedim
rue Riad Zitoune Jdid

11

av. Houmman el Fetouaki

10

rue Imam el Rhezali

9

8 **MELLAH**
place des Ferblantiers

rue du Mellah

5 6
7

rue Dar Adou

rue Berrima

1 rue
☆ 2
start here 3 4

de la Kasbah

KASBAH

Royal Palace (Dar el Makhzen)

rue de Bab Ahmar

rue de Bab Irhli

Aguedal Gardens

1 Bab Agnaou
2 Rue de la Kasbah
3 Mosque of the Kasbah
4 Saadian Tombs
5 Rue Dar Adou
6 Rue du Mellah

7 El Badi Palace
8 Place Kzadrya
9 The Souks
10 El Bahia Palace
11 Medersa El Bahia
12 Musée Dar Si Said (Museum of Moroccan Art)

13 Grand Bijouterie
14 Islamic cemetery
15 Rue Riad Zitoune Kedim
16 Restaurant Dar Es Salaam
17 Jemaa el Fna

After you exit the tombs, retrace your steps beside the southern foundation of the white-sided Mosque of the Kasbah, and return to the base of Bab Agnaou. Don't exit from the confines of the Medina by passing beneath it. Instead, turn right just before you pass underneath it, and first pass beneath one archway and, a short distance later, a more ornate second archway. Beyond this second archway is an airy promenade lined with trees, and a distant view of the soaring Koutoubia Minaret.

Take the first right-hand turn from this promenade onto:

5. rue Dar Adou. The sienna-colored *pisé*-sided building on your left (without an identifying sign or house number) is a modern 20th-century medersa (Koranic school) built by the Moroccan government in the 1950s.

You will now begin a hot and rather dusty four-block promenade past dozens of shops. At the end of the street, jog left, and a few paces later, jog right onto:

6. rue du Mellah. This marks the beginning of what formerly served as the Jewish quarter, although very few Jews remain here today. Within two blocks, rue du Mellah opens onto place du Mellah (some maps and some signs might identify it as place des Ferblantiers). On your left is the simple Mosquee du Mellah.

From here, you'll notice discreet signs pointing to your next destination, El Badi Palace. Follow them onto rue Touarga, which becomes rue Barama. The gate at the end of rue Barama pierces a forbiddingly high pisé wall, marking the beginning of:

7. El Badi Palace. Enter the forecourt of the most tragic building in Marrakesh, and turning right, walk uphill to the entrance. When it was built by Ahmed el Mansour late in the 1500s to celebrate a decisive victory over the Portuguese, it was the most exquisite and opulent palace compound in the Islamic world, loaded with marble slabs and columns carved in Italy. Within a century of its construction, sultans of later dynasties (especially Moulay Ismail), jealous that its glories might overpower the architectural accomplishments at Meknes, ordered the palace stripped of its marble, ebony, ivory, and gold leaf for use in other building projects, and its gardens destroyed. The destruction of El Badi Palace required 10 years of constant labor. Today, the vast compound is a crumbling masonry shell. Many of the region's annual folkloric performances are presented within these ruins.

Leaving the ruins of El Badi Palace, walk straight across the gently sloping terrain of the square (there may be some tour buses parked there) and take the second (not the first) arch that pierces the wall on your left. You'll suddenly enter, once again, a bustling commercial zone of the Mellah district, which street signs will identify as:

8. place Kzadrya. Walk straight through it (unless you choose to stop at some of the shops along the right-hand side), then fork right onto the continuation of a street you already know, rue du Mellah. Turn right into a very narrow covered alleyway that may or may not be identified as the Haij es Salaame (it begins right after the Douirya Restaurant); you are now at the beginning of the most congested section of:

9. The Souks. You can explore them leisurely later during your stay in Marrakesh. For now, proceed down a corner of the section where fruits and vegetables are sold. Kiosks, itinerant farmers, veiled women, and cassock-robed merchants will be on all sides of you. Ahead of you, as the alleyway curves gently to the left, you'll see sunlight and open space. When you reach it, turn right. About a hundred paces ahead of you, behind a portico capped with green tiles, is the entrance to:

10. El Bahia Palace. Translated from the Arabic as "brilliance," it has only a limited number of courtyards and apartments open to visitors. Its interior gives an idea of the wealth and grandeur of the 19th-century pashas of Marrakesh. Exit from the main gate you entered, and turn hard right onto rue Riad Isitoune Jdid.

Note the charmingly decorated Moorish post office on your left. Within a short distance, you'll reach a wide plaza, place Riad Isitoune. The sienna-colored building on the opposite edge of where you are standing is the Koranic school, which was long ago associated with the palace. It was known as the:

11. Medersa El Bahia. A few paces later, turn right beneath a narrow archway that will begin on the right side of the square, then turn left onto an alleyway identified as Dar Si Said. The streets at this point are very narrow, lined with unusual shops, and famous as the historic and oldest part of the Medina. Bypass the entrance to the Restaurant Palais Gharnatta, but continue straight along the same street. At the end of this labyrinth of narrow alleyways is the ornate gateway leading into the Medina's most famous museum, the:

12. Musée Dar Si Said (Museum of Moroccan Art). Filled with historic artifacts and cultural exhibits showcasing the region, it's contained within a building erected late in the 19th century.

After your visit, exit from the door you originally entered and turn right onto Dar Si Said. At the first opportunity, turn right onto another alley, Darb Zaouia. It will jog to the left, and then shortly after, to the right. Within a short walk, the beginning of another covered souk will loom before you. Turn left (the street is technically still the Darb Zaouia). Walk a block past merchants selling household goods and kitchenware. At the next T-junction, go left. You'll notice the Moorish entrance to the local Lion's Club, then the façade of the previously mentioned Medersa El Bahia. Suddenly you'll recognize a broad street that you've previously followed, rue Riad Zitoune Jdid.

Continue retracing your steps along this street, past the entrance to El Bahia Palace. Several steps later, rue Riad Zitoune Jdid will turn sharply right. Continue following it to where it will once again, within about 100 yards, make a sharp turn to the left. Just at that point, notice the ornate plasterwork detailing above a doorway on the right-hand side of the street. It will be labeled:

13. Grand Bijouterie, and it contains as many as 50 jewelers. Originally staffed by Jews, and replaced after 1956 and 1968 by Moroccan entrepreneurs who adopted many of their skills, this market contains the single most valuable repository of gold and silver ornamentation in Marrakesh. Detour briefly inside (and be forewarned that you might be sorely tempted to buy something) and then exit via the same door you entered. Turn right. The street will have suddenly changed its name to a street you've already explored, rue du Mellah. Within a short walk, behind the crumbling wall on your right, will appear the:

14. Islamic cemetery, with the characteristically modest flat tombstones.

You will come to a busy and confusing traffic circle that funnels traffic from six different streets. This is known as place du Mellah. Take the first street entering this square on your right:

15. rue Riad Zitoune Kedim. Walk north in a straight line past shops and cafés toward your ultimate destination, the most central and most famous plaza in Marrakesh, the Jemaa el Fna. Midway along this street, you'll come to your much-deserved:

REFUELING STOP   16. Restaurant Dar Es Salaam, Riad Zitoun Kedim, 170 bis (tel. 44-35-20). Built late in the 17th century as a palace for one of the city's important families, it was one of the locations for the filming of Hitchcock's *The Man Who Knew Too Much* in the 1950s. Today, it is an undeniably romantic and cool refuge from the glaring sun, with lavishly adorned high ceilings and symmetrically elegant arcades. Fixed-price meals range from 140 to 190 DH ($17.50 to $23.75), and the menu lists typical Moroccan specialties—tajine with prunes and almonds, couscous with either chicken or mutton, chicken with olives, and brochettes of meat. Moroccan spectacles are presented nightly at 8:30pm. Lunch is served daily from noon to 3pm and dinner from 8 to 10:30pm, but you can drop in at any time during the day for mint tea (or mineral water) and pastries.

After you exit the restaurant, turn right, and continue walking along your original path until you enter the confusion, color, and exoticism of the:

17. Jemaa el Fna. During the 19th century, you could have bought anything from a slave to a colony of snakes within this square. Today, it's considered the top tourist attraction of Marrakesh. Avoid anything blatantly illegal, and celebrate the end of your walking tour.

5. SAVVY SHOPPING

Recommending a suitable collection of shops in Marrakesh is a lot like trying to identify grains of sand on a beach. In the souks of the Medina, you'll discover a staggering display of handcrafts, lots of them sold by aggressive merchants who will often literally pull you into their shops. As at any other Moroccan shop, you should bargain, and bargain hard, for the best values.

THE SHOPPING SCENE
BEST BUYS & WHERE TO FIND THEM

Most of the major Moroccan handcrafts are sold in the souks of the Medina, including store after store devoted to Moroccan carpets. Most stores in Guéliz are found along avenue Mohammed V, or in streets branching off from that main artery.

The principal street is **rue Souk Semarine,** which contains a spice and pottery market at its entrance. Cloth merchants dominate this street, where endless bolts of bright silks and embroidered cloth for kaftans are sold.

Following rue Souk Semarine, take the first and then the second right to **Rahba Kedima,** site of the old corn market, which is today peppered with jewelry shops and spice merchants. Beware of some of those "amber" necklaces here—"plastic" is more accurate. All those drying lizards, snakes, eagles, whatever, you see are blended to make a "love potion." There is serious belief in many of these ancient aphrodisiacs, and sometimes they can command a good price.

On the opposite of Rahba Kedima is the **Criée Berbère,** filled with kilim cushions, kilim carpets, and other items made from kilim weaves. This was—at least until the French did away with them in 1912—the site of the former slave auctions.

Going beyond Rahba Kedima, rue Souk Semarine divides into **Souk Attarine** and **Souk el Kebir** on the left. Many Western-made items, including clothes, are sold here, and the area no longer has the character it did decades ago.

Continue to the end of the souk and bear left for the labyrinthine **Souk Cherratin,** featuring metalwork, wood, and leather. You soon come to the alleys of the kissaria, the traditional heart of the Medina. Here you enter the **Souk des Babouches,** where many slippers, mainly in yellow and white, are sold.

At the end of the Souk des Babouches, head west to the famed **Souk des Teinturiers,** the dyers' souk. Flamboyantly colored dyed wool dries in the Sahara air. It is every camera-toting visitor's dream.

North of the kissaria you'll find souks devoted to coppersmiths and metalworkers, as well as carpenters. You'll also see many shoemakers (this is the place to come for shoe repairs).

TAXES & HOURS

There is no recovery of the government tax of 17% to 19% added to goods and services in Morocco. Bargaining is acceptable in all stores that don't have fixed prices. Stores that publicize fixed prices usually include various government-operated artisan centers. Traditionally, the best trading period in the souks has been in the morning, any time daily after 8am.

SHOPPERS BEWARE

There are some pitfalls to shopping in the souks—buying fake merchandise, for example. You might think you're getting silver, but it turns out to be pewter. Many major purchases are paid for by credit cards, and alterations of the amount on the credit-card voucher are commonplace. This has become such a problem that many people prefer to pay cash for their purchases.

Some stores will arrange shipment and bill you on the spot for air freight, but will then send the merchandise "collect," even though you've already paid for it. Sometimes they don't even bother to send the merchandise at all, thinking you will never return to Marrakesh. More and more people are taking their goods with them, even if they have to pay extra on the airplane.

Of course, anything you buy with your guide in a shop will include his "commission" from the store. It's merely added to your bill, and the guide, after dropping you off, returns to collect it from the merchant. Obviously, deals made without a guide are the cheapest deals. Only problem is, it's hard for first-time visitors to find a particular store in the Medina without a guide. Even if you go alone, you'll be besieged all the way by young men offering to become your guide.

To complicate matters, there is also the problem of theft from pickpockets so skilled that the practice is almost a state-of-the-art profession. Sometimes purse snatchers race by on a motor scooter and disappear in the labyrinthine alleyways.

If you hear someone behind you yelling "Balek! Balek!" heed the warning. It means "Get out of the way," and is usually uttered by a man on a donkey. In these congested streets, where there's hardly any room to walk, men and boys riding bicycles often ring bells to warn of their approach.

All these warnings are not meant to discourage you from shopping in the Medina. A visit here is one of the highlights of a trip to Morocco. They are meant as precautions—prior knowledge of what can go wrong will often prevent something from actually going wrong.

SHOPPING A TO Z
Artisan Centers

L'ARTISANAT DE L'OR, Mouassine, 120. Tel. 434-75.
Its inventory is vast and unusual—a reflection of this store's status as one of the major privately owned artisanal emporiums within the Medina. Although it sells many of the small items you might have already seen in great profusion, it also sells major pieces of sculpture, including large replicas of camels, lions, and gazelles in hollow ironware inlaid with masses of silver. Upstairs is a selection of carpets from throughout Morocco. The store is recommended for large purchases. To get here, take bus no. 1 or 20 to the Jamaa el Fna, then walk.

COOPARTIM ENSEMBLE ARTISANALE, av. Mohammed V (without number). Tel. 436-64.
Within a cool, tiled pavilion in the Ville Nouvelle, a 15-minute walk from the Koutoubia market, you'll find what might be the best-stocked and most interesting government-run cooperative for handcrafts in all of Morocco. Everything on the two floors is sold for a fixed price. Before you begin bargaining in the souks, you might check out the going rates for similar merchandise at this store. Behind the showroom, within the garden-style courtyards, a handful of craftsmen ply their trades, giving you the chance to watch their creativity. One of them is a luthier, making a living solely from crafting the delicate stringed instruments that contribute to the distinctive sounds of Moroccan music.

A second, less well stocked branch of this establishment is in the heart of the Medina, on the Jemaa el Fna (tel. 428-48). To get to either branch, take bus no. 1 or 20, both of which stop in front of the stores.

CARPETS

PALAIS LES ALMORAVIDES, Derb Lagnaïz Mouassine, 3. Tel. 437-84.
To find this shop, along the twisting and dusty streets of the Medina, you will almost certainly need a guide. From an unlikely low doorway, a passage expands into

a huge, high-ceilinged room filled with rows of second-floor balconies. Dozens of carpets are on sale from throughout Morocco. Hard bargaining is recommended. To reach this place, take bus no. 1 to the Jemaa el Fna.

LA PORTE D'OR, Souk Semarine, 115. Tel. 454-54.
A 15-minute walk north of the Jemaa el Fna, it boasts a huge inventory of carpets. Salesmen are well informed, and don't mind pulling out and unfolding many of their wares. Also for sale are copper vessels and antique jewelry. Mr. Lioua, one of the co-owners, is especially helpful. To get here, take a petit taxi, or bus no. 1 or 20, to the Jemaa el Fna then walk.

CERAMICS

BAZAR CHICHAOUA, Souekt Laksours, 57. Tel. 437-17.
Brightly colored ceramic vases—in a wide range of colors, each laboriously painted by hand in floral or geometric designs—are the specialty here. A favorite color is the shade of iridescent turquoise known as Safi blue. To get here, take a petit taxi to the Jemaa el Fna, then walk.

LEATHER GOODS

KHIAM CUIR, rue Rif, route de Agadir. Tel. 467-33.
Outside the Medina in the Quartier Industriel, this is a factory making leather goods. Gone are the days when Moroccan leather meant only overstuffed cushions and embroidered belts. Khiam Cuir offers a huge selection of leather pants, jackets, and overcoats perfectly suited to sophisticated tastes; however, prices are about half (or less) of what you'd pay back home. The showroom on this establishment's second floor is often filled with buyers from chic boutiques in France or Italy. To get here, take a petit taxi.

METALWORK

L'ART MAROCAIN, place Kzadrya, 50. Tel. 412-46.
Near El Badi Palace, it's a showroom of sophisticated metalwork, beautifully crafted into exotic shapes and vessels. Some of the best merchandise is at the top of a flight of winding stairs. To get to this place, take a petit taxi to Bab Agnaou, then walk.

6. EVENING ENTERTAINMENT

THE ENTERTAINMENT SCENE

For such a big resort city, the most important in Morocco outside of Agadir, Marrakesh seems at first to have very little nightlife. The Ancien Casino de Marrakech (see below) is its major nighttime venue. Nearly all big hotels feature folkloric entertainment, including Moroccan music and dance. If your hotel has both a Moroccan restaurant and an international restaurant, go to the Moroccan one, because that is where the entertainment will be.

Aside from the hotels, many of the finer restaurants in the Medina also present Moroccan dancing and music along with dinner. So your choice of restaurant becomes not only your dining selection for the night, but your "nightclub" choice as well. In essence, you get two for the price of one, both food and amusement.

All the best and most comfortable bars are also in the big hotels, notably the Mamounia. If your hotel doesn't have suitable entertainment, you can always go to one that does.

There are no publications to guide you; you have to ask around to find out what's happening. See also "Accommodations" and "Dining," above, for tips.

THE PERFORMING ARTS

Concerts and classical music entertainment as Westerners tend to know them are not part of the city's allure. Concerts here tend to be infrequent, and if any are held, it's usually in the high-season winter months. Inquire at the tourist office for details.

LOCAL CULTURAL ENTERTAINMENT

The folkloric entertainment in the city's hotels has already been cited. See also the remarks regarding the Ancien Casino de Marrakech, below.

Although *fantasias* in Marrakesh are nearly always held for the benefit of tourists, they still make a good show with tribal dancing, music, and regional food—all that combined with the charge of the Berber cavaliers. Bookings are often made through your hotel. A major center for this type of amusement is the recommendation immediately following.

RESTAURANT CHAOUIA, Rouge de Guemassa. Tel. 429-15.

This restaurant is in Menara, close to the airport (1½ miles outside of town), and it caters to groups who usually arrive en masse by motorcoach in time for the elaborate displays of horsemanship, dancing, swordplay, exhibition combat, and music. Call ahead for show times, then reserve a private table for yourself and your group. Dinner (daily 8:30pm to midnight) is served either in an indoor restaurant or in tents flanking the edges of a playing field. The menu includes typically Moroccan tajines, brochettes, and grills; a complete meal costs 130–150 DH ($16.25–$18.75). Transportation: Grand taxi.

ANCIEN CASINO DE MARRAKECH, av. el Kadissia (without number). Tel. 488-11.

Its name is deceptive because there is actually no gambling of any kind. Nonetheless, it offers one of the most comprehensive exposures to the folkloric arts of Morocco anywhere in the country. Although you might object to the touristic overtones, you'll see, crammed into one *spectacle*, as many as nine different acrobats, a team from the Rif mountains dancing with candles, jugglers, snake charmers, Bedouin dancers, "blue men" (simultaneously bathed in blue light) from the deep south dancing the legendary *guedra* with sabers and veils, plus a selection of the region's best belly dancers. This cabaret is housed within an annex of the Hotel Es Saadi. Some guests come for the fixed-price four-course dinner, costing 270 DH ($33.75). If you've already eaten and just want to see the show, you can just buy drinks. It opens for dinner daily at 9pm; shows are daily from 10:30 to 11:45pm. Transportation: Petit taxi.

Admission: 100 DH ($12.50), including first drink.

THE BAR & DISCO SCENE

PIANO BAR, Hotel Mamounia, av. Bab Jdid (without number). Tel. 489-81.

Located off the lobby of the Hotel Mamounia, it's without equal in Marrakesh for sophisticated Western urban flair. The interior is deliberately underlit except for the brilliant spotlights focused upon a very large piano. A series of entertainers supplies a warm, soulful, unapologetically North American sound. Notice especially the very good portraits of past jazz artists hanging above the bar. Drinks are 90 DH ($11.25) and beer is 40 DH ($5). It's open daily from 6pm to 1am. Transportation: Petit or grand taxi.

DISCO PARADISE, Hotel Club Pullman Mansour Eddahbi, av. de France (without number). Tel. 482-22.

Reputed to have one of the best sound systems in Marrakesh, the Paradise is connected to the massive conference hotel already described. Jackets and ties are not required for men, and the clientele—perhaps more than at any other disco in town—will vary according to whichever convention group happens to fill the hotel. Average drinks cost 75 DH ($9.40). It's open daily from 10pm to 7am. Transportation: Petit taxi.

Admission: 80 DH ($10), including first drink.

BAR ACAJOU, Hotel Imperial Borj, av. Echchouada (without number), Quartier Hivernage. Tel. 473-22.

Despite the name, French for "mahogany," you'll find far more brass, granite, and leather at this bar than wood. The staff is charming, and the view extends out onto a swimming pool designed like a desert oasis, barricaded from the rest of the hotel by an ever-blooming rose garden. There is no admission charge. Drinks cost 50 DH ($6.25), and beer is 20 to 30 DH ($2.50 to $3.75). The place is open daily from 9am to 1am. Transportation: Petit taxi.

COTTON CLUB, Hotel Tropicana, Semlalia. Tel. 339-13.

In this busy and animated disco within the least expensive of a trio of adjacent hotels, the music is loud and the ambience amusing. Although there's a restaurant on the premises, many guests arrive only to drink and dance. Drinks cost 40 DH ($5). The Cotton Club is open daily from 9pm to 5am. Transportation: Petit taxi.

Admission: 60 DH ($7.50), including first drink.

MORE ENTERTAINMENT
CASINO

LE GRAND CASINO DE LA MAMOUNIA, Hotel Mamounia, av. Bab Jdid (without number). Tel. 489-81.

Entrance to the only casino in Morocco is through the lavishly decorated public rooms of the legendary Hotel Mamounia. The low-ceilinged room is slightly claustrophobic. Bets are limited to 50 DH ($6.25) each. No passport is necessary, and there is no dress code, though clients are requested not to wear jeans or espadrilles. Formally dressed croupiers tend baccarat, roulette, and blackjack tables, but the main diversion here seems to be the incessant clanging of the Atlantic City–style slot machines. There's a small and very informal restaurant within the casino. Closing time is when the last high rollers depart in the early morning air. There is no admission charge. The casino is open in summer from 8pm to "closing," in winter from 9pm to "closing." Transportation: Petit or grand taxi.

7. EASY EXCURSIONS

One of the most popular excursions to take is south of Marrakesh through the Ourika Valley (see Chapter 9).

TIZI N'TICHKA PASS & TELOUET

Reached along route S501, the pass can be visited on a day trip from Marrakesh. From a height of 7,415 feet, it offers a panoramic view of the Atlas range. From December to April, the pass may be closed until snowplows clear it. The road was constructed before World War II. Before that, it took almost two weeks to cross the pass, and travelers were often robbed by mountain bandits.

From the pass, you can travel to Telouet. The round-trip journey from Tizi n'Tichka is less than 35 miles, and the road climbs to 5,900 feet. Once at Telouet, you'll find one of the most elaborate kasbahs in Berber country. At the end of the road stands Dar Glaoui, the rambling former residence of the *caid,* on a hill overlooking the valley. After a simple lunch in this large village on the south slope of the Atlas range, you can journey back to the pass and return to Marrakesh, having traveled a distance of about 180 miles.

THE HIGH ATLAS & THE DEEP SOUTH

- **WHAT'S SPECIAL ABOUT THE HIGH ATLAS & THE DEEP SOUTH**
- **SUGGESTED ITINERARY**
1. **VALLÉE DE L'OURIKA**
2. **ASNI**
3. **OUARZAZATE**
4. **ZAGORA**
5. **EL KELÂA DES M'GOUNA**
6. **BOUMALNE DU DADÈS**
7. **TINERHIR**
8. **ER RACHIDIA**
9. **ERFOUD**

The most legendary mountains of North Africa, the High Atlas range separates Marrakesh from the Sahara desert. Some destinations can be reached as day trips from Marrakesh, while others can be combined into a trip of several days' duration. For example, you can take a 5-hour drive over the High Atlas to the walled city of Ouarzazate, gateway to the Sahara. This old town lies at the crossroads of the desert road to Agadir, the Tizi n'Tichka Pass, the Drâa Valley, and the Dadès Valley.

After exploring Ouarzazate, you can head east. The mud-red houses look even redder under clear skies of piercing blue. This is the trail Marlene Dietrich took when she followed Gary Cooper into the desert in the 1930 version of *Morocco*. The Deep South—south of the Atlas mountains—is just the place to experience that Foreign Legion–style exotica.

Many of the dynasties that later dominated all of Morocco originated here. A few comfortable government-built hotels are found along this trail, but you must always call ahead for reservations, since many places are completely booked by French-speaking tour groups. The heat is dry, although in summer the mercury is likely to hit 107°F.

In your journey through the Deep South of Morocco, with the desert outpost of Erfoud as your final destination, you cross a vast desert plateau relieved by kasbahs and oases with welcoming palm groves. As you make your way through the valleys, you'll be taking the same roads traveled by ancient trading caravans from black Africa.

SEEING THE HIGH ATLAS & THE DEEP SOUTH

GETTING THERE

The fastest way is on a direct flight to Ouarzazate on Royal Air Inter from Marrakesh (the major gateway), Agadir, or Casablanca. Ouarzazate can also be visited on a daily bus ride from Marrakesh and can be your gateway for exploring the rest of the Deep South, where there is no train service. However, Marrakesh is the major launching pad for car trips through the area. From Ouarzazate, the P32 leads you across the Route of the Kasbahs.

WHAT'S SPECIAL ABOUT THE HIGH ATLAS & THE DEEP SOUTH

Great Towns/Villages

☐ Erfoud, a frontier town, gateway to the Sahara, evoking memories of the French Foreign Legion of the 1930s.

☐ Zagora, best center for the Drâa Valley and the last stop before "gazelle country."

Ace Attractions

☐ Vallée de l'Ourika, one of the most popular excursions south of Marrakesh; among Morocco's most beautiful valleys.

☐ Gorges du Dadès, one of the most stunning natural attractions of Morocco.

☐ Gorges du Todra, 9 miles north of Tinerhir; Morocco's answer to the Grand Canyon.

The Best Kasbahs

☐ Kasbah of Taourirt at Ouarzazate, a Saharan-style fortress, one of the most beautiful kasbahs of Morocco.

☐ Kasbah of Tiffoultoute, outside Ouarzazate, once the residence of the powerful Glaoui, "lords of the Atlas."

Great Routes

☐ Route of the Kasbahs, which cuts east through southern Morocco, filled with tribal strongholds and oases.

☐ Drâa Valley, rising in the High Atlas mountains, a series of canyons and narrow valleys known for their cliffs of black or green rocks.

SUGGESTED ITINERARY

Day 1: While based in Marrakesh (see Chapter 8), explore the Vallée de l'Ourika (Ourika Valley).

Days 2–3: Journey south to Ouarzazate. You'll spend most of the day just getting there. Use the following day to explore the Kasbah and attractions in the environs.

Day 4: Take the secondary road, the P31, south to Zagora for the night. Spend what remains of the day and the following morning sightseeing.

Day 5: Drive back to Ouarzazate but cut east before reaching the town; stay overnight in El Kelâa des M'Gouna.

Day 6: Continue to Boumalne du Dadès and use it as a base for exploring the first part of the Gorges du Dadès. Continue to Tinerhir in the east for the night.

Day 7: Venture into the Gorges du Todra, then continue east to Er Rachidia for the night.

Day 8: Drive south from Er Rachidia to Erfoud. There are many interesting excursions using Erfoud as a base. Give it another day if you have the time to spare.

A NOTE ON ARCHITECTURE

During your visit to this arid sub-Sahara region of southern Morocco, you'll be very aware of a style of Berber architecture more plentiful here than anywhere else. Fortresses known as *ksour* (singular, *ksar*) were built by local chieftains to protect their tribes from invaders. Many sociologists cite them as examples of the aesthetic durability of Berber art forms, since they have descended virtually unchanged for thousands of years.

Construction is of sun-dried mud, sometimes mixed with a binder of chopped straw or pulverized palm trunks. The local word for the building material is *pisé*. The structures are easily damaged by water and windstorms, and require constant maintenance. Windows are rare, although a central courtyard admits light and air into the interior. Access is via one monumental door.

These are not museums but places where families live. Admire them from a distance. Nonetheless, a view of dozens of these ksour along the valleys of southern Morocco is one of the most memorable sights in all of Africa.

DESERT TRAVELING TIPS

The best way by far to reach each of the destinations in this chapter is by car. Weighed against the inconvenience and discomfort of other modes of transportation, the cost of a rental car is well worth the expense.

Local buses and perhaps *grands taxis* are available at major town centers. These taxis are shared; you pay only for your seat. Most bus trips, especially those in midsummer, begin very early in the morning to avoid the intense heat. Buses are not air-conditioned and tend to be overcrowded, making it an exhausting way to travel.

If you do rent a car, make sure it is in good working order. If you break down along the road in the intense desert heat, you might find it difficult to reach a garage for repairs. Sometimes you'll have to wait until a police car comes along. Gasoline is occasionally in short supply at certain places, and stations tend to be far apart, so never let your gas gauge fall below the halfway mark.

Always carry plenty of water, which you should drink even if you don't feel particularly thirsty. (You can get dehydrated very quickly here.) Extra bottles of water are also useful if your car radiator overheats.

Surprisingly, the desert highways are excellent, well maintained by the Moroccan government as part of their national security system. Secondary roads are less so. Make sure your spare tire has the correct pressure; flats are not uncommon.

Avoid driving during midday in midsummer. Temperatures can reach 120°F. Winter is the preferred time to travel here. Even then, the days are hot; the nights, however, are cool.

Regardless of how tempting an oasis looks, don't stop to cool your feet in some river or stream. The water could be swarming with a nasty little parasite, bilharzia, that is so powerful that it can enter your bloodstream through the soles of your feet.

---

1. VALLÉE DE L'OURIKA

42 miles S of Marrakesh

GETTING THERE   By Grand Taxi   In lieu of any adequate public transportation, you can rent a grand taxi from Marrakesh for a day tour of the valley. If you can bargain, prices tend to be reasonable, depending on how many are in your group. A single seat usually costs no more than 15 DH ($1.90).

By Car   This is a far more reliable way to see the valley. Head south from Marrakesh along route S513, entering the valley at Dar Caid Ouriki.

ESSENTIALS   If you attempt to make calls to hotels in the valley, you will have to go through the telephone operator, since, at press time, there's no direct-dialing system in this area.

A motor jaunt to the cool highlands of the narrow Vallée de l'Ourika (Ourika Valley), which cuts deeply into the High Atlas, has always been the most popular excursion from Marrakesh. In summer, its cooler temperatures and groves of eucalyptus, oleander, and almonds give respite from the blast furnace of the desert.

WHAT TO SEE & DO

The valley technically begins 20 miles southeast of Marrakesh. **Dar Caid Ouriki**, noted for its painted minaret, is one of the first Berber villages you'll encounter. The road narrows significantly at this point, and the dusty flatlands become cooler. At the town of Arhbalou, the road will fork, leading west to the ski resort of Oukaïmeden or east to the less developed holy village of **Setti Fatima**. Most visitors opt for Setti Fatima, which marks the end of human habitation within the Ourika Valley, at a point 42 miles from Marrakesh.

The final half mile of the ascent to Setti Fatima requires a strenuous walk, and the path is frequently washed away by floods. If you're especially adventurous, you might attempt the climb, but most motorists admire the panorama from the end of the road, then very wisely turn back. Setti Fatima is the site of an annual *moussem* (pilgrimage) to the shrine of the Islamic saint for whom the town is named, and is known for its waterfalls and streams.

If you do choose to visit Oukaïmeden, you'll continue 20 miles beyond Arhbalou, along a road that climbs dramatically with hairpin turns and frightening cliffs. There is a continually unfolding view of the High Atlas mountains, Berber settlements clinging to cliffs, and intricately terraced gardens.

Oukaïmeden ("the meeting place of the four winds") is the centerpiece of Morocco's fledgling ski industry, and the departure point for several wintertime chair and ski lifts. It contains a not-very-memorable collection of modern chalets, lots of rock, and cement pylons for the ski lifts. You'll pay 5 DH (65¢) to enter the resort. There is no particular view of anything from Oukaïmeden itself, but a sweeping panorama is available from the Tizerag TV relay station, about a mile's drive along the continuation of the road you used to enter the resort. A handful of badly eroded prehistoric rock carvings exist nearby, but you'll need a local guide to find them.

WHERE TO STAY & EAT

INEXPENSIVE

HOTEL OURIKA, Vallée de l'Ourika, route S513, Arhbalou. Tel. 339-93.
22 rms (all with bath). **Transportation:** Grand taxi from Marrakesh.
$ Rates: 215 DH ($26.90) single; 265 DH ($32.50) double. Breakfast 21 DH ($2.65) extra. MC, V.

An unexpected island of sophistication at the foothills of the High Atlas range, 28 miles southeast of Marrakesh. On a ledge above the road that splits the Ourika Valley, the hotel offers mountain views from nearly every bedroom window. There's even an alpine-inspired fireplace in one of the sunny public rooms, to take off the afternoon chill in the high altitudes. Most of the pine-trimmed bedrooms have terraces. Fixed-price meals in the pleasant dining room go for 110 DH ($13.75). Even if you can't stay overnight, I recommend a stop for lunch.

HOTEL RAMUNTCHO, Vallée de l'Ourika, route S513, Arhbalou par Marrakech. Tel. 118 Arhbalou. 12 rms (all with bath). **Transportation:** Grand taxi from Marrakesh.
$ Rates (including half board): 245 DH ($30.65) per person. MC, V.

A roadside inn on the lower portion of the winding road cutting through the Ourika Valley, it has been known for four decades for its hearty food and pleasant rooms. The terrace dining room, partially shaded by orange trees, overlooks the river. A country tavern atmosphere prevails, with rugged stone walls, a raised hearth, and large windows. Meals are served daily from 12:30 to 3pm and 7:30 to 10pm; a six-course meal costs 110 DH ($13.75), including a wide choice of hors d'oeuvres; a fish or egg dish; one of eight main-course choices, such as *tajine* (lamb, veal, or chicken cooked with prunes or onions); a salad course; and dessert.

---

2. ASNI

32 miles S of Marrakesh

GETTING THERE **By Bus** Six buses daily from Bab Doukkala, the principal bus station in Marrakesh, the trip taking 2 hours.

By Car   South from Marrakesh along route S501 toward Tizi n' Test.

ESSENTIALS   Phone calls to this area require operator assistance.

_____

Many city dwellers escape in the summer to this Berber village, noted for its kasbah. At an altitude of 4,000 feet, surrounded by the highest peaks of the High Atlas (Mount Toubkal, 13,665 feet), the view is impressive. The town is easily reached on a morning's excursion.

From Asni you can continue southwest on the Taroudannt road to Tizi n'Test, at 6,890 feet, one of the most magnificent mountain panoramas in the High Atlas, with the Souss Valley spread out before you.

WHERE TO STAY & EAT

INEXPENSIVE

GRAND HOTEL DU TOUBKAL, km. 45, route de Taroudannt, Asni. Tel. 3 Asni. 31 rms (all with bath). **Transportation:** Bus from Marrakesh.
$ Rates (including half board): 320 DH ($40) single; 430 DH ($53.75) double. MC, V.

This kasbah hotel, built in 1945 and restored in 1970, retains the building's original filigreed stone ceilings, the exposed wood, and the patterned mosaics. The establishment's reception desk fills an unlikely corner of the high-ceilinged dining room, where big windows provide views of the snow-covered peaks of the High Atlas mountains. Each of the 31 bedrooms is clean and sunny, with handwoven bedspreads and tile floors; some rooms have balconies. Even if you don't stay overnight, the courteous staff will welcome you to lunch. There are tables beside a rose garden and a grove of apple, pear, and cherry trees. Fixed-price meals cost 115 DH ($14.40) and feature Berber specialties.

AN EXCURSION TO VAL D'OURIGANE

Eight miles south of Asni, on the road to Tizi-n-Test (S501), is one of the loveliest and most tranquil retreats near Marrakesh—Val d'Ourigane. There is no direct-dial phone service. The operator will place your call.

WHERE TO STAY & EAT

Moderate

LA ROSERAIE, Val d'Ourigane, km. 60, route de Marrakesh— Taroudannt. Tel. 4 Ourigane. 30 rms (all with bath). **Transportation:** Bus from Asni.
$ Rates: 425 DH ($53.15) single; 730 DH ($91.25) double. Breakfast 25 DH ($3.15) extra. MC, V.

⭐ Established shortly after World War II by the German-born Count Meckenheim, who lavished time and money on the 54 acres surrounding it, the property was bought in the 1970s by a Moroccan entrepreneur who built a cluster of well-furnished bungalows, added a rectangular swimming pool, and transformed it into one of the most charming hotels in all of Morocco. A dozen gardeners maintain the thousands of roses. Brick sidewalks connect the many outbuildings, a sauna, clay tennis courts, and a stable of horses for rent. The lushness of the grounds is striking, given the dusty countryside that surrounds them. Of the 30 rooms contained in the outlying bungalows, most have kitchens and a few have fireplaces; all have private bathrooms. There are two restaurants—one European and the other Moroccan. The honey served at breakfast comes from bees kept on the property, where many of the teas, tisanes, and herbs that are served are also cultivated and collected.

FARTHER AFIELD TO TOUBKAL NATIONAL PARK

Its major village is Asni, and its centerpiece is the highest mountaintop in North Africa, **Mount Toubkal,** at 13,665 feet above sea level. Some visitors enjoy the climb, which, while relatively safe in summer, is ice-covered and treacherous in winter and suitable only for experienced climbers.

A round trip from Asni requires a local guide with a mule and at least 18 hours. It's usually broken up into two days, with an overnight stay at a mountain shelter in a hamlet called Nelter. Without a guide, the trails are baffling. You can arrange for guides at the **Grand Hotel du Toubkal,** in Asni, or at the **Centre National des Sports de Montagne,** B.P. 672 (tel. 04/44-74-48), in Marrakesh.

Less ambitious climbers usually head for the small village of **Imlil,** which offers a series of trails for day hikes along the mountain's lower altitudes.

---

3. OUARZAZATE

127 miles S of Marrakesh

GETTING THERE   By Plane   An airport is half a mile northeast of Ouarzazate. There are flights from Marrakesh, Casablanca, Agadir, and Er Rachidia. For tickets and flight **information,** call 146.

By Bus   Four buses leave Marrakesh daily, heading south to Ouarzazate and taking 4 to 5 hours, depending on the connection.

By Car   Take the winding route P31 southeast of Marrakesh.

ESSENTIALS   Orientation   Once in Ouarzazate, you can walk to most places or rent a grand taxi leaving from place Mouhadine. Make sure that you get into a taxi servicing the town, as some of these vehicles go all the way to Marrakesh.

Information   The **Ouarzazate Tourist Office** is found on avenue Moham-med V (tel. 088/24-85), open Monday through Friday from 8:30am to noon and 2:30 to 6pm.

Fast Facts   Area code is 088. For a drug store, try **Pharmacie de Nuit,** on avenue Mohammed V (tel. 27-08) across from the post office; open daily from 8am to 7:30pm. The **Ouarzazate Police Station** is also on avenue Mohammed V (tel. 19), as is the **Ouarzazate Post Office** (don't try to call—show up in person). The latter is open in summer Monday through Saturday from 7am to 2:30pm; from mid-September through June, Monday through Saturday from 8:30am to noon and 2:30 to 6pm. It is next to the tourist office (see above) and near the bus station.

Reached after a half day's journey through the High Atlas mountains from Marrakesh, it appears as an oasis of palm trees—surrounded by the endless desert. Because of its position near the junction of the Drâa and Dadès valleys, it has a good selection of hotels.

Although the ramparts look older, Ouarzazate was built by the French as a military garrison in 1928. Some visitors consider it a look-alike for a movie set (in fact, David Lean shot many scenes for his classic *Lawrence of Arabia* here) until the dust and grime and color of its shops, souks, and medinas bring it into a vivid and immediate reality.

Today, Ouarzazate is something of a tourist boom town, with the largest population in the region, almost 65,000. Also the capital of a sun-baked district containing more than a half a million inhabitants, the city gives its name to a desirable style of carpet—*les tapis de Ouarzazate* or *les tapis Ouzguita,* named after the tribe that developed the original forms. Dotted with geometric forms and occasionally depicting men, camels, and even cows (technically not permitted within the Islamic canon), they are loosely woven and make charming souvenirs of a trip to the region.

WHAT TO SEE & DO

About a mile east of Ouarzazate on the Boumalne road stands the **Kasbah of Taourirt,** a richly decorated (though much restored) Saharan fortress. This is one of the most beautiful kasbahs in Morocco, characterized by angled walls and square-based towers, each pierced with openings and having crenellated tops. It was the residence of the Glaoui, the "lords of the Atlas," and the family home of the pasha of Marrakesh. Private houses are built around the base, almost one on top of the other, rising up the slope. You can see the rooms used by the Glaoui, including a chamber reserved for "the favorite." Admission is 10 DH ($1.25), and daily hours are 8am to 6pm.

Two miles beyond the town is a **film studio** you might visit (open daily from 8am to 8pm). *Lawrence of Arabia, The Jewel of the Nile,* and *Jesus of Nazareth* were shot in the area.

Eight miles west on the route to Zagora stands the **Kasbah of Tiffoultoute** (take the turnoff onto route P31, the Marrakesh road, for 2 miles). It dominates the palm-fringed valley of Ouarzazate. From here you'll have a beautiful view of the High Atlas. Open daily from 8am to noon and 3 to 7pm; admission is 10 DH ($1.25). To get to Tiffoultoute by public transportation, you need to rent one of the grands taxis leaving from Ouarzazate. Your single share is about 65 DH ($8.15) for a round trip.

WHERE TO STAY & EAT

EXPENSIVE

HOTEL KARAM PALACE, bd. Prince Moulay Rachid (without number), Ouarzazate. Tel. 088/22-25. 150 rms (all with bath). A/C TV TEL **Transportation:** Grand taxi.
$ Rates: 650 DH ($81.25) single; 700 DH ($87.50) double. Breakfast 50 DH ($6.25) extra. AE, DC, MC, V.

On a plateau above the oldest part of the city, the hotel was designed to look as much like a modernized version of a kasbah as possible. Inside you'll find one of the most luxurious modern interiors in southern Morocco. There's a rectangular swimming pool near the terrace, where the enclosing wall looks out over an arid valley and part of the mud-walled city beyond. There's a lattice-ringed outdoor café-bar, as well as landscaping and arbor-covered walkways. The modern accommodations are located in two-story bungalows, connected by passageways and Moorish courtyards. Rooms have radios and TVs. A fixed-price lunch or dinner goes for 120 DH ($15).

MODERATE

HOTEL AZGHOR, bd. Prince Moulay Rachid (without number), Ouarzazate. Tel. 088/26-12. 150 rms (all with bath). A/C TEL **Transportation:** Grand taxi.
$ Rates: 300 DH ($37.50) single; 378 DH ($47.25) double. AE, DC, MC, V.
The Azghor sits in a Europeanized suburb on a hillside away from the oldest part of the Medina. Its earth-colored tower is part of an older mud-brick hotel built in 1953; the better-maintained newer sections were constructed about 10 years later. There's a rectangular swimming pool with a breathtaking view over the valley and the mountains nearby. The rooms have a simple and functionally modern decor, with lots of wooden trim. Fixed-price meals cost 120 DH ($15), and there's a bar on the ground floor with modern furniture and Moroccan-made brass chandeliers.

HOTEL ZAT, Aït Gief (without number), Ouarzazate. Tel. 088/25-21. 60
rms (all with bath). A/C TEL **Transportation:** Grand taxi.
$ Rates: 300 DH ($37.50) single; 368 DH ($46) double. Breakfast 31 DH ($3.90)
extra. AE, DC, MC, V.

Ⓢ Modern, pleasant, and clean, it not only serves the best food in town—fixed-
price meals start at 105 DH ($13.15)—but boasts a swimming pool, a gift shop,
and a bar. Rooms are functionally furnished, made even more comfortable
following a 1990 renovation.

BUDGET

**HOTEL GAZELLE, av. Mohammed V (without number), Ouarzazate. Tel.
088/21-51.** 30 rms (all with bath). **Transportation:** Grand taxi.
$ Rates: 94 DH ($11.75) single; 112 DH ($14) double; 148 DH ($18.50) triple. No
credit cards.
Built in the mid-1970s, this hotel is for serious economizers. Still, the staff is friendly
and cooperative, and the plain dining room serves well-prepared dinners—inside
under plaster-filigree friezes, as well as outside on the pleasant terrace. Fixed-price
meals begin at 65 DH ($8.15).

---

4. ZAGORA

107 miles SE of Ouarzazate; 225 miles SE of Marrakesh

GETTING THERE   By Bus Two buses daily between Ouarzazate and Zagora,
taking 4 hours. From Ouarzazate, bus connections can be made to Marrakesh.

By Car From Ouarzazate, continue southeast along route P31.

ESSENTIALS Zagora cannot be dialed directly, and can be reached by phone
only through the state operator.

A thriving village in the Drâa Valley, Zagora is the last stop before gazelle country
and the desert. From the top of Djebel (Mount) Zagora, you have a panoramic
view of desert and valley. The town, whose main boulevard is avenue Mohammed V,
contains the ruins of a **fortress** built in the 11th century by the Almoravids. The very
existence of its foundations is considered unusual, because the Almohads, who
supplanted the Almoravids, usually destroyed all architectural remains. To reach the
ruins of the stone fortress, cross the Drâa Bridge and walk in the direction of the sign
pointing to *Camping Montagne,* a site in the foreground of the sugarloaf Mount
Zagora.

Market days at the souks in Zagora are Wednesday and Sunday, when special dates
from the desert are sold. A local date called *boufeggous* is said to be the best-tasting
in Morocco. You'll also see some souks selling the indigo-dyed cotton cloth of the
"blue men" of the desert, so named because the dyed cloth acts to discolor the skin.

From Zagora, go to **Tamegroute,** 10 miles south, to view the **Zaouia
Nasseria,** an ancient library containing illustrated antique Korans written on gazelle
skin—the oldest dating from the 13th century. Non-Muslims are allowed into the
library, a historic center of Islamic monasticism. The village also has several potteries
in a small souk. Metal goods and rather reasonably priced carpets are also sold.

The highway doesn't actually end in Zagora, or even in Tamegroute, but continues
to **M'hamid,** the final outpost before the desert. If you're traveling south from
Zagora, you must apply for special permission at the police barricade beside the traffic
circle south of the center of town (Cercle de Zagora).

The 59-mile journey to M'hamid takes you over rough roads (you are likely to be
stopped by the police several times on the way there). At M'hamid, the water of the
Drâa Valley comes to an end and the vast wasteland of the Sahara begins.

At this military outpost, camel rides in the desert can be arranged—you'll see the animals waiting near the old fort of M'hamid. On camelback you're taken past ruined ksour. Once at an oasis, you can lounge on layers of carpets and flamboyantly covered pillows for a "picnic under the palms," finishing with sticky sweet almond pastries and the traditional mint tea.

Back in Zagora, you'll note a famous sign on the main square, TIMBUKTU 52 JOURS—that's 52 days by camel across the desert to this legendary city.

WHERE TO STAY & EAT
EXPENSIVE

PULLMAN HOTEL REDA, Zagora. Tel. 149 ("par la poste"). 155 rms (all with bath). A/C TEL **Transportation:** Petit taxi.

$ Rates: 560 DH ($70) single or double. Breakfast 50 DH ($6.25) extra. AE, DC, MC, V.

Built in 1987 as one of the most stylish hotels in the region, it's a short walk south of the town center. Each of the modern bedrooms is simply but comfortably furnished, with a modern bathroom, and each has a balcony. There are two swimming pools, plus tennis courts. A fixed-price meal in the hotel dining room costs 130 DH ($16.25).

INEXPENSIVE

HOTEL TINSOULINE, Zagora. Tel. 22. 90 rms (all with bath). A/C TEL

$ Rates: 222 DH ($27.75) single; 234 DH ($29.30) double. Breakfast 31 DH ($3.90) extra. AE, DC, MC, V.

In the center of town, this hotel offers 90 adequate rooms, each with private bath or shower. Try for a room overlooking the gardens. The swimming pool is a welcome sight after a trek through the desert. The bar, the lounges, and the restaurant are appealing. A tourist dinner costs 100 DH ($12.50).

5. EL KELÂA DES M'GOUNA

31 miles E of Skoura; 57 miles E of Ouarzazate

GETTING THERE **By Bus** El Kelâa des M'Gouna lies on the main bus route between Ouarzazate and Er Rachidia.

By Car Follow the P32 east, passing through Skoura, the first main town you approach on the Route of the Kasbahs. Continue east from Skoura until you reach El Kelâa des M'Gouna.

ESSENTIALS The area code is 088.

The oasis at El Kelaa des M'Gouna, with its huge accumulation of nearby ksour, makes a good stopover between Ouarzazate and Tinerhir. The town is famous for the rose bushes that line the main roads and for the massive quantities of rose water produced by the town's only industry. Local shops are amply stocked with what seem to be thousands of bottles of it. Set upon a Saharan plateau, the town is also known for its annual springtime rose festival. Wednesday is souk (market) day.

WHERE TO STAY & EAT
MODERATE

KTH HOTEL DES ROSES DU DADÈS, El Kelâa des M'Gouna. Tel. 088/18. 102 rms (all with bath). A/C TEL

$ Rates: 264 DH ($33) single; 322 DH ($40.25) double; 446 DH ($55.75) triple. Breakfast 31 DH ($3.90) extra. AE, DC, MC, V.

The KTH is so isolated, and the town around it is so dusty, that you'll be surprised at the elegance here. Visible from its perch on a plateau dominating the town, the main building contains a pair of inviting courtyards and a cool decor of tile, wood, and marble. A spacious modern dining room offers views of the desert; fixed-price meals begin at 120 DH ($15). Upstairs, on a raised terrace, the lovely pool offers relief from the scorching sun. There's an unusual bar with lots of exposed wood and a lively ambience, especially when tour buses stop by. The rooms are Spartan, with tile surfaces and simple furniture.

The well-stocked gift shop offers some of the best values in the region on handwoven Bedouin carpets, although you'll have to negotiate hard to get a really good price. There are two tennis courts, and horseback riding through the valley can be arranged by the hotel.

AN EXCURSION TO THE DADÈS VALLEY

★ If you return to Ouarzazate in the northwest, you can take an entirely different route this time, heading east into one of the most visited regions in the south of Morocco, the world-famous Route of the Kasbahs, which follows the path of the Oued Dadès (Dadès River.)

Of the several different valleys that irrigate the sun-blasted landscapes of the northern Sahara, the Dadès is the widest and most fertile. Its waters begin as a mountain stream flowing southwest from the High Atlas. Famed for its roses, which have thrived under irrigation for hundreds of years, the valley has traditionally served as a busy thoroughfare for east-west transit through this part of the desert. Thanks to irrigation, the valley has a healthy diversity of crops, a permanent population of 80,000 residents, and some of the most interesting rural architecture in Morocco.

6. BOUMALNE DU DADÈS

72 miles E of Ouarzazate

GETTING THERE   By Bus   Boumalne du Dadès is on the bus route linking Ouarzazate to Tinerhir (see below). Three buses leave Ouarzazate daily, taking 2½ hours.

By Car   From Ouarzazate, continue along the Route of the Kasbahs (P32), passing through Skoura and El Kelâa des M'Gouna, until you come to Boumalne.

ESSENTIALS   Telephone calls to this town require operator assistance.

As you continue along the Dadès Valley, the road takes you past several imposing ksour, ranging from splendid palaces to medieval fortresses, that seem to emerge from palm groves and tamarisks. The narrow road has many hairpin turns. The mountain scenery is exceptionally beautiful, and the gorges are lush and green. The rocks glow red or mauve, depending on the light and the time of day.

WHERE TO STAY & EAT

MODERATE

PLM HOTEL MADAYEQ, Boumalne du Dadès. Tel. 31. 100 rms (all with bath). A/C TEL
$ Rates: 264 DH ($33) single; 322 DH ($40.25) double. Breakfast 31 DH ($3.90) extra. MC, V.
From the outside, the hotel looks like a heavily fortified kasbah, but inside, you'll find

a handful of courtyards filled with plants, a spacious cafe, and a collection of well-decorated public rooms. Bedrooms are comfortable, with tile baths, small terraces, and phones. There's a swimming pool on the rooftop terrace. At the pleasant restaurant, well worth a luncheon stopover, fixed-price meals cost from 120 DH ($15).

AN EXCURSION TO THE GORGES DU DADÈS

Boumalne du Dadès is considered the departure point for visits to the famous Gorges du Dadès. Considered one of the geological oddities of Morocco, they are dramatically beautiful canyons carved out of the limestone bedrock of the High Atlas mountains by erosion of the Dadès River. They stretch over more than 30 miles of the river's uppermost region, only part of which can be traveled in a conventional vehicle. Despite the wildness of the terrain, the district is heavily populated by mountain tribespeople, who inhabit and maintain the dozens of kasbahs that line the sides of the road and seem to emerge like natural extensions of the rocks and sands upon which they were built. Few (if any) of the individual villages have names signposted beside the road.

The gorges begin about a mile northeast of Boumalne, following the path of route 6901. Most visitors enjoy the view from their cars, although some explore parts of the area on foot. (This is recommended only for the most hardy and experienced climbers.)

Although intrepid motorists and hikers can continue along this road until it degenerates into a barely navigable path best traversed by army vehicles, most visitors end their foray at the only bridge that traverses the gorge, at the village of Aït Oudinar, 15 miles northeast of your starting point at Boumalne. (Although the path theoretically continues for another 18 miles beyond the bridge, it grows increasingly narrow and potholed, with a constant danger of rock slides and springtime floods. In fact, the road is so notoriously bad that the insurance policies on many rental cars do not apply to treks into the gorges several miles beyond the bridge.)

7. TINERHIR

33 miles E of Boumalne du Dadès;
105 miles E of Ouarzazate

GETTING THERE   By Bus   Three buses daily from Ouarzazate, taking 5 hours. Several connections a day are possible from Boumalne du Dadès, taking 50 minutes.

By Car   Continue along the P32 from Boumalne du Dadès to the next major stopover at Tinerhir.

ESSENTIALS   Because there is no direct dialing to Tinerhir, telephone calls must be made through the operator.

The capital of Tafilalet province, with a population of less than 3,000, is built on a hill above an oasis, and was once a garrison for the French Foreign Legion. The **Kasbah of Tinerhir**, now ruined and awash with graffiti, was once controlled by the Glaoui tribe. In the environs of the town, numerous ksour overlook palm and olive groves and walnut trees. The flowers from the walnut trees are processed here to extract the oil.

WHERE TO STAY & EAT
MODERATE

HOTEL SARGHO, Tinerhir. Tel. 01. 60 rms (all with bath). A/C **Directions:** Follow signs to the hotel at the western approach to town.
$ Rates: 262 DH ($32.75) single; 328 DH ($41) double. Breakfast 31 DH ($3.90) extra. MC, V.

S At first glance, you might have thought that the red-ocher walls of this hotel contained an inhospitable ksar similar to the many ancient ones that surround the rest of the town. Inside, however, you'll find comparative luxury, with cool and comfortably furnished bedrooms. Facilities include a swimming pool, a bar, and a restaurant where the tourist menu starts at 120 DH ($15). From its terraces there's a panoramic view of the surroundings.

AN EASY EXCURSION

★ From Tinerhir, you can visit the **Gorges du Todra,** the "Grand Canyon of Morocco," beginning 9 miles north of the town. Chiseled from the rocks by the life-sustaining waters of the Oued Todra (Todra River), the gorges' banks are lined with palms. The contrast of the vibrantly green vegetation against the reddish-brown rocks is memorable. The tarmac road leading from Tinerhir to the mouth of the gorges is lined with family-dominated kasbahs, and what seems to be a perpetual and uninterrupted palm grove. Two miles from the mouth of the gorges, 7 miles north of Tinerhir, is the Zaouia (religious college) of Sidi Abdelali, with a nearby spring that reputedly cures female infertility.

There is no real road within or atop the gorges. The tarmac road leading from Tinerhir ends abruptly at a rock face, then continues in the form of a gravel track skirting the river. Rock cliffs rise dramatically more than 1,000 feet on either side, and vegetation thrives within the cool moist confines of the canyons. According to local legend, this abyss was created when a djin attacked the mountains with his saber.

---

8. ER RACHIDIA

110 miles E of Ouarzazate; 316 miles E of Marrakesh

GETTING THERE By Bus   Two buses daily from Tinerhir, taking 3 hours. Three buses daily from Fez (8½ hours) and 1 from Meknes (8 hours).

By Car   From Tinerhir, the P32 (Route of the Kasbahs) continues its run to Er Rachidia.

ESSENTIALS   The area code is 057.

Once known as Ksar-es-Souk, Er Rachidia is essentially a large palm grove, with a bustling market on the main square. It's in the valley of the Ziz, at the crossing of two ancient routes—the road from Meknes to the oasis of Tafilalet and the Deep South Atlas Highway to southern Algeria. It became important when it served as a supply base for the French Foreign Legion.

If you're coming from Erfoud, you can visit the **Blue Springs** at Meski, 11 miles north of Er Rachidia. The **Cirque de Jaffar,** a natural amphitheater near Midelt, 75 miles from Er Rachidia, is another possible excursion.

WHERE TO STAY & EAT

MODERATE

HOTEL RISSANI, Er Rachidia. Tel. 057/21-86. Fax 057/25-85. 60 rms (all with bath). A/C TEL
$ Rates: 310 DH ($38.75) single; 398 DH ($49.75) double; 484 DH ($60.50) triple. Breakfast 31 DH ($3.90) extra. No credit cards.
Surrounded by lovely gardens, this modern hotel is east of the town center, at the

bridge spanning the Oued Ziz (Ziz River). It has a rectangular swimming pool, an outdoor terrace overlooking the nearby village, and rooms with terrazzo floors and big windows. Fixed-price meals go for 109 DH ($13.65) to 140 DH ($17.50).

INEXPENSIVE

HOTEL MESKI, Er Rachidia. Tel. 057/20-65. 25 rms (9 with bath).

$ Rates: 85 DH ($10.65) single without bath; 102 DH ($12.75) single with bath; 102 DH ($12.75) double without bath; 122 DH ($15.25) double with bath. Breakfast 15 DH ($1.90) extra. No credit cards.

S A true no-frills bargain, the Meski is on the P32 at the western approach to town. There's a second-floor guest lounge with a sunny terrace, as well as a small oval swimming pool with an intermittent supply of water. Rooms are simple but comfortable. There's a ground-floor café.

---

9. ERFOUD

234 miles E of Ouarzazate; 48 miles S of Er Rachidia

GETTING THERE   By Bus   Four buses daily from Er Rachidia, taking 1½ hours.

By Car   From Er Rachidia, take route P21 south.

ESSENTIALS   The area code is 057.

This town (population 5,000) of oxblood-red buildings—shaded by pepper trees and eucalyptus—was built by the French in the 1930s as a gateway to the Sahara. At an altitude of 3,051 feet, Erfoud stands near the Ziz (Gazelle) River, at the foot of the Djebel Erfoud. You can explore its crowded souks and see the desert sunsets over the palm groves. The best vantage point is the **Borjd Est**, an old fortress 2 miles from the center, a long uphill walk from the main square.

South of Erfoud lies a charming oasis, **Tafilalet**, which lends its name to part of the outlying region. It's kept green by the underground waters of the Ziz and Rheris rivers. Beyond this point vegetation ceases, but the oasis itself is glorious and ancient, with fruit trees, tamarisks, and date palms. It is 9 miles wide and 12 miles long.

Drive 14 miles south to **Rissani**, with its 18th-century ksar, barracks, and souk (Tuesday or Thursday morning around 10am). On Sunday, there's an authentic Saharan camel market.

From Rissani, it is 1½ miles to the venerated and much restored **Mausoleum of Moulay Ali Cherif**, the ancient and devout ancestor of the Alaouite dynasty.

To the west of Rissani lie the ruins of **Sijilmassa**, the famous "red town." Transdesert caravans of long ago used to arrive at this most westerly Saharan terminus, bringing gold from the Sudan. Its counterpart was Timbuktu in the south.

From Erfoud you can make a dramatic and difficult excursion 31 miles south to **Merzouga**, where civilization ends and the vast wilderness of the Sahara begins. You may already be familiar with the scenery, as it was used in such films as *The Little Prince* and *Marco Polo*. It's customary to go with a guide at dawn and watch the sun rising over the Sahara.

You'll need a guide because the road is not clearly marked. You can drive to Merzouga in a regular vehicle, but because of poor road conditions, it's risky and you might find your tires sinking into the sand.

WHERE TO STAY & EAT

MODERATE

HOTEL SALAM, route de Rissani, Erfoud. Tel. 057/66-65. Fax 057/64-26. 160 rms (all with bath). A/C TEL

$ Rates: 296–475 DH ($37–$59.40) single; 368–475 DH ($46–$59.40) double. Breakfast 31 DH ($3.90) extra. AE, MC, V.

Directly south of town on the road to Rissani, this four-star hotel, which opened in 1986, looks traditional because it was constructed in Berber style, with the cement core covered with dried mud and chopped straw. A swimming pool and gardens make it feel like an oasis. Each of the small but cozy bedrooms has a beamed and plank-covered ceiling, tile-covered floors, and a Bedouin decor. The most luxurious rooms are in a new wing built in 1989. Fixed-price meals cost 120 DH ($15).

INEXPENSIVE

HOTEL TAFILALET, av. Moulay Ismail (without number), Erfoud. Tel. 057/60-36. Fax 057/60-36. 70 rms (all with bath). A/C TEL
$ Rates: 168 DH ($21) single; 210 DH ($26.25) double; 283 DH ($35.40) triple. Breakfast 30 DH ($3.75) extra. No credit cards.

On the north side of town, beside the road leading into Erfoud from Er Rachidia, this hotel has a triangular swimming pool in a pleasant garden, and an exterior designed like a modernized version of a kasbah. Rooms are simple and clean, each with a balcony. The concierge can arrange half-day Land Rover tours to nearby oases for 450 DH ($56.25) per person. Fixed-price meals cost 95 DH ($11.90) each.

CHAPTER 10

THE WESTERN SAHARA

- **SUGGESTED ITINERARY**
- **WHAT'S SPECIAL ABOUT THE WESTERN SAHARA**
- **1. GOULIMINE**
- **2. LAAYOUNE**

Isolated, inaccessible, and unlivable are three adjectives frequently applied to the vast landscape southwest of Agadir. Known today as Morocco's Western Sahara, it sprawls over an undulating, almost unbelievably harsh terrain, without many distinguishing characteristics—a wilderness of stony soil without vegetation. Its immensity is matched only by that of the undrinkable waters of the Atlantic, which flank its western edge, and the relentlessly blue skies above.

Except for the presence of the world's richest phosphate deposits, which were only discovered in the 1960s, and the force of will of the Moroccan monarch, the territory would probably have remained uncharted, unwanted, and unexplored for decades.

SEEING THE WESTERN SAHARA
GETTING THERE

Goulimine can be visited by bus or private car from Agadir, but it is best to fly to Laayoune deep in the Western Sahara from such cities as Casablanca and Agadir.

SUGGESTED ITINERARY

Day 1: Explore Goulimine and its famous camel market with so-called blue men from the desert.

Day 2: Return to Agadir and make plane connections to Laayoune, where you should book into a hotel for at least two nights.

Day 3: Explore the minor attractions of this unusual city in the desert and ask the tourist office or a local travel agency to arrange an excursion for you into the desert.

1. GOULIMINE

125 miles S of Agadir; 69 miles S of Tiznit

GETTING THERE   By Bus   Six buses daily from Tiznit, taking 2½ hours, and 2 buses daily from Agadir, taking 4½ hours.

By Car   From Agadir, continue south along the P30, passing through Tiznit. South of Tiznit at the junction with the P41, head southwest for the final lap to Goulimine.

ESSENTIALS   The area code is 087.

A thousand years ago, Goulimine was one of the desert's busiest watering holes for caravans traveling to and from Timbuktu. As late as the early 20th century, you could still buy gold, salt, silks, ivory, ebony, and slaves within its marketplace from caravan drivers from Mali, the Sudan, and the banks of the Niger.

WHAT'S SPECIAL ABOUT THE WESTERN SAHARA

Beaches
- ☐ Uncrowded beaches on the Atlantic coastline of the Western Sahara. But beware of undertows and the blistering sun.

Great Towns/Villages
- ☐ Goulimine, popular for a thousand years as a watering hole for caravans from Timbuktu.
- ☐ Laayoune, a city of 100,000 created in a vast desert wilderness once viewed as uninhabitable.

Ace Attractions
- ☐ If you've wondered what the Old Testament was talking about when saints met sinners beside desert wells, the Western Sahara is the place to see them. Nothing could be more unexpectedly verdant.
- ☐ The camel market at Goulimine, where the so-called blue men of the desert barter furiously over the perceived value of a one-humped beast.

- ☐ The souks of Laayoune. Note especially weavings designed to adorn camels and their drivers.
- ☐ The land isn't densely populated, but the offshore sea is, offering state-of-the-art deep-sea fishing trips.
- ☐ A Fleur du Desert trip, arranged by travel agents in Laayoune, takes you back to Biblical times as you live in tents of accommodating Bedouins.

Special Events/Festivals
- ☐ The *moussems* of Sidi Ahmed Rguibi, Sidi Ahmed Laaroussi, and Cheikh M'Rabbih Rabbou at Laayoune in January, February, and April, when local tribespeople gather to showcase some of their decorative arts.

Goulimine today is a dull desert outpost whose uninspiring cement-and-mud buildings shelter a population of 150,000 who spend most of the day seeking shelter from the blistering sun. Though much of its attraction—its marketplace—was dealt a serious blow during the region's guerrilla warfare, Goulimine is still famous for its **Reguibate tribesmen** ("blue men," whose skin usually bears a bluish tinge from the dyes of their traditional indigo-colored robes). Although their numbers have greatly diminished, they are the most visible early in the morning on Saturdays in winter. (There is no souk held here in summertime.) Then, they congregate for their camel market, which is held within a fenced-in stockade a short walk north of town. Another attraction is the slow and sinuous dance of the heavily veiled women, which is performed on their knees and accompanied by the insistent rhythms of a terra-cotta and animal-skin drum called a *guedra*.

WHERE TO STAY & EAT

INEXPENSIVE

HOTEL SALAM, av. Youssef Techfne (without number), Goulimine. Tel. 087/20-57. 20 rms (none with bath).
$ Rates: 108 DH ($13.50) single; 134 DH ($16.75) double. Breakfast 15 DH ($1.90) extra. No credit cards.

In the center of this small town, the Salam is the only acceptable place to stay. Its simple bedrooms are arranged around a central enclosed courtyard one floor above the reception area. Fixed-price meals in the Moroccan restaurant go for 61 DH ($7.65). A sunny terrace on the top floor has panoramic views of the town. The staff is well informed and helpful.

2. LAAYOUNE

345 miles S of Tiznit; 402 miles S of Agadir;
719 miles S of Casablanca

GETTING THERE By Plane The only way to go that I'd endorse. **Laayoune Airport,** to the east of town (tel. 22-33-46), receives flights from Agadir and Casablanca, even from Las Palmas, capital of Spain's Canary Islands, lying off the coast to the west. **Royal Air Maroc**'s booking offices are on place Bir Anzarane (tel. 22-40-77).

By Bus Buses from Agadir head south to Laayoune, passing through Goulimine, Tan Tan, and Tarfaya. However, I do not recommend traveling by bus.

By Car From Goulimine, continue south into the desert along the P41 all the way to Laayoune. Fill up the tank and take plenty of water with you, and make sure that you are driving a reliable vehicle.

Information The **Délégation du Tourisme** is on avenue de l'Islam (tel. 33-75); for tours, go to the **Agence Sahara,** located on Zeknat Kadi Ghellaoui (tel. 31-33).

ESSENTIALS

Fast Facts You can get currency exchanged at the **Banque Populaire,** bd. Mohammed V, 9 (tel. 45-11), or at the **Banque al-Maghrib,** bd. Mohammed V, 16 (tel. 41-190). You cannot telephone Laayoune directly, but only through an operator-assisted call.

Located 15 miles inland from the sea, a fortress of Moroccan nationalism within a newly populated wilderness, Laayoune is the largest, busiest, and most impressive of the new cities of the Western Sahara. Since 1976, Morocco has poured an estimated billion dollars into the town, which today has a population of 100,000. Many of its residents were lured there from more verdant parts of Morocco by double wages, tax-free imports, government loans for new businesses, and construction jobs or government building projects.

The city survives on grit and national will. It has the excitement of a new frontier ready to be tamed.

WHAT TO SEE & DO

Laayoune was designed along European lines on a rectangular grid pattern, beside the valley of a frequently dried-out streambed. There is no medina in the form you might have come to expect after visiting the north, and the town's most visible monument, the rectangular minaret of its blue-and-white mosque (built in 1983, and closed to non-Muslims), is unashamedly new. Many of its low-slung concrete buildings are capped, perhaps as a reminder of the town's Islamic origins, with cupolas and domes. A notable exception is a modest and not particularly inspiring **cathedral** (permanently closed), which was built in the Iberian style during the Spanish occupation after 1956.

On the outskirts, there's a concrete **sports stadium** with frequently watered grass and enough seats for 30,000 spectators. The **Bou Craa phosphate mine,** several miles east of town, contains only a fraction of the phosphate reserves (3%) of the entire region.

Near the base of the mosque is the town's main attraction, the **Hall of the Green March,** which is set to the side of the verdantly landscaped place Mechouar. A glass-sided pavilion, it contains an exhibition of photographs that convey some of the history and passions of the mass demonstration in 1975 that made Laayoune possible. **Place Mechouar** itself can be illuminated from giant cement pylons for the political rallies that sometimes take place here.

Within the town, the most memorable marketplace is the **Souk of Domesticated Animals.** Selling mainly caged birds, it provides a charming oasis in the midst of the dusty heat.

IN THE ENVIRONS

Although the human population diminishes as you go south within the Moroccan mainland, the Atlantic coast provides ever-increasing quantities of fish. Some anglers claim excellent results in the waters off the **Port of Laayoune,** 18 miles to the southwest of the town. Likewise, mullet sometimes work their way up the narrow streambed to breed in the brackish lagoon near the town center. (Your competition there, however, from the locals will be fierce.)

There are **beaches** stretching north and south. Because of an occasionally dangerous undertow, only some of the region's many beaches are specifically recommended by local authorities. Highly attractive are the beaches at Naylat and Foum-El-Oued, both of which lie 12 miles from the Port of Laayoune, alongside the road leading south to Boujdor. Others include beaches 60 miles north of Laayoune, at Tarfaya, where ruins of an ancient fortress and a monument to French aviator Antoine de Saint-Exupéry provide quiet diversions. Local travel agencies can provide a guide or driver to accompany you on full-day excursions to these beaches. By all means, take proper precautions from the blistering rays of the sun, and realize that you're much safer with your clothes on than with them off.

One local curiosity is the geological depression at **Sabkhat Tah**—located 7 miles inland from the sea, near Laayoune—whose lowest point is 180 feet below sea level. A plaque placed there marks the visit by Moroccan monarchs Hassan I and Hassan II, in 1885 and 1985, respectively.

Another excursion is the half-day tour of the **Oasis of Lamsyed.** Although it's only 10 miles from the town center, its lack of modern amenities might just as well place it in the central Sahara. At this and any other pocket of water that manages to percolate through the mud to the surface, flocks of birds (including the region's pink flamingos) will flock for nourishment.

Finally, for the most adventurous, there's the possibility of a **Fleur du Desert trip,** which can be arranged for durations of between 4 and 15 days, by air or by land, with accommodations in camping tents or (if you want to rough it) in the tents of friendly Bedouins. Many different beaches, oases, and geological oddities are visited during these extended trips, which are recommended only for visitors who have already sated themselves with the more frequently visited sections of Morocco, and who are very hardy, very patient, and very tolerant.

Don't overlook the region's five artisanal cooperatives scattered throughout Laayoune and its surrounding region. Craftspeople will display their wares (leather goods, jewelry, and weavings) at many different souks and stalls within the town.

Islamic festivals within the region take place in January, February, and April, with the Moussem of Sidi Ahmed Rguibi, the Moussem of Sidi Ahmed Laaroussi, and the Moussem of Cheikh M'Rabbih Rabbou, in that order. Although not as crowded and dramatic as some of the moussems farther north, they gather together local tribespeople and offer a showcase of some of their decorative arts.

WHERE TO STAY & EAT

MODERATE

HOTEL AL MASSIRA KHADRA, rue de la Mecque (without number), Laayoune. Tel. 22-42-25. 72 rms (all with bath); 3 suites. A/C TEL **Transportation:** Petit taxi.

$ Rates: 420 DH ($52.50) single; 470 DH ($58.75) double; suites from 820 DH ($102.50). Breakfast 30 DH ($3.75) extra. AE, DC, MC, V.

In the center of town, near the landmark Hotel Parador, this place is usually booked up by tour groups, many of which arrive from the Canary Islands. It has a swimming pool and a bar, but its restaurants are open only when there is tour-group business. Bedrooms are comfortably furnished.

HOTEL PARADOR, rue Okbaa Ign Nafeh. (without number), Laayoune. Tel. 22-45-00. 31 rms (all with bath). A/C MINIBAR TV TEL **Transportation:** Petit taxi.

$ Rates: 420 DH ($52.50) single; 470 DH ($58.75) double; suites from 820 DH ($102.50). Breakfast 30 DH ($3.75) extra. AE, DC, MC, V.

⭐ Built in 1970 as a Spanish parador, this is a low-lying building painted green in honor of the Green March through the desert. It caters to individual travelers, rejecting tour groups, who head instead for its neighbor next door, the Hotel Al Massira Khadra. In the geographic center of town, the Parador has a five-star rating and a categorization of *luxe*, remarkable for a place so far out in the desert, where the swimming pool is a welcome relief and a real luxury. Rooms are attractively furnished, comfortable, and well maintained. Fixed-price meals in the hotel's restaurant, costing from 100 to 200 DH ($12.50 to $25), are served daily from noon to 3:30pm and 8pm to midnight. The bar is a popular local gathering place.

APPENDIX

A. GLOSSARY OF TERMS

Agadir fortified granary built communally by Berber tribes

Agdal/Aguedal enclosed park or garden with a water basin

Aïn spring

Argan oil-producing tree, notable for the hardness of its wood, indigenous to the Souss Valley

Attarine spice market

Bab gate

Babouche flat leather slipper, sometimes embroidered

Bled semiwilderness; bush country, often used only for grazing

Burnoose man's hooded cape

Caftan woman's dress

Caïd tribal chieftain, usually empowered with responsibility for maintaining order within his territory by a faraway sultan

Caliph a spiritual heir of the Prophet Muhammad (in Morocco, the Almohads were the first dynasty to claim this designation)

Damascene decorative etchings, usually upon weapons, in a style that originated in Damascus

Dar imposing building or palace, the term applying to the building and to the immediate neighborhood that surrounds it

Darb street, usually covered, as in a souk

Dirham Moroccan currency

Djeballa tribes occupying mountainous regions, but specifically the western Rif

Djebel/Jebel mountain or mountainous region

Djellabah loosely fitting cotton or wool garment with sleeves and a hood

Djin/Djinn a spirit, usually warlike, often evil

Enshallah/Inshallah "If God wills it"

Fantasia exhibition of horsemanship

Ejben camel-milk cheese, more pungent than goat's cheese

El Hamdillaa "Thanks be to God"

Fassi resident of Fez

Gnaoua religious brotherhood composed of descendants of former slaves of the sultans, known for their acrobatic skills, music, dance, and (in the eyes of the Berbers) occult powers

Haj a pilgrimage to Mecca, one of the pillars or commandments demanded of all Muslims

Hegira the Islamic era, beginning with the flight of the Prophet Muhammad from Mecca to Medina in A.D. 622

Henna common plant that, when dried and powdered, is used as a russet-colored dye for hair, hands, and feet

Idrissid first Arab dynasty, founded by Moulay Idriss I in A.D. 788 at Fez

Islam submission to God as described in the Koran

Istiqlal independent political party, established in 1943, that spearheaded the resistance against the French Protectorate

Jedid/Djedid new

Jihad holy Islamic war, sometimes infused with nationalistic politics

Ka'aba a black meteorite forming the central shrine of Mecca (Muslims walk around it seven times as part of the rituals connected with a *haj*)

Kasbah/Casbah walled fortification within the setting of a larger city or town

Kef/Kif hashish; illegal in Morocco

Kissaria section of a souk devoted to the sale of jewelry and fabrics

Kohl pulverized antimony, used as an eyeliner since before the days of Cleopatra

Koran/Qur'an Muslim holy testaments containing the orthodox doctrines of Islam

Koubba domed shrine, usually containing the tomb of an Islamic saint

Ksar (plural, Ksour) fortified adobe village in southern Morocco

Kufic style of Arabic script whose bold angles can be gracefully incised into plaster and rock

Lalla female saint, or title of respect for an Islamic woman

Maghreb northwestern Africa ("land where the sun sets"), the term also referring to the fourth prayer of a Muslim's day

Medina literally city, but in Morocco referring to the oldest and most labyrinthine part of town

Mellah neighborhood of a Moroccan city originally built as a Jewish quarter

Merenid Moroccan dynasty that replaced the Almohads, ruling from 1248 to 1465

Mihrab decorative prayer niche within a mosque or Koranic school, indicating the alignment of the building with Mecca

Minzah garden pavilion, usually with a panoramic view

Moulay honorary title for a saint or the descendant of a saint

Moussem religious festival involving a communal pilgrimage to the tomb of an Islamic saint

Muezzin chosen for the volume and melodiousness of his voice, the man who calls the Faithful to prayer from the minaret of a mosque

Oued river

Pasha governor of a city

Pisé packed wet clay scooped from a riverbank, sometimes mixed with chopped straw or palm fronds as a binder, and baked in the sun; the standard building material of the Moroccan south

Protectorate period of French colonial rule in Morocco, lasting from 1912 to 1956

Rabat/R'bat fortified Islamic monastery

Ramadan ritualized month of penitence and communal acknowledgment of the structures of Islam, involving denial of food, water, and carnal pleasures during daylight hours

Saadian Moroccan dynasty established in 1541, ruling first from Taroudannt and then from Marrakesh

Sanhaja largest of the Berber ethnic groups occupying the Sahara and parts of the Atlas mountains

Sidi honorary title for an Islamic saint or the descendant of a saint

Souk/Suq marketplace

Sufi mystical Islamic brotherhood

Tajine/Tagine traditional earthware casserole with a teepee-shaped top, the standard method of food preparation in Morocco; typical tajines include versions with chicken, mutton, lamb, fish, vegetables

Thuya hard, worm-resistant wood known for its lemon scent and suitability for carving

Tizi mountain pass

Vizier chief minister of a sultan

Wadi dried-out riverbed

Zaouia rural Koranic school or sanctuary around the tomb of an Islamic saint

Zakat an Islamic tax sanctioned by the Koran

Zellig/Zellij geometric mosaic pattern, usually pressed into wet plaster, composed of glazed and carefully chipped tiles

B. THE METRIC SYSTEM

LENGTH

1 millimeter (mm)	=	.04 inches (*or* less than 1/16 in.)
1 centimeter (cm)	=	.39 inches (*or* just under ½ in.)
1 meter (m)	=	39 inches (*or* about 1.1 yards)
1 kilometer (km)	=	.62 miles (*or* about ⅔ of a mile)

To convert kilometers to miles, multiply the number of kilometers by 0.62. Also use to convert speeds from kilometers per hour (kmph) to miles per hour (m.p.h.).

To convert miles to kilometers, multiply the number of miles by 1.61. Also use to convert speeds from m.p.h. to kmph.

CAPACITY

1 liter (l)	=	33.92 fluid ounces = 2.1 pints = 1.06 quarts
	=	0.26 U.S. gallons
1 Imperial gallon	=	1.2 U.S. gallons

To convert liters to U.S. gallons, multiply the number of liters by 0.26.

To convert U.S. gallons to liters, multiply the number of gallons by 3.79.

To convert Imperial gallons to U.S. gallons, multiply the number of Imperial gallons by 1.2.

To convert U.S. gallons to Imperial gallons, multiply the number of U.S. gallons by 0.83.

WEIGHT

1 gram (g)	=	0.035 ounces (*or* about a paperclip's weight)
1 kilogram (kg)	=	35.2 ounces
	=	2.2 pounds
1 metric ton	=	2,205 pounds = 1.1 short ton

To convert kilograms to pounds, multiply the number of kilograms by 2.2.

To convert pounds to kilograms, multiply the number of pounds by 0.45.

AREA

1 hectare (ha)	=	2.47 acres		
1 square kilometer (km²)	=	247 acres	=	.39 square miles

To convert hectares to acres, multiply the number of hectares by 2.47.

To convert acres to hectares, multiply the number of acres by 0.41.

To convert square kilometers to square miles, multiply the number of square kilometers by 0.39.

To convert square miles to square kilometers, multiply the number of square miles by 2.6.

TEMPERATURE

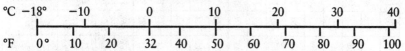

To convert degrees Celsius to degrees Fahrenheit, multiply °C by 9, divide by 5, and add 32 (example: 20°C × 9/5 + 32 = 68°F).

To convert degrees Fahrenheit to degrees Celsius, subtract 32 from °F, multiply by 5, then divide by 9 (example: 85°F − 32 × 5/9 = 29.4°C).

C. MILEAGE BETWEEN MOROCCO'S MAJOR CITIES

DISTANCE IN MILES

Zagora	Tiznit	Tetuán	Taroudannt	Tangier	RABAT	Ouarzazate	Melilla	Meknes	Marrakesh	Fez	Essaouira	Er Rachidia	Erfoud	El Jadida	Ceuta	Casablanca	Agadir	
338	56	562	50	552	381	234	691	470	190	490	108	423	474	263	590	323		Agadir
377	379	239	373	229	58	274	393	138	147	182	218	308	370	60	349		323	Casablanca
645	646	26	639	63	209	534	295	187	414	205	484	397	466	355		349	590	Ceuta
347	332	299	313	289	118	243	455	205	122	242	158	432	412		355	60	263	El Jadida
158	516	386	418	422	334	234	355	273	355	261	461	63		412	466	370	474	Erfoud
220	477	317	373	559	272	189	292	210	310	198	416		63	432	397	308	423	Er Rachidia
331	164	456	158	446	275	227	611	362	106	399		416	461	158	484	218	108	Essaouira
526	547	172	441	203	124	422	201	37	301		399	198	261	242	205	182	490	Fez
225	238	522	140	371	200	121	502	280		301	106	310	355	122	414	147	190	Marrakesh
505	518	180	420	174	87	401	238		280	37	362	210	273	205	187	138	470	Meknes
526	740	270	642	306	335	623		238	502	201	611	292	355	455	295	393	691	Melilla
104	288	497	184	492	171		623	401	121	422	227	189	234	243	534	274	234	Ouarzazate
425	437	182	430	171		171	335	87	200	124	275	272	334	118	209	58	381	RABAT
596	608	35	601		171	492	306	174	371	203	456	559	422	289	63	229	552	Tangier
288	98	600		601	430	184	642	420	140	441	158	373	418	313	639	373	50	Taroudannt
603	618		600	35	182	497	270	180	522	172	456	317	386	299	26	239	562	Tetuán
386		618	98	608	437	288	740	518	238	547	164	477	516	332	646	379	56	Tiznit

INDEX

GENERAL INFORMATION

Accidents and health, 42–3
Accommodations:
   for children, 213
   money-saving tips, 81, 210
Adventure/wilderness travel, 48
American Express, 59
   traveler's checks, 34
Antimalarials, 41
Architecture, 19–21
   Berber, 19–20, 243–4
   books about, 29
   Spanish, 20–1
Art, 17–19
   books about, 29

Banks, 59
Bars, 59
Berber architecture, 243–4
Beverages, 26–8
   alcoholic, 28
   liquor, 28
   nonalcoholic, 27–8
   water, 27–8, 41, 63
Blue men: *see* Reguibate tribesmen
Books about Morocco, 28–30
Business hours, 59

Calendar of events, 37–40
Camping, 59
Car rentals, 54–5
Cars and driving:
   breakdowns/assistance, 57
   car rentals, 54–5
   driving rules, 56
   gasoline, 55
   international driver's license, 56
   mileage chart, 264
   road maps, 56–7
Climate, 36–7
Clothes, 44
Consulates and embassies, 60
Cuisine, 26–7
Currency, 33–5
Customs, 33, 60

Dining customs, 25
Dirham (DH), 33–5
Disabled travelers, tips for, 45–6
Documents of entry, 32–3
Dress code, 44
Driver's license, international, 56
Driving rules, 56
Drug laws, 60
Drugstores, 60

Educational travel, 47
Electricity, 60
Embassies and consulates, 60
Emergencies, 60
Entry requirements, 32–3
Etiquette, 60

Families, 47
Fast Facts, 59–63
   banks, 59
   bars, 59
   drugstores, 60
   electricity, 60
   embassies and consulates, 60
   emergencies, 60
   etiquette, 60
   guides, 60–1
   hairdressers, 61
   hitchhiking, 61
   language, 61
   laundry, 61
   legal aid, 61
   liquor laws, 61
   mail, 61
   maps, 61
   newspapers and magazines, 62
   offices, 59
   pets, 62
   police, 62
   radio and television, 62
   religious services, 62
   rest rooms, 62
   safety, 62
   taxes, 62

Fast Facts (*cont'd*)
  telephone, telex, fax, 62
  time, 62
  tipping, 62
  tobacco, 63
  water, 63
  Yellow Pages, 63
Fax, 62
Festivals and special events, 38–40
First aid, 40–1
Food, 25–7, 41–2

Gasoline, 55
Geography, 2–3, 6–7
Glossary of terms, 261–2
Guided tours, 60–1

Hairdressers, 61
Health and accident insurance, 42–3
Health concerns, 26, 40–2
Historical figures, 22–3
History, 7–16
  books about, 28–9
Hitchhiking, 57, 61
Holidays, 37
  Ramadan, 38
Homestays, 47
Hostels, youth, 47

Insurance, 42–3
  accident and health, 42–3
  lost luggage, 42–3
  trip cancellation, 42–3

Koran, The, 25

Language, 61
  Arabic, 22
  Berber, 22
  glossary of terms, 261–2
Laundry, 61
Legal aid, 61
Liquor, 28
Liquor laws, 61
Literature, 21–2, 28–30
Lost luggage insurance, 42–3

Magazines, for disabled travelers, 45
Mail, 61
Maps, 4–5, 56–7, 61
Measurements: *see* Metric system
Medicines, 40–1
Metric system, the, 263
Mileage chart, 264
Money, 33–5

Moussem of Moulay Idriss, 39
Moussems, 38–40
Music, 30

Newspapers and magazines, 62

Offices, 59

Passports, 32
Pets, 62
Photographic needs, 59
Planning and preparing for your trip:
  alternative/adventure travel, 47–8
  currency, 33–5
  Customs, 33
  entry requirements, 32–3
  information sources, 31–2
  what to pack, 44–5
  when to go, 36–40
Police, 62
Politics, 16–17
Publications:
  for disabled travelers, 45
  for senior citizens, 46

Radio and television, 62
Ramadan, 38
Reguibate tribesmen, 257
Religion, 23–5
  The Koran, 25
Religious services, 62
Restaurants:
  for children, 222
  money-saving tips, 89, 219
Rest rooms, 62
Road maps, 56–7

Safety, 32, 62
Senior citizens, 46
Singles, 46
Students, 47
Suggested itineraries, 57–9

Taxes, 62
Tea-making ceremony, 26
Telephone, telex, fax, 62
Time, 62
Tipping, 62
Tobacco, 63
Tourist information, 31–2
  for disabled travelers, 45
  for senior citizens, 46
Tours:
  for disabled travelers, 45–6
  package, 51

tours (*cont'd*)
guided, 60-1
Transportation within Morocco:
    by bus, 53
    by car, 54
    breakdowns/assistance, 57
    driving rules, 56
    hitchhiking, 57
    by plane, 52
    by taxi, 53-4
    by train, 52-3
Traveler's checks, 34
Traveling companions, for singles, 46
Traveling

with children, 47
in the desert, 244
to Morocco: by bus, 51; by car, 51;
    package tours, 51; by plane,
    48-9; by train, 50
to Spain, by ferry, 57
Trip cancellation insurance, 42-3

Vaccinations, 41

Water, 41, 63
Weather, 36-7

Youth hostels, 47

DESTINATIONS

AGADIR, 184–93
accommodations:
Agadir Beach Club (*M**), 188
Argana, Hotel (*I$*), 188
Atlas, Hotel (*M*), 188
Atlas-Amadil, Hotel (*E*), 187
Club PLM Dunes d'Or (*VE*), 186
Europa Hotel Safir (*VE*), 186–7
Mabrouk, Hotel (*I$*), 189
Royal, Hotel (*I$*), 189
Sahara Agadir (*VE*), 187
Tamlelt, Hotel/Hotel Agador (*E*), 187–8
entertainment and nightlife, 192–3
Fast Facts, 185
orientation, 185
restaurants:
Belle Epoque, Restaurant (*M*; international), 190
Chez Jo Restaurant Cacher (*I*; Kosher/Sephardic), 191
Chez Redy (*I*; international), 191–2
Darkhoum Restaurant Marocain (*M*; Moroccan), 190
Du Port, Restaurant (*I**; seafood), 192
Golden Gate (*VE*; international), 189
Jardin D'Eau (*M*; French), 190
La Pampa (*I**; international), 192
La Tour de Paris (*VE*; French), 189–90
Le Dome (*M*; international), 190
Marine Heim, Restaurant (*M*; German), 191
Via Veneto (*M*; international), 191
shopping, 192
sights and attractions, 185–6
tourist information, 185
transportation within, 185
traveling to, 184–5
AGADIR, THE SOUSS & THE ANTI-ATLAS, 183–98
Agadir, 184–93
mosques, 196
suggested itineraries, 183
Tafraoute, 197–8
Taroudannt, 193–6
Tiznit, 196

traveling to, 183
what's special about, 184
see also specific places
AÏN DIAB, 150
ANFA, 150
ASILAH, 122–4
ASNI, 245–7
AZROU, 166

BOUMALNE DU DADÈS, 251–2

CAPE SPARTEL, 110
CASABLANCA, 140–53
accommodations:
Basma, Hotel (*M$*), 146
Bellerive, Hotel, Aïn Diab (*I*), 151
Casablanca Hyatt Regency (*VE**), 144
El Mansour (*VE*), 144–5
Georges V, Hotel (*I*), 146–7
Holiday Inn Crown Plaza Hotel (*VE*), 145
Kandara Hotel (*M$*) j, 146
Les Almohades, Hotel (*M$*), 146
Riad Salam Le Meridien, Aïn Diab (*E*), 151
Safir, Hotel (*E*), 145
Salam Doukkala, Hotel Club, El Jadida (*M*), 153
Sheraton Casablanca (*VE*), 145
Toubkai, Hotel (*M$*), 146
bars, 149–50
churches and cathedrals, 143
entertainment and nightlife, 149–50
excursions from, 150
El Jadida, 152–3
Fast Facts, 142–3
history of, 140
orientation, 140
map, 141
restaurants:
Al Mounia (*M**; Moroccan), 148
Dar Beida (*E**; Moroccan), 147
Des Fleurs, Restaurant (*I$*; French/Moroccan), 149
Douira, Restaurant (*E*; Moroccan), 147

CASABLANCA (cont'd)
   La Cambuse, Aïn Diab (M*; seafood), 151
   La Corrida (M; Spanish), 148
   La Mer, Restaurant, Aïn Diab (M*; French), 151–2
   Ma Bretagne, Aïn Diab (M*; French), 152
   Petit Poucet (I$; French), 149
   Valentino, Restaurant (M; Italian), 148
   Wong Kung, Restaurant (M; Chinese), 148
  shopping, 149
  sights and attractions:
   Cathédrale du Sacré-Coeur, 143
   Hassan II Mosque, 143
   New Medina, 143
   Notre-Dame de Lourdes, 143
   Old Medina, 143
   United Nations Square, 143
  tourist information, 140
  transportation within, 140, 142
  traveling to, 140
  what's special about, 128
CEUTA/SEBTA (SPAIN), 112–17
  accommodations, 116
  Fast Facts, 115
  history of, 112–13
  orientation, 114–15
  restaurants, 116–17
  sights and attractions:
   Our Lady of Africa, Church of, 115–16
   Plaza de Africa, 115
   Sala Arqueológica, 115
  tourist information, 115
  traveling to, 112–13
CHAOUEN (CHEFCHAOUEN), 120–2
COSTA DEL SOL (SPAIN): see Ceuta/Sebta

DADÈS VALLEY, 251

EL HAJEB, 164
EL JADIDA, 152–3
ERFOUD, 254–5
ER RACHIDIA, 253–4
ESSAOUIRA, 153–4
FEZ, 166–81
  accommodations:
   Fes, Hotel de (E), 175
   Le Grand (I$), 176
   Les Merinides, Hotel (VE*), 174
   Mounia Fes, Hotel (I), 176

   Paix, Hotel de la (I$), 176
   Palais Jamaï (VE*), 174–5
   Zalagh, Hotel (M), 175–6
  entertainment and nightlife, 180–1
  Fast Facts, 167
  maps, 165
   walking tour, 171
  mosques, 169–70
  museums, 168, 170
  orientation, 166
  parks and gardens, 173
  restaurants:
   Al Fassia (M*; Moroccan), 176–7
   Café Restaurant Lanoria (B; Moroccan), 173
   Dar Saada, Restaurant (M; Moroccan), 177
   Dar Tajine (M*; Moroccan), 177–8
   Djenina Restaurant (M*; international), 178
   El Minzah, Restaurant (M; French), 178
   Firdaous, Restaurant al (M*; Moroccan), 177
   L'Adour Restaurant (I; French/ Moroccan), 180
   La Kouba du Ciel (M*; Moroccan), 178
   La Tour Merinide (M; French), 179–80
   Nejjarine, Restaurant (M*; Moroccan), 178–9
   Palais de Fes (M; Moroccan), 179
   Palais Mnebhi (I; Moroccan), 180
   Pavilion Lambra (M*; Moroccan), 179
  shopping, 167–8, 172, 180
  sights and attractions:
   ancien avenue des Français, 173
   Andalusian Quarter, 168
   Armory Museum, 170
   Attarine Medersa (*), 168–9
   Bab Boujeloud, 174
   Bab es Seba, 173
   Bab Semmarin, 172
   Bou Inania Medersa, 168
   Dar el Makhzen, 169
   Dyers' Street, 168
   Fès el Bali, 167–9
   Fès el Jedid, 169–70
   fruit and vegetable market, 172
   Gare Routière, 173–4
   Great Mosque, 169–70
   Jardin Publique/Jardin de Boujeloud, 173
   The Medina (*), 167

FEZ (*cont'd*)
Mellah, or Jewish quarter, 169, 172
Merenid necropolis, 170
Moroccan Art and Handcrafts, Museum of, 168
Old Mechouar courtyard, 169
Orchard Path (Jnane Sabile), 172–3
Place Nejjarine, 169
Royal Palace, 172
rue de Fès al Jedid/grande rue, 172
Seffarin Medersa, 169
Souk el Henna, 167–8
Tanners' Quarter, 168
Tetuani Fondouk, 169
Vieux Méchouar, 173
Ville Nouvelle, 170
Zawiya of Moulay Idriss II, 169
tourist information, 166
tours, 170
transportation within, 166–7
traveling to, 166
walking tour, 170, 172–4
map, 171

GOULIMINE, 256–7

HIGH ATLAS & THE DEEP SOUTH, 244–55
architecture, 243
Asni, 245–7
Boumalne du Dadès, 251–2
Dadès Valley, 251
Erfoud, 254–5
Er Rachidia, 253–4
El Kelâa des M'Gouna, 250–1
Ouarzazate, 247–9
suggested itineraries, 243
Tinerhir, 252–3
traveling to, 242
Val d'Ourigane, 246
Vallee de l'Ourika, 244–5
what's special about, 243
Zagora, 249–50
see also specific places

EL KELÂA DES M'GOUNA, 250–1

LARACHE (EL ARAÏCH), 124–6
LAAYOUNE, 258–60
LIXUS, 126

MARRAKESH, 199–241
accommodations:
Atlas Asni (*M$*), 212
Chems (*I*), 213
for children, 213
Club Les Almoravides, Hotel (*I*), 213
Club Pullman Mansour Eddahbi, Hotel (*E*), 210–11
El Andalous (*I$*), 213
Grand Imilchil, Hotel (*I$*), 214
Imperial Borj, Hotel (*E**), 211
Le Koudou, Hotel (*E**), 211
Le Marrakech, Hotel (*I*), 214
Le Meridien Marrakech (*E*), 211–12
Mamounia, Hotel (*VE**), 207, 210
map, 208–9
Palais El Badia, Hotel (*M*), 212
PLM N'Fis Hotel (*M**), 212
Tafilalet, Hotel (*I*), 214
Tichka, Hotel (*M$**), 212–13
Toubkal, Hotel (*I$*), 214
bars and discos, 239–40
calendar of events, 39–40
cars and driving, 204
casinos, 240
cost of everyday items, 35
drugs, 200
entertainment and nightlife, 238–40
excursions from, 240–1
Fast Facts, 205–7
Frommer's favorite experiences, 225
getting around:
by bicycle, 204
by bus, 203–4
by car, 204
on foot, 204
by horse and buggy, 204–5
by taxi, 204
layout of, 202–3
maps:
accommodations, 208–9
dining, 216–17
sights and attractions, 226–7
walking tour, 233
metalwork, 238
mosques, 228
museums, 230
orientation, 200–1
parks and gardens, 230–1
performing arts, 239
restaurants:
Al Fassia (*E*; Moroccan), 215
Bagatelle, Restaurant (*M*; French), 219
Brasserie des Négociants (*B$*; café), 223
Café de France (*B$*; café), 223
Chez Jack'line (*B$*; international/fast food), 223

MARRAKESH (*cont'd*)
for children, 222
Dar Fez (*E**; Moroccan), 220–1
El Bahia (*E*; Moroccan), 220
Foucauld, Restaurant de (*I$*; Moroccan), 221
Iceberg (*I$*; Moroccan), 221–2
La Trattoria de Gian Carlo (*E**; Italian), 218
Le Calèche, Restaurant (*M*; French), 222
Le Jacaranda (*E*; French), 215
Le Koudou, Restaurants (*E**; French/Moroccan), 215, 218
Mamounia, Hotel (*B$*; mint tea), 223
map, 216–17
Marocain du Mamounia, Restaurant (*E**; Moroccan), 218
Palais Gharnatta, Restaurant (*VE*; Moroccan), 220
Petit Poucet (*I$*; French), 220
Relais al Baraka, Restaurant (*I–M*; Moroccan), 222–3
Restaurant Dar Es Salaam (*I–M*; Moroccan), 235
Rôtisserie du Café de la Paix (*M*; Moroccan), 219
Stylia, Restaurant (*E*; Moroccan), 221
Villa Rosa (*E*; Italian), 218–19
Yacout, Restaurant (*E**; Moroccan), 221
shopping, 225, 228–9, 232, 234
artisan centers, 237
best buys, 236
for carpets, 237–8
caveat emptor, 236–7
for ceramics, 238
for leather goods, 238
taxes & hours, 236
sights and attractions:
Bab Agnaou, 232
for children, 231–2
El Badi Palace, 234
El Bahia Palace, 229, 234–5
Dar el Makhzen (Royal Palace), 230
Dar si Said, 230
gardens, 230
Grand Bijouterie, 235
Islamic cemetery, 235
Jemaa el Fna*, 225, 228, 231, 235–6
Koutoubia Minaret, 228
map, 226–7
Medersa Ben Youssef, 229
Medersa El Bahia, 235
Mellah, 230
Moroccan Art, Museum of (Musée Dar Si Said), 235
Mosque of the Kasbah, 232
Musée Dar Si Said (Museum of Moroccan Art), 235
place Kzadrya, 234
Ramparts, 232
rue Dar Adou, 234
rue de la Kasbah, 232
rue du Mellah, 234
rue Riad Zitoune Kedim, 235
Saadian tombs,* 229, 232
scenic routes, 231
Souks, 234
Souks of the Medina*, 228–9, 232
souks, 225, 228–9, 232, 234, 236–7
suggested itineraries, 224–5
tourist information, 202
tours, guided, 200–1
transportation within, 200–1, 203–5
traveling to, 201
walking tour, 232, 234–7
map, 233
what's special about, 200
MEKNES, 156–66
accommodations:
Bab Mansour, Hotel (*M*), **161**
Grand Hotel Volubilis (*M*), **161**
Nice, Hotel de (*I$*), 162
Palace, Hotel (*I*), 162
Rif, Hotel (*E*), 161
Transatlantique, Hotel (*VE*), **160–1**
Zaki, Hotel (*E*), 161
excursions from:
Azrou, 166
El Hajeb, 164
Moulay Idriss, 164
Volubilis, 163–4
Fast Facts, 158
history of, 156, 158
map, 157
orientation, 158
restaurants, 162–3
sights and attractions:
Bab Er Rih, 160
Bab Mansour, 159
Bordj el Ma, 160
Christian Prison, 160
Dar el Beida, 160
Dar el Makhzen, 160
Dar Jamaï, 159
Dar Kebira, 159
Heri Es Souani, 160
Imperial City, 159–60
Kasbah of Hedrache, 160

MEKNES (cont'd)
   Koubbet El Khiyatine, 160
   Mausoleum of Moulay Ismail, 160
   Méchouar, 160
   Medersa Bou Inania, 159
   Medina of Meknes, 159
   Mosque of Bab Berrima, 159
   Mosque of Er Rouah, 160
tourist information, 158
transportation within, 158
traveling to, 156
**MEKNES, FEZ & THE MIDDLE
   ATLAS,** 155–82
Azrou, 166
El Hajeb, 164
Fez, 166–81
maps:
   Fez, 165
   Meknes, 157
Meknes, 156–66
mosques, 159–60, 169–70
Moulay Idriss, 164
museums, 168, 170
parks and gardens, 173
suggested itineraries, 156
Taza, 181–2
traveling to, 155
Volubilis, 163–4
what's special about, 156
see also specific places
MOULAY IDRISS, 164

NORTHERN COAST, 111–26
accommodations, 119–20
Asilah, 122–4
beaches, 119
Ceuta/Sebta (Spain), 112–17
Chaouen (Chefchaouen), 120–2
churches and cathedrals, 115–16
Larache (El Araïch), 124–6
Lixus, 126
museums, 115, 119
suggested itineraries, 112
Tetuán, 117–20
traveling to, 111–12
what's special about, 112
see also specific places

OUARZAZATE, 247–9

RABAT
accommodations:
   Balima, Hotel (I$), 135
   D'Orsay, Hotel (I$), 135–6
   La Tour Hassan, Hotel de (E), 134–5
   Oudayas, Hotel (M), 135
   Rabat Chellah Hotel (M), 135
   Rabat Hyatt Regency (VE*), 134
   Safir Rabat (E), 134
   Sheherazade, Hotel (I), 136
entertainment and nightlife, 139
excursions from, 139
Fast Facts, 130–1
history of, 130
map, 129
mosques, 139
museums, 132–3
orientation, 130
restaurants:
   Balima, Restaurant (I; continental),
      137–8
   Café Restaurant Saadi (I; Moroccan),
      138
   El Andalous (VE*; Moroccan), 136
   Justine's (VE*; French), 136
   Kanoun Grill (M; Moroccan), 137
   Koutoubia (M; Moroccan), 137
   La Couronne and El Mansour (E;
      Moroccan/international), 136–7
shopping, 138
sights and attractions:
   Bab Oudaïa, 132
   Kasbah des Oudaïa, 132
   Medina, 131–2
   Musée Archéologique, 133
   Museum of Oudaïa, 132
   Necropolis of Challah, 133
   Tower of Hassan/Mausoleum of Mo-
      hammed V, 132–3
tourist information, 130
traveling to, 128, 130
what's special about, 128
**RABAT, CASABLANCA & THE
   ATLANTIC COAST,** 127–54
Aïn Diab, 150
Anfa, 150
Casablanca, 140–53
churches and cathedrals, 152–3
El Jadida, 152–3
Essaouira, 153–4
maps:
   Casablanca, 141
   Rabat, 129
mosques, 143
museums, 132–3
Rabat, 128, 130–9
Salé, 139
suggested itineraries, 128
traveling to, 127–8
see also specific places

SALÉ, 139
SEBTA (SPAIN): *see* Ceuta/Sebta

TAFRAOUTE, 197–8
accommodations, 197–8
excursions from, 197–8
Fast Facts, 197–8
festivals and special events, 197–8
traveling to, 197–8
TANGIER, 64–110
accommodations:
  Africa Hotel (*M*), 79
  Bristol, Hotel (*I$*), 81–2
  Chellah Hotel (*I*), 79
  Continental, Hotel (*B$*), 82
  D'Anjou, Hotel (*B$*), 82
  El Minzah, Hotel (*VE**), 75
  El Oumnia, Hotel (*M*), 79
  Grand Hotel Villa de France (*I*), 79
  Les Almohades, Hotel (*VE**), 80
  map, 76–7
  Panoramic Massilia, Hotel (*B*),
    79–80
  rates & reservations, 77, 78
  Rembrandt, Hotel (*VE**), 78–9
  Rif Hotel (*E*), 80
  Shéhérazade, Hotel (*M*), 80–1
American Express, 72
area code, 72
baby-sitters, 72
bookstores, 72–3
cafés, 102, 104
car rentals, 73
cars and driving, 72
churches and cathedrals, 100, 102
doctor & dentist, 73
drugstores, 73
electricity, 73
embassies and consulates, 73
emergencies, 73
entertainment and nightlife:
  belly dancing, 106–7
  dance clubs, 107
  nostalgic & expatriate bars, 108–9
  pubs/wine bars, 107–8
  supper clubs, 107
excursions from:
  Cape Spartel, 110
  Caves of Hercules (*), 110
Fast Facts:
  American Express, 72
  area code, 72
  baby-sitters, 72
  bookstores, 72–3
  car rentals, 73

currency, 73
doctor & dentist, 73
drugstores, 73
electricity, 73
embassies and consulates, 73
emergencies, 73
hairdressers/barbers, 73
hospitals, 73
laundry/dry cleaning, 73–4
libraries, 74
lost property, 74
mail, 74
newspapers and magazines, 74
photographic needs, 74
radio/television, 74
religious services, 74
rest rooms, 74
safety, 74
shoe repair, 74
taxes, 74
taxis, 74
telegrams/telex/fax, 74
transit information, 75
weather, 75
hairdressers/barbers, 73
history of, 65–7
hospitals, 73
laundry/dry cleaning, 73–4
layout of, 69–71
  street maps, 71
libraries, 74
lost property, 74
mail, 74
maps:
  accommodations: 76–7
  restaurants, 83–4
  sights and attractions, 92–3
  street, 71
  walking tour, 101
mosques, 96–7
museums, 94–5, 97, 98, 103–4
neighborhoods:
  the Kasbah, 70
  La Plage, 70
  the Medina, 70
  the Port of Tangier, 70–1
  Ville Nouvelle, 70
newspapers and magazines, 74
orientation, 67
parking, 72
parks and gardens, 95, 96, 99–100
photographic needs, 74
radio and TV, 74
religious services, 74
restaurants:

TANGIER (cont'd)
Africa, Restaurant (I$; International), 88
Big Mac (B; hamburgers), 90
Café Central, 102
for children, 82, 90
Damascus (M; Moroccan), 86
El Erz (VE*; French), 85
El Korsan (VE*; Moroccan), 85
Emma's B.B.C. (M; international), 87–8
Granada, Restaurant (M; Spanish/Moroccan), 88–9
Hamadi, Restaurant (I$; Moroccan), 89
La Grenouille (M$; French), 86
Le Detroit (I; Moroccan/pastries), 104, 89–90
map, 92–3
Osso-Bucco (M$; international), 86
Patio Wine Bar (E; French), 85–6
Raihana (I; Moroccan), 87
Romero, Restaurant (I$; Spanish/Moroccan), 87
San Remo (M$; Italian), 86–7
Sun Beach (M; international), 88
Windmill (M; international), 88
rest rooms, 74
safety, 74
shoe repair, 74
shopping:
for antiques, 105
best buys, 104–5
for carpets, 105
for ceramics, 105
for embroideries, 105
for handcrafts, 105–6
for leather products, 104
for silver, 105
sights and attractions:
Café Central, 97
The Caves of Hercules, 98
Centre Culturel Français, 99
for children, 98
Dar el Makhzen, 94, 103
El Minzah, 99
English Church, 98–9
Ethnography and Archeology, Museum of, 103–4
Forbes Museum of Military Miniatures, 97, 98
Frommer's favorite experiences, 100
Garden of the Sultan, 95
Grand Socco, 96
The Kasbah, 98
Kasbah of Tangier, 103
The Kasbah Quarter (*), 91, 94–5
Le Musée des Antiquités, 94–5
Le Musée des Arts marocains, 94–5
map, 92–3
The Medina (*), 95–7, 100
Mendoubia Gardens, 96, 99–100
Mendoubia Palace, 96
New Town (Ville Nouvelle), 98
Old American Legation, 97–8, 102
Petit Socco, 97, 102
place Amrah, 103
place de France, 99
place de la Kasbah, 95, 103
place du Grand Socco, 99
Praça de Faro/place El Maguise, 99
rue Dar Dbagh, 103
rue de Almouades, 103
rue es Siaghin, 102
rue iskiredj, 102
rue Mokhtar Ahardan or rue des Postes, 102
rue Riad Sultan, 104
rue Sidi ben Raissouli, 103
rue Semmarine, 100
Spanish Cathedral, 100, 102
suggested itineraries, 91
Villa "Sidi Hosni," 103
Ville Nouvelle (New Town), 98
taxes, 74
taxis, 74
telegrams/telex/fax, 74
tourist information, 69
tours, guided, 67
transit information, 75
transportation within, 67–8, 71–2
traveling to:
by bus, 68
by car, 68–9
by ferry & hydrofoil, 69
by plane, 67–8
from Spain, 68–9
by train, 68
walking tour, 99–104
map, 101
weather, 75
what's special about, 65
TAROUDANNT, 193–6
accommodations, 194–5
Fast Facts, 193
orientation, 193
restaurants, 195
shopping, 195
sights and attractions:
place Assarag, 194

TAROUDANNT (*cont'd*)
  place Tamoklate, 194
  souks, 194
  walls of Taroudannt, 194
traveling to, 193
TAZA, 181–2
TETUÁN, 117–20
Fast Facts, 118
history of, 117–18
orientation, 118
restaurants, 120
sights and attractions:
  Archeological Museum, 119
  Exposition Artisanale, 119
  Medina of Tetuán, 118–19
  Musée d'Art Marocain/Musée Eth-
    nographique, 119
  Royal Palace, 119
tourist information, 118
transportation within, 118

traveling to, 117
TINERHIR, 252–3
TIZNIT, 196

VAL D'OURIGANE, 246
VALLEE DE L'OURIKA, 244–5
VOLUBILIS, 163–4

WESTERN SAHARA, 256–60
Goulimine, 256–7
Laayoune, 258–60
Reguibate tribesmen, 257
souks, 259
suggested itineraries, 256
traveling to, 256
what's special about, 257
see also specific places

ZAGORA, 249–50

NOW, SAVE MONEY ON ALL YOUR TRAVELS!
Join Frommer's™ Dollarwise® Travel Club

Saving money while traveling is never a simple matter, which is why the **Dollarwise Travel Club** was formed 31 years ago. Developed in response to requests from Frommer's Travel Guide readers, the Club provides cost-cutting travel strategies, up-to-date travel information, and a sense of community for value-conscious travelers from all over the world.

In keeping with the money-saving concept, the annual membership fee is low —$20 for U.S. residents or $25 for residents of Canada, Mexico, and other countries—and is immediately exceeded by the value of your benefits, which include:

1. Any TWO books listed on the following pages.
2. Plus any ONE Frommer's City Guide.
3. A subscription to our quarterly newspaper, *The Dollarwise Traveler*.
4. A membership card that entitles you to purchase through the Club all Frommer's publications for 33% to 40% off their retail price.

The eight-page **Dollarwise Traveler** tells you about the latest developments in good-value travel worldwide and includes the following columns: **Hospitality Exchange** (for those offering and seeking hospitality in cities all over the world); **Share-a-Trip** (for those looking for travel companions to share costs); and **Readers Ask . . . Readers Reply** (for those with travel questions that other members can answer).

Aside from the Frommer's Guides and the Gault Millau Guides, you can also choose from our Special Editions. These include such titles as **California with Kids** (a compendium of the best of California's accommodations, restaurants, and sightseeing attractions appropriate for those traveling with toddlers through teens); **Candy Apple: New York with Kids** (a spirited guide to the Big Apple by a savvy New York grandmother that's perfect for both visitors and residents); **Caribbean Hideaways** (the 100 most romantic places to stay in the Islands, all rated on ambience, food, sports opportunities, and price); **Honeymoon Destinations** (a guide to planning and choosing just the right destination from hundreds of possibilities in the U.S., Mexico, and the Caribbean); **Marilyn Wood's Wonderful Weekends** (a selection of the best mini-vacations within a 200-mile radius of New York City, including descriptions of country inns and other accommodations, restaurants, picnic spots, sights, and activities); and **Paris Rendez-Vous** (a delightful guide to the best places to meet in Paris whether for power breakfasts or dancing till dawn).

To join this Club, simply send the appropriate membership fee with your name and address to: Frommer's Dollarwise Travel Club, 15 Columbus Circle, New York, NY 10023. Remember to specify which single city guide and which two other guides you wish to receive in your initial package of member's benefits. Or tear out the next page, check off your choices, and send the page to us with your membership fee.

FROMMER BOOKS
PRENTICE HALL PRESS
15 COLUMBUS CIRCLE
NEW YORK, NY 10023
212/373-8125

Date_____

Friends: Please send me the books checked below.

FROMMER'S™ GUIDES

(Guides to sightseeing and tourist accommodations and facilities from budget to deluxe, with emphasis on the medium-priced.)

☐ Alaska	$14.95	☐ Germany	$14.95
☐ Australia	$14.95	☐ Italy	$14.95
☐ Austria & Hungary	$14.95	☐ Japan & Hong Kong	$14.95
☐ Belgium, Holland & Luxembourg	$14.95	☐ Mid-Atlantic States	$14.95
☐ Bermuda & The Bahamas	$14.95	☐ New England	$14.95
☐ Brazil	$14.95	☐ New Mexico	$13.95
☐ Canada	$14.95	☐ New York State	$14.95
☐ Caribbean	$14.95	☐ Northwest	$16.95
☐ Cruises (incl. Alaska, Carib, Mex, Hawaii, Panama, Canada & US)	$14.95	☐ Portugal, Madeira & the Azores	$14.95
		☐ Scandinavia	$18.95
☐ California & Las Vegas	$14.95	☐ South Pacific	$14.95
☐ Egypt	$14.95	☐ Southeast Asia	$14.95
☐ England & Scotland	$14.95	☐ Southern Atlantic States	$14.95
☐ Florida	$14.95	☐ Southwest	$14.95
☐ France	$14.95	☐ Switzerland & Liechtenstein	$14.95
	☐ USA	$16.95	

FROMMER'S $-A-DAY® GUIDES

(In-depth guides to sightseeing and low-cost tourist accommodations and facilities.)

☐ Europe on $40 a Day	$15.95	☐ Israel on $40 a Day	$13.95
☐ Australia on $40 a Day	$13.95	☐ Mexico on $35 a Day	$14.95
☐ Costa Rica; Guatemala & Belize on $35 a day	$15.95	☐ New York on $60 a Day	$13.95
		☐ New Zealand on $45 a Day	$14.95
☐ Eastern Europe on $25 a Day	$16.95	☐ Scotland & Wales on $40 a Day	$13.95
☐ England on $50 a Day	$13.95	☐ South America on $40 a Day	$15.95
☐ Greece on $35 a Day	$14.95	☐ Spain on $50 a Day	$15.95
☐ Hawaii on $60 a Day	$14.95	☐ Turkey on $30 a Day	$13.95
☐ India on $25 a Day	$12.95	☐ Washington, D.C. & Historic Va. on $40 a Day	$13.95
☐ Ireland on $35 a Day	$13.95		

FROMMER'S TOURING GUIDES

(Color illustrated guides that include walking tours, cultural and historic sites, and other vital travel information.)

☐ Amsterdam	$10.95	☐ New York	$10.95
☐ Australia	$10.95	☐ Paris	$8.95
☐ Brazil	$10.95	☐ Rome	$10.95
☐ Egypt	$8.95	☐ Scotland	$9.95
☐ Florence	$8.95	☐ Thailand	$10.95
☐ Hong Kong	$10.95	☐ Turkey	$10.95
☐ London	$10.95	☐ Venice	$8.95

(TURN PAGE FOR ADDITONAL BOOKS AND ORDER FORM)

FROMMER'S CITY GUIDES

(Pocket-size guides to sightseeing and tourist accommodations and facilities in all price ranges.)

☐ Amsterdam/Holland	$8.95	☐ Minneapolis/St. Paul	$8.95
☐ Athens	$8.95	☐ Montréal/Québec City	$8.95
☐ Atlanta	$8.95	☐ New Orleans	$8.95
☐ Atlantic City/Cape May	$8.95	☐ New York	$8.95
☐ Barcelona	$7.95	☐ Orlando	$8.95
☐ Belgium	$7.95	☐ Paris	$8.95
☐ Berlin	$8.95	☐ Philadelphia	$8.95
☐ Boston	$8.95	☐ Rio	$8.95
☐ Cancún/Cozumel/Yucatán	$8.95	☐ Rome	$8.95
☐ Chicago	$9.95	☐ Salt Lake City	$8.95
☐ Denver/Boulder/Colorado Springs	$7.95	☐ San Diego	$8.95
☐ Dublin/Ireland	$8.95	☐ San Francisco	$8.95
☐ Hawaii	$8.95	☐ Santa Fe/Taos/Albuquerque	$10.95
☐ Hong Kong	$7.95	☐ Seattle/Portland	$7.95
☐ Las Vegas	$8.95	☐ St. Louis/Kansas City	$9.95
☐ Lisbon/Madrid/Costa del Sol	$8.95	☐ Sydney	$8.95
☐ London	$8.95	☐ Tampa/St. Petersburg	$8.95
☐ Los Angeles	$8.95	☐ Tokyo	$8.95
☐ Mexico City/Acapulco	$8.95	☐ Toronto	$8.95
☐ Miami	$8.95	☐ Vancouver/Victoria	$7.95

☐ Washington, D.C. $8.95

SPECIAL EDITIONS

☐ Beat the High Cost of Travel	$6.95	☐ Motorist's Phrase Book (Fr/Ger/Sp)	$4.95
☐ Bed & Breakfast—N. America	$14.95	☐ Paris Rendez-Vous	$10.95
☐ California with Kids	$16.95	☐ Swap and Go (Home Exchanging)	$10.95
☐ Caribbean Hideaways	$14.95	☐ The Candy Apple (NY with Kids)	$12.95
☐ Honeymoon Destinations (US, Mex &		☐ Travel Diary and Record Book	$5.95
Carib)	$14.95	☐ Where to Stay USA (From $3 to $30 a	
☐ Manhattan's Outdoor Sculpture	$15.95	night)	$13.95

☐ Marilyn Wood's Wonderful Weekends (CT, DE, MA, NH, NJ, NY, PA, RI, VT) $11.95
☐ The New World of Travel (Annual sourcebook by Arthur Frommer for savvy travelers) $16.95

GAULT MILLAU

(The only guides that distinguish the truly superlative from the merely overrated.)

☐ The Best of Chicago	$15.95	☐ The Best of Los Angeles	$16.95
☐ The Best of France	$16.95	☐ The Best of New England	$15.95
☐ The Best of Hawaii	$16.95	☐ The Best of New Orleans	$16.95
☐ The Best of Hong Kong	$16.95	☐ The Best of New York	$16.95
☐ The Best of Italy	$16.95	☐ The Best of Paris	$16.95
☐ The Best of London	$16.95	☐ The Best of San Francisco	$16.95

☐ The Best of Washington, D.C. $16.95

ORDER NOW!

In U.S. include $2 shipping UPS for 1st book; $1 ea. add'l book. Outside U.S. $3 and $1, respectively.
Allow four to six weeks for delivery in U.S., longer outside U.S.
Enclosed is my check or money order for $_____

NAME_____

ADDRESS_____

CITY_____ STATE_____ ZIP_____

0391